Traders in Motion

Traders in Motion

Identities and Contestations in the Vietnamese Marketplace

Edited by Kirsten W. Endres
and Ann Marie Leshkowich

SOUTHEAST ASIA PROGRAM PUBLICATIONS
an imprint of
Cornell University Press
Ithaca and London

First published 2018 by Cornell University Press

Printed in the United States of America

Library of Congress Cataloging-in-Publication Data

Names: Endres, Kirsten W., editor. | Leshkowich, Ann Marie, editor. |
    Container of (work): Turner, Sarah, 1970– Run and hide when you see the police.
Title: Traders in motion : identities and contestations in the Vietnamese
    marketplace / edited by Kirsten W. Endres and Ann Marie Leshkowich.
Description: Ithaca : Cornell University Press, 2018. | Includes
    bibliographical references and index.
Identifiers: LCCN 2017042001 (print) | LCCN 2017045614 (ebook) |
    ISBN 9781501721342 (pdf) | ISBN 9781501721359 (epub/mobi) |
    ISBN 9781501719820 | ISBN 9781501719820 (cloth : alk. paper)
    | ISBN 9781501719837 (pbk. : alk. paper)
Subjects: LCSH: Markets—Vietnam. | Merchants—Vietnam. | Street
    vendors—Vietnam. | Small business—Vietnam. | Business networks—Vietnam.
Classification: LCC HF5475.V52 (ebook) | LCC HF5475.V52 T73 2018
    (print) | DDC 381/.109597—dc23
LC record available at https://lccn.loc.gov/2017042001

CONTENTS

Chapter 5

Chapter 6

Chapter 7

Chapter 8

PART III. BORDERWORK

Chapter 9

Chapter 10

Chapter 11

Chapter 12

PREFACE

In Vietnam today, people are making markets, but markets are also making people. As anthropologists, we coeditors routinely seek to make sense of complex dynamics that extend across vast swaths of time and space by considering how they emerge in and through the lives of particular actors who are navigating particular spatial and temporal contexts. While international and national policies may seem to be the primary forces shaping the markets in which a street trader in Hanoi plies her wares, what those markets actually are, physically and conceptually, are every bit as much the product of her daily actions and the subjectivity that informs them. Trade and traders co-constitute each other.

The vibrancy of trade in market socialist Vietnam drew each of us independently to the study of marketplaces. Leshkowich began research in Ho Chi Minh City's Bến Thành market in the 1990s, where the opportunity and uncertainty posed by newly enacted market-oriented policies sparked struggles over class, property rights, social relationships, and memories of the past. These dynamics often centrally involved gender, as traders articulated identities as women that both worked to enhance their bottom lines and were personally meaningful ways of becoming proper, socially legitimate moral subjects in a palpably volatile economic and social environment (Leshkowich 2014a).

For Endres, markets moved to the center of attention when she joined the Max Planck Institute for Social Anthropology in 2009. Her research group Traders, Markets, and the State in Vietnam, generously funded by the Max Planck Society and the Max Planck Institute for Social Anthropology in Halle/Saale, investigated market development policies as part of complex infrastructural planning assemblages aimed at national development, with a special focus on the entangled webs of social ties, state structures and discourses, and economic forces in which the lives of small-scale traders in market socialist Vietnam are situated. The group's researchers focused on local markets and other sites of small retail trade in different locations across contemporary Vietnam: the capital city, Hanoi (Lisa Barthelmes); a peri-urban village in the Red River Delta (Esther Horat); the northwestern uplands (Christine Bonnin); and two trading hubs on the Vietnam-China border (Kirsten Endres, Caroline Grillot).

In seeking to engage with the complexity of "market making" in a single country, Endres's research group purposefully took a different approach from those of prior projects and edited volumes that have tended to focus on a particular aspect of trade, such as street trade, marketplaces, or a commodity type, in order to generate comparative case studies from different contexts around the world. Nonetheless, a comparative enterprise, albeit of a different kind, lies at the heart of the group's work and also inspires the present volume. Given the ongoing central role of nation-states or regions in shaping the legal and political environment for trade, it is analytically important to examine these dynamics, their impact on small-scale traders, and their uneven effects across time and space within one context. Doing so shows that markets evolve in unpredictable and uneven ways through uncertainty or, as we write in the introduction to this volume, through friction. Thus, while this volume certainly contributes to Vietnamese studies in an ethnographic and analytical sense, it has been explicitly designed to spark comparison by illuminating dynamics of spatialization, mobility, and borderwork that, we propose, shape trading contexts around the world.

To enable this comparative conversation, we have organized the volume into three thematic parts. These speak to each other, but they also can stand on their own. Each section has its own introduction that, along with the introduction to the volume as a whole, explicitly explores what Vietnamese trade, traders, and marketplaces—in all their rich specificity—might reveal about trade, traders, and marketplaces beyond the borders of this particular nation-state.

The contributors to this volume first presented their chapters at the conference "Traders in Motion: Networks, Identities, and Contestations in the Vietnamese Marketplace," hosted by the Max Planck Institute for Social Anthropology in September 2014. The goal of this conference was to examine how Vietnamese small-scale traders experience, reflect upon, and negotiate current state policies and regulations that affect their lives and trading activities. By looking at various types and places of small-scale trade in contemporary Vietnam, the conference sought to shed light on local-level economic agency in the seemingly paradoxical context of Vietnam's continuing socialist orientation, on the one hand, and contemporary neoliberal economic and social transformations, on the other. We here take the opportunity to extend our warm thanks to Chris Hann, director of the department Resilience and Transformation in Eurasia at the Max Planck Institute for Social Anthropology, for his enthusiastic support of this project. Special thanks go to Bettina Mann, Anke Meyer, and Berit Westwood for their excellent organizational and logistical work behind the scenes that enabled the conference to run smoothly. The event kicked off with a lively keynote lecture by Gracia Clark, who kindly agreed to provide the afterword to this book. We are particularly grateful to the team of discussants who supplied valuable food for thought: Regina Abrami, Chris Gregory, Gracia Clark, Erik Harms, Sarah Turner, and Vương Xuân Tình. Special thanks to Lale Yalçin-Heckmann, Thomas Sikor, Oliver Tappe, and Roberta Zavoretti for chairing the sessions and sharing their views during the discussions. We also wish to thank Gita Rajan for language editing some of the chapters, Thi Thu Trang Nguyen for assisting in formatting and proofreading, and Jutta Turner for preparing the map.

At Cornell University Press, Sarah Grossman deserves special credit for her stewardship of this book from proposal to finished volume. We would also like to thank Karen Hwa for her work as production editor, Romaine Perin for copyediting, Fred Conner for his assistance with maps, illustrations, and other details of production, and Rachel Lyon for preparing the index. Our sincere gratitude extends to the anonymous reviewers of the book manuscript for their careful reading, insightful comments, and helpful suggestions. Finally, we editors would like to extend our appreciation to all of the volume's contributors for so enthusiastically embracing this collaborative enterprise. Scholarship, much like the trade that this volume chronicles, becomes all the more rewarding when it emerges through long-term relationships of exchange.

Field site locations in Vietnam. Map by Jutta Turner,
Max Planck Institute for Social Anthropology.

Traders in Motion

Introduction: Space, Mobility, Borders, and Trading Frictions

Ann Marie Leshkowich and Kirsten W. Endres

Marketplaces are fixed locations, but in Vietnam they are on the move, literally and figuratively. In Lào Cai, a northern upland city and provincial capital, a new, bigger market building is currently under construction. "Building a new market means there will be even more traders competing for customers," one vendor muses. "The new market will make things even more difficult for us." In Sa Pa, a popular tourist destination in the same province, traders are not happy with the local government's plan to relocate the town's bustling central market. "While the government is trying to create economic opportunities, the traders don't see any opportunities in this relocation plan," a seller of medicinal herbs argues. Elsewhere in the northern uplands, some of the newly built or relocated marketplaces already lie fallow, the victim of high rents and out-of-the-way locations. Similar dynamics also plague Vietnam's capital, Hanoi. Several old-style marketplaces have been turned into upscale shopping malls, with former vendors consigned to the basement. A trader in one of these markets reports that she has lost many of her former clients. She now has so much time on her hands that she can even prepare the family meals during her working hours at the market.

In other contexts, it is traders who are on the move. In Hanoi, a fruit vendor sits on the pavement and anxiously observes the street. If the police turn up today, she will have to run or else risk her goods being confiscated. Each day, the vendor commutes from her home in a peri-urban zone. Her family's agricultural land has been rezoned to make way for expanding industry and housing, so her family depends on her income from petty trade. Other rural areas have witnessed more extensive labor migration. In a village on the south-central coast of Vietnam, approximately one-quarter of the active labor force hawks sunglasses, lighters, and souvenirs to tourists and migrant laborers as part of a vast mobile trading network encompassing the entire southern half of Vietnam, from Huế to Cà Mau. That this kind of arduous work can also expand horizons becomes clear if one listens as other migrants, in this case men who have now settled down to raise families on the outskirts of Hanoi, reminisce about the cosmopolitan pleasures of peripatetic youths spent pursuing the junk trade in Ho Chi Minh City.

With all this mobility come boundary making and border transgression. As political tensions between Vietnam and China over the South China Sea intensify, Vietnamese and Chinese traders along the Sino-Vietnamese border struggle to cooperate in order to exploit market gaps and circumvent regulations. It is like "holding a knife," one Vietnamese seafood trader says. "The Chinese hold the handle and we hold the blade." Other boundaries are conceptual. As part of government attempts to regulate currency markets, Ho Chi Minh City police raid a private shop suspected of illegally trading in gold bars, the currency of choice for transactions involving real estate and other valuable property. An online forum erupts in protest after the shop owner claims that the gold seized was in fact a lawful family inheritance. Twenty kilometers outside Hanoi, property dilemmas of a different sort trouble a village that has become home to the biggest wholesale fabric market in northern Vietnam. Newly prosperous residents worry that their wealth will invite moral critique in a village that cherishes communal solidarity and traditional rural values. The modern and traditional clash in the center of Hanoi as well. Visions of a beautiful, civilized capital render certain things out of place. These include the beehive coal briquette, as well as those who trade or use this still-popular cooking fuel.

Compiled from the chapters in this volume, these vignettes from Vietnam highlight the dynamics of emplacement, mobility, and boundary making through which a market economy emerges. They tell a familiar story. Around the world, modernization, industrialization, and urbanization have shaped new forms of production, consumption, and the distribution of goods and services. These developments bring about new forms of *spatialization*, a term that refers both to the physical distribution of people, things, and activities across the landscape and to the meanings, often hierarchical, associated with these patterns. Commerce and finance become concentrated in downtown skyscrapers, marketplaces, and malls. Production increasingly takes place in new economic zones or large industrial plants. Spaces devoted to work become distinct from those devoted to family or leisure. Some people come to be increasingly mobile, perhaps because they wish to capitalize on new markets or because the loss of a prior livelihood strategy forces them to search for work. Others may be trapped in locations now deemed traditional or peripheral to the futures being imagined in the corridors of power. Spatialization, then, is fundamentally also about mobility and differentiation, boundary making and borderwork along multiple axes: not just location or region, but also gender, class, ethnicity, and age.

These processes have been particularly accelerated and visible in market socialist contexts such as Vietnam and China, where the bureaucratic tools of central planning—five-year plans, production targets, and so on—have been applied to new domains of private enterprise or joint ventures. Yet the impetus to develop a market economy has not emanated solely from on high. Fence breaking and individual or familial entrepreneurial energy seem to have been just as much the motor driving change in Vietnam (see, e.g., Kerkvliet 2005). Wherever the momentum may have originated, it gets picked up by officials and transformed into a techno-political "will to improve" (Li 2007; see also T. Mitchell 2002; Rose 1999) that corrals the welter of market energy into the rational discourse of projects and targets, of specialized and formalized markets, and of bureaucratic oversight and accountability. Yet these very dynamics of governmentality also mean that "the market" in Vietnam is not a singular entity. Its diverse modalities emerge out of complex interlinkages between global challenges and local dynamics of economic transformation that are subject to equally diverse forms of encouragement, regulation, and policing at national and local levels.

In Vietnam, as in other late and post-socialist settings, new horizons of market profitability have sparked complex contestations over the regulation of trade activities, institutionalization of control of marketplaces, and use of public space. The multiple dynamics of market socialist economic growth, urban and rural economic transformation, and state efforts to implant a "modern" (*hiện đại*) or "civilized" (*văn minh*) lifestyle have profoundly affected the ways in which Vietnamese small-scale traders have participated in, and benefited from, commercial activities since the introduction in the 1980s of the market-oriented reforms known as Đổi mới. As terms such as *modern* or *civilized* imply, these processes are not simply technical or economic; they are also moral, as people develop notions of what is right and good that propel and justify their activity as market actors. How do entrepreneurial or potentially entrepreneurial subjects make sense of the world? What do they desire? What forms of activity seem reasonable or appropriate to them? How do their actions and perspectives create a market economy?

The chapters in this volume address these questions through finely grained ethnographic studies of trade, traders, and marketplaces throughout Vietnam and across its borders. They vividly explore the micropolitics of local-level economic agency, as Vietnamese traders and marketeers, like their counterparts around the world, experience, reflect upon, and negotiate current state policies and regulations that affect their lives and trading activities. The contributors show how trading experiences shape individuals' notions of self and personhood, not just as economic actors, but also in terms of gender, region, class, ethnicity, and age, and how these forms of personhood in turn work to challenge or naturalize aspects of a market economy. Focused on one country, these contributions highlight how what may seem a singular market economy is in fact composed of shifting and internally diverse constellations of political economy constructed through quotidian interactions between traders, suppliers, customers, family members, neighbors, and officials at various levels—in contested spaces; through expanding and contracting circuits of mobility; and across physical and conceptual borders that are fixed yet porous. The rich stories these chapters tell are particular to Vietnam, but the dynamics of spatialization, mobility, and borderwork that they illuminate (and which serve, respectively, as the themes for the volume's three parts) will undoubtedly afford comparative insight into other rapidly shifting trade contexts: in China, Southeast Asia, formerly socialist Eastern and Central Europe, Cuba, and beyond.

SPACE, PLACE, AND CONTENTIOUS POLITICS

Vietnam's shift from a centrally planned toward a market-oriented and globally integrated economy has effectively contributed to the "production of new spatialities and temporalities" (Sassen 2000, 215) that interact with complex reconfigurations of social, economic, and power relations. Whereas small-scale, marketplace-based trade received relatively little governmental attention during the first fifteen years of the Đổi mới era, since the early 2000s Vietnam has pursued ambitious programs aimed at modernizing the nationwide network of marketplaces. These top-down planning policies have affected the socio-spatial dimensions of small-scale trading practices in complex and dynamic ways. In many places throughout the country, the demolition and reconstruction or relocation of public marketplaces became focal points of intense struggles over livelihoods, the control and use of public urban space, and, more generally, the meaning of development. As Kalman Applbaum succinctly puts it, "Marketplace relocation, reconfiguration and, ultimately, trade concentration illuminate a part of the trajectory of the convergence of marketplaces and market principle" (2005, 276). The chapters in the book's first part show that this trajectory is not free of tensions, conflicts, and contradictions. These tensions may best be seen as an effect of Vietnamese political decision makers' efforts to "fix" the economy, both as a conceptual and as a regulatory domain, by "embedding certain twentieth-century practices of calculation, description, and enumeration in new forms of intellectual, calculating, regulatory, and governmental practice" (T. Mitchell 2002, 118).

Marketplaces have historically been "defined by the movement of people and commodities" (Agnew 1986, 23) from and between various places of production, distribution, and consumption. With the advent of modern, industrialized nation-states, the control over such movement and mobility became a central concern of rule and governance (Salazar and Smart 2011, iii; Scott 1998). While the regulation and policing of marketplaces (regarding, for example, market locations and times of access, quality and measurement standards, prices, and common rules of fairness) has a long record in human history, their efficiency as "important nodes, obligatory points of passage for the development of new modes of [social] ordering" (Kevin Hetherington 1997, 36) subsequently took on new forms and dimensions. The famous Parisian market of Les Halles serves as a case in point. Originally constructed in the eighteenth century so as "to confine activities deemed potentially dangerous to the overall population (faulty commerce, disease) by putting in place an architecture to incite circulation" (TenHoor 2007, 76), extensive renovations a century later "provided an excuse to 'clean up' the behaviors and morals of its largely female merchants, limiting their economic power as a class and providing an opportunity to further manage the behavior and morality of those attempting to participate economically in marketplace exchanges" (79). Finally, in the 1960s, the removal of Les Halles to the suburbs signaled that large-scale food trade no longer belonged in the center of a global metropolis. In each moment, the form and location of Les Halles were extensively debated and planned to "accommodate and/or produce shifting notions of architectural, social, and financial order" (73).

Marketplaces in Vietnam have similarly gone through different epochs, each with its own top-down (and bottom-up) spatial logic. In the late nineteenth and early twentieth century, the French colonial regime sought to modernize indigenous Kinh (ethnically Vietnamese) commerce through the construction of rational, hygienic market halls, such as Đồng Xuân market in Hanoi (1889) and Bến Thành market in Saigon (1914). During socialist transformation, vendors in public markets were encouraged to join cooperative trading groups (*tổ hợp tác*) and marketing cooperatives (*hợp tác xã mua bán*) (Abrami 2002b, 140; Leshkowich 2014a, 139–41). Although private economic activity was severely restricted by the legal and ideological underpinnings of central planning, it was never completely eliminated. On the contrary, its prohibition even seemed to have the opposite effect. As Regina Abrami notes, "Indeed, central state attempts to control illegal trade in Vietnam only brought further protection from local commune officials and enhanced synergy and integration of the public and private economies" (2002b, 416). These everyday politics of economic subversion, including both unplanned fence-breaking activities "from below" and unorthodox ad hoc measures "from above," ultimately turned out to be a major trigger of the economic reforms inaugurated in 1986 (Kerkvliet 2005). Throughout the reform period, small-scale and marketplace-based trade experienced an unprecedented surge in growth, not only as a channel for the distribution of consumer goods and a means of (additional) income, but also as a source of economic creativity, flexibility, and maneuvering. Although the state (initially, at least) invested substantially in the refurbishment of preexisting market buildings and the construction of new ones in order to "realize a diversified economic development, meeting the hopes and expectation of the people" (Báo Lào Cai 1996, 267, translation by authors), market vendors remained enframed as "objects of ambivalence who, in contrast to modern entrepreneurs or businesspeople (*doanh nhân* or *thương gia*), are critiqued as backward, uneducated vestiges of tradition, unable to contribute to economic development" (Leshkowich 2011, 278). Not surprisingly, then, marketplaces served as instructive ethnographic sites for investigating the interaction between the material and ideological components of marketization, particularly in terms of gender, class, and ethnicity, during the first two decades of Đổi mới (Abrami 2002b; Leshkowich 2014a; Michaud and Turner 2000, 2003; Pettus 2003).

During the first two decades of the twenty-first century, the government's attempts at civilizing the marketplace have reached a new level of bureaucratization and regulation. Since the central government issued its first decree on the development and management of marketplaces in January 2003 (Chính Phủ 2003), the relevant ministries have spawned numerous decisions and regulations with regard to marketplace classification; distribution network planning; investment into the construction, repair, and upgrading of marketplaces; and general market management. In line with these centrally issued policies, the provincial and municipal people's committees subsequently launched their own market development projects (*quy hoạch phát triển chợ*) as part of their general, local-level socioeconomic development strategy. These policies have worked toward creating a broader classificatory movement in which markets of different kinds, and hence economic activities and people within them, became a proper concern of the government "at all levels" as part of a nation-wide marketplace network (*mạng lưới chợ*) that needs to be developed "in a civilized, modern direction" (Bộ Công Thương 2015). These top-down planning policies may be seen as a technology of governance by which imaginings of "state verticality and encompassment become real and tangible" (Ferguson and Gupta 2002, 985). Kirsten Endres's chapter shows that bureaucratic documents, including master plans, government circulars, and local performance and project implementation reports, play a significant role in producing an image of the state as an autonomous, abstract source of power that is set apart from society, or what Timothy Mitchell calls a state effect resulting from "detailed processes of spatial organization, temporal arrangement, functional specification, and supervision and surveillance" (T. Mitchell 1991, 95). Besides asserting the conceptual boundary between state and society, bureaucratic documents shape the experiential reality of the marketplace by enabling state officials to establish their positions and authority through paperwork. The meaning of the marketplace thus becomes part of a circulation of documents that contributes to the construction of hierarchies through which markets are run, the positioning of subjects within those hierarchies, and the imaginings of the market's future.

The spatial reconfiguration of small-scale trade has not gone uncontested. Sarah Turner's contribution explores how official attempts to control access to public spaces for commercial purposes have led ethnic minority traders in the popular upland tourist town of Sa Pa (Lào Cai province) to diversify their selling strategies in markets, along thoroughfares, and on trekking routes. Ethnic majority Kinh from the lowlands make up only 16 percent of the population, but they dominate the ranks of local officials. Kinh traders often have preferential access to market stalls and lucrative street vending locations. Meanwhile, ethnic minority Hmong, Yao, and Giáy face more disadvantageous conditions. Officials want to concentrate them in a new marketplace, but traders find this location to be too far from the main tourist areas. Having to commit to a fixed schedule in the marketplace also prevents them from pursuing other livelihood strategies or attending to family needs. Many prefer trading along the streets, only to become vulnerable to unannounced raids and seizures of wares directed against them, but not against Kinh traders. Sa Pa's markets, streets, and mountain paths have become ethnically patterned trading microgeographies in which people struggle to define the meaning of public space and who has what kind of access to it.

Elsewhere in the province of Lào Cai, the government has poured vast sums of money into the upgrading of upland markets. Yet, as Christine Bonnin's chapter shows, the on-the-ground realities reveal a clear disconnect between the markets imagined and promoted by the state and the livelihood needs of local upland traders. As a result, many of these newly built markets have been "left fallow" (*bỏ hoang*). Whereas both Kinh and ethnic minority traders criticized the poor implementation of market development policies by local state authorities, ethnic minority traders felt that the state does little to integrate their needs and flexible trading schedules, instead imposing a system of permanent market structures where traders rent fixed stalls, sell on a daily basis, and pay fees and taxes to the state.

Gertrud Hüwelmeier's chapter similarly focuses on the problems of ambitious top-down development plans that leave traders, particularly women, behind and create empty "ghost markets." In Hanoi, processes of market rebuilding seeking to make the capital "clean and green" require temporary relocations that disrupt the relationships with vendors that traders have cultivated over the years. By exploring three markets in different stages of redevelopment, Hüwelmeier shows the crucial spatial and temporal dimensions of clientelization. Municipal spatialization practices that attempt to create the appearance of modernity by putting traders into supposedly rationally designated locations in fact involve traumatic processes of displacement: physical, social, and economic. The experiences that Hüwelmeier describes suggest that cleaning and greening the city is in fact a process of expropriating space from traders so that someone else can profit.

Circuits of Mobility, Identities, and Power Relations

As these accounts of marketplace redevelopment suggest, attempts to fix traders in place or confine them to regulated spaces also involve the creation of particular circuits of mobility. At first glance, the term *mobility* pulsates with promises of economic profit and cosmopolitan pleasure. Engaging in global flows can be particularly alluring in formerly socialist societies, where central economic planning had adopted a "gardening" approach that rooted people in place and circumscribed movement as part of the state's "exceptional concern with pattern, regularity and ordering" (Urry 2000, 186; see also Nyíri 2010, 3). Over the past several decades, traders have been one of the more visible groups to capitalize on new opportunities to be on the move. For example, Vietnamese students and workers living in the German Democratic Republic, the Soviet Union, Hungary, Poland, and Czechoslovakia during the Cold War as part of fraternal socialist exchanges often supplemented their incomes through informal production and trade. In the late 1980s, some took advantage of arbitrage opportunities created by economic and political changes in both home and host countries to expand these activities. After the collapse of communism in Eastern Europe, they were joined by a second wave of economic migrants, sometimes connected to the first wave through family or social relations (Hüwelmeier 2015a; Nowicka 2015; Schwenkel 2014, 2015b; Williams and Baláž 2005). Even larger movements are occurring domestically, with the possibility of making money and becoming the kind of modern person who knows how to navigate urban lifeways prompting rural residents to move to cities.

Vietnamese are by no means unique in experiencing an impetus toward mobility. Mimi Sheller and John Urry (2006, 207–8) note prominent global dynamics that have propelled people, things, ideas, and money to be increasingly on the move: Legal international arrivals have consistently increased since the mid-twentieth century; so, too, have other forms of movement across national borders. The Internet and mobile communication devices enable virtual mobility and facilitate interaction while one is literally on the go. Goods, both legal and contraband, circulate through increasingly rapid multinational supply chains. Microbes travel quickly as well, sparking fears of global pandemics, from SARS to Ebola and Zika. The "new mobilities paradigm" emerged in the 1990s across numerous fields, including anthropology, sociology, geography, science and technology studies, and cultural studies, precisely to analyze these complex developments. According to Sheller and Urry, this paradigm also addressed a gap in the social scientific conception of space, namely, "how the spatialities of social life presuppose (and frequently involve conflict over) both the actual and the imagined movement of people from place to place, person to person, event to event" (2006, 208).

The concept of mobility has considerable attractions, but the large body of scholarship resulting from the "mobilities turn" in the social sciences rightly cautions against easy celebration.[1] As Noel Salazar observes, "The very processes that produce movement and global linkages also promote immobility, exclusion, and disconnection" (2014, 60). Mobility is thus "a contested ideological construct" (61; see also Salazar 2011). This requires that we explore what Doreen Massey terms the *"power-geometry"* of space and mobility that considers how "different social groups and different individuals are placed in very distinct ways in relation to these flows and interconnections" (1993, 61). As Julie Chu notes for marginalized Fuzhounese in China, "Being stuck in place while others all around were moving to broaden their spatial-temporal horizons" could itself become a form of dislocation (2010, 12). Scholars now tend to pluralize the term as "mobilities," explicitly to reference diverse forms of mobility, their causes, their effects, and their significance.

Mobilities scholarship raises three points that are especially germane to this volume's ethnographic exploration of Vietnamese traders and trading. First, mobility needs to be understood as central to contemporary governmentality. Celebratory rhetoric of global flows notwithstanding, nation-states remain key gatekeepers defining forms of transnational and domestic mobility and permitting or forcing their pursuit. Some individuals or groups may choose to be mobile, but others are forced: "'Mobility is a resource to which not everyone has an equal relationship'" (Skeggs 2004, 49, quoted in Sheller and Urry 2006, 211; see also Cresswell 2010, 21). State management has the effect of legalizing and valorizing certain kinds of mobility and the subjects that embody it.

This leads to a second key insight: forms of mobility and immobility both reflect and produce complex hierarchies. Clearly, mobility can be status enhancing. The rich and educated become model citizens who participate in forms of movement that increase their privilege (Ong 1999; Nyíri 2010). Allison Truitt has cogently observed that visibly riding around Ho Chi Minh City on a motorbike symbolizes the allure of various forms of physical and social mobility, including "the promise of individual freedom and autonomy associated with the market, newfound urban mobility, and the formation of new hierarchies of who (or what) has the right-of-way" (2008, 14). Likewise, immobility can lock one into subordinate status. This is particularly true in Vietnam, which, like China, maintains a household registration system (*hộ khẩu* in Vietnam, *hukou* in China). Originally introduced in the mid-1950s as a development strategy to keep people in place, to restrict urban growth, and to enable central economic planning (Hardy 2001), household registration requirements can now impede the mobility required by market capitalism. Although the *hộ khẩu* is no longer connected to food rations, domestic migrants to the city can find themselves without the paperwork needed to gain access to health, education, or welfare services (Hardy 2001; Karis 2013; Locke, Nguyễn Thị Ngân Hoa, and Nguyễn Thị Thanh Tâm 2012; Small 2016, 83; Winkels 2012). In China, migrants from rural and ethnic minority regions have become a "floating population" on the move from their villages of origin to the cities in search of better livelihood options (L. Zhang 2001).[2] In spite of even life-threatening hardships, domestic and international mobility may be the only perceived pathway to upward mobility. In Fuzhou, China, planning and undertaking dangerous mobility has become compulsory if one wishes to display oneself as possessing the appropriately modern aspirations that now characterize proper moral personhood in a market context, thus displacing other forms of personhood based on reciprocal relationships within a community of origin (Chu 2010). At the same time, "peasant" status brands domestic or transnational migrants as "backward," marginal, and of low quality (*suzhi*), subjecting them to intensive suspicion and surveillance at borders and in the places in which they attempt to reside (Chu 2010; see also Ong 1999). It also creates enormous pressure for peasants to stay in place (Chio 2014). As Chio notes, the irony is that the distances that modern mobility might seem to reduce in fact can be experienced as greater distance in socioeconomic and cultural terms (182).

Third, mobilities scholars point out that (im)mobility is not just spatial; it is also temporal (Chu 2010; Harms 2011; Massey 1993). Mobility often results from inability to make a living in one's prior profession or place of residence. The Vietnamese students and workers in Central and Eastern Europe who took up trade or expanded trade activities after the collapse of communism often did so because the emergence of a market economy led to their loss of employment in centrally planned industry (Hlinčíková 2015, 43; Schwenkel 2014, 252). Within the trading profession, opportunities caused by gaps in knowledge, prices, or supply may prove short-lived. Competition intensifies as other groups enter the marketplace or supermarkets and transnational hypermarkets replace street markets and itinerant peddling. Meanwhile, as contemporary processes of (im)mobility laud certain kinds of movement through time and space, they render invisible or meaningless other forms of mobility and temporality. Domestically, teleological state-sponsored visions of development rest on spatial designations that locate desired future progress and modernity in urban or industrial zones, while defining rural areas, their agriculture, and their residents as somehow in the past. State classification in both China and Vietnam ironically erases histories of peasants' former mobility and flexibility in livelihood strategies and instead depicts them as somehow autochthonous of a land that they have occupied since time immemorial (Chu 2010; Vu and Agergaard 2012). Where peasant mobilities are acknowledged, as in itinerant peddling, they are viewed as traditional and hence something to be curbed so that modern forms of mobility—pedestrian tourism in downtown areas, flows of motorbike or automobile traffic—can be promoted (Turner and Oswin 2015; see also Truitt 2008). Peasants are consequently sedentarized, physically and conceptually, as part of development plans. Chio (2014) provides a fascinating discussion of how such peasant immobility in China is key to state promotion of domestic and international tourism. Far from a preexisting, static state, attractive rurality is in fact something that peasants need to be taught to embody, thus allowing them to become modern—to a certain extent, at least—by seeming to be traditional and in place. Persistent mobility in such a context can therefore be a problem. For example, as Turner and Oswin point out, officials in Vietnam's northern uplands seek to curb the trading mobility of ethnic minorities: "While mobility helps these vendors maintain a presence on the streets, a strong state preference for either immobile, regulated trade or other forms of mobility deemed 'modern' impedes ethnic minority mobile traders from achieving steady incomes or secure livelihood options" (2015, 395). Looking transnationally, celebrations of globally mobile market development make it easy to forget that in Vietnam, as in China, Cuba, and Central and Eastern Europe, the global socialist ecumene involved significant movement of people and attendant promise of enhancing social, economic, and cultural capital (Bayly 2009). Temporal and spatial shifts from relatively privileged "socialist mobilities" to those of the market economy can involve dislocation and loss of status (Schwenkel 2014, 2015b).

The volume's second part advances discussion of these three themes of governmentality, hierarchy, and spatial temporalities to explore how movements of traders and goods between localities, regions, and nations occur within "zones of graduated sovereignty" (Ong 1999, 217). Aihwa Ong originally defined this term in a spatially circumscribed sense, as "a series of zones that are subjected to different kinds of governmentality and that vary in terms of the mix of disciplinary and civilizing regimes" (7). States such as China have created regions in which they cede authority over economic development to enterprises, either directly or indirectly through special tax or labor codes, while retaining government control over resources and populations. Similar forms are in place in Vietnam, although not as extensively as in China. We nevertheless find the concept of "'zones of graduated sovereignty'" useful in the sense that "sovereignty is manifested in multiple, often contradictory strategies that encounter diverse claims and contestations, and produce diverse and contingent outcomes" (Ong 2006, 7; see also Labbé 2014, 170). As the foregoing discussion makes clear, we view the act of establishing or defining such zones as a form of spatialization that also compels (im)mobility between spaces. Graduated sovereignty thus directs movement by attracting or trapping particular kinds of actors.

This mobility is both physical and ideological. Ong places particular emphasis on the gendered nature of mobility hierarchies, especially how family regimes and government plans combine to valorize "mobile masculinity and localized femininity" (1999, 20).[3] Two of the chapters in the second part of this volume likewise explore how gender shapes mobility and its effects, but they focus instead on migrant masculinity at the lower end of the socioeconomic ladder. In Vietnam, petty trade, both mobile and in marketplaces, is stereotyped as essentially feminine and hence appropriate for women (Leshkowich 2014a). Hy Van Luong points out, however, that the expansion of vast mobile trading networks over the past few decades has created opportunities for central Vietnamese villagers, both men and women. This is difficult, low-status work, but the men who sell lighters, wallets, and trinkets to tourists and migrant laborers also enact a kind of masculine ethos of braving physical hardship to support their families. Minh T. N. Nguyen's chapter chronicles what happens when these kinds of men return home, in this case to a village in the Red River Delta, after some years of junk trading in Hanoi and Ho Chi Minh City. As they marry and have families, they might seem to embody immobility—a settling down—associated with normative, mature masculine responsibility. Yet they continue, often quite obviously, to display such cosmopolitan habits as drinking coffee in cafés that they acquired as young men traveling for the junk trade. Although these men are marginalized in class terms, they nonetheless make a temporal, embodied claim to gendered cosmopolitanism by positioning themselves with respect to prevailing imaginaries of mobility (Salazar 2011).

The two chapters that follow focus on the repercussions of mobility, particularly rural to urban, necessitated by livelihood needs. Nguyễn Thị Thanh Bình conducted her research in a peri-urban community outside Hanoi in which agricultural land had been reallocated for industry and housing. Peasant households may receive some temporary cash from the involuntary "sale" of their land, although nowhere near the profit subsequently netted by developers and their government associates.[4] What's more, as Nguyễn Thị Thanh Bình shows, they lose the ability to depend on agriculture or to make a living through flexible combinations of farming, handicraft production, and trade. They have little choice but to become itinerant peddlers who strive to make a living closer to the city. Her chapter provides a poignant example of Chio's (2014) point that the lessening of spatial distance from the city begets mobilities that are productive of socioeconomic difference. Lisa Barthelmes's chapter focuses on how similarly positioned mobile traders experience their daily lives selling wares along Hanoi's thoroughfares. Facing myriad impediments and legal restrictions, traders develop a vast array of tactics to evade police, who view them as obstacles to the modern flow of traffic and hence as a lucrative source of income from fines—a dynamic characteristic of street trade around the world (see, e.g., K. T. Hansen, Little, and Milgram 2013; Graaff and Ha 2015). In Barthelmes's account, traders' tactics include performatively emphasizing their feminine marginality and the small scale of their businesses, thus reinforcing state developmentalist logic that would depict women's entrepreneurial mobility as backward and marginal.

Taken together, these four chapters consider the impact of (im)mobility as temporal and spatial, as material and ideological, and as profoundly context dependent. Once mobilities become required or valued—economically, politically, socially, or personally—they lend themselves to techno-governmental projects of spatial differentiation, particularly in terms of urban and rural or local and global, that are bound up with the production of class, gender, ethnic, and other forms of differentiation. Personal mobility projects often work to reproduce the logic of state developmentalist policies, but they can also present possibilities for unruliness and unpredictability that might ultimately "heighten people's susceptibility to new ideas and interpretations of the world and relax the boundaries of what is socially acceptable" (Nyíri 2010, 139). While the chapters in this section primarily focus on the problematic side of mobility, they also indicate that small-scale traders' mobility strategies grant individuals and communities income, status, or experiences that they find worthwhile.

BORDERWORK

Dynamics of spatialization and mobility frequently play out through constructing and navigating borders—physical, material, and conceptual. As Chris Rumford notes, "To theorize mobilities and networks is at the same time to theorize borders" (2006, 155). Mobility can rescale borders, delineate networks, and hence invite new forms of policing (156–57; Walters 2006). The grid of a new marketplace building that allocates merchandise types to stalls of fixed dimensions draws a physical and conceptual boundary between the ordered, rational trade of a civilized market economy within its walls and the disorderly, premodern trade on the streets outside. Regulation of domestic migration from countryside to city demarcates that which is rural and that which is urban, a boundary that is spatial, temporal, and moral. Moving up in scale to national borders, the globalization that seemed to be about borderlessness appears instead to be rebordering the world, although in ways that are selectively permeable and hence harder to see as absolute (Rumford 2006, 159; Newman 2006, 172). Their management has diversified, with border control no longer the province of solely nation-states and those acting directly on their behalf (Cresswell 2010, 26; Rumford 2006; Walters 2006).[5] Vietnam's own shifting geopolitical position provides further evidence of the fluid temporal dimensions of perceived spatial borders. The removal of the "iron curtain" that had placed Vietnam in the so-called Second World might now seem to locate Vietnam in time as postsocialist, even as, like China, it technically is not so in a political sense.

Physical and political acts of bordering are often accompanied by profoundly social, moral, and temporal acts of boundary making.[6] Yet borders and boundaries are not coextensive. Migrants, for example, may cross a territorial border, only to find themselves facing boundaries of identity (see, e.g., Fassin 2011). Part of the power of borders lies in their capacity to provide clarity, something that Anne Fadiman describes with appreciation: "I have always felt that the action most worth watching is not at the center of things but where edges meet. I like shorelines, weather fronts, international borders. There are interesting frictions and incongruities in these places, and often, if you stand at the point of tangency, you can see both sides better than if you were in the middle of either one" (1997, viii). Fadiman's quote suggests that the allure of borders lies in showing us where one thing ends and another begins. But this may also be where they prove illusory. Where is the point of tangency as waves and land meet? Does the line on a map that separates China and Vietnam in fact correspond to where the border crossing is placed? And do either of these points reflect what political leaders negotiated? That the significant international boundary represented by "kilometer zero" on Vietnam's main highway may not be where it is said to be has fueled conspiracy theories that Vietnamese leaders may have given territory away to China, which in turn has prompted officials to crack down on the online circulation of unofficial border maps, stories, and photos (MacLean 2008). The proliferation of permeable or fuzzy, yet decisive, borders of all kinds thus raises ontological questions about our place in the world and our orientation in space, time, and social and moral orders. It also increases the stakes for those trying to establish or navigate borders and calls upon scholars to pay attention to these contexts of borderwork.

The term *borderwork* has been employed by anthropologists and sociologists interested in understanding how interactions across lines of difference such as ethnicity or gender that might signal the porousness of these distinctions in fact tend to have the opposite effect of consolidating the border between them (see, e.g., Barth 1969 and Thorne 1993). How can borderwork help us to understand the contemporary development of a market economy in Vietnam? Timothy Mitchell's historical analysis of the creation of "the economy" proves instructive in this regard. In Mitchell's view, the conception of the economy as a coherent and distinct domain of human activity was an act of defining borders that bifurcated the world into the material and cultural, real and abstract: "It was both a method of staging the world as though it were divided in this way into two, and a means of overlooking the staging, and taking the division for granted" (2002, 82–83). Mitchell's argument is complex and detailed in its historical specificity, but the key outlines merit brief summary here: Prior to the mid-twentieth century, writers in English did not use the definite article *the* before the word economy. Instead, they referred to economy (without a definite article) as processes of maximizing resources and available means to achieve desired ends. Economy in this sense could occur in specific forms, such as money economy in commercial exchange (81). Momentum toward the inclusion of the definite article began in nineteenth- and early twentieth-century imperial regimes, as leaders and bureaucrats developed techniques of calculation to regulate economic and political processes in colonized territories that then shaped how the world could be known and viewed. Mitchell documents these transformations in Egypt, where cadastral maps replaced registries that had formerly simply listed landholdings. The visual technique of mapping made it possible to represent the size of plots owned, to see how they related to each other, to determine whether fertility-based taxation rates in fact logically corresponded to the actual spaces those holdings occupied, and to identify "empty" spaces that might then become objects to be incorporated into economic processes (89). In short, the cadastral map not only made political power rest on "knowledge and command of space" (90) but also separated reality from its representation, the land from the map. This separation, Mitchell argues, allows "the economy" to emerge as a thing precisely because it could be represented through maps, as well as through statistics about crop yields, the volume of money in circulation, the value of currency, and so on. Taken together, such methods of calculation worked to construct "the economy" as a thing that is knowable, even as they appeared only to be measuring that thing. The definite article becomes necessary and so natural that we cannot imagine a time when "the economy" did not exist as such.

The chapters in the third part of this volume similarly focus on how acts of borderwork performed by traders and officials—the "art of neighboring" across national boundaries; challenging or reinforcing cultural stereotypes through cross-border trade relations; establishing boundaries of moral conduct and business ethics, the boundaries of currency realms, and the (blurred) boundaries between the legal and the illegal—construct the market economy in Vietnam by rendering it knowable and legible. While this certainly is happening through production targets, measures of inflation, and statistics about foreign direct investment, the chapters here suggest that borderwork often rests on more qualitative assessments of the kinds of trading activity that are deemed appropriate for "the market economy" and hence should be encouraged or regulated in order to foster its emergence.

Gold, for example, has in the past functioned as a currency in Vietnam that was used for high-value transactions in real estate, to circumvent the official economy, or to protect wealth from the volatility of state-issued paper notes. But what does the ongoing significance of gold bars as an alternative currency to the đồng suggest about the status of Vietnam's market economy? Allison Truitt's chapter addresses this question by exploring the effects of state efforts to regulate gold bars by outlawing their trade in private gold shops. After police in Ho Chi Minh City raided a shop in 2014 and confiscated the gold bars and Vietnamese and U.S. currency that they found there, the owner protested that the bars were private property, an inheritance from her parents. Online reaction to the raid seems sympathetic to the shop owner and highlights the problem of drawing distinctions between gold as commodity/currency, versus gold as private property. Indeed, the attraction of gold lies in its liquidity, its ability to cross precisely these boundaries. Although the development of a market economy entails notions of rationality and techniques of bureaucratic management that bring particular aspects of trade under state control, those crying foul over the raid suggest that such distinctions are arbitrary, and thus implicitly question the legitimacy of state attempts to manage the economy based on those distinctions.

In countering the accusation that her lucre was illegally acquired on the market by instead claiming it to have been a kinship bequest, the gold shop owner references a much broader debate in Vietnam about the moral values of private accumulation in the market economy. Scholarship on China and Vietnam traces the particular moral dilemmas that a market economy can pose in a socialist political context in which entrepreneurship and the generation of wealth had previously been labeled as corrupt. In her study of small-scale entrepreneurs in China, Carolyn Hsu explores how class differentiation becomes moralized as normal or appropriate. In popular discourse, the petty trading street vendor, or *getihu*, becomes a "stock character"—an object lesson in the dangers of market accumulation by individuals who are low status, uneducated, and lacking in morality (2007, 20). "Respectable entrepreneurs," in contrast, are seen as possessing quality (*suzhi*) (22). Their global market successes advance China's national interest (141).

Ann Marie Leshkowich's (2014a) study of Ho Chi Minh City's Bến Thành market similarly explores how smaller-scale traders navigate characterizations that they are greedy cheats who "talk nonsense." For the predominantly female cloth and clothing traders with whom she conducted research, gender became a salient personal and rhetorical resource. Through price negotiations and other marketplace performances, traders emphasized that they were just women running small stalls in order to support their families. Traders relied on social networks for access to capital, merchandise, and information, but they viewed these relationships as also based on mutual support and interpersonal sentiment (*tình cảm*), both touchstones of proper Vietnamese femininity. Many Bến Thành traders had become well off, but emphasizing particular aspects of gender worked to downplay their success and hence cast their profit as virtuously acquired.[7] But these self-portrayals carried a price. With limited means to assess marketplace trade by tracking capital investment, profit margins, labor practices, and so on, officials also were likely to read gender as a sign of an enterprise's scale. Their characterizations may have lessened traders' tax burdens, but they worked to denigrate stallholders as uneducated, backward, and insignificant—thus placing them on the wrong side of moral and economic boundaries and making it unclear whether they would be included in future plans to develop the market to promote tourism.

Esther Horat's chapter in this volume offers a rich complementary perspective on how traders in one of Vietnam's largest wholesale fabric markets define and navigate the boundaries between the moral and immoral. Traders in the Red River Delta village of Ninh Hiệp articulate moral claims that help them to make sense of their economic activity, their social community, and a broader context in which their economic success is sometimes used to critique their values and lifestyles. As traders' market activities and lifestyles become increasingly similar to those in nearby Hanoi, some of the more successful among them visibly and audibly assert their identity as villagers. While "the village" can be perceived as a space of backwardness, it is also seen as the repository of time-honored Vietnamese traditions. Being "just a villager" can, like being just a woman petty trader or just a daughter who has inherited gold, place one's wealth (and oneself) on the right side of a boundary between moral rectitude and depravity.

Horat's analysis of city-village distinctions recalls earlier work by Erik Harms, who studied how a peri-urban district in Ho Chi Minh City experienced the arbitrary boundaries that can naturalize social distinctions. Starting from the premise that the actual edges between urban and rural are quite fuzzy, Harms explores how the fringe of a city is in intimate relationship with its center as a supplier of food, labor, and housing for that labor. Nevertheless, the presumably clear distinction between city and country is "used to codify everything from different social types and lifestyles to poverty indexes and living standards, from differential access to health care and education to general quality of life" (2011, 2). Conceptual distinctions imperfectly capture a much more complex and less bifurcated reality, yet they also get used strategically to make claims that advantage some by disadvantaging others. This creates what Harms calls "spatiotemporal oscillation": ideal categories create oppositions—of geography, class, gender, and ethnicity—that allow people to act, yet everyday life moves productively between these categories.

Those who trade in and use coal briquettes in Hanoi are experiencing precisely this kind of spatiotemporal oscillation. In her chapter, Annuska Derks chronicles how this inexpensive cooking fuel has become branded as backward and dirty in comparison with gas and other modern fuels. It is thus deemed out of place and out of time in a capital city that aspires to be green, clean, and beautiful. Even so, the briquette continues to be widely used and its trade lucrative. Derks traces the briquette's commodity chain backward, from stove to trader to production site, in order to shed light on "how the dynamics and networks of small-scale commercial activities are inherently linked to the changing uses and meanings of place and space in urban Vietnam." The briquette thus daily crosses precisely the boundaries of space and time that its existence is used to delineate.

Caroline Grillot's chapter on trade between Vietnam and China focuses squarely on the kind of international boundary that the term *border* evokes. The decisiveness of this line—claims about "kilometer zero" notwithstanding—makes trade across it complex and dangerous, but also highly lucrative. The demarcation of a national boundary creates differential markets and hence the opportunity for arbitrage by moving particular kinds of goods across them. Grillot details the cat-and-mouse game that Vietnamese and Chinese traders play with officials, plus the opportunity for collusion that can bring profit to them all. The border may be relatively permeable, but it also creates distinctions between legal and illegal goods and between legal and illegal means of circulating them that seem to advantage Chinese traders.

According to Chris Rumford, "All borders, each act of debordering and rebordering, and every border crossing are constitutive of social relations, and, as such, help us orientate ourselves to the world" (2006, 167). The chapters in this section show us that the borderwork performed through trade, traders, and their trading networks works toward constructing the material and conceptual distinctions that are then taken as indexical of the emergence and development of "the market economy." Physical, temporal, and conceptual boundaries define the market economy and render it knowable, even as the market's functioning rests on the daily blurring and contesting of precisely those boundaries.

Trading Frictions

"The market economy" has emerged in Vietnam over the past thirty years through complex, shifting processes of emplacement, mobility, and borderwork. While state agents may invoke logics of calculation, rationality, and utility to fix people in place, direct circuits of mobility, and establish clear physical, social, and conceptual boundaries, the detailed ethnography featured in the twelve studies collected in this volume highlight considerable unevenness in how these approaches are applied. Rather than hampering the emergence of "the market economy," these chapters suggest, such inconsistencies may in fact work to encourage it by generating "productive friction" (Tsing 2005, 3). Friction creates danger and uncertainty, but it also transforms both trading activity and the subjectivities of traders and officials. While Anna Tsing's influential formulation of friction focused on global encounters across differences, this book explores the construction, exacerbation, and bridging of differences within a single country through complex configurations—or what might be called assemblages—of graduated sovereignty, spatialization, movement, temporality, and bordering. The contours of friction that the contributors outline may be particular to Vietnam and their field sites, but they offer a broader lesson: markets form and transform in uneven ways through the interplay between global processes and local trajectories of economic and social development that interact with changing—and not always consistent—regimes of state regulation at various levels of implementation. Rather than obstacles to market formation or its workings, the shifting dynamics of contestation and uncertainty—trading frictions—are the necessary ground on which new forms of political economy emerge.

NOTES

1 For a detailed, insightful overview of "the new mobilities paradigm," see Sheller and Urry 2006.
2 Nyíri characterizes the situation in China as follows: "In sum, the function of the *hukou* system has shifted from preventing population mobility to controlling access to economic resources, and finally to class and subject formation. It exercises this function by limiting the social rights, expectations, and status of most while granting exception to an elite minority who conform to the imaginary of modernization and success" (2010, 23).
3 Interestingly, Nyíri notes that migrant Chinese women can "evade regimes of discipline" and hence challenge gender hierarchies (2010, 119–21).
4 For further discussion of the role of land expropriation and conversion in prompting labor migration and downward social mobility, see Kim 2011; Nguyễn Thị Nguyệt Minh 2012; and Turner and Oswin 2015.
5 For example, Walters observes that airline agents at the site of departure now do the work of inspecting travel documents such as passports. Prescreening helps traffic flow more freely over borders (2006, 194–95).
6 Eder analyzes this relationship by distinguishing between hard and soft borders: "Europe can be taken as a case of how border discourses on imaginary boundaries (i.e. soft facts) can play a causal role in the making of institutional (hard) Europe which we call the European Union" (2006, 256). This example is particularly resonant as we complete this introduction, for different countries in Europe are at this moment reconsidering their union and reworking their borders in response to a refugee crisis.
7 Kate Jellema (2005) offers a parallel case of how newly prosperous families in a Red River Delta village remoralize their wealth through merit donations to temples and community events.

PART I

SPACE, PLACE, AND CONTENTIOUS POLITICS OF MARKET REDEVELOPMENT

Introduction: The Spatial Politics of Marketplaces

Linda J. Seligmann

The chapters in this part address the dynamics of displacement and resettlement under way among market traders in Vietnam. Three of the chapters are based on field research among traders in the upland province of Lào Cai, home to multiple minority groups, an increasingly popular tourist destination, and the site of substantial cross-border trade with China. The fourth chapter is centered on marketplaces in Hanoi. The majority of policies aimed at defining, altering, and destroying market space are put into place by state officials and implemented by market managers, yet these policies do not go uncontested. Kirsten Endres's ethnographic fieldwork and scrutiny of archival documents on the daily management of Lào Cai City's central market and long-term plans for it demonstrate the significant and patterned ways that bureaucratic documents serve both performative and coercive functions to perpetuate state control over market spaces, as well as traders and their activities. At the same time, however, Endres, by tracking between the documents and her interactions with traders and managers, traces how these routinized and formulaic exercises of bureaucratic language and rationality frequently make the state less rather than more legible to people. Much is excluded from the documents or erased because of the direct involvement of state authorities, for example, in their misconstruing of financial data, corruption, and collection of bribes, resulting in a disjuncture between formulaic documents and lived sociality. Endres shows how the state's efforts to make Lào Cai City market traders pay for their own displacement and the renovation of the central market, as outlined in documents, led small-scale traders to challenge the documents when they became aware of what they were obfuscating and of how state officials were devolving unfair and sometimes fabricated costs onto traders.

Sarah Turner examines the efforts of minority traders of different kinds—specifically mobile street vendors, more established traders, and wholesale traders—in Lào Cai to contest state control and authority. Not only does she ask what "the street" means as a defining characteristic of traders, but she also documents how ethnicity and tourism intervene in the ways traders are treated, where their activities transpire, and how traders, in turn, attempt to evade state surveillance in creative but limited fashion.

Christine Bonnin deconstructs the kinds of development ideologies that catalyze the state infrastructural projects to build, relocate, and manage markets, calling attention to disconnections between the state's compulsion to alleviate poverty and achieve modernization and its simultaneous lack of communication regarding marketing culture and livelihood practices with upland traders and local market managers. These failures of communication are not inadvertent; they are compelled by deepseated perceptions of upland traders as chaotic and in need of instruction. As both Turner and Endres also observe, while traders do not accept these characterizations, they nevertheless experience economic and political hardships as a consequence of these costly policies of displacement and resettlement.

Finally, Gertrud Hüwelmeier stresses how markets constitute socially constructed spaces and a distinctive culture that was long ago described by Clifford Geertz (1978) as a "bazaar"—a site of economic exchange and myriad social networks that serve purposes of information sharing and patron clientelism, among other functions. These sites are also highly politicized, and Hüwelmeier illuminates the struggles over the control of space, the consequences of failed state projects in the name of market socialism, and the merging of the licit and illicit among traders and officials in the sprawling, opaque flea market.

There are intriguing similarities between the dynamics of displacement and resettlement underway among these market traders and those found among traders in many other world regions, despite the distinction that Vietnam is a socialist country (Brown 2006; Cross and Morales 2007; K. T. Hansen, Little, and Milgram 2013; Lindell 2010b; Roy and AlSayyad 2004; Seligmann 2013; Seligmann and Guevara 2013). I first want to call attention to these commonalities and then elaborate on some of the methodological, theoretical, and ethnographic strengths of these chapters by discussing three principal themes: (1) the rationales that states offer for their policies of displacement, dislocation, and enforced fixity; (2) the consequences these policies have for vendors and why it is that, in general, state officials and ideology tend to ignore these consequences; and (3) the ways traders shape and contest these policies in practice, but also how scale, as well as ethnic and class stratification, intervene in traders' strategies to alter state policies. I conclude by outlining future research directions that these contributors point us toward.

Roughly around the same time—the end of the twentieth and beginning of the twenty-first century—many states, regardless of whether they were officially socialist or not, embraced ideologies of modernization and development that went hand in hand with neoliberal economic policies. Eviction, restructuring, and, not uncommonly, an intensification of surveillance and law enforcement took place at this moment in time in informal markets and among mobile traders worldwide. The impact of these policies was shaped by the existing palimpsest of the social, cultural, and institutional landscape in which they were implemented. In the cases that Endres, Turner, Bonnin, and Hüwelmeier describe, the rationales for the policies varied. In some instances, the emphasis was on the need to tear down preexisting strata of flexible and apparently chaotic economic and social trading regimes in order to replace them with practices and processes well framed within the tenets of bureaucratic rationality. In other instances, the discourse specifically emphasized development as a poverty-reduction mechanism, focusing more intently on the racial or ethnic composition of those who traded and the need to instruct them in proper economic thinking, etiquette, and practice. That is, ethnic ranking itself according to superiority and inferiority was embedded in the discourse, policies, and practices of modernization. The state's assumption was that new and permanent well-defined markets would lift people out of poverty and teach them how to properly engage in market transactions and economies. Yet other reasons given for displacing or anchoring vendors to one permanent site called attention to the need for environmentally enlightened restructuring of the urban land-scape in order to make it "greener." As Turner observes, this went hand in hand with state visions that sought to attract tourists as a source of foreign exchange by providing them with an experience that, while different from their everyday lives, nevertheless offered them comfort and safety.[1]

The curious thing about these justifications for uprooting traders from their locus of livelihood is that, almost to a one, they rarely met their objectives and often did very much the opposite, as recounted by the authors. Hence, even though the state, in its multiple manifestations, desired to accumulate revenues through controlling licensing, taxation, and the purchase and leasing of market stalls, the opposite occurred. Spanking-new "ghost" markets, as Hüwelmeier describes them, attracted neither vendors nor clients and were even repurposed for other social functions that vendors and residents thought were more useful and significant. Traders who have been relocated or displaced have rarely viewed their changed circumstances in a positive fashion and few traders have benefited economically from these changes. Stalls remain empty and business has declined precipitously. According to data cited by Christine Bonnin, in the upland Lào Cai province of northern Vietnam, fifteen marketplace infrastructural projects that were built have failed, costing VNĐ11.5 billion (US\$589,744). Ten of these markets are completely empty and the other five are "less efficient," with fewer traders and, therefore, fewer revenues entering the coffer of the state.

Given these outcomes, there are at least four reasons that may help to explain why these policies have persisted despite their failure, at least from the vantage point of stimulating and improving the livelihoods of vendors. First, and most obviously, while traders may find these arrangements to their disadvantage, the state, according to an imagined aesthetic schema and ideal notions of economic rationality, is actually not particularly interested in improving vendors' livelihoods per se but rather in improving how urban centers and the nation, as a whole, are viewed by foreign investors and visitors. Second, state agents, at each step along the way, have been able to siphon off revenues for themselves and have done so, ironically, in many cases, through existing patron-client ties they had already established with vendors. That is, even if policies are not particularly effective, they persist because they generate revenues for those who are charged with enforcing them and the agents themselves have undergone, increasingly, a professionalization process as official bureaucrats. Third, the state aims for legibility of its population, a long-standing concern. Homogeneity, permanence, stability, accountability, and acquiescence are all aspects that lend themselves to legibility, and thus to people and markets that are not fluid (Scott 1998). These criteria contrast sharply with how traders view their optimal conditions for making a living, although one must be cautious about overgeneralizing, since traders themselves are stratified—by how permanent their businesses are and where they are located, and by age, gender, and ethnicity. Fourth, as Das and Poole have shown, the state actively strives to create margins and these margins are not necessarily located along territorial borders but rather carve up social and political spaces such that a topography of power structures social, political, and economic relationships that include or exclude some populations but not others. Nevertheless, even as the state may seek to consolidate state control over subjects, populations, territories, and lives, rather than the state being "about" its legibility, there are many spaces, forms, and practices through which "the state is continually experienced and undone through the illegibility of its own practices, documents, and words" (Das and Poole 2004, 10).

The success of market traders depends on their command of a subtle and rich knowledge of spatial relationships and their capacity to use mobility to their advantage. One can sharply juxtapose the fluidity of many retail, and even wholesale, traders in upland Vietnam to the fixed marketplaces that are the objective of state projects of modernization and supported by international lending agencies and private investors. The specific grammar of mobility among traders depends upon a number of variables—access to clients, access to products, knowledge of the marketing environment—that is, the layout of cities and the networks between city and countryside—the locus of residence and marketing operations, the periodicity of markets, the web(s) of social relationships that facilitate information sharing and support systems, and the intervention of ethnicity.

Bonnin and Turner most explicitly delineate how nonfixed trading is also elaborately intercalated with other kinds of livelihood activities. Temporality is as important as spatial relations in these calculations. Trade—including careful attention to the timing of periodic markets, agricultural cycles, and craft production—provides multiple streams of income. It would require systematic data gathering to discern whether or not trading (and possibly craft production) subsidize agricultural production and whether or not the establishment of fixed markets may thereby undermine the ability of traders to farm. That is, periodic marketing and other kinds of temporary migrant labor not infrequently permit impoverished peasants to continue to cultivate and remain on their lands (Collins 1988). This is something that few government officials necessarily realize. Further, the very movement of vendors is intimately tied to the cycles of production and the locus and availability of the particular commodities they are acquiring and selling.

Mobility fosters distinctive kinds of relationships with clients and other traders at retail and wholesale levels, and it is important to remember that some vendors combine or alternate between operating as wholesalers and retailers. Ethnic discrimination is apparent in the manner in which traders of different kinds are treated, where they are located, and how stable their operations are. Upland ethnic minority traders are the target of market displacement and conversion into fixed vendors or, alternatively, they are prevented from entering urban centers altogether, whereas this same focus has not extended to lowland Kinh traders, who are viewed as already incorporated into state mores of modernity and development (see, especially, Turner's chapter in this volume). Hence, state policies with respect to market restructuring also have embedded within them a kind of social engineering that envisions an ideal citizenry that the state will more easily be able to control. At the same time, as Turner shows, even these policies take unexpected turns as tourists embrace the indigeneity represented by upland, rural ethnic traders and demonstrate a preference for their handicrafts, hence countering the hegemonic vision of citizenship and urban spatial design that the state seeks to assert. Turner shows how Hmong and Yao traders who were evicted and displaced from their selling "places" or who simply cannot find a niche in the now-transformed urban trading environment have worked creatively (and out of necessity) to elaborate new "places" to sell their wares by following tourist routes, becoming mobile wholesalers of handicrafts, and establishing temporary secondary marketplaces. These efforts to reestablish their livelihoods have not been without conflict. Competition has increased *within* ethnic groups that are attempting to benefit from tourism in different ways.

Policies of displacement, re-placement and enclosure/permanence are about more than meets the eye. Most urban planners would agree that the flows of mobile traders in urban centers that are experiencing increasing population density and vehicular traffic contribute to hazards for pedestrians and to greater congestion. Yet these policies are about the expansion of bureaucratic rationality, the state's capacity at multiple levels to capture taxes and other kinds of loyalties from the general population, and the efforts of representatives of the socialist state to shape and manage a controllable capitalist economy. It is not evident that they serve the needs of all consumers. This is something that would entail additional research—that is, to discern if permanent markets cater to particular populations and not to others—and if they do, what the characteristics of those consumers are. Research done in other world regions, especially Latin America, suggests that the cheaper outlays for traders' informal operations make their products more affordable for poorer populations *and* that poorer populations may benefit from provisioning such traders, and from bartering or purchasing from them (e.g., Babb 1998; Cross and Morales 2007; Ødegaard 2010; Seligmann 1989, 2004, 2013; see also Brown 2006; Clark 1994; and K. T. Hansen 2004, for Africa).

The state policies with reference to traders that I have sketched out above are surprisingly limited in their effectiveness in reaching their intended goals. The contributors to this part offer excellent reasons for why and how they fall short that give us great insight into the cultural dimensions of trading in Vietnam. Endres carefully examines the disarticulation between what is laid out in "the archive"—legal, regulatory, and policy documents—and how things *actually* work in markets, that is, who gets what and who gets to do what in light of the occupation of party committee and management organizations, the enactment of patron-client relationships, the deployment of highly gendered behaviors, and greasing of wheels through the subterranean yet well-understood flow of personal favors that circulate in the form of loyalties, commodities, information, and networks that are transacted and converted into symbolic, political, or economic capital, as the case may be. This "roster" of debts and credit is complex and traders and officials alike make elaborate calculations and keep track of them in a manner that constitutes a powerful yet quite invisible alternative archive. One of the consequences of the ongoing intermeshing of official and hidden archives is that the practices that emerge from this articulation are not transparent, predictable, or easily legible to "the state" as a unified entity and, therefore, policies, as enforced by state officials, are rarely coherent. While official archives often appear rather mundane, reviewing them in conjunction with how they are employed, interpreted, and evaded in daily practices makes them invaluable as ethnographic sources. Interviews with the individuals who produce these documents provide yet another lens through which to view the competing and sometimes overlapping bureaucratic fields within which vendors operate (Riles 2006a).

"The state" is highly critical of initiatives to create workable markets that emerge from below or of grassroots transformations of spaces that were intended for markets but were never successful into useful community places for athletic fields, child care facilities, or meetings. Failed place-making on the part of the state, converted into community functions, challenges the public face of the state.

Sometimes, state policies are explicitly resisted through demonstrations and mobilizations. Interestingly, these mobilizations often initially take the form of rumors that circulate. Bonnin explains how the deliberate exclusion of upland residents and traders from planning decisions about the markets, for example, led to rumors that the market would be torn down to make way for a mega-supermarket owned by a Chinese company or that a fancy upscale tourist market with exceedingly high rents would be established. Ultimately, these rumors catalyzed a major mobilization of both Kinh and minority traders to make a three-hundred-kilometer journey to Hanoi to appeal to the central government not to destroy the market. How rumor sparked a more heightened degree of action and agency among traders is akin to some of the examples that James Scott (1990) has described of the ways that apparently minor language exchanges or practices that are often hidden from public view may create explicit challenges to the status quo. These "rumors," it turns out, reveal the more deeply analytical grasp that people have of economic policies and of state regulatory and enforcement mechanisms.

An important variable that intervenes in the livelihoods of traders and the ways that they contest policies leveled against them is scale. Alan Smart and George Lin (2007) and Neil Brenner (2000) and Brenner, Jamie Peck, and Nik Theodore (2010) have written at length about scale, specifically with reference to those working in informal economies and living in urban spaces, respectively, while James Ferguson and Akhil Gupta (2002) and Michael Smith (2001) have discussed the effects of scale, in general, on understanding the workings of sociopolitical and cultural interconnections. All these authors argue that it is a mistake to correlate physical distance with social space, particularly because of the flows of people, both permanently and temporarily, from one locus to another, and because of the ways in which local interactions and interpersonal relationships, as well as specific cultural milieus, fracture entities thought to be unitary and coherent, such as "the state." This is important because, increasingly, traders operate across substantively different geographical extents that range from the very local to the transnational, global, or both. These complex interconnections are not homogeneous and, in fact, Michael Smith prefers to refer to these movements as translocal rather than as transnational. For example, although a Hmong trader in Vietnam might be purchasing wares from a supplier in China across the border, the supplier could very well be from the Hmong trader's hometown and, therefore, provide invaluable connections and information that serve the mobile trader well. These border populations and crossings clearly also call into question national loyalties. In a very different vein, what appears small scale may be immensely consequential because of face-to-face interactions. On the other hand, as a Hmong trader lobbies for a lower monthly stall rent or license in a newly renovated market, despite geographical proximity of the market committee, its members could hail from Hanoi or be Kinh Vietnamese, thereby creating far greater sociopolitical and economic hurdles and distance. In a similar fashion, local state agents tasked with enforcing regulations may not conform to central state mandates in their everyday practices. These are not given conditions. Scale has a critical interpersonal variable that influences mobility pathways, access to information, patron-client ties, and the clamping down or ignoring of corruption.

The *processes* that create interconnections across space are impeded or facilitated by existing economic, social, and cultural practices and ties, such that it is impossible to assume that what is "local" is near and what is distant geographically is not. As Smart and Lin (2007, 284) point out, a grammar of "insiders" and "outsiders" remains but it is not necessarily correlated with spatial locus. Kinship ties across space, ethnic affiliation, and patron-client networks intervene in structuring how scale affects vendors and how such sociability and interconnections create "family" that serves economic purposes in many instances and, just as important, may contribute to how traders calculate the risk they are willing to take. Smart and Lin (2007, 287) point out that those investors with social relationships and cultural affinities are more willing to undertake risky endeavors, a point that Hüwelmeier also makes in her chapter. In similar fashion, vendors may invest heavily in expanding the reach of their kinship or lineage ties in order to conduct business at greater scales. The *shaping* and *impact* of policies—such as neoliberal economic projects—and their *enforcement* hinge on the question of scale. All the contributors to this part demonstrate well the value of fine-grained field research in understanding how scale operates to affect networks, alliances, factions, and exchange circuits. Their findings make it clear why so many state policies intended to restructure and discipline traders such that they become more legible to authorities and conform to state (as well as private) objectives of development rarely succeed. Their findings also demonstrate how traders themselves have a canny comprehension of the way scale works on the ground and are able to use that knowledge for purposes of fortifying clientelism, extending networks, and skirting state control.

In short, the volume editors and contributors to this part have emphasized the unexpected ways in which movements and policies come together in trade economies to bring about, on the one hand, displacement and precarious livelihoods and, on the other, a fragile yet evident resilience among vendors as they manipulate (often because they are forced to) these flows for purposes of acquiring information, products, brokering deals, and evading state demands and coercion.

The nuanced ethnographies of each of the chapters in this part emerge from on-the-ground field research, together with the use of middle-range theory. Future directions for research that these contributions set the groundwork for are three aspects of how control and power work together through space. The first is whether traders will embark upon more explicit modes of political mobilization and resistance to state policies in the future or whether the stratification among vendors, the force of the state, and even consumer demands will impede such actions. Or perhaps it is the case that more subtle kinds of resistance that are more difficult to trace are underway (some are described in these chapters), such as those that take advantage of the uneven, nonbounded nature of scale and networks as they combine. It would be fascinating to know more about these and what roles space, place, and flows play in these actions.

Second, and closely related to the first point, it would be worthwhile to examine how official authorities perceive traders' bodies in accordance with traders' locus—on the street, inside a warehouse, in front of a hotel, or mingling with tourists—the positioning of their bodies—standing, sitting, crouching, or moving—and even the dress and condition of their bodies. Likewise, how do traders themselves understand and use their bodies to contest constraints on their activities and to make a livelihood? What are the cultural, economic, and political roots of these distinctive grammars of the body? This is one aspect of the biopolitics of the market that is deserving of more attention.

Finally, with the shift in how the state envisions social and economic space and its optimal utility, will the discourse that is employed in interactions between vendors and state agents, local market committees, clients, store owners, and tourists and among vendors themselves also undergo patterned transformations or modifications? Pierre Bourdieu's extensive work on how discourse itself is converted into economic and social capital is worth considering as yet another variable in examining how the discontinuities of scale will affect the livelihoods of traders in these changing conditions.

NOTE

1 Ray Bromley offers an excellent, succinct list of arguments, in general, that have been set forth both in favor of and against street vendors in cities (2000, 4–10).

CHAPTER ONE

MAKING THE MARKETPLACE: TRADERS, CADRES, AND BUREAUCRATIC DOCUMENTS IN LÀO CAI CITY

Kirsten W. Endres

It was a chilly January evening in 2011. Darkness had fallen early over the city of Lào Cai on Vietnam's northern border with China. The electric heater started circulating warm air as I made myself comfortable with a cup of hot tea and a stack of official reports I had obtained from the management board of Lào Cai's largest market, the main field site of my research. I was aware that the written administrative records would differ from the complex picture that had emerged from my conversations and interviews with market vendors and management officials over the past three months, but I nevertheless hoped to gain some further insight into the local handling of public market management. I started flicking through the pages. The opening sentences seemed identical in all six documents in front of me. "Listen to that," I said to Tâm, my research assistant, who was relaxing on the other bed in our sparsely furnished room. "The staff's ideological standpoints are steadfast, sufficient for the work. Internal solidarity and collective strength is high. Within the unit, clear guidance . . ." With a mischievous grin, Tâm chimed in, ". . . is provided by the leadership, and the staff has performed its duties with excellent results!" "Oh," I asked in surprise, "you have already read the document?" Tâm answered, "Not yet! But I'm quite familiar with bureaucratic reports, and their wording is pretty much the same in all government institutions."

The role of written documents has long been understood as essential to modern bureaucratic practice (Weber 1978, 956–1005). As "paradigmatic artifacts of modern knowledge practices" (Riles 2006b, 2), documents are important tools in the exercise of governing authority and in the mediation of state-society relations. They do not necessarily, however, reflect the social reality that engenders them. Instead, they are implicated in "the construction of a distinctive documentary reality" (Atkinson and Coffey 2004, 66). This is, in part, achieved by employing and adhering to specific conventions of textual form, content, and style that belong to the wider tool kit of simplification techniques through which states attempt to render the complex social realities of their subjects legible (J. C. Scott 1998). As such, written documents can be powerful tools in the creation of what David Dery has termed "papereality"—that is, the production of binding representations "that take precedence over the things and events represented" (1998, 678). This may then also have effects in the opposite direction, namely, the creation of illegibility. In his 2013 book *The Government of Mistrust*, Ken MacLean has convincingly shown that the incongruity between (top-down) governing documents and (bottom-up) reported outcomes in pre-reform socialist Vietnam in fact disrupted legibility from within, rendering the bureaucracy "partially illegible to itself due to differences between what low-level cadres claimed and what was achieved" (2013, 9).

Topical work in the emerging anthropology of documentation also urges us to consider the role that the production and circulation of bureaucratic paperwork plays in actually shaping experiential and social realities. As "material objects of law and governance" (Navaro-Yashin 2007, 81) endowed with both performative and phantasmatic qualities (80), bureaucratic documents, from government decrees to administrative reports, are likewise "constitutive of broader associations of people, places, and other things" (Hull 2012, 18). From this Latourian perspective (Latour 2005), anthropologists have approached bureaucratic documents as "graphic artifacts" that facilitate the formation of networks and coalitions among people and groups both within and outside the bureaucracy (Hull 2003, 291; see also Harper 1998), as material objects with a potential quality of information that emerges in unpredictable ways from social interactions and power relations (Kregg Hetherington 2011; Leshkowich 2014b) or as forms of bureaucratic inscription through which structural violence is inflicted upon the poor (Gupta 2012).

Building on these insights, this chapter examines the relationship between the documentary—or representational—reality created in the market management reports, and the everyday market sociality in which encounters between market management officials and vendors take place. Following Hull's contention that "documents, like other forms of material culture, . . . are central to the everyday representation and, thereby, the reproduction of states" (Hull 2012, 26), I argue that written reports, as part of wider bureaucratic assemblages of circulating documents (Schwenkel 2015a, 213), play an important role in fortifying the elusive line that makes state and society appear as two separate, autonomous entities (T. Mitchell 1991, 90). After all, "the state" does not exist in and of itself, above and distinct from the people who constitute "society" (Abrams 1988; Trouillot 2001). Instead, it is continuously performed into being through complex sets of bureaucratic practices, routines, and encounters (Bierschenk and Olivier de Sardan 2014; Krupa and Nugent 2015; Mathur 2016). Written reports contribute to this process not so much through their content as through their mundane production, authoritative form, and vertical movement within the administrative hierarchy (MacLean 2013, 18). The cases presented in this chapter show that ordinary people have little opportunity to insert themselves into these streams of bureaucratic paperwork through which authority is established, subjects are governed, and marketplaces are made. In the experiential reality of the everyday market bustle, however, the boundary between formal state rule and informal social and economic practice often gets blurred (Gupta 1995). Below I explore two different, yet interrelated forms of blurring (or crossing) such boundaries. The first two cases presented show how market officials establish their positions through paperwork, and how these documents in turn enable bureaucrats to have authority that the traders can then undermine (or bolster) by paying bribes in order to circumvent the rules. The third ethnographic example looks at the ways in which bureaucratic documents such as master plans, government decrees, and written reports also shape the experienced reality by contributing to "the realization of state projections and revenues" (Bear

2011, 57), in this case marketplace redevelopment. While the traders were excluded from the decision-making processes affecting their lives and futures, they were able to insert their objections through petitions and media coverage.

The main research for this project was carried out from October 2010 to March 2011, with brief follow-ups in subsequent years until December 2016.[1] Much of my daily fieldwork routine consisted of hanging out in the market's various sections and observing the ebb and flow of trading activities and social interactions among and between vendors, market administration personnel, and law enforcement officials. Data collection also involved a representative questionnaire survey among sixty stallholders, countless informal conversations, and sixteen in-depth ego-network interviews with traders, transporters, and intermediaries. Semi-structured interviews were conducted with seven officials at province and city level, including two market managers.

PLANNING ASSEMBLAGES AND MARKETPLACE POLICIES IN LÀO CAI CITY

Market management reports, or any other kinds of bureaucratic documents, do not exist in and of themselves. They are entangled in wider paperwork-producing bureaucratic structures and processes and constitute "a crucial means for exerting and sustaining power" (Espeland 1993, 298) by enabling government officials to establish their positions and authority through paperwork. In the following paragraphs, I briefly sketch the contours of Vietnam's planning assemblages in the early 2000s of which marketplace policies form part. In the words of Simone Abram and Gisa Weszkalnys, the central aims of such assemblages "include assumptions of a possible or idealized congruence between architectural and built form and the social order; attempted mediation between public and private interests and powers; efforts to improve forms of spatial control and regulation, with all their intended and unintended consequences; and finally, a rationalization and comprehensive integration of different elements of state provision to ensure the welfare of the greatest number" (2013, 8).

Vietnam's current national and provincial market redevelopment policies aim at developing the national market network "in a civilized, modern direction" (Bộ Công Thương 2015, Art.1/d) with the overall goal of "ensuring social security and stable livelihoods" (Art.2/a). Although rural markets are part of the agenda, these policies are most intricately linked with the government's accelerated efforts to speed up urbanization and urban development, both of which are seen as crucial conditions for successful industrialization and modernization. In 2001, the country adopted a hierarchical classification system for cities (updated in 2009 and 2011), defined by a number of criteria, including urban infrastructure facilities and approved schemes of urban expansion (World Bank 2011, 10). Higher-grade cities enjoy not only a higher administrative status but also greater access to and control over financial resources. According to Coulthart, Quang, and Sharpe (2006, 4), this explains why attaining promotion to the next grade apparently became "a major preoccupation of local government authorities." As a consequence of this ambition, many investments in prestigious infrastructure projects, including new public market buildings, primarily aim at meeting the criteria of the next-higher classification level rather than at responding to the more immediate needs of the urban population.

Much in common with that of other cities in the country, Lào Cai's history has been marked by repeated episodes of urban destruction and renewal (see, e.g.,

Schwenkel 2012, 446). During the brief but violent border war with China in early 1979, the town was bombed to the ground and left largely abandoned and derelict for the years to follow. After the normalization of Sino-Vietnamese relations in the late 1980s, the town was rebuilt from scratch. Throughout the 1990s and early 2000s, the growing economic opportunities for cross-border trade attracted new waves of Kinh migrants from the lowland regions and fueled the rapid transformation of Lào Cai's urban landscape. Upon its merger with the district-level town (*thị xã*) of Cam Đường in 2004, Lào Cai was recognized as a grade 3 city (*đô thị loại III*).[2] An impressive complex of multistory buildings housing the provincial administration emerged along the highway that connects the two formerly independent towns, and a number of new residential areas (*khu đô thị mới*) were established as architectural playgrounds of the newly rich and modern urban planners. The beautification of Lào Cai's historical center included building a promenade along the banks of the Red River and the redevelopment of the river embankment area into a modern, upscale urban residential district. Ten years after its elevation to grade 3, in 2014, Lào Cai was upgraded to a grade 2 city. As one media report noted, "After ten years of steadfast effort, Lào Cai has effectively created the image of a civilized, beautiful, and rich city" (Thu Phương 2014). Meanwhile, on the other side of the river, a skyline of Chinese high-rise buildings has been emerging. In light of all this urban renewal, Lào Cai's central market seemed clearly out of date.

When the Zone A market building was inaugurated in 1996, it was seen as "an important step towards realizing a diversified economic development, meeting the hopes and expectations of the people" (Báo Lào Cai 1996). As mentioned above, the new livelihood opportunities that were expected to open up with the facilitation of cross-border trade had already drawn many settlers to the town under construction. Once a marketplace characterized by "its diversity of autochthonous races," as noted in the French colonial Guide Alphabetique Taupin (1937, 176), Lào Cai's central market now turned into a modern public market facility dominated by Kinh small-scale traders. Throughout the 1990s and early 2000s, small-scale cross-border trade flourished and fortunes were made. The Lào Cai central market soon became too crowded, and in 2004 a second two-story building (Zone B) was constructed with a total floor space of twenty-five hundred square meters. A year earlier, in January 2003, the central government had issued a first comprehensive decree aimed at improvements in the following areas: marketplace network development, investment into marketplace construction and repairs, market organization and management, and regulatory control over business activities in the marketplace (Chính Phủ 2003). In 2007, the Ministry of Industry and Commerce approved a first master plan toward the year 2020 that targeted a total of 914 markets throughout the country for "development," including both the upgrading of previously existing marketplaces and the construction of new ones (Bộ Công Thương 2007).[3] Curiously enough, in this master plan, the Lào Cai central market was listed as one of the fifty-six class 1 markets in the country that were to be left in their then-current condition (*giữ nguyên*).[4]

When I started research in Lào Cai in October 2010, however, the central market was already buzzing with rumors about the local government's plan to reconstruct the Zone A market building. To that end the market management board was looking for an investor (*chủ đầu tư*). The 2007 master plan formulated by the Ministry of Industry and Commerce had already pushed for the privatization of local market renovation and upgrading, "with the motto of state and people working together on a voluntary basis for mutual benefit" (Bộ Công Thương 2007, Art. 8.2). In 2009 the government issued a new decree, as an amendment to its 2003 decree on the development of markets (Chính Phủ 2003), stipulating that only class 2 and class 3 markets would be financed through the state's development investment budget (Chính Phủ 2009, Art.1/4).[5]

Many Lào Cai traders I talked to expressed mixed feelings about the central market reconstruction project. On the one hand, they said they would appreciate a more spacious stall, additional storage facilities, and, more generally, a cleaner and more modern market environment. On the other hand, however, they worried not only about the time they would have to spend in a temporary location during the time of construction but also about the negative effects of additional competitors on their profits in the market. In the middle years of the 2000s, their businesses had already become less profitable than they used to be. I asked Mr. Hung, who traded in household electronics, "How do you feel about the plans for constructing a new market?" He answered, "What do we know about the state's policy; they do whatever they see fit [*họ làm thì làm thôi*]. We worry because we are already many traders, and building a new market means there will be even more traders competing for customers. Business is already difficult enough these days, and the new market will make things even more difficult for us." I prodded further: "Has anybody actually asked your opinion on that matter?" "Nobody has asked us," he said; "they just proceed with their plans. They will hold meetings and announce their decisions by loudspeaker, that's how we will learn the news."

Market Management and Bureaucratic Reporting

With more than seven hundred registered vendors operating permanent stalls in the two separate buildings (Zone A and Zone B), the Lào Cai central market is the largest public market in the whole province. The market area was more or less clearly divided into different sections categorized by the type of goods sold there, for example, fresh and dried foods, medicinal herbs, household items, electronics, Vietnamese wooden handicrafts, souvenirs and refreshments, children's toys, textiles, garments, and shoes. In common with other major urban markets along the Vietnam-China border, the product range was dominated by Chinese imports, including low-quality items and counterfeit or fake goods that did not conform to existing product standards and certification requirements. In addition, the market had gained dubious fame among visitors for the easy availability of strictly prohibited or so-called hot goods. These goods included dangerous weapons (Tasers, guns, sharp knives, etc.) as well as items regarded as morally harmful, such as adult toys and sexual-enhancement products.

This bustle of legal and illegal vending activities was administered by a management board (*ban quản lý chợ*) comprising a director and vice director, an administrator, three accountants, one treasurer, and a general manager for security in charge of the security and parking-service teams. Operating under the authority of the local municipal People's Committee,[6] the Lào Cai central market management board's main tasks were (1) to assist the city administration in managing all ongoing market activities, including the commencement of stall rental agreements, the collection of monthly fees, and the coordination of repair and construction works; (2) to implement the relevant state policies; and (3) to make sure that stallholders abide by the rules and regulations governing the marketplace (see figure 1.1). As a street-level administrative unit, the market management board was naturally confronted with the dilemma of striking a reasonable balance between "compassion and flexibility on the one hand, and impartiality and rigid rule-application on the other hand" (Lipsky 1980, 15–16).

The following statement from a special 2010 performance report alludes to this dilemma by pointing out that the board's primary duties were difficult to reconcile: "The administrative specificities [of the market management board] are very complicated and involve direct contact with subjects from all levels of society. In our activities we have to ensure state administration and social management on the one hand, and on the other we have to ensure stable business activities and increase revenue for the state budget" (Báo Cáo 2010). The annual performance and accountability reports submitted to the city People's Committee, however, did not provide insights about how this dilemma was solved. Instead, they assessed the implementation of (state) policies that control and regulate economic activities in the marketplace, listed the revenue collected from stallholders, outlined the board's tasks during the upcoming year, and highlighted the main difficulties that interfered with the performance of duties.[7] The reports examined in this chapter document the activities of the Lào Cai central market management board for the years 2005 to 2012. They were signed by the board's director and followed a standardized outline of headings and subheadings. Their dry, repetitive jargon is not only typical of the Vietnamese bureaucratic system but also an effective tool for establishing authority. To set the stage for my subsequent ethnographic cases, a brief summary of the reports' content is in order.

A typical report first lays out the general responsibilities of the market management board and confirms the latter's ability to master these tasks, in spite of various difficulties concerning the deteriorating material conditions of the market. It then moves on to report the "results of performing duties," including (1) public order, hygiene, and safety; (2) prevention of illegal activities; (3) vendor management/control; (4) revenue collected; and (5) budget spent. The next section lists the common duties of the market management board for each month of the upcoming year and is basically identical in all the reports at hand. The report then reviews specific difficulties and potential solutions. This part invariably starts with the sentence "Although the market management board has admonished all sectors to carefully implement all tasks and targets, there still remain some shortcomings." The most pressing issue, repeated in all the reports, concerned the (growing) presence of street vendors in front of the market and on the street and pavement. As a standard solution for tackling the space issue, the reports suggest the construction of a third market building (Zone C). Another frequently mentioned issue was that some traders sold goods for which they were not licensed. The 2008 report stated that several market vendors traded in prohibited items, such as weapons and sex toys. The final section, "Petitions, Requests," basically lists (or repeats) all necessary repairs and other desired improvements (e.g., additional fire extinguishing equipment). It also suggests reconstructing Zone A (2010) or, during the time when this cannot be done yet, considering upgrading the building (2011, 2012).

By emphasizing the board's commitment to ensuring efficient rule-based market management, the documentary reality created in the written report asserts that government cadres exercise control over the economic activities of market vendors by enacting the state's relevant policies and guidelines. It does not, however, and for obvious reasons, shed light on the vast realm of discretionary decision making, informal negotiations, and the blurring of boundaries between public and private interests that keep the market running. To grasp the reality of lived experience, we therefore need to turn to other sources. In the following case studies, I contrast specific passages from the reports with ethnographic accounts of conversations with vendors and market management staff at the Lào Cai central market.

Figure 1.1. Marketplace rules and regulations displayed in front of the main entrance. Photograph by K. W. Endres.

ESTABLISHING AUTHORITY, GOVERNING SUBJECTS

> The administrative apparatus has been strengthened and assigned tasks to the staff according to their professional specialization and knowledge. The staff's ideological standpoints are steadfast, sufficient for the work. Internal solidarity and collective strength is high. Within the unit, clear guidance is provided by the leadership, and the staff has performed its duties with excellent results. (Market reports 2008–12, point I/1, "Achievements")

Mrs. Cúc had been working in the market administration for many years until she was promoted to director of the market management board in 2011. Her flamboyant personality, reflected in the way she dressed and groomed herself, did not really fit the stereotypical mold of a Vietnamese bureaucrat, but it blended in well with the youthful and modern style that prevailed among the female vendors at the market. According to her, the market was like a miniature society. "There are all sorts of good and bad people," she explained. "They're usually very gentle, but there are moments when they fight with each other, when they quarrel and compete for customers or vending space in the aisles." Moreover, she hinted at the presence of criminal elements, thugs, and hoodlums. A market official, Mrs. Cúc argued, needed to have certain characteristics in order to tame the unruly nature of the marketplace: "As a market official you need to have a 'mafia temperament' [*máu xã hội đen*], you need to be able to tie their wrists and ankles, otherwise you can't do the job." Whereas, on the one hand, she thought it was important to be authoritative and resolute "like a man," on the other, she emphasized that a market official must be "close to the vendors" and act with sentiment (*tình cảm*). While working in close contact with the people and acting with reason and sentiment are among the ideal attributes of a Vietnamese government official (Malarney 1997; Endres 2014b), Mrs. Cúc claimed that the relations between traders and officials at this market were particularly close compared with those at other border markets: "The relationship between traders and the management is friendlier and more human," she reasoned. "Other markets are managed according to strict principles, and traders are not in close contact with the authorities and the administration."

An official from the city's People's Committee saw things a bit more critically. "The overall market management [in Lào Cai City] is sluggish and inefficient," he ranted. "Staff members are idlers [*người ăn không ngồi rồi*]," he went on, "kings and queens who rule their subjects and enjoy life." The majority of market management personnel allegedly got into their position by way of connections and favoritism, not because of their education and knowledge. "Most of them are children of big men [*con ông to*] or relatives of leaders [*người lãnh đạo*]," the city official pointed out. Mrs. Cúc (whose husband was a high-ranking cadre in the city administration) confirmed these allegations: "Look, our accountant T. is a relative of an army general, the other accountant is the sister-in-law of the director of the internal affairs division, the husband of Mrs. M. is director of the Lào Cai border gate economic zone management board, [and] Mrs. O. is the granddaughter of the director of the foreign affairs office. All of them are relatives of 'big men'—in case of any wrongdoing, nobody dares to punish them."

Besides criticizing the staff's immunity to punishment gained through the "protective umbrella" (*ô dù*) held over them by high-ranking benefactors, Mrs. Cúc thought the actual workload of market management did not justify the amount of staff in the board. "So there are all these people who have nothing to do," she concluded. "Like our two accountants, they're only busy for five days per month, the rest of the time they just sit around. Our state is feeding an apparatus of unnecessary officials, it's such a waste." While the report naturally does not refer to the practice of patronage that characterizes public-sector employment in Vietnam, it alludes to some of its effects by self-critically noting that "professional standards [within the board] are not uniform and administrative work mainly relies on experience; work is constrained by low professionalism and a lack of method and proper handling" (Market reports 2005–12, point I/2, "Difficulties"). The verbatim repetition of these "shortcomings" in each of the reports, however, reveals the ritual nature of self-assessment practices in the Vietnamese bureaucratic system as much as it inscribes the market management board's authority as an administrative unit of the local government that does its best, in spite of certain constraints, to implement its duties and responsibilities. As I show in the following section, this authority, established to some considerable extent through paperwork, can then be undermined—or perhaps also bolstered—by the traders who pay the cadres bribes in order to circumvent the rules.

CIRCUMVENTING THE RULES

It also frequently occurs that vendors trade in goods for which they are not licensed. This has a large [negative] effect on the market management as well as on market activities. . . . The [vendors'] sense of compliance with the rules is still limited and the market management is not yet strict enough, which is why [such incidents] are still common and vendors complain about each other. (Market reports 2007 through 2012, section V, "Meeting Difficulties, Reasons, and Solutions")

Mr. Thanh's stall was conveniently located in the market's entrance hall and accessible from three different sides. Together with his wife he mainly traded in mats, pillows, and musical instruments. Besides that, he retailed a small range of household goods, such as rice cookers and lamps. In 2011, the neighboring vendor decided to move to Hanoi and sold his stall use rights to Mr. Thanh, who then took the opportunity to expand his assortment of merchandise to include children's toys.[8] When I asked him to assess his relationship with the market management board, he spoke in very positive terms. "The market management board provides the conditions for me to sell many different kinds of goods," he explained. "According to the regulations I'm only entitled to sell the goods I am registered for, but if I[followed that rule] I would not have enough to eat and would starve to death," he stated, continuing to defend himself. "In order to ensure an appropriate living standard for my family, I need to sell many other goods as well. The market management board has created the necessary conditions for me so that my goods don't get confiscated." Whereas Mr. Thanh did not elaborate on the necessary steps for these conditions to apply, conversations with vendors trading in prohibited items provided further clues. In the reports, this issue is touched upon in a cursory manner: "Some vendors secretly sell goods that the state prohibits, such as weapons, [sex toys], fake goods, contraband, and substandard items. . . . [Law] enforcement is still slack and lacks professional knowledge about fighting [these violations]. . . . Due to the lack of cooperation between local authorities and the infrequency of inspections, the perpetrators still continue to bring in fake and prohibited goods for sale inside the market" (Market reports 2008 through 2012, section V).

Vendors in the market's souvenir section were notorious for trading in weapons and sex toys under the counter, and the market management was well aware of this (see figure 1.2). Every once in a while, a vendor was caught in the act and had to face punishment. Mrs. Mai, for example, was caught selling sex toys to a group of male tourists. Her stall was closed down, but three days later she was back at her stall. "I had to prepare an envelope for the [market management] director," she explained. "If not, they would have closed my stall for a whole week." Mr. Thọ, director of the market management board in 2010, was in fact frequently seen strolling around in the market, sometimes in the company of his little grandson. He often sat down at one of the refreshment stalls from which he could watch the flow of customers in the souvenir section while having a free cup of tea and a cigarette. "Mr. Thọ roams around the market in order to loot," one of the vendors nagged. "He smokes for free, drinks for free, whatever his grandson likes he gets for free. Or he buys things he likes, but then he does not pay for them." Moreover, he was said to observe the stalls selling prohibited items in order to make some extra money by issuing fines. "This usually happens to those who haven't 'made law' [i.e., negotiated a bribe; see Endres 2014b] with him, they are fined and have their stalls closed for a week," Mrs. Mai related. A bribe arrangement, however, did not entail a guarantee that no more bribes and fines would be demanded. "It also happens to vendors who have already 'made law' with [the director] for the whole year," Mrs. Mai added. "That's why he often cruises around that section. No matter if it's a rainy day, a hot day, or a holiday, Mr. Thọ always shows up at the market."

Figure 1.2. Illegal goods are available at many stalls in the souvenir section. Photograph by K. W. Endres.

Yet Mr. Thọ, or, more generally, the market management board, was but one node in the wider local network of corruption that facilitated cross-border trade in Lào Cai City (Endres 2014b). This network included the customs office, the border police, the municipal Market Control Department, the Office for Standards, Metrology and Quality, the local police station, and the tax department. Whereas bribe arrangements were usually made on an individual basis (i.e., between an individual trader and state officials), some of my research data are also suggestive of the role of the market management board in coordinating bribe negotiations with other official agencies—at least during the time of Mr. Thọ: "When Mr. Thọ was the director it was easier [to trade in prohibited items]," Mrs. Mai said. "He acted more in the interests of the traders [than the new director], we could breathe more easily at the market." She went on explaining: "Before a police raid, a tax inspection, or a quarantine check, the officials would first have to 'work' with Mr. Thọ," hereby implying that the director made his own arrangements with the relevant authorities in favor of those traders who had bribed him beforehand. "Business was easy, because he took bribes [*ăn tiền*]. Whatever we wanted to do, we just had to give him some money, that's it—no more worries!"

Mrs. Mai's propositions reveal that "lack of professional knowledge and cooperation" were certainly not the main reasons why law enforcement in the marketplace had still remained "slack." Instead, they point to a "shadow reality" (Nordstrom 2000) in which state officials collude in informal and illegal practices in order to sustain the local economy (i.e., "ensure stable business activities") while reaping material benefits for themselves. Yet the line that distinguishes "legitimate" corruption for a mutual "benefit" from morally condemnable corruption for personal enrichment is a thin one (Endres 2014b). As I shall demonstrate in the following section, unveiling and reporting corruption therefore became a useful negotiating tool for the traders to advance their interests in the face of marketplace reconstruction.

"Market Making" through Documents

Because of the combined effects of Vietnam's harsh climate, poor materials used in postwar construction, and lack of maintenance, the T-shaped Zone A building of the Lào Cai central market already looked dated and weatherworn in 2010, only fourteen years after its construction. The management board had noted the market's material deterioration since the mid-2000s:

> After many years of use, the material condition of the market has deteriorated, and large amounts of capital are necessary in order to renovate, repair, and upgrade [a number of things], such as the main building of the market [Zone A]; the fire alarm system, the roof and the toilet of [Zone B]. (Market reports 2008–11, point I/2, "Difficulties")

> Zone A needs to be rebuilt because it has deteriorated a lot, the demand for more vending space is very high. (Market report 2010, "Petitions/Requests")

In December 2013, the People's Committee decided to push ahead with its plan to reconstruct Zone A with additional space for more than one hundred vendors. The city's efforts over the past years to mobilize funds from private investors for the construction of a new market building on a BOT (build-operate-transfer) basis had not been successful, though. In August 2012, Mrs. Cúc had explained to me that a number of stakeholders and companies had considered investing, but then shied away from the risk, especially with regard to the unstable business conditions of small-scale traders. The traders, in turn, would rather invest their money in their children's education or in buying land in Hanoi. "Quite unlike the Chinese," Mrs. Cúc said, "the Vietnamese invest in all sorts of things rather than in their shops and businesses."

Without funding, however, the project could not proceed as planned in time for Lào Cai's upgrade to a grade 2 city. The solution adopted by the provincial People's Committee was therefore to impose the costs of the new market building on the traders. In order to retain their guaranteed space in the new market, the current stallholders were asked to contribute 190–240 million đồng each (approximately US$8,800–11,000), in return for which they would be exempt from paying stall use fees for a period of ten years. To facilitate the funding process, the Lào Cai provincial government entrusted the Local Development Investment Fund (LDIF) with the implementation of the project. LDIFs are "locally based state financial institutions" that allow provincial governments "to invest in urban and economic infrastructure that provides a satisfactory return on investment" (Albrecht, Hocquard, and Papin 2010, 33). LDIFs may be financed through share capital subscribed by the province, through bonds, or through domestic or (via the Ministry of Finance) Official Development Assistance loans. In the case of the Lào Cai central market, however, the LDIF acted as an investor (*chủ đầu tư*) who, rather than asking for funds from financial institutions, forced (most of) the traders to take substantial bank loans in order to raise capital for constructing the new market. In other words, the state shifted the responsibility for realizing its ambitious urban development plans to the people, at their own risk.

While the funding of state-owned markets through trader contributions is a long-established practice in Vietnam (see note 8), the amount required was perceived by the traders as "way above the sky" (*giá trên trời*). When the authorities announced the decision in early June 2014, the traders staged a series of angry protests, including a strike that lasted several days, and entered into intense negotiations with representatives of the local government.[9] In the course of these negotiations, the traders expressed their distrust of the city and provincial leadership regarding legal and budgetary issues and demanded a significant reduction in their contribution payment. The traders also unveiled a number of irregularities pertaining to the unofficial selling of so-called ghost spaces by the market management board and demanded further investigations into the matter.

Mrs. Cúc had apparently "sold" additional spaces in the old market (some as tiny as twenty by thirty centimeters) with the promise that the stallholders would later receive "preferential treatment" in the new market. The money received for these spaces had, of course, not entered the state budget but disappeared in private pockets. When the scheme was uncovered through the traders' initiative (recordings of staged phone calls and visits to the parties involved), Mrs. Cúc was transferred to another position in the city administration, while two staff received disciplinary warnings. The traders, however, were not satisfied with this outcome. They argued that this was a case of embezzlement that should be brought before the law instead of being handled internally by the Lào Cai provincial People's Committee. When all their pleas for fair treatment and justice at the local level had been rebuffed, a group of trader representatives went to Hanoi to protest in front of the Government Inspectorate (Thanh tra Chính phủ).[10] They had signed a petition to "complain and denounce" the abuses they had faced and implored the central level to take action and bring all irregularities before the law, "so that we, the people, can firmly believe in the leadership of the Party and in the Constitution of the Socialist Republic of Vietnam." Like many such appeals (Gillespie 2009, 214), however, the Government Inspectorate rejected their case and referred them back to the provincial authorities in charge of their cause. The only concession the traders were ultimately able to obtain was the promise that the rent-free period for their stalls in the new market would be extended to twelve years (instead of the fifteen years they had bargained for). In September 2014, one month before the prime minister recognized Lào Cai as a grade 2 city per decision 1975/QĐ-TTg, the traders were relocated to the temporary market on the banks of the Red River.

In this chapter I have argued that bureaucratic documents hold an important place in the tool box of state rule techniques through which the conceptual boundary between state and society is maintained and (re)asserted. Official documents should therefore not be dismissed as irrelevant in anthropological research, as they provide important insights about the ways in which the "myth of the state" (T. B. Hansen 2001) as a rational, unified entity that exercises effective control by implementing its policies and laws is created and reinforced. The representational reality created through paperwork necessarily simplifies, and at times even obscures, the lived, experienced reality of everyday interactions between state officials and citizens/subjects in the marketplace. Yet as I have shown, the two realities may in fact not be as distinct and separate from each other as they might seem. Written documents not only enable government officials to establish their positions and authority vis-à-vis their subjects but also shape the market's future, and hence the concrete steps that are taken to construct that future. Power therefore concentrates in the hands of those who actively participate in the production of bureaucratic paperwork—whereas traders may get marginalized in part because they cannot as easily insert paper into these flows of documentation. When they do, however, as through written petitions, they often get referred back down to the lower administrative level (e.g., province or municipality) that had made the determination in the first place.

"We always trust in those who hold pen and ink," the Lào Cai central market traders wrote in a letter titled "Urgent Cry for Help" that they sent to a number of journalists in order to alert them to their case. The traders' anger and feeling *bức xúc*, that is, a "distressed sense of oppressive exasperation" (Harms 2012, 739) over the provincial government's decision to place all costs for building the new market on their shoulders and the overall lack of transparency in the planning and budgeting process sparked numerous incidents of collective resistance in the form of going on strike, organizing meetings with government officials, drafting and filing a petition to the Government Inspectorate, and sending letters to various newspapers known for their investigative reporting. I thus agree with Christina Schwenkel's contention that official documents are to be seen not just as "tools of coercion and control" but also as "productive of particular affects that [inspire] new collectivities and forms of political subjectivity" (2015a, 213; see also Leshkowich 2014b, 145). In spite of the traders' agency, expressed in the acts of petitioning the government for the redress of their grievances and use of the press to air their discontent, the changes brought to Lào Cai City by the planning assemblages of which market development policies are part suggest that the position of small-scale market traders will continue to deteriorate in the near future. Yet during my visit to Lào Cai in March 2016, many traders seemed surprisingly confident. "Other markets may be deserted, but [this one] will always be crowded with customers," one of my interlocutors said. The (temporary) market was indeed bustling with domestic tourists arriving in busloads after a trip to the nearby tourist town of Sa Pa and its 2016 inaugurated three-rope cable car up to Vietnam's highest summit, Mount Fansipan. Some vendors claimed their sales were even better now than at the old (demolished) market. They were, however, well aware that the market upgrade would accelerate ongoing processes of retail gentrification whereby less affluent vendors are gradually displaced from their stalls and replaced by those who are able to pay off their bank loans and afford higher rents while still making a decent living.

NOTES

1 I am deeply grateful to all participants in this research who have shared with me their time, stories, insights, and views. All individuals mentioned in the text have been given pseudonyms to protect their privacy and anonymity.

2 Vietnamese cities and towns are classified into six grades based on population size, population density, infrastructure, and other urban development indicators. There are currently twenty-five grade 2 cities. Fourteen cities have so far been recognized as grade 1 provincial cities, and another three (Haiphong, Danang, and Cần Thơ) are administered by the central government. Only Hanoi and Ho Chi Minh City have "special city" status (*đô thị loại đặc biệt*).

3 In its assessment report preceding the new 2015 master plan (Bộ Công Thương 2015), the Ministry of Industry and Commerce admitted that these aims had been way too optimistic (Bộ Công Thương 2014, 64–70).

4 According to the three-tiered market classification system in place at least since 1996 (Bộ Thương Mại 1996) and revised in 2003 (Chính Phủ 2003), class 1 markets are defined as centrally located commercial facilities that accommodate more than four hundred vendors and meet certain service criteria, such as parking and storage facilities, quality control, food hygiene, and safety requirements.

5 This amendment was also reflected in the resolutions on market development issued by the People's Committee of Lào Cai province, albeit a few years later. Following the 2003 government decree (Chính Phủ 2003), the 2008 resolution stated that the state budget would only finance class 1 markets "planned at key economic and commercial positions of the province" (UBND Tỉnh Lào Cai 2008, Art. 5). In the 2013 resolution, however, class 1 markets are no longer listed as beneficiaries of state funding. Instead, the People's Committee "encourages organizations and individuals and businesses of all economic sectors to invest in, or contribute capital to, the construction of marketplaces in the province" (UBND Tỉnh Lào Cai 2013, Art. 5/4).

6 Local government at the province, city, district, and commune (*xã*) or municipal ward (*phường*) level consists of a People's Council, a People's Committee, and branches of the Communist Party and its mass organizations (Kerkvliet 2004, 4). The People's Committee is in charge of implementing state laws and regulations at the local level and manages everyday administrative and governmental affairs. It is accountable to the People's Council at the same bureaucratic level and to the People's Committee at the next higher level (7).

7 The reports did not assess the impact and general effectiveness of marketplace-related policies, though. See Turner et al. (2016) for a fascinating account of the "rightful criticisms" that local government officials raise about development policies in the northern uplands.

8 Strictly speaking, traders do not own their stalls but have rental agreements with the market management board based on the legal framework in place. These rental agreements are usually signed for a certain time period (one year in Lào Cai). The reality, however, is more complicated. First, traders may contribute capital toward the construction of state-run markets by paying the rent for a specified time in advance. Second, stall rental contracts can also be auctioned (*đấu giá, đấu thầu*) to the highest bidder in case the demand exceeds the availability of stalls in a newly constructed market. Many vendors have thus invested large sums into bidding for the right to operate a stall. This right is transferable, that is, vendors can also "sell" their stall use right or sublet the stall to someone else. Moreover, it can be used as collateral for a bank loan to raise capital for trading purposes. A stall in the market therefore represents an asset value even though the trader is not its proper owner.

9 While some of these hearings were open to all traders, during other hearings the traders were represented by the market's twelve section heads (*tổ trưởng ngành hàng*). The section heads are commonly elected by the traders and act as intermediaries to the market management board. Unlike, for example, in India or the Philippines, restrictions on the formation of associations persist and effectively block more organized avenues for Vietnamese market and street vendors to pursue and safeguard their interests (cf. Anjaria 2011; Milgram 2011).

10 The Government Inspectorate is "a state investigation agency" responsible for resolving "'hard' cases that are not directly covered by statute" (Gillespie 2009, 215). In the 2000s, sending letters and petitions to higher administrative levels has become a widespread means of drawing attention to grievances, especially with regard to land issues (Kerkvliet 2014).

CHAPTER TWO

"Run and Hide When You See the Police": Livelihood Diversification and the Politics of the Street Economy in Vietnam's Northern Uplands

Sarah Turner

It has been suggested that until World War II the northern Vietnam uplands were a "zone of refuge" for those not wishing to live under the state's lowland-centric gaze (J. C. Scott 2009). While such conceptual notions can be debated ad infinitum, it is known that lowland Vietnamese (Kinh, Việt) state officials were not particularly keen to be stationed in these mountainous uplands, and even during the early collective period, many upland residents were able to continue to farm as households, as they had for decades (Poisson 2009; interviews). Yet, since the initiation of Đổi mới (economic renovation) in the mid-1980s, the 1992 launch of the Greater Mekong Subregion by the Asian Development Bank and partner countries, and the lifting of the U.S. trade embargo in 1994, these uplands have been increasingly targeted for state interventions. Upland infrastructure such as roads, communication networks, and fixed marketplaces are being widely promoted by the Vietnamese state and its development partners, along with the extensive inauguration of hybrid-seed technology and cash cropping, with shifting cultivators strongly encouraged to become settled farmers. Extractive industries such as mining are multiplying, while hydroelectric operations appear to be the flavor of the month. These northern uplands—home to eleven million upland residents, including six million ethnic minority individuals— are also experiencing something of a tourism boom, especially of domestic tourists from the lowlands, with the establishment of new casinos, golf courses, and even mountain cable cars (Michaud and Turner 2017).

As part of its Đổi mới reforms, the Vietnamese state initiated a pro-urban policy to entice foreign investment. Witnessing the rapid socioeconomic transformations occurring in the capital Hanoi and in Ho Chi Minh City (formerly known as Saigon), in 1998 the government introduced the "Master Plan for the Development of Vietnam's Urban Centres until 2020." One of the plan's aims was the establishment of a number of medium and small urban centers to encourage rural urbanization (DiGregorio

2011). This planning initiative has occurred as waves of Kinh lowlanders migrate to the uplands, with entrepreneurs taking advantage of lucrative new trade deals with China and various investment opportunities.[1] Work by Trincsi, Pham, and Turner (2014) has found that Lào Cai province, where this study is situated, has experienced important rural-to-urban land use change at an average rate of 18 percent each year between 1999 and 2009. Yet, while urbanization has been building momentum, we still know little about the emergence of, and state control over, urban public space in these uplands. Nor do we know how upland residents react to controls over what they consider to be their right to create a range of urban livelihoods in these expanding small towns and cities, including street vending.

The focus of this chapter is Sa Pa town and district, a popular tourist destination in Lào Cai province, close to the Sino-Vietnamese border. The town received over one million tourists in 2016 (Lào Cai Department of Culture, Sports and Tourism, pers. comm., 2016), while Sa Pa district's population stands at around 54,000 (GSO 2010). Male and female ethnic minority residents of this district are diversifying their livelihoods with some attempting to trade to tourists in Sa Pa town's public spaces. These street vendors and their wholesalers now face a political environment where fines and retribution for their trading livelihoods can shift on a daily basis depending on the whims of state officials. But how do these traders react to such limitations? And how do their acts of negotiation and resistance challenge state understandings of public space? As these vendors' rights to be part of a street economy have become increasingly constricted, some have decided to resist the increasing controls over their livelihoods via a range of subtle, in situ tactics, while others have become more mobile, following tourists on treks to nearby villages. Yet ethnic relations and tensions also play a central role in determining who gets to trade where and how.

The street economy in Sa Pa district can be roughly divided into five groups of traders linked to specific ethnically rooted livelihood approaches. First are ethnic minority itinerant and stationary street vendors selling on the main streets, sidewalks, and public spaces of Sa Pa town. These include Hmong and Yao women selling textiles, tourist trinkets, and seasonal fruit; Giáy women selling agricultural produce; and Hmong men selling orchids, honey, and songbirds. Second are ethnic minority textile wholesalers who sell to local ethnic minority women, often from sidewalks, on their market day visits to the town. Third are ethnic minority women accompanying tourists trekking to nearby minority villages. These women occupy what could be labeled "shifting insurgent spaces." They do not partake in the *urban* street economy while on the move, yet their new trading regimes—what could be considered a rural trail economy—are a direct response to state directives over urban public space. This chapter focuses on how these first three groups claim and maintain their rights to trade. Discussed briefly for comparative purposes, the fourth group are Kinh street vendors who operate small stationary stalls in the town selling grilled food snacks (locally called BBQ), *Bia hơi* (draft beer), and lottery tickets. Fifth and finally are ethnic minority traders with rented, fixed stalls, in the town's marketplace, some of whom take to the streets at specific times to engage in itinerant trading.

This chapter is based on fieldwork conducted in Sa Pa town and in other locales in Lào Cai province annually since 1999. For this project, I completed over 120 conversational interviews with ethnic minority (Hmong, Yao/Dao, Giáy) and Kinh street and market vendors. The vendors interviewed were overwhelmingly female—reflective of the overall vending population in the town—and ranged in age from eighteen to eighty-six years old. In addition, I collected conversational interviews, oral histories, and life stories with thirty Kinh long-term residents, both male and female. Two Kinh marketplace officials participated in semistructured interviews, and the changing spatial patterns of vendor trade and enforcement of urban space regulations were observed yearly.[2]

CONCEPTUALIZING THE ROLE OF THE STREET ECONOMY FOR DIVERSIFYING RURAL LIVELIHOODS

Conceptually, rural livelihood diversification is understood to encompass the ways by which rural households bring together a diverse set of activities and social support to be able to survive and attempt to improve their standards of living (Ellis 1998). Such diversification options and routes for individual and household livelihoods are shaped by "local and distinct institutions (e.g. local customs regarding access to common property resources, local and national land tenure rules), and by social relations (gender, caste, kinship and so on), as well as by economic opportunities" (Ellis 2000, 6; Turner, Bonnin, and Michaud 2015). Livelihood diversification takes many shapes, including the introduction of cash cropping, nonfarming activities located on farm (e.g., producing goods for sale at markets), or off-farm activities, including small-scale trade or waged labor such as factory work or public-sector employment (Chambers and Conway 1991; Rigg 2006). In the Global South, rural livelihood diversification occurs for a number of complex reasons, among them the decline of farm profits, land shortages, environmental degradation, increasing extreme weather events, and the closure of land frontiers. New nonfarm opportunities are driving livelihood diversification trends alongside social and cultural changes influenced by media, education, and new consumption trends. The rising necessity for financial capital resulting from development programs and the agrarian transition also plays an important role (de Haan and Zoomers 2005; Eakin, Tucker, and Castellanos 2006).

In many urban and peri-urban locales across the Global South, a possible route to household livelihood diversification is to join the street economy. Following Brown, Lyons, and Dankoco (2010, 667), the street economy is defined here as "economic activity that depends for its existence on access to the street or other publicly accessible spaces." Bhowmik (2005, 2256) suggests that the street economy includes vendors who sell from either a stationary stall or itinerantly, defining a street vendor as someone "who offers goods for sale to the public without having a permanent built-up structure from which to sell." Brown (2006) proposes that the street economy also encompasses individuals who supply those trading on the streets, such as wholesalers and porters. Other authors have focused more on the legality of the street economy, with Cross (1998) noting that street vending occurs when there is a lack of appropriate permits, a violation of zoning codes, or noncompliance with a range of other regulations (labor laws, taxation, and so on). In this chapter, the focus is on both locale and legality, as Brown, Lyons, and Dankoco (2010) have also emphasized in their work on the street economy in African towns.

CONTEXTUALIZING URBAN TRADE DYNAMICS IN THE UPLANDS

Over six million ethnic minority individuals call the uplands of northern Vietnam home, with most practicing semi-subsistence livelihoods (General Statistics Office [GSO] 2010). Rice and maize constitute the local agricultural staples, supplemented by home gardens, livestock, forest products, and small-scale trade and barter. For as long as records have been kept, marketplace trade has taken place in these uplands. Salt was historically the most important necessity, bringing traders together in imperial and colonial times (Michaud and Turner 2003). Following the Đổi mới market reforms starting in 1986, marketplace trade has become more significant than ever for upland households (see Michaud and Turner 2003; Bonnin and Turner 2014). The introduction of state-endorsed hybrid rice and maize seeds and the subsequent need for cash to purchase yearly seed, fertilizer, and pesticide inputs have encouraged upland minority farmers to expand the cash portion of their livelihood portfolios (Bonnin and Turner 2012; Turner, Bonnin, and Michaud 2015). Contemporary upland marketplace trade is therefore dynamic and growing, while supporting a rapid agrarian transition, yet little is known about the emergence of a street economy among upland traders, distinct from officially sanctioned marketplace sites.

Situated forty kilometers from the Sino-Vietnamese border, the case study locale of Sa Pa town has grown swiftly since 1992, when the region reopened to independent foreign tourists for the first time since the colonial period. International visitors now arrive seeking trekking adventures and interactions with ethnic minorities, while lowland Vietnamese (Kinh) predominantly vacation in the town to enjoy the cooler climate and, since 2016, to ride a cable car to the top of Mount Fansipan, the highest peak in mainland Southeast Asia outside Burma. The development of commerce, infrastructure, and the service economy has boomed, and demand for agricultural produce for numerous hotels and restaurants is rising. Incoming Kinh traders and intermediaries with networks in the lowlands have filled much of this produce demand, edging out local minority producers. Yet demand for traditional ethnic minority handicrafts—authentic or fake—has also increased, promoting a niche trade opportunity for ethnic minority women (Turner 2007). In general, these two groups—local Kinh and ethnic minority residents—tolerate or ignore each other, unless specific events disrupt this balance, as noted below.

The People's Committees of Lào Cai province and Sa Pa district are influential in shaping trade opportunities, urban planning, and infrastructure development in Sa Pa town. Though lowland Kinh make up only 16 percent of the district's population, Kinh representatives control the key positions in the local government and Kinh businesspeople operate the majority of hotels and restaurants (GSO 2010). Ethnic minorities have few opportunities to participate meaningfully in district politics and find it difficult to make their voices heard, more so as many do not speak Vietnamese. Not helping this situation is the pervasive opinion among Kinh that upland ethnic minorities are backward, unmotivated, or lazy (McElwee 2004; van de Walle and Gunewardena 2001; World Bank 2009). Moreover, the Vietnamese state keeps a close watch on the activities of upland ethnic minority groups, especially Hmong and Yao, who are not considered to have strong loyalties to the state project in the wake of their transnational histories in China and beyond.

This majority/lowland-minority/upland dichotomy becomes increasingly apparent when looking at ethnic minority access to vending livelihood opportunities, and it is not surprising that rights to the street economy in urban areas in the uplands are highly inequitable. Social connections, ethnicity, and political institutions play a strong role regarding who has the right to trade in Sa Pa town's public spaces (cf. Henaff and Strong 2001). While public space making and practice across the Global South have long been partially exclusionary, often on the grounds of gender and specific social groups, this can be argued to be especially acute in socialist settings where official public spaces are closely controlled by the state (Hou 2010). Despite the liberalization of the Vietnamese economy, one finds that public space remains closely regulated. Moreover, as for all citizens in Vietnam, ethnic minority groups have extremely limited rights to engage in overt collective action.

STREET ECONOMIES IN THE UPLANDS

THE MARKETPLACE FILLS UP

As tourism in Sa Pa started to escalate in the late 1990s, young Hmong women began wandering the town's main streets greeting newly arrived tourists, mostly Western backpackers. These young Hmong women wanted to make new friends, learn some English (among other foreign languages), and sell small trinkets (interviews, 1999, 2000). Elderly or divorced Hmong and Yao women, or those with time off from household and agricultural tasks, also began to sell homemade textiles itinerantly on the streets, carrying their wares in woven baskets on their backs. This merchandise consisted mostly of secondhand homemade hemp or cotton embroidered jackets, and intricately embroidered collars and patches, along with simple bags refashioned from this embroidery. Both groups of women tended to gather where minibuses dropped off backpackers after the hour-long road trip from Lào Cai city train station, a transfer point on the overnight trip from Hanoi.

Sa Pa town's central marketplace was renovated during the same time (1997–98), transformed from a series of small one-story halls without walls into a significantly larger two-story concrete building (see fig. 2.1). Over the next five years, half of the top floor gradually filled with ethnic minority textile vendors, mainly Hmong and Yao women between twenty and sixty years old.[3] Demand for trading spots in the market began to exceed supply, and those who could not access a spot in the market sold on the town's main streets instead. Thus while the number of ethnic minority youth befriending tourists on the streets of Sa Pa has remained fairly stable over time, the number of textile sellers on the sidewalks and streets has increased. By 2015, about two hundred textile vendors (along with other vendors, including Giáy selling fruit) lined the sidewalks of the main streets and clustered in the town square/park, where pedestrian flows are high on weekends.

Police and district officials wanted Hmong and Yao textile vendors in these public spaces to return to their villages or trade in the marketplace, with one official noting, "They cannot run after tourists like this on the street, because the tourists get annoyed" (2006). Yet minority traders were not overly enthusiastic about being based in the central Sa Pa marketplace. On the one hand, it provided a stable location that was locked at night and where goods could be stored in metal boxes (albeit that traders had to purchase). The marketplace was also preferred when it rained or was cold outside. Yet, on the other hand, with around eighty to ninety traders packed into a space roughly fifty meters by thirty meters, vendors who managed to secure a spot there reported far lower sales than on the street, noting that there was too much competition because "we all sell the same thing together" (Yao trader, 2013).

These concerns were soon to be dwarfed, however. In a major upheaval in late December 2014/early January 2015, all central marketplace traders (Kinh and ethnic minority) were shifted to a brand-new marketplace over one kilometer from the town center (see figure 2.1). While the new marketplace has more space, ethnic minority traders are extremely unhappy, as few tourists venture into this part of the town, and sales have plummeted even further.

Paradoxically, town officials want vendors to become sedentary yet officials create conditions that discourage ethnic minority women from selling in the state-controlled marketplace. As well as now being located far from the town's center, marketplace sellers are expected to be trading at their stalls on a fixed daily schedule, with no consideration given to the multiple productive and reproductive tasks that vendors must undertake. Traders are also required to write down their name and village for marketplace officials, when few ethnic minority Hmong and Yao women in this district above the age of thirty are literate. One female Hmong interviewee, Sho,[4] explained that she prefers to sell outdoors from a small stationary spot on the sidewalk, rather than in the marketplace, because "if you sell in the market, you have to write your name down and sell there every day. I don't have enough time for that, so I just sell in the street." She added that her trading time is limited and must remain flexible because her daughter-in-law had passed away, and she is helping her son with household duties, including the care of her grandchildren. Since early 2017, ethnic minority traders have had to pay a monthly fee to trade in the new market, a cost that had initially been waived for them after the market's move. This is further negatively affecting their livelihoods.

Itinerant and Stationary Street Traders

From the early 2000s onward, Sa Pa police and officials have clamped down erratically on ethnic minority traders selling itinerantly or from small roadside trade spots, often displaying goods on embroidered blankets or plastic sheets (see figure 2.2). This official response is partially a consequence of growing numbers of both vendors and tourists, but officials also cite concerns over increased congestion for "essential" tourist vehicles, including more and more full-sized coaches and minibuses. Heavy machinery and trucks also pass through the town on an ongoing basis as the construction of hotels, new roads, and nearby dams is prioritized in the area.

The official stance toward street sellers is inconsistent over both time and space. Before special events such as conferences, dignitary visits, or national holidays, street vendors—both stationary and itinerant—are usually cleared, with their trade curtailed. Although vendors are sometimes warned of such clearances over the town's loudspeaker address system, the messages are in Vietnamese, which not all minority vendors speak. Minority vendors must therefore scramble to collect their goods and retreat from the street when police carry out sudden street sweeps. As Ly, a Yao informant noted in 2009, "If an important person is coming to town or an important event, then we're told to get off the streets. Nowadays it's about one or two times per month. Police don't usually give us any warning, they just come and take our stuff." Kinh street vendors, who can understand and react to official broadcasts, are at an advantage in these situations. Other raids are unannounced, yet Kinh who operate portable street stalls selling grilled snacks, beer, and small souvenirs, and who are technically subject to the same dispersal orders as minorities, are rarely targeted.

Furthermore, since the mid-2000s, police began to focus on clearing the streets on weekends, when ethnic minority traders with small stationary trading spots cater to the weekend "market rush." From Friday to Sunday, minorities from surrounding villages arrive in town for the weekend market to trade and socialize among themselves and to cater to the influx of tourists. Police have been more zealous in some years than others in patrolling the streets on the weekend, and the severity of punishment has also largely depended on the individuals involved. For example, some officers have

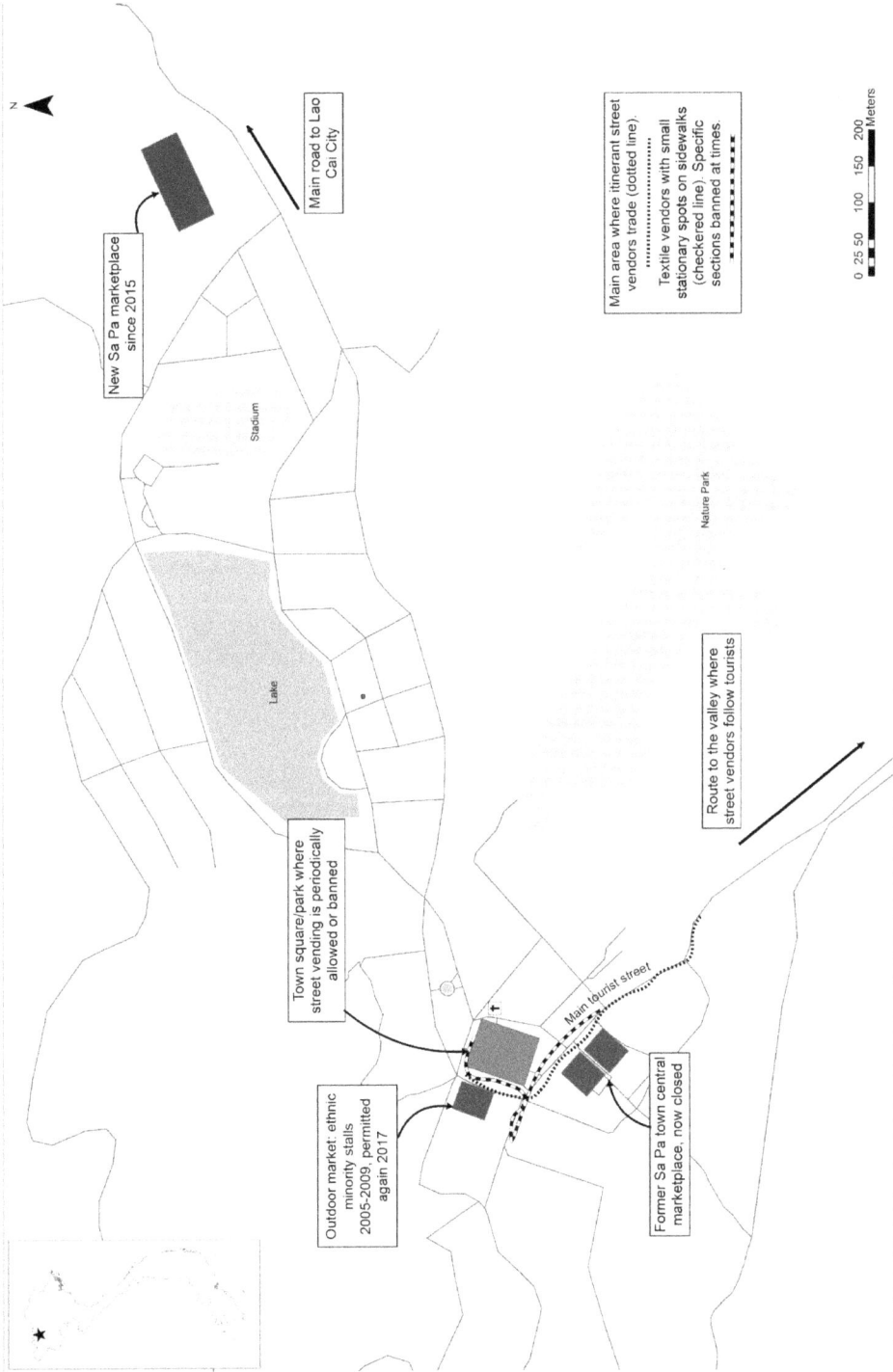

Figure 2.1 Sa Pa town, with marketplaces and itinerant street trading locales highlighted.

Map by Kate Trincsi and Jean Michaud.

N

New Sa Pa marketplace since 2015

Main road to Lao Cai City

Main area where itinerant street vendors trade (dotted line).

Textile vendors with small stationary spots on sidewalks (checkered line). Specific sections banned at times.

0 25 50   100   150   200
Meters

Stadium

Lake

Nature Park

Town square/park where street vending is periodically allowed or banned

Route to the valley where street vendors follow tourists

Main tourist street

Outdoor market: ethnic minority stalls 2005-2009, permitted again 2017

Former Sa Pa town central marketplace, now closed

been more sympathetic to older street sellers or realize that there is a lack of space in the marketplace, while others act harshly toward all ethnic minority vendors.

Just as surveillance and enforcement can change unpredictably from month to month and as a result of special events, the government is constantly and arbitrarily changing the public spaces where stationary vending is permitted. In 2014, Fey, a young Yao woman, noted, "If we walk in the streets to trade, or over there [in the town square], we can get into trouble. The police come and take our stuff." Then, in 2015 a Hmong vendor, Mang, explained, "This year the police have started to give us a small area from where we can sell on this street [on the main street north of the town square], but this is new and there's not enough spots anyway. I share this with my mother and sister. If we move outside this area we get fined. I don't know what will happen next year." By April 2017, this specific option had been prohibited again, while another limited trading space was approved (figure 2.2), but only for two nights a week.

Officials' erratic reactions to vendors attempting to trade from small stationary spots in public parks, sidewalks, and streets keep these women on their toes (oftentimes literally). Hmong interviewee Sho explained, "If you sell just walking around it's OK, but if you sit around the top of the square then they come and take your things. You can't sit there, the policemen will come and take your goods." Twice this Hmong woman in her late-sixties had had her goods confiscated and noted, "You've just got to run." The first time she was caught, the police seized a large embroidered blanket from her with no warning. When she went to the police station with a friend, she explained that she did not know she could not sell in that location and begged for her blanket back. Although she had been warned that a bribe would be necessary, the officer took pity on her because of her age. The second time her goods were confiscated, she feared that the police would recognize her and decided not to try to recover them. The vast majority of Hmong and Yao women traders interviewed confirmed that they have had to pay to have their goods returned if confiscated by police. These "fines" vary, with 2015 rates ranging from VNĐ100,000 (US$4.50) to VNĐ300,000 (US$13.50) depending on how the police rank the quality of the goods.[5] One Hmong vendor, Shu (2015), noted with contempt that when her goods were last seized, she had had no money to pay the fine and the Kinh official had given her goods to his wife, who then sold them from her own shop.

As already noted, the customary response to a police raid is to gather up one's goods as quickly as possible and run. Hmong and Yao women live in fear of the police, with one Yao interviewee noting, "If you don't run away, then they take everything, they grab everyone's things" (2009). In 2013, Lan, a Hmong woman who has relatives who trade, noted with some pride that vendors selling on the streets "know to run and hide when the police come around." Additionally, in 2015, some vendors noted that they were focusing on making smaller products than in the past specifically to be able to bundle their goods up and move more quickly to avoid a police sweep.

As a livelihood coping strategy and covert resistance measure, Hmong and Yao street vendors have also come to remember which times and days police and town officials are likely to patrol, avoiding the town then if possible (cf. Eidse and Turner 2014). For instance, a few vendors noted that police sweeps tend to happen around 10:00 a.m. However, such avoidance strategies are often not profitable, especially since tourist numbers rise so dramatically over the well-patrolled weekends.

While Hmong and Yao interviewees commented that trading itinerantly in public spaces makes them less susceptible to police action than trading from a small

Figure 2.2. Since 2016, ethnic minority traders selling on Sapa's main tourist street, near to the town square, are closely monitored and permitted to sell from small stalls only on Friday and Saturday evenings. Photograph of Hmong traders by S. Turner.

stationary space, this is only a possibility for a few. These Hmong and Yao trade from the marketplace during the day and then walk the streets in the evenings with their less heavy items for sale. This evening trade is limited to a specific subset of individuals who, since the early 2000s, have started renting rooms in town after their families agreed that they could be away from the village overnight.

It is not only state officials who wish to curb vendors' access to public trading spaces however. In 2011, Kinh shopkeepers, supported by the local People's Committee, argued that their businesses were suffering because of street traders. In Sa Pa town as well as in nearby villages, it was broadcast over the loudspeaker systems that selling in the town's streets would be henceforth forbidden. The number of vendors momentarily dropped, yet it had risen again by the next year.

Emphasizing the ethnically divided right to trade in the town, in 2005, land for a new outdoor market was cleared near the town square, and a semi-permanent collection of stalls made of wood, bamboo, corrugated asbestos tiles, and tarpaulins was constructed (see figure 2.1). Many Hmong, Yao, and Kinh vendors unable to secure a spot in the town's central marketplace at that time, and who had been selling from nearby sidewalks, quickly set up shop in this market, paying a small fee. Trading from this outdoor market, where some minority traders also cooked and slept overnight, was a tenuous affair, and after a few years of uncertainty, the semi-permanent structures were demolished in 2009 to make way for a "permanent" Kinh cooked-food market with large, permanent, enclosed stalls. No ethnic minority individuals were allowed to remain to trade as they had been—even though the Kinh food stalls were often deserted, even on weekends—and no minorities could afford to rent the larger stalls. Ethnic minority traders displaced from this market space either gave up and went back to their villages (where some now sell to trekking tourists passing through, discussed shortly) or returned to itinerant trading on the streets. When asked about the obvious ethnic change in the space's occupants, one Hmong woman shrugged her shoulders, saying, "There's nothing we can do."

Revisiting this same space in mid-2017, it was surprising to see ethnic minority vendors trading there again, from sheets of plastic on the ground, while all the Kinh traders had closed up shop. A large construction company, Sun Group, is rumored to have purchased this site with plans for a new tourism development. In the meantime, minority traders selling from a previously permitted pavement space during the week (noted earlier in the quote by Mang) had been told by the town's authorities to move to this site in early 2017. When asked why this might have occurred, one young Yao woman stated, "I think the local Kinh shopkeepers didn't like that there were minorities selling on that sidewalk because the Kinh shops couldn't make sales. They [Kinh shopkeepers] probably paid money to the police, and then the police moved the vendors." While this claim has yet to be substantiated, the result certainly reflects the 2011 temporary ban, mentioned earlier, that was initiated by nearby Kinh shopkeepers. Hmong and Yao traders interviewed in this soon-to-be-private space reported the move to be dire for their trade, as the entrance to the area is small and few tourists are venturing in. They also have no idea how long they are going to be permitted to trade here again.

ETHNIC MINORITY TEXTILE WHOLESALERS

Extending the street economy in Sa Pa town beyond daily vendors are approximately 20–30 Hmong wholesalers, mostly women, from around Lào Cai province as well as the neighboring provinces of Lai Châu and Yên Bái. Traveling to Sa Pa town once every two to three weekends by bus or with their husbands on motorbikes, these wholesalers bring used textiles from rural villages to sell to local Hmong traders, who then sometimes also act as intermediaries with Yao and Kinh town traders. The wholesalers leave home as early as 1:00 a.m. to arrive in Sa Pa in time for a frenetic morning of trading in the main town square, on central sidewalks, or in the main market before returning home (interviews, 2009 and 2013).

These wholesalers obtain old textiles from remote villages that can be refashioned into tourist commodities, paying with cash or bartering with plain black cotton or synthetic skirts from China. Most of these women walk several days to visit villages, where they stay overnight with distant relatives. Hmong wholesaler Pang explained, "We can stay with family in other villages, we might take two to three days to do a trip buying old skirts" (2013). These wholesalers tend to be ignored by police during their trips into Sa Pa town, perhaps because of their very temporary nature or because they trade fairly early in the morning. Nonetheless, these men and women keep a sharp eye out for police and have their goods ready to move instantly if necessary.

CREATING A RURAL TRAIL ECONOMY

As the number of street vendors in Sa Pa continued to rise through the mid-2000s and police raids increased accordingly, some entrepreneurial minority women identified a possible new trade niche. They determined that if they followed Hmong or Yao guides leading tourist groups on rural trails down the nearby valley on day treks or to overnight homestays, they could try to convince overseas tourists to purchase their merchandise en route.[6] Informally accompanying a tourist group, these women initiate conversations if their English language skills are good enough and help tourists cross streams and muddy paths. At an opportune time, often during lunch or a drink break, they begin a fervent sales pitch and tourists often feel pressured to buy a few textile items. To date, local officials have not clamped down on this tactic, focusing on street traders in Sa Pa town instead. This is rather ironic, given tourists' complaints on social media that highlight how these interactions are rather intimidating, as one noted on Facebook: "Local vendors follow you all the way on Sapa track—yes, even up to 5 hours—and help you while walking, climbing up and down, explain about your surroundings but expect you to buy something at the end. They are very insistent" (Facebook page for local trekking company, 2015).

A number of vendors talked about this as a useful strategy to make tourists "feel guilty." Hmong textile trader Khu noted, "It's better to follow the tourists to the villages and engage with them, because then the tourists feel guilty and will buy something. In the [Sa Pa] market, the tourists are only looking, and they only buy if they see something that they like." This tactic has created new, often uneasy relations between mobile vendors and the young Hmong and Yao women leading trekking groups. Guides note that tourists will sometimes ask them to tell the women traders to stop hawking their goods, but when guides pass this information on, the sellers (with limited English) often do not believe that the tourists are asking this, and argue with the guides that they are being selfish. As this can foster ill will between young guides and sellers who are often older and sometimes kin, guides noted that they are disinclined to enter these negotiations and, while mediating cultural norms as best they can, usually say something unrelated to the traders instead.

Another group of Hmong and Yao women have started to sell from their homes if they live in a village visited by trekkers. New resentments have also started in these cases, as village-based traders are unhappy with traders following tourists and vice-versa. "I walk with you, why you no buy from me?" is a common refrain from mobile vendors. The number of mobile vendors operating along the main trail into the valley from Sa Pa has grown so large that some women who initially traded from villages have switched to selling on the streets of Sa Pa instead. In this case, one form of itinerant trading, and its surrounding cultural and village politics, has reinforced a different trading niche in the town, in the face of official opposition.

POLITICS OF THE STREET ECONOMY

With cash needs rising because of agrarian transformations, rural households near Sa Pa town with spare labor during off-peak farming seasons are increasingly considering vending as a livelihood diversification option to gain financial capital. Vendors have also noted an additional need for cash to offset food shortfalls caused by extreme weather events, such as late rains in 2012 that resulted in diminished rice harvests. Yet a strong state preference for immobile, regulated trade in state-sanctioned marketplaces impedes many traders from achieving steady incomes. Ethnic minority traders deem the town's new marketplace too remote and inaccessible for tourists, while livelihood options in the urban street economy are constantly under threat. This has led some to innovate and take up an itinerant-vending approach along trekking trails, allowing these vendors to secure a viable yet physically and time-demanding trade option. Others maintain a presence on the town's streets, drawing on a range of tactics to continue their trade while facing ever-changing rules and regulations.

It has become clear that vending in the urban public spaces of these uplands is marked by the intersectionality of ethnicity, gender, space, local politics, and livelihood diversification strategies. Rights to Sa Pa town's streets and sidewalks are politically constructed and ethnically biased. District and provincial state officials argue that street vendors are disrupting traffic and pedestrian flows, making the streets "messy," particularly during visits of senior state delegations. More broadly, street vending is deemed informal and traditional, while modern uses of this public space such as vehicle movement are prioritized. Police raids, fines, and confiscations thus become instruments to restrict certain public space practices. Local government officials and police, overwhelmingly Kinh men, target ethnic minorities—overwhelmingly women—far more frequently than they do Kinh traders (men and women), reflecting decades of prejudice against ethnic minorities and a strong gender bias (World Bank 2009). Adding to the complexity of who gets to trade where, *within* ethnic minority communities there exist differences in language ability, road access, reproductive duties at home, and social networks that all influence opportunities, and create new intra-ethnic tensions for some.

At the same time, ethnic minority traders are not backing down from their perceived right to be part of the street economy, creatively blending active engagement, cautious choices, and, at times, resistance. While it might be too extreme to call street vending in this upland boom town an act of insurgency or urban space hijacking, these traders do inject new meaning into Sa Pa's public spaces. They challenge official regulations and use their agency to shape trade approaches and livelihood diversification strategies that work for them, sometimes with subtle yet perceptible signs of dissent and questioning of state authority and control. It remains to be seen whether these vendors can rely on such tactics in the future.

Notes

1 Previously, in the 1960s and 1970s, waves of lowland migrants arrived in these uplands as part of state-sponsored New Economic Zones (Hardy 2000).
2 Interviews were completed with Hmong and Yao traders with the aid of research assistants/interpreters of the same ethnicity, and with Vietnamese or Giáy traders with the help of Vietnamese interpreters or independently. This chapter draws from and extends Turner and Oswin 2015.
3 Giáy have not become involved in the tourist-oriented textile trade, perhaps because they do not grow hemp or weave textiles like the Hmong, nor do they intricately embroider their clothes like Yao and Hmong.
4 All names are pseudonyms.
5 I hypothesize that, as in Hanoi and Ho Chi Minh City, the majority of these "fines" are quasi-legal and help to supplement the salaries of local police and officials (see Leshkowich 2005; Turner and Schoenberger 2012).
6 It should be noted that relatively few Vietnamese tourists go on such hikes, and when they do, minority women seldom try this approach, given historical inter-ethnic antagonisms and the negative stereotypes Kinh often hold of minorities.

CHAPTER THREE

GRAND DESIGNS? STATE AGENDAS AND THE LIVED REALITIES OF MARKET REDEVELOPMENT IN UPLAND NORTHERN VIETNAM

Christine Bonnin

In the northern mountainous province of Lào Cai, Vietnam—a multiethnic space that is home to a majority of the nation's fifty-three official ethnic minority groups—vast sums of money have been poured over the last decade by the government and international development institutions into market improvement schemes. As part of the Vietnamese state's efforts since 2003 to promote market modernization, this process is not unique to these uplands (see Barthelmes 2013; Endres 2014a). Yet while many of the processes, outcomes, and trader responses associated with marketplace transformations here appear to be shared with those in lowland centers, there are some noteworthy differences. In particular, market modernization and improvement schemes for the uplands are—on paper, at least—being drafted and performed under the label of "development" (Bonnin 2012).

In upland areas like Lào Cai where ethnic minorities constitute the bulk of the population, this nuance to the national agenda is reflected by a focus on poverty alleviation, as well as by frequent state misconceptions of these groups as poor at market interactions and needing help to be "taught" how to trade with outsiders (McElwee 2008; World Bank 2009; Bonnin 2012). With a lack of market integration being identified as a key factor behind persisting levels of poverty in these uplands, the Vietnamese state has attempted to "bring the markets to the people," mainly through the construction, modernization, and formalization of physical marketplaces (Chính Phủ 2003; Phan Si Man 2005; World Bank 2009). Explicit importance is attached to marketplaces located in upland ethnic minority communes, where the government sees them as an "urgent need" (Chính Phủ 2004).

This creation and upgrading of marketplaces as part and parcel of the state's approach to helping the uplands "catch up" with the lowlands has occurred alongside the development of and investment in other infrastructure also geared to improving access to markets. This includes "distance demolishing" connective infrastructure such as roads, highways, public transport, and telecommunications—particularly mobile phone services—that improve physical mobility and information flows and overcome the "friction of terrain" (J. C. Scott 2009, 45–47).

Yet in most cases the economic benefits intended by these grand designs have not materialized. In many instances, market redevelopment projects aimed at encouraging economic development and trade have done precisely the opposite. Indeed, many of these "modernized" markets either have witnessed declining numbers of traders or have been left entirely vacant. In this chapter, I explore the reasons why so many new markets have not worked, in order to understand the complexities of this very expensive upland development failure. I concentrate on the building and upgrading of local marketplace infrastructure as important arenas of struggle over livelihoods and the meaning of development. The on-the-ground lived realities of these development projects reveal a stark disconnect between the kinds of markets being imagined and promoted by the state and the livelihood needs of local traders, both ethnic minorities and Kinh alike.

I also draw attention to how important ethnic-based differences that exist in marketplace trade may hold a number of implications for how traders are able to use or gain access to new market infrastructure. Upland market redevelopment schemes are not experienced equally by traders, nor are their benefits collective. Such projects can have differential impacts on different groups, something that appears to be entirely off the state's radar, and at times seems at odds with the officially stated poverty alleviation agenda aimed at benefiting ethnic minority residents. This chapter draws useful insights from studies on the politics of infrastructure (Larkin 2013). Here, infrastructure is often conceptualized as "in the background," gaining visibility when it comes under threat, such as with the privatization of public services like water or electricity (Star 1999). At the same time, in many parts of the Global South, people's experiences of infrastructure have often been far from "invisible" (Kregg Hetherington and Campbell 2014). Grand public building projects for hydroelectric dams, roads, and bridges executed with the goal of economic development have served as powerful reminders of the presence of states, multinational lenders, or colonizers, "establishing the hand of human intervention in areas that were considered too 'natural' and therefore developmental failures" (192).

This scholarship also draws our attention to infrastructure as being far more than simply material form, highlighting how projects are heavily laden with a politics of inclusion and exclusion (Ferguson 2012). It examines how infrastructural development is linked to a redistribution of resources and who is best positioned to benefit from this. Marketplace redevelopment schemes in Vietnam's upland periphery clearly illustrate how wider processes of marginalization can become operational through infrastructure, as well as how cultural and political assumptions are often built into its designs, something that has been well demonstrated with regard to the urban context (Rodgers and O'Neill 2012).

This chapter draws on over eighteen months of fieldwork undertaken between 2007 and 2011 as part of a doctoral thesis on marketplaces and small-scale trade livelihoods in Lào Cai province, as well as follow-up visits in 2012, 2014, 2016, and 2017. I undertook intensive participant observation in fourteen rural, upland markets in Lào Cai, also visiting other markets in the province, in neighboring provinces, and across the border in Yunnan China. I also conducted over two hundred conversational interviews with a diversity of marketplace traders (of Hmong, Tày, Yao, Giáy, Nùng, Kinh, and Han Chinese ethnicity) and over twenty semi-structured interviews with marketplace, district, and provincial officials. According to the latest national census, the population of Lào Cai is just over 610,000, with ethnic minorities accounting for 64 percent. The Hmong (22 percent), Tày (15.8 percent) and Yao (Dao) (14.5 percent) constitute the largest ethnic groups, while Kinh lowlanders make up 35.9 percent of the provincial population (General Statistics Office [GSO] 2010).

Locating Lào Cai's Upland Marketplaces and Traders

Since at least the mid-1800s, Lào Cai's marketplaces have provided important spaces for economic and sociocultural exchanges with kin, neighbors, and others. Here, ethnic minority, Kinh, and Han Chinese traders have engaged in a vibrant cross-border market network, with trade links reaching far north into Yunnan China and south to Vietnam's lowland delta (Turner 2010; Salemink 2011; Li Tana 2012; Bonnin 2012; Bonnin and Turner 2014). Although various colonial and postcolonial power holders have long sought to regulate various dimensions of these upland tradescapes, overall until very recently many of Lào Cai's periodic markets remained fairly autonomous and informal, adapting seasonally, cyclically, or when needed to changing local conditions, opportunities, and requirements.

Prior to around 2005 a number of marketplaces remained in a fairly basic condition. Trade continued to be conducted on earthen grounds with market structures erected by traders themselves from local materials such as bamboo and thatch to shield people and goods from hot or wet weather. However, since this time most of the province's markets have undergone structural improvements by the state, which have involved the construction of more permanent, concrete buildings. The typical market layout today is based on one or more concrete buildings, supported by pillars, sheltered by a tiled or corrugated iron roof, and set within the paved grounds of an enclosed plaza. Traders rent either a fixed stall or a space and offer a range of daily necessities for sale to upland consumers. Nevertheless, within this general plan there can be a great deal of variation in terms of sophistication, design, and size. On the one hand, some of the new market buildings in many of the more remote upland communes and border areas are little more than a concrete market hall. On the other hand, upland markets in district towns can be very large, multistory structures with clearly demarcated stalls, indoor food courts, and sometimes even CCTV cameras installed for surveillance by market management officials.

A total of seventy-one marketplaces in Lào Cai province are currently officially recognized. These channel nearly half of all goods traded within the province, adding almost VNĐ10 billion (US$475,403) annually to the provincial state budget (UBND Tỉnh Lào Cai 2012). Yet there is a noteworthy spatial and temporal variation regarding how these markets are organized that parallels important ethnic-based differences in marketplace trading and holds a number of implications for livelihoods and how market infrastructure is used. The main division is between markets that take place on a daily basis and those that function periodically, usually only once a week. Spatially, daily markets are the more centrally located, found in the main towns of each upland district, while the majority of periodic markets lie outside these centers in the more remote communes. Periodic markets are the most prominent, accounting for around 63 percent of all marketplaces in the province (Hùng Mạnh 2008).

These temporal and spatial distinctions are further reflected by trader ethnicity and type of trade. Overwhelmingly, ethnic Kinh make up the bulk of traders at the daily, district town markets in Lào Cai. These traders originate from lowland provincial towns in the Red River Delta and have arrived over the past fifty years during different migratory periods.[1] The majority either rent permanent market stalls from the government or are shopkeepers running trade stores. Although there are a few exceptions—such as the stallholding handicraft traders in the Sa Pa town market, discussed below—only a very small number of ethnic minorities are engaged in this type of daily, fixed trade. This ethnicized division in upland trading is significant, and Kinh have become a major force within the province's upland markets. Furthermore, Kinh are often at a great advantage over ethnic minority traders through their spatially extensive social networks, a better ability to communicate with state officials, relatively larger financial capital, and greater mobility. As such, Kinh have tended to end up dominating and monopolizing upland trade and business (World Bank 2009).

Kinh market traders do not usually sell what they themselves produce, instead purchasing goods from wholesalers or producers, which they resell in retail quantities to rural consumers. Common commodities that Kinh vendors specialize in include produce of Vietnam lowland or Chinese origin, a range of manufactured clothing, meats and fish, dried foods, packaged foods, and housewares. These traders have played a key role in the accessibility and spread of lowland commodities and Kinh consumer preferences to upland residents—such as fruit originating from southern Vietnam and up-to-date urban fashions. Kinh traders have also become the key actors within a wide variety of commodity chain networks for ethnic minority products, including handicrafts, cardamom, plums, and maize. Yet while Kinh assume a decisive role in linking ethnic minority producers and traders to wider markets, they also tend to retain an overall larger share of the financial earnings.

With regard to Lào Cai's upland periodic markets, ethnic minorities form the main groups of traders and visitors. Most of these individuals are from neighboring hamlets and trade goods that they often produce or collect themselves, such as seasonal produce, forest products, home-distilled rice and maize liquor, livestock, textiles, and specialty minority foods. In markets that receive tourist visitors, some ethnic minority traders—and increasingly also Kinh—sell handicrafts. Finally, improvements in upland connectivity since 1998 resulting from enhanced roads and the advent of the motorbike have also facilitated the activities of a small but important group of mobile minority traders who follow a weekly circuit of periodic markets. These traders supply a range of ethnic minority-oriented commodities, among them Hmong textiles imported from China, agricultural equipment, traditional medicines, buffalo livestock, and VCDs/DVDs of minority-oriented films and music videos (Bonnin 2018). Kinh from upland towns—most of whom are landless economic migrants arriving since Đổi mới in search of new livelihood opportunities—create a different group of ambulant traders. These traders ply a similar periodic market itinerary and travel to more remote commune periodic markets to sell manufactured clothing, dried foods, utensils, and produce.

Periodic markets display important seasonal changes, with higher trader and customer numbers in the months following the harvest and in the period leading up to Lunar New Year, when people need to purchase items for the festivities and are in a mood to celebrate. It should be noted that daily upland town markets can often also act as periodic markets (*chợ phiên*), so that once or twice each week the market expands dramatically, and the number of ethnic minority traders arriving from the district and remote hinterlands swell to outnumber daily Kinh traders.

Traders pay different fees to sell in the market, depending on type of trade (daily, weekly, cross-border, and so on), the size of the stall, the merchandise sold, and the trader's location in the marketplace.[2] Moreover, in some daily town markets, the rights to trade have been more permanently regularized through lump sum payments for long-term use contracts. When compared with the case of daily market trading, a key advantage for traders who sell in periodic markets either once or several days a week (in the case of mobile traders) is the much lower cost. While daily traders must pay a monthly stall rental as well as other fees, periodic market traders need pay only a fee for that day. Moreover, traders who follow a weekly market circuit are able to avoid paying any monthly or other fees that permanent daily traders are obligated to pay, while benefiting from periodic markets packed with visitors.

The State's Vision versus Local Realities

In Lào Cai, specific targets were established for upgrading, renovating, and building new markets in the province, as well as to ensure that all "makeshift markets" would be completely abolished (Chính Phủ 2008). Impressive steps have been taken toward these goals, as more than thirty permanent market buildings have been built in commune centers, while a total of twenty-three market buildings have undergone modernization since 2005 (Lục Văn Toán 2012). Capital funds for these construction projects in Lào Cai come from a number of sources: central, provincial, and district budgets; international development lending agencies; private investors; and contributions collected from traders and the local population (Chính Phủ 2003; Provincial Department of Commerce and Tourism, interview, August 4, 2007). International lenders have supplied funds for these projects primarily through Programme 135 (1998–2010), a poverty-alleviation development program that has remained very much focused on the provision of basic infrastructure in the uplands. The government also strongly encourages private enterprises and organizations to invest or join the state in investing in marketplace construction (Chính Phủ 2003).[3]

Provincial and district officials have often acted with haste to put national plans into effect, rushing to get projects under way quickly.[4] Yet these plans are often poorly communicated to local officials and traders. While market officials usually knew that market redevelopment plans were in the works, they could rarely confirm when, why, or how this was going to happen. In one upland town where I attempted to ask a market management official about plans to build a new central market, he replied: "At what time the new market will open depends on a lot of things. I am not allowed to take part and give my ideas to the committee for the new market because there is a board to negotiate and discuss the plans and I am not a participant on it." The exclusion of these market officials from the planning process is particularly concerning because they act as the face of the state in the market and as traders' key official sources of information. One provincial official noted:

> The reality is there are just too many leading players and investors involved in the business of building markets in remote areas: the district People's Committee; managers of the poverty reduction program, the Department of Agriculture and Rural Development, and the immigration and resettlement of ethnic minorities program. Most of these players have little specialized knowledge; their site survey and construction plan may not follow correct procedures. Their building design can end up being inappropriate for locals' practical needs. The end result is an irony that some markets get built but nobody comes to them! After a review, it is later revealed that the wrong location was picked or that the size of the market is inadequate, so nobody ends up trading there.

With upland residents left out of the decision making, markets have been constructed in poor locations where they are not wanted or needed, leading to a situation of barren markets and wasted funds.[5] In Lào Cai province, the situation is particularly serious. The Lào Cai Department of Trade and Industry (DTI) reports that fifteen marketplace infrastructure projects built under this scheme have failed, at a cost of VNĐ11.5 billion (US$589,744). The DTI states that of these fifteen markets, ten remained completely empty after completion, while five were active but are now "less efficient," with fewer traders than at the previous market (Quốc Hồng 2011).

According to one news report from 2010, the situation is even more extreme than the DTI claims. The article cites at least a dozen newly built but completely abandoned market structures in Lào Cai province. Some of these have been referred to as "left fallow" or as places now appropriated by locals to dry cassava and for children to play football (Ngọc Triển and Ngọc Bằng 2010). Indeed, as an attempt to transform the outputs of these projects so that they are not an entire waste of funds, the DTI has recommended that barren markets be converted to other (nonmarket) purposes. New market infrastructure has thus been put to entirely different uses than intended, including as storage space for agricultural materials and tools; a vocational training center; or, as in the case of one market located on the border with Yunnan, as a station for guards who patrol the border (Quốc Hồng 2011).

One such example of a project that never took off is the newly built market in Thanh Phú commune, Sa Pa district. Built in 2007 at a cost of VNĐ1.16 billion (US$66,358), this market was intended to meet the trading needs of local ethnic minorities and bring in revenue for the commune. However, of the very small number of traders, merely eight, working in this market, only five are actually from Thanh Phú commune, with the rest from other localities. Traders in this new market are expected to pay VNĐ150,000–200,000 (US$6.60–8.80) a month for a stall. The market management accounts for the low numbers of traders by explaining that these market fees are far too high for people from the area to be able to afford. In addition, with a much larger market only fifteen kilometers away, many customers prefer to bypass Thanh Phú for the more popular and vibrant established venue.

An even greater flop is the handicraft market built in Tả Phìn commune, Sa Pa district. On a daily basis Tả Phìn receives a substantial number of tourist visitors, who arrive with the purpose of visiting a "typical" ethnic minority Hmong and Yao village. Slightly different from the other market projects in the province geared at modernization, this market—built with the support of the Netherlands Development Organisation—was made to represent an apparently more "traditional" style to appeal to tourists. Yet when I last visited in 2012, it was clear that as with the other market upgrading schemes, this new market had not taken hold. Local Yao and Hmong handicraft traders explained that they preferred to maintain a more "active" mobile approach of following tourists on a village walk to persuade them to visit their homes for a sale, or to wait near the car park where tour buses unload (also see Turner, chapter 2).

Despite the overt development intentions and promises of these schemes, traders' negative experiences of these upgrades make it quite evident that provincial and local state planning is at stark odds with traders' livelihood needs. A lack of communication, delays in market construction and relocation, and the poorer trade conditions found in the new and supposedly "improved" market environments leave market traders frustrated, angered, and often resistant to the changes. The following case studies of two of the most high-profile upland marketplaces in the province shed light on the on-the-ground realities of these development plans.

PLANNING DILEMMAS AND CONSTRUCTION DELAYS IN THE
BẮC HÀ MARKETPLACE

The drawing on a sign that hung in the ruins of the old Bắc Hà town marketplace—which for much of the time of my research had been a dusty construction site—suggested a large bastion of commerce. The full-color drawing displayed the ambitious plans for Bắc Hà's new market: a two-story structure with gleaming white pillars and a tiled, almost pagoda-like roof set in a beautiful parklike surrounding. Yet the fact that the sign was hanging quite askew hinted that it had been there some time. Indeed, my visit to the site in August 2008 came nearly a year after the completion date that the sign announced of December 2007, and a full two years since the project initially began in 2006. For the traders of Bắc Hà market, the discrepancy between the promises made by the sign and the lived reality of this VNĐ12 billion (US$754,053) market overhaul was the key point of contention. For the past two years, traders had been housed by the district in a temporary market set in a sloping, often muddy field, with their stalls covered by only tarpaulin (see figure 3.1).

Nam, a male Kinh daily market trader in his forties, was fed up with the state's handling of the project.[6] In particular, he spoke of the failure of local cadres to make good on their promises to traders, as well as the injustice of having to pay for a temporary stall space to which he himself had to make major improvements for it to be useable:

I'm very upset with the temporary market we were relocated to. Before we were moved, the government promised we'd be given support with a small amount of

Figure 3.1. The temporary market during construction of Bắc Hà marketplace. Photograph by C. Bonnin.

money. We were also told we wouldn't be asked to pay rent for our stalls while in the new temporary market. But in fact, the market board still collects money from us for fees and rental space! So in comparison with the old market, the total amount of money we have to pay now is even greater than before. My wife and I paid a lot of money to rent our stall for a fixed period [here]. In the new market we should [still] be entitled to have a spot for a few more years. The district [told us that] people who still have time left over on their rental agreement will be reimbursed a certain amount of money. Or they will be provided a spot in the new market for the duration they have left, [but only] if there's room. But me and most of the others don't want the money back and prefer to be given a new spot for trading in the new market.

Similarly, daily Kinh trader Đặng remarked upon the very shoddy temporary market that the district had provided, entirely lacking in waste disposal or sanitation facilities. He explained how security had also become a major concern for traders: "Many of [us] sleep in the marketplace because [we] need to protect [our] goods from being destroyed or stolen since the stalls are so flimsy. In the old market, we could feel safe to lock the door and keep our goods in the market at night." For traders like Nam and Đặng, this "development" project is anything but improvement, coming as an unfair intrusion into their ability to make a living.

Such striking sentiments were also voiced by another male Kinh trader, Thanh, who feels that the district's actual priorities lie more with developing the area for tourism than where its obligations should lie, in improving the Bắc Hà marketplace to assist its petty traders:

I think that the government's main purpose for building the new market is to draw more tourism because we already had a good market here! But in reality, tourists were coming to Bắc Hà market because they were attracted by the traditional characteristics of it and the culture of the people, so they don't want to see it change. Traders here called the District People's Committee to the Provincial Courts in order to complain about having to relocate to this temporary market because the compensation and the design of the temporary market were unacceptable to us. I feel that the state policy is often good, but in practice the actions of the People's Committee are not good.

While the state's clear intent is to advance rural trade and marketplaces—and, therefore, overall socioeconomic development—examples such as the Bắc Hà market renovations illustrate how these projects are often carried out in a haphazard manner. Plans are not communicated properly to traders, often leaving them in a worse financial situation than they were in to begin with.

THE CONTESTED RELOCATION OF THE SA PA MARKETPLACE

Other conflicts between state development goals and local interests have occurred over marketplace relocation decisions. This is clearly illustrated in the case of the Sa Pa market, another extremely long, drawn-out project spanning 2005–14, that involved a highly contested market closure and relocation. The historical central marketplace in this upland tourist town dates back to the French colonial period, while the structure to be demolished, located in a prime spot in the center of town, was built in 1996

(Michaud and Turner 2000). This central market included a multiethnic mix of close to four hundred registered traders, including around forty ethnic minority daily traders (mainly Hmong and Yao), and was a popular draw for tourists. In addition to providing for the daily necessities of locals, the market was famous for the sale of ethnic minority handicrafts and relied heavily on the tourist trade.

District plans for a new two-story market complex based one kilometer away on the very edge of the town had been officially approved by the provincial People's Committee since 2005. Yet because of a number of issues—including ongoing contestations over the land acquisition and compensation of households residing on the land where the market was to be built—the project was stalled for almost a decade (Mạnh Hưng 2015). Given traders' temporal experience of this stalled plan as an enduring state of affairs, many did not really believe the new market would ever be built and were not too worried about an impending relocation. Nevertheless, this time frame was still characterized by both limbo and uncertainty as traders were kept in the dark about when the market would be completed and whether they would have to move. Many commented that "we hope it'll take at least another five years" so that trade could continue at the existing market spot.

During my visit in autumn 2012, it appeared that construction had again commenced in earnest, leading to mounting speculation over the new market and the fate of the much beloved old market. In the absence of any official information, rumors abounded. Some traders stated that the market would be torn down and turned into a modern supermarket "that no locals could afford," owned by a Chinese company. Others believed that it might be rebuilt as a fancy tourist market with rents markedly hiked up. However, traders all agreed that the new marketplace was very poorly situated, well out of the way for customers to reach. Hạnh, a Kinh tourist trader, emphasized the importance of the current market location for gaining access to tourist sales: "[The other market] is so far away! There's no point—it's on the other end of town and no one's going to go there. Only some locals would ever go to that market to buy fresh fruit, and that's not what this market is about!"

Moreover, some ethnic minority traders, like Hmong trader Vu, felt wary of losing access to market space, as this is something that has happened to them in the past when a new market was built: "Around 2006, a new outdoor market was built that was supposed to be for us minorities to sell in. However, soon fancier stalls were rebuilt where our stalls used to be. These stalls were for the Vietnamese people selling barbeque, and minority people ended up being kicked out. Maybe the same thing may happen again."

Such statements echo important concerns raised by many other ethnic minority traders who perceive themselves as being displaced from newly improved, more highly regulated markets by Kinh traders who tend to be more adept at dealing with state officials and regulations. Experiences such as these serve to expose how the market engages different categories of social actors in different ways, something that market development plans have not taken sufficiently into account.

Once again, as with Bắc Hà and other new markets, there also appears to have been very minimal consultation with traders and locals over the Sa Pa market project. According to Bích, a Kinh medicinal herbs trader:

> The government doesn't provide information to the people. While the government is trying to create economic opportunities, the traders don't see any opportunities in this relocation plan, so there is a total mix-up and people are unwilling

to move. It's a pity that this brand-new expensive development creates no benefit for locals whatsoever. People are just suspicious of this white elephant. It will destroy the livelihoods here that are thriving and lively with tourists passing by. It's like the government just thought, "Oh, let's build something here and they will come."

Significantly, a number of minority traders in the same town also highlighted ethnic based barriers to accessing state planning information. As Hmong trader Kou stated: "We'd love if someone came here to tell us what's happening—to explain if we'll have to move, pay more fees, and how we can deal with this change—but so far no one has come. Something might have been said on the public loudspeaker but that's only in the Vietnamese language, which many of us can't understand."

Similar ethnic minority–based access barriers to state information are a common occurrence in other project areas such as health care provision (Bonnin 2013) and agricultural extension (Bonnin and Turner 2012). By 2014, the market building seemed to be very much completed when I visited in July. However, it remained locked up and empty. A few Kinh traders who lived in the direct vicinity were selling meat, fruit, and vegetables outside, on the market's periphery, but aside from that it was quite empty. Back at the old market, both Kinh and ethnic minority traders explained that they had been requested to move, but were going to stay put for as long as possible. Responding to my question of why, one long-term Kinh trader in the market, Thùy offered, "It's a trust issue. People here don't have any more faith in the follow-through of the government. Plans are on paper only but they never seem to materialize. So . . . maybe we can keep postponing this move."

Many ethnic minority and Kinh traders were particularly concerned over what appeared to be much smaller stall sizes and increased trade fees at the new market—conditions that are far from an improvement from the perspective of local livelihoods. For example, Kinh handicraft trader Vân explained: "All the people here got together to tell the district People's Committee that we won't go to the new market. The new market is more expensive and the stalls there are also smaller. Here, I have eighteen meters [stall length], but there I would have only seven meters. And it costs me VNĐ3 million to trade here for one month, while over there it costs VNĐ5 million." Likewise, Hmong handicraft trader Mi said: "Two months ago we were asked by the People's Committee to go look at the new market and to sign a paper to agree to sell there. They promised us that we would get 2.25 meters, but when we went there to look at it, it was only 1.20 meters. The costs for rent were VNĐ460,000 including electricity, sanitation, and cleaning. However, here we only pay VNĐ150,000 per month. We refuse to relocate there and will stay here for as long as possible . . . or until the People's Committee agrees to their promise of 2.25 meters!"

During the autumn and winter of 2014, traders attempted a number of appeals to the provincial and district state to overturn the market relocation decision. One of these involved a meeting held between a group of market traders and the People's Committee of Sa Pa district in early December. At the meeting, traders requested a response to an official letter they had written to the provincial People's Committee to reconsider the relocation but to which they hadn't receive a response. The answer from the district state representative was that there was "no need to ask for people's opinions. We can do whatever we like. It is the right of the authorities and the final decision is that the market must be moved according to the plan" (UBND Huyện Sa Pa 2014).

Following this unsuccessful attempt, Sa Pa market traders decided to launch a market relocation appeal at the central government level. In a highly significant effort, a group of around one hundred marketplace traders, both Kinh and ethnic minority (Hmong and Yao) made the three-hundred-kilometer journey in order to petition the government in Hanoi to halt the relocation. According to Traynor, "The Kinh [traders] seemed to treat the minority traders as equals as they all travelled together and slept in the same hotel. The Kinh encouraged the minority traders to hold up banners even though these were [written] in Vietnamese which they couldn't understand because the Kinh said it was the minorities' market too. [Some vendors] made a financial contribution to pay for the group to get to Hanoi, especially the minorities who could not afford to go. One Kinh family even contributed US$500" (2015, 29).

The complaints of the Sa Pa market traders lay with the nonexistent local consultation on the project and the lack of clarity by the district over what would happen to the old market and to their businesses. These collective actions taken by traders should be recognized as a remarkable show of solidarity. Although in many past instances, ethnic Kinh and minority traders have had rather strained relationships in the market, here they were able to align in defense of their livelihoods (Turner 2007; Bonnin 2012). Unfortunately, none of the traders' numerous efforts to appeal the relocation proved successful in the end and the Sa Pa market was closed down on December 17 at 6:00 p.m. As a last attempt at foot dragging, some traders had left their wares in the market, thinking that this would delay things further. However, all their goods were loaded onto trucks and carted away by authorities. The next day the traders found that the market had been emptied and locked and the electricity cut, and they realized that they finally had to move.

At present, the new Sa Pa market has opened and is functioning, but the traders' worst predictions appear to have come true. While Kinh trader Chi explained that "we do like the appearance of the new market[;] . . . it is modern, clean, safe, and bright," she went on to say, "The problem is that very few customers come here because of the location, while the rent for trading is twice what it was in the old market. . . . Local Kinh people don't shop here because it is not in the center of town, while tourists do not know about it or do not know how to get here because there are no signposts and it is not found on any maps" (interview in Traynor 2015, 28).

As the Sa Pa market now receives so much less tourist footfall, many of the minority handicraft traders who worked in the old market have now moved their trade to join the ranks of vendors on Sa Pa's streets. Hmong and Yao handicraft traders I spoke with in the summer of 2016 were very upset with the location they were assigned in the new market: up toward the back of the second floor, dark, and hidden from tourists' view. Whereas in the old market the layout was such that customers had to pass each and every stall in order to move through the handicrafts section—raising the likelihood of a sale—now tourists are able to just browse at the first row of stalls. Moreover, as part of their desire to ensure that the new market appeared modern and orderly, Sa Pa market management officials restricted ethnic minorities' displays to the use of tabletops, preventing them from using the wall and rails, as they were accustomed to in the old market, to exhibit their larger handicrafts such as skirts and wall hangings. However, during a brief visit in March 2017, it appeared that traders were nevertheless ignoring these regulations and were once again hanging their wares as they were used to doing previously. Nevertheless, such concerning outcomes once again call into question the degree to which market redevelopment serves the interests of upland livelihoods or contributes to the objective of poverty alleviation.

Inappropriate Standardized Marketplace Models for the Uplands?

Further evidence of incompatibilities between state marketplace development agendas and traders' livelihood priorities emerges when we consider how markets are actually used by different groups of social actors in this multiethnic space. The modern, daily market structures with fixed stalls and rental fees that are prioritized in the Vietnam state's market development agenda are not always the best replacement for upland periodic market fairs that have featured for centuries in ethnic minority trade and socialization (Bonnin 2012; Trần Hữu Sơn 2014). This approach also seems paradoxical, given that a number of markets in Lào Cai have been officially designated by the province as "cultural markets"—including Bắc Hà and Sa Pa—apparently on the basis of their long histories. These markets are considered to be "authentic sites" where ethnic minority "culture" is on display and thus part of the province's cultural heritage. As cultural tourism is an economic sector that the provincial state and private interests are keen to encourage, this does not seem to translate with how some ethnic minorities find themselves being increasingly marginalized from these markets (Chính Phủ 2008).

For many Hmong and Yao ethnic minority households in Lào Cai, the agricultural basis of their livelihoods is prioritized and deeply embedded in local understandings of wealth and well-being, and livelihood diversification strategies are adjusted around this core. Plans for new markets that do not permit a flexible engagement with trade limit the activities and participation of ethnic minorities who carefully shift their livelihood activities according to their seasonal agricultural calendars.

Despite a long history of involvement in wider trade networks, development failures like these can fuel misunderstandings and stereotyping of ethnic minorities as lacking business interest or skills (McElwee 2008; World Bank 2009; Bonnin 2012; Bonnin and Turner 2014). For instance, when I asked a Kinh People's Committee member why plans drawn up for a commune market had not yet been implemented, he responded, "[It's] because the local people [ethnic minorities] in this area still do not understand the concept of daily trading from a fixed selling space." As such, he felt that ethnic minorities would not use a new market efficiently.

This notion that ethnic minorities need to be educated in how to trade was clearly illustrated by another official from the Chamber of Commerce and Tourism. This Kinh official explained that because ethnic minorities tend to have much less financial capital than Kinh, "they should not have to pay taxes. . . . However, they should be shown the proper way to be involved in the business sector, have the correct documents, and be provided with the information on how to do business in the correct way." Here, the state representative identifies the "correct way" to trade as through formal official channels and as full-time trading with the right legal documents.

The Vietnamese state's emphasis on physical marketplaces and the trade that occurs in them serves to perpetuate the stereotypes and rhetoric noted above. This approach defines a marketplace trader as someone who sells in the market year-round on a daily basis from a fixed location and has good capital flows—and not one who trades weekly, on a seasonal basis, or according to a more flexible schedule. Yet this model does not represent the diversity of trade strategies that are adopted and works to exclude a great deal of alternative exchange and commerce that occurs both inside and outside of official marketplaces (Bonnin 2012).

This chapter has revealed the conflicting aims of official development procedures, from the local to provincial to national levels. At the local level, ethnic minority traders are faced with a lack of information regarding market reconstructions and relocations that directly affect their daily livelihoods. The market management is left unclear about plans, and there is little communication between state representatives and traders. When relocations do occur, they have been disorganized, with no consistent information provided about new trade conditions and infrastructure. National-level plans for market infrastructure redevelopment, when carried out at the very local level, thus have numerous unforeseen, unequal, and often unwanted consequences. The most telling "development failures" are those markets that have been rejected by traders and that remain entirely empty or else are creatively adapted to serve a range of other functions.

These infrastructure projects are of tremendous interest to traders and local residents, and especially so for those living on the margins. With poorly executed plans and outcomes that result in further socioeconomic exclusion, a great deal of cynicism and frustration has been directed toward the local government. I have demonstrated how the lack of proper implementation and communication of market plans to officials and traders at the local level has led to heightened livelihood vulnerability and uncertainties for upland residents. Traders reveal their agency through their efforts to contest market redevelopment, whether in terms of more organized protest and public media arenas or via more subtle methods such as "foot dragging" and feigned accommodation. While for some traders, the issue lies with how markets have been poorly implemented in practice, for others, this shift to more modern, fixed markets is problematically one that corresponds more with an idealized "one size fits all" development model than with upland realities, while state-sanctioned markets do little to integrate traders' actual needs.

The chasm that lies between the enthusiasm of national and provincial government officials to build upland marketplaces vis-à-vis their underuse after being built opens the door for lingering qualms that these infrastructures might represent something more or something else altogether, although it remains beyond the scope of my research to offer concrete findings in this direction. As Mbembe's (2001) work highlights, infrastructures may harbor hidden agendas and opportunities for elite actors. Larkin describes this work in his annual review on infrastructure and says: "States put forth other sorts of objects—roads, factories, bridges—that also profess to have a technical function but in fact operate on a different level at the same time. Mbembe points out that often the function of awarding infrastructural projects has far more to do with gaining access to government contracts and rewarding patron-client networks than it has to do with their technical function. This is why roads disappear, factories are built but never operated, and bridges go to nowhere" (2013, 334). Indeed, these upland marketplace infrastructural projects seem to not only be about the tangible gains, in terms of increasing the livelihoods of traders or appearing modern, but also about the possibility of benefits that are less visible.

Furthermore, as Larkin argues, "Infrastructures also exist as forms separate from their purely technical functioning, and they need to be analyzed as concrete semiotic and aesthetic vehicles oriented to addressees. They emerge out of and store within them forms of desire and fantasy and can take on fetish-like aspects that sometimes can be wholly autonomous from their technical function" (2013, 329). I suggest that these marketplaces also symbolize something rather different for government officials so that their failure does not seem to matter as much. It is being able to build these grand designs as a sign of progress, and not the project's actual outcomes, that is the point. The fact that new and upgraded markets are then left barren or taken over for other uses speaks not to the failure of these development projects and the Vietnamese government but to the lack of progress or level of civilization on the part of the traders who have refused to occupy these modernized spaces. While I have shown how in some instances, such as that of the Sa Pa marketplace, traders were effectively forced out of the old market and into the new one, overall, the dispossession we are witness to here is a bureaucratized one that reinforces and is legitimized through mechanisms of moral categorization (see Harms 2012) and a state enclosure of upland trade practices (Bonnin and Turner 2014). Upland traders resist these assertions by continuing to not occupy these new market spaces or by reworking the spaces of control within them as they strive to maintain culturally appropriate and livelihood-relevant trading approaches.

NOTES

1 Kinh migrants concentrated mainly in upland towns and areas with greater physical accessibility. Many of the more established marketplace traders were part of the earlier state-sponsored New Economic Zones mass movements of the 1960s and 1970s. More newcomers since the 1990s have come independently, seeking new upland livelihood opportunities made possible by the state's greater relaxation on internal migration following Đổi mới in the late 1980s. Compared with the earlier migrants, many of this later group are landless, lack official residency, and are highly dependent upon trade for their livelihoods. Migrants from different lowland areas have tended to settle together in upland districts, and hometown ties remain a crucial livelihood asset supporting their trading activities.

2 The fees that market traders must pay are as follows: (1) a daily amount to trade in the marketplace for all traders; (2) a monthly amount for renting the market stall for those with a business license and a signed contract with the market board; and (3) service fees for sanitation (cleaning and waste collection), water, and electricity and for keeping order and security.

3 Incentives for marketplace construction investors include preferential policies for their activities (see Chính Phủ 2003).

4 The widely acknowledged kickbacks available in the construction industry in Vietnam may be linked to this eagerness to start construction. In addition, it has been suggested that the speed with which some projects are started is to ensure the continuance of funding dispersals from international lending agencies.

5 In particular, it is the new markets being constructed in upland communes and villages—rather than the central marketplaces in upland towns, which are highly depended upon as trade spaces—that tend to remain barren after they are built.

6 All informant names are pseudonyms.

CHAPTER FOUR

GHOST MARKETS AND MOVING BAZAARS IN HANOI'S URBAN SPACE

Gertrud Hüwelmeier

In 2012, when I first visited the location of the chợ Mơ (Mơ market) as part of my ethnographic fieldwork on marketplaces in Hanoi, the market structure had already been demolished. Where once a traditional market had sprawled, a twenty-story building was under construction, the future Mơ Commercial Center. Chợ Mơ was one of the biggest markets in Hanoi, and its redevelopment, along with that of several other market sites, was part of the city's plan for making Hanoi a "green and clean" metropolis. Urbanites in the neighborhood explained to me that chợ Mơ had been transferred to another place a few kilometers away from the original area to allow business to continue during construction. The provisional site, a moving bazaar, resembled some of the traditional markets, in this case an enclosed place with its entrance from the street, characterized by rows of market stalls between which customers drive in on motorbikes to buy fruit, vegetables, and other products and leave without ever getting off their bikes. Traders in this temporary marketplace, most of them women in their forties and fifties, were not informed about when exactly they would be able to return to the former site, and in particular, where exactly their stall would be located in the redeveloped place. For some of them it was not even clear if they would be able to continue trading at all in the reconstructed chợ Mơ, as they had already lost many of their former clients because of the market relocation.[1]

As this small vignette illustrates, markets in Vietnam are on the move, which creates precarious situations for a majority of traders. Many people I spoke with in Hanoi are not at all optimistic regarding the future development of the new marketplaces. Over the past few years, Vietnam's central government and the municipal authorities in Hanoi have sought to create an economic hub and to develop the capital into a more "civilized and modern" place. The policy is guided by ideas about the "clean and green city," which are part of socialist modernization and urban planning (DiGregorio, Rambo, and Yanagisawa 2003; DiGregorio 2012). This policy aims to transform not only the capital city, Hanoi (Labbé and Boudreau 2011), but also Ho Chi Minh City (Harms 2011, 2016), and its famous Bến Thành market (Leshkowich 2014a); secondary cities such as Vinh in north-central Vietnam (Schwenkel 2012), the homeland of Hồ Chí Minh; and other places, such as upland northern Vietnam (Bonnin and Turner 2014). One of the key projects of the Vietnamese government as part of this policy is the replacement of some traditional urban markets with supermarkets, hypermarkets, and new commercial centers. These new shopping localities embody the intersection of "capitalist forms of globalization and market socialism" (Schwenkel and Leshkowich 2012, 380). This policy has an impact not only on the physical spaces of the markets but also, in particular, as I will argue in this chapter, on social and economic ties between vendors and buyers and on trader-to-trader relationships.

By conceptualizing marketplaces as sites of exchange in which the social, cultural, political, and economic aspects of everyday life have an impact on the encounters between various groups, such as clients, traders, market management, and political authorities (Hüwelmeier 2013a, 2013b, 2015a, 2015b), this chapter aims to contribute to a research agenda on markets and diversity in urban spaces (Hiebert, Rath, and Vertovec 2015), which focuses on the relationship between the economy and society and investigates cultural diversity and neoliberal state regulatory structures. Using Geertz's (1978) concept of clientelization, in which the development of ongoing, reciprocal, but competitive relationships is central to marketplace dynamics, I will take a closer look at the transformation of the relationship between vendors and buyers and the loss of regular customers as a result of market relocation. As the complex processes and dynamics of everyday interactions in Hanoi's bazaars are affected by the spatiality of markets and the state regulations within which they operate, I draw on an understanding of space as socially produced (Lefebvre 1991; Massey 1993) to argue that the redevelopment, the temporary moving, and the later relocation of vendors to now renovated marketplaces pose great challenges to the trading activities and survival strategies of vendors, especially those of female traders.

Based on multi-sited ethnographic fieldwork in a number of Hanoi's marketplaces, this contribution focuses on three places, each in a different stage of renovation: one postrenovation locality, one being considered for renovation, and one in transition at the time of my fieldwork in 2012–13.[2] By investigating several localities, each of which is affected by urban redevelopment or rumors about future demolition, I will analyze perspectives on how different actors' views shape the present and future vision of being a petty trader in some of Hanoi's marketplaces. First, by drawing on encounters with stallholders in the Hàng Da market, I will trace women's experiences and their economic losses after the reconstruction of the market. Second, by analyzing Hanoi's most famous "flea" market (chợ Trời), long on the city government's list of markets to be removed, I will illuminate the view of a male representative of the market management with regard to rumors of the market's demolition. Finally, referring to experiences of petty traders in chợ Mơ, a market that was moved to another place for a temporary period, I will explore the fragility of the trader-client relationship when vendors have to relocate.[3]

GHOST MARKETS

Developments in Vietnam's capital, not least resulting from the economic transition known as market socialism (Beresford 2008), point to the fact that Vietnam's central government and the municipal authorities in Hanoi aim to create an economic hub in order to transform the capital into a more civilized and modern place (Turner and Schoenberger 2012, 1029). The development policy draws on ideas about the "clean and green city," which include reducing traffic chaos, eliminating indiscriminate parking, and ensuring that pavements are free of informal street vendors. One main element of urban development policies is market redevelopment. In the capital, the Hanoi People's Committee has started implementing this policy by replacing traditional fresh markets with supermarkets and hypermarkets (Söderström and Geertman 2013, 251). However, this policy was not successful, as I will illustrate in my ethnographic examples. On the contrary, it has presented street vendors and small traders in local fresh markets with great challenges in regard to their ability to conduct business.

Chợ Hàng Da, located near the ancient quarter, an area where small entrepreneurs have been trading since the thirteenth century (Turner 2009, 1204), provides an excellent example of the Hanoi People's Committee's drive for rapid redevelopment. This trading place was one of the oldest markets in Hanoi (Geertman 2011) and was renovated as a roofed market in the late 1980s. For decades, a thriving market existed here, but over the past few years, this site as well as a number of similar markets, described by the authorities as "chaotic" (Drummond 2012, 79), have been completely destroyed or renovated. Hàng Da market was demolished in 2008 and construction of a new building, financed by private investors, started that same year.

Reopened in 2011 and officially called Hàng Da Galleria, the new site was redesigned as an upscale shopping mall, thereby totally losing its former character. Small-scale traders from the old market were relocated into the basement of the new mall. While processes of market redevelopment are part of urban development policies (Endres 2014a, 98), these policies are not entirely new in the Socialist Republic of Vietnam, as illustrated by the work of Ann Marie Leshkowich (2014a). Since 1995, Leshkowich has been carrying out long-term ethnographic fieldwork on women traders in the famous Bến Thành market in Ho Chi Minh City. The market, which opened in 1914, has long been a fixture in the urban space. Leshkowich reported hearing rumors of development plans in the 1990s (195) and noted that similar plans had been discussed even before 1975. However, the Bến Thành market survived, not least because of its growing popularity as a tourist destination, similar to the famous Đồng Xuân market in Hanoi, built by the French in 1889. Moreover, Bến Thành market became a symbol of Ho Chi Minh City, and, in conjunction with an unforeseen rise in urban property values, planners reevaluated this place and their former assessments about female traders as being backward, small-scale entrepreneurs unable to participate in modern life.

Urban market redevelopment in Hanoi is part of extensive processes of spatial reconfiguration, with implications for the social and economic ties of vendors and customers alike. During my five months of ethnographic fieldwork in late 2012 and early 2013, various people I spoke with in Hanoi, among them small traders, retailers, and former clients of the Hàng Da market, reported that the market has become a *chợ ma*, a ghost market, with broken windows in abandoned shops. When I started fieldwork in September 2012, the escalator in the new Hàng Da shopping center did not work, but a few shops selling expensive shoes and textiles were open on the first and second floors, though with no customers. However, when I returned in January and February 2013, all these shops were closed and private security guards were monitoring each floor and instructed me not to take photographs. In the basement, however, a number of traders were selling fresh food, such as vegetables and meat, and other items, such as secondhand textiles, in narrow spaces of about three square meters. Most of the retailers were just sitting around and there were only a handful of clients present. The basement market has completely lost its aura of a traditional market, with its smells, sounds, and the hustle and bustle of large numbers of people.

As the new building was designed as a shopping center and had completely lost its traditional character, not all the former vendors moved back in 2011. Since then, many traders have started selling fresh food in small, newly created street markets with stalls on the side around the old market site. Others finally gave up their business, while some traders rented shops in the side roads. I met a poor woman in her sixties, who had been a vendor in the former Hàng Da market, and was serving tea and selling tea leaves next to a friend's street market stall. As the woman was not able to continue her business in the old Hàng Da market, her trader friend had given her permission to "use" a small space next to her stall at the Phùng Hưng Street, which received a lot of traffic and where many customers on motorbikes stopped to buy fresh food. This is but one example of solidarity among female traders, based on long-term relationships in the former marketplace.

The market redevelopment has affected not only traders but also investors, such as Mrs. Thúy, a businesswoman in her fifties. She had invested US$200,000 to have twenty square meters at her disposal in the new shopping area. However, she has lost her investment, as nobody wants to rent space in the new building. Moreover, in her view, the investment will be a total loss for her, as she cannot find another customer for this vacant business space.

One of the big problems associated with the relocation of marketplaces is the loss of clients, which before the demolition of the marketplace most traders in the Hàng Da market suspected would happen and which they did indeed experience after the redevelopment. As noted by Clifford Geertz, an essential aspect of bazaar life, in addition to bargaining and the exchange of information, is clientelization. He defines clientelization as "the tendency . . . for repetitive purchasers of particular goods and services to establish continuing relationships with particular purveyors of them, rather than search widely through the market at each occasion of need. . . . Its buyers and sellers, moving along the grooved channels clientelization lays down, find their way again and again to the same adversaries. 'Adversaries' is the word, for clientship relations are not dependency relations, but competitive ones" (1978, 30).

The moving and renovating of traditional markets results in a breakdown of these relationships, as illustrated by the cases of women traders from the Hàng Da market with whom I spoke after they had returned to the new building. They complained that they had lost nearly all their regular clients, whom they had known for many years, and they attributed this loss to the way the new space forced customers to adopt new shopping behavior that was less convenient to their lifestyles. Mr. Thanh, who was a customer in the Hàng Da market for more than fifteen years, explained to me, "I used to drive through the food section with my motorbike every day on my way home, like many Hanoians did. It was convenient, because I just stopped, and while sitting on my motorbike, I could bargain and then drive home." Motorbikes, as Allison Truitt has brilliantly analyzed for Ho Chi Minh City, "have become indispensable vehicles in altering the boundaries of the 'private' and the 'public' . . . , thus constituting a Vietnamese urban middle class" (Truitt 2008, 3). Motorbikes are part of urban mobilities, and while driving such a vehicle, "a person can stop by a street vendor to purchase fruit or check the day's winning lottery numbers" (5). Likewise, most middle-class households in Hanoi own one or more motorbikes, and women and men usually use their motorbikes to drive into small street markets; stop at stalls near the street; or purchase fresh food, vegetables, fish or meat in traditional marketplaces. Mr. Thanh was not pleased with the site's redevelopment into a shopping mall, noting that "the market is not a market any more. You have to park your motorbike in the back of the building, you have to pay for parking, and you have to walk down the stairs to reach the basement, where prices are high and where there is no market atmosphere."

Mr. Thanh's experiences correlate with the narratives of many traders, who told me that only a few customers still visit the food section in the basement of the building, which can be entered only on foot, as there is now a staircase, unlike the previous food section, where clients were able to drive in by motorbike or bicycle. When I first met the trader Mrs. Hà in the basement, she was busy cutting hundreds of onions, as her business consists of supplying two restaurants with onions and meat. She said that she had lost many of her former clients, who had been coming to her several times a week for many years, while briefly chatting about family news or health issues. Her customers used to drive into the old marketplace by motorbike to buy fresh meat for cooking at home, but they stopped shopping at her stall after the relocation of the market. Mrs. Hà now makes her living predominantly from two restaurants, whose owners buy bigger portions of meat. The restaurant owners do not visit her stall the way regular clients would; instead, Mrs. Hà purchases the meat from a wholesale market and then delivers it to the restaurants by motorbike in the early morning. She told me she currently has a lot of time on her hands and that she even prepares her home cooking at her work place, as she has fewer customers since moving into the basement.

Mrs. Hà reported that before the redevelopment of the Hàng Da market there had been around five hundred traders on the site. She declared that after the rebuilding and reopening only 10 percent of the retailers who had been trading in the Hàng Da market since the early 1990s had returned and were selling goods in the basement. While other research suggests that a larger proportion of long-term traders may in fact have moved into the new market (Endres 2014a), Mrs. Hà and a number of traders in this place have observed a dramatic difference between the past and the present situations. According to Mrs. Hà, many vendors now trade outside the building, in an area near the locality, or have given up their businesses entirely. Petty traders operating outside the market do not pay rent or taxes, as Mrs. Hà noted, and their products, including meat, are not controlled by the authorities. While the social relationships between Mrs. Hà and the traders next to her stall seemed to be quite relaxed, such as joking and chatting, despite the fact that they were selling similar products, they perceived the street vendors outside the market as competitors. Next year, Mrs. Hà told me, she will give up her business because of the loss of clients and will spend more time with her grandchildren, as many middle-class women in their fifties and sixties do in contemporary Hanoi. In 2016, when I revisited the market, traders next to her stall said that the place of Mrs. Hà is empty and that she could not sell the use rights for the trading place, as nobody wants to buy them, because of the decline of business in this market.

The redevelopment of Hàng Da market may have resulted in some positive changes, but, for the traders in the basement at least, these do not seem to outweigh the disadvantages. In their study on retailers' degree of satisfaction with the new market site, Endres (2014a, 105) and her collaborators in Hanoi found that retailers in the basement were highly satisfied with the safety and hygiene of the place but that overall they were less satisfied with their levels of profit. My informants seemed even more disappointed. They complained of conflicts with the market management; high rents; receiving disinformation about the current situation; the high cost of electricity because of the new air conditioning system; and the monthly fees they must pay for freezers, the cleaning of the market, and the toilets. These aspects make it far more difficult for the traders to earn a living from their work in a place without windows and fresh air than was the case in the roofed market. Contrary to the statements by some government officials, many traders and those people I know from my personal networks, including former clients of this site, cannot see any positive developments for the future of the Hàng Da market.

OPEN AIR AND FLEA MARKET

The most famous, but simultaneously infamous, market in contemporary Hanoi is chợ Trời. This locality is considered "dark" or "opaque," for various reasons. First, some people would never go there because of their anxieties about thieves and fences at work in the market and the chance that they themselves could be robbed while shopping there. It is said that most of the goods here are stolen and that this site is a "black" market, where people can even "place an order" for things they need, which will then be illegally obtained for them. Other people, however, are happy to get a good bargain or find everything they need, in particular spare parts for cars and motorbikes. Clients buy secondhand goods such as radios, TVs, and computer equipment, as well as such smaller goods as nuts and screws and anything made of metal, including nails, tools, and so on. According to the market manager of chợ Trời, in previous times there were more secondhand goods to buy in this place; nowadays, however, many products are new and imported mostly from China and Japan, but some are also produced in Vietnam. These products include aggregators, electrical spare parts for machines, ball bearings, and automobile and motorbike accessories, as well as CD players and CDs.

Chợ Trời is an open-air market and a street market, so no car can pass through. There is no fixed roof, but tarpaulins, and there are no halls such as in chợ Hôm, chợ Đồng Xuân, or other markets. In the middle of some narrow streets one finds small boxes of about three square meters, made from wood or metal and established on public space. The boxes are placed in two rows in the middle of the street, so motorbikes can drive through the market on the right and left sides of the street. Traders, most of them female, open the boxes early in the morning, take the goods from inside the boxes to the outside so that the box looks like a table, and then trade until five in the afternoon, when the market closes. In the evening, traders lock their boxes and leave them there until they come back the next morning.

Mr. Nguyên is the third manager since the establishment of the market as a state market in 1985 and has been working there for seven years. The market management consists of the male manager and five female assistants, and their office was under renovation at the end of 2012, which to me was an indication that the market would not be moved to another site. But, as the manager recounted, plans to transfer the market do exist. The authorities have long wanted to close chợ Trời, as it is considered dirty and "dangerous" and does not correspond to state policies and laws, such as those banning trading in the streets. The practice of selling goods on the sidewalk, by using public space and partly the space in front of peoples' private houses, for example, sitting on the stairs and selling vegetables, is generally discouraged and subject to different enforcement practices, as has also been discussed for Ho Chi Minh City (Kim 2015). However, this kind of trading happens in many places and requires various agreements with the owner of the house, neighbors, other traders, and local authorities.

According to Mr. Nguyên the market was already in existence before 1954, the year when the French left the country. Having been established during French colonial times, but without any state control, it was always a spontaneous market, a place where secondhand objects were traded. Even after 1954, chợ Trời had the negative reputation of being a place where stolen goods circulated. The local authorities had already thought about closing the market in the late 1970s and early 1980s, the manager said, but they had never gone through with the project. Some informants, who have been living near the market around Huế Street from the 1950s onward, told me that the market already existed when they were small children and had to pass those streets on their way to school. At that time, people had been trading in secondhand goods more from their front doors, not on the open street as they do today.

The government started controlling the space in 1985, as Mr. Nguyên reported. Before this time, there were no documents and no lists about people trading in this place, and, as a result, vendors did not pay taxes. Nowadays, tax officials perform a special kind of job. According to traders I met in chợ Trời and other markets, a tax official will visit a vendor and will estimate the sales and then determine the amount of tax after the trader has bargained over the tax amount by offering an amount of money or a bottle of expensive whiskey or other "gifts" to the tax official. In general, informal practices such as giving money to state authorities are considered "economies of favor" and have been analyzed for the cases of Russia (*blat*) and China, where they are known as *guanxi* (Ledeneva 2008). In contemporary Vietnam, there are a number of services for which most people have to have "beneficial relations" (*quan hệ*). Thus, social networks, based on "beneficial relations," as have been described for rural-urban migration in Hanoi's informal sector (Jensen and Peppard 2003) and analyzed in particular with regard to female porters in the Long Biên market (Agergaard and Vu 2011), are likewise important for inner-city mobile street vendors (Leshkowich 2005; Drummond 2000) and traders in Hanoi's marketplaces.

Concerning the market organization, Mr. Nguyên explained that chợ Trời is special because there are no market halls. There is no enclosed space as in other markets, such as the Long Biên market, so the market management cannot appoint its own guards. Furthermore, chợ Trời closes at five o'clock and all the traders put away their goods, so there is no market in the evening. As the market is located in the streets, and as such is an open-air market, the market management is dependent on local police and law enforcement forces for security and surveillance.

At present, the market director explained, there are nearly eight hundred stalls in the chợ Trời, and the rental agreements are for only one year, as the local authorities are thinking about moving this market to another place. Mr. Nguyên further reported that the local city administration plans to withdraw from the market management, because it intends to transfer the management to a state-owned trade company called Hapro, as it has already done with other marketplaces. According to Mr. Nguyên, in the near future, the city's plan is to relocate chợ Trời to the south of the city. In the case of relocation, the market management, simultaneously representing its own interests and those of the traders, will discuss the issue of a bazaar on the move and its consequences with the local authorities. Female traders in chợ Trời are not overly worried about the rumors of being relocated: too often the plans to relocate the market have come to nothing. As this market is unique in Hanoi, vendors are not scared of losing buyers in the case of relocation. Although purchasers do not visit the market on a daily basis, they have long-standing ties to particular traders, who specialize in certain products. Most of the customers own motorbikes and come to chợ Trời because they know that this is the only place where they will find everything they need in order to repair their vehicles. Again, the high appreciation for motorbikes in contemporary Hanoi, as mentioned above, sets this secondhand market with its focus on spare parts apart from all other markets in the city.

MOVING BAZAARS

The case of chợ Mơ (Mơ market) further illustrates how a market's move to another locality for purposes of redevelopment results in a loss of client-trader relationships. This marketplace had already been relocated to another site when I started fieldwork in September 2012 and was moved again after the Mơ Commercial Center opened in 2014. As I mentioned in the beginning of this chapter, a large building was under construction on Bạch Mai Street, on the grounds of the former market, when I first visited this place. Vendors I met in the temporary chợ Mơ a few kilometers away from the original place hoped to soon return to the old site. The temporary market was arranged like many other markets in the city (DiGregorio 2012), quasi-provisional, half covered, and perfect to drive in by bicycle or motorbike (see figure 4.1). There were also some small covered restaurants in the transient place, as visitors will find in many traditional marketplaces in Hanoi. When I first arrived in this market, there were almost no customers around, as it was raining. But it was not just rain that kept clients from visiting the new locality, it was also distance and the spatial change. Sellers complained that since the relocation of the market to the temporary site, business had gone down because they had lost nearly all their regular customers.

Trader-customer ties are long-established connections shaped by various factors, including the location of a shopping site and the associated convenience for customers in regard to time spent traveling and shopping. These ties are based on reciprocal relations and cannot be replaced within a few weeks or months. For example, traders who sell fresh food have daily or weekly contact with customers and might know about the family of the client and ask about the well-being of family members. If the client arrives early in the morning, the trader will sell him or her the best-quality product to

Figure 4.1 Chợ Mơ (temporary market), February 2013. Photograph by G. Hüwelmeier.

demonstrate that this client holds a favorite place in the order of customers. In some cases, vendors announce the supply of special fruit from other parts of Vietnam for the next day and in this way entice a certain client to come back early, or they offer to reserve the goods for this customer. When this is taken into consideration, it becomes clear that the moving of a market has a negative impact on clientelization, as previously illustrated in relation to the Hàng Da market. Moreover, some traders I spoke with in 2012 and early 2013 were afraid that after they move back to the renovated, that is, newly built, chợ Mơ, there will be just as few clients as in the current Hàng Da market, since their former regular customers might have formed business relations with traders elsewhere.

According to the market management in the transferred chợ Mơ, there were about twelve hundred traders in the old marketplace. However, after the relocation, only seven hundred remained. One trader reported that those who were no longer dependent on trading to earn a living accepted a compensation payment. The female representative of the market management explained that after the expected move into the new Mơ market building later that year, vendors would trade in the basement, with upper floors reserved for offices. The new market would be organized according to product groups, with one row for fish vendors, the next row for secondhand clothing, the next row for broom vendors, then suitcase vendors, and so on. There are currently sixteen product groups in the marketplace. In addition to the traders, there are forty-seven employees working in the temporary market, such as people in the market management, but also guards, cleaning personnel, and others. Only seventeen out of all employees are state officials paid by the government. Asked if there were any conflicts among traders, the market representative said there are only a few problems. If any, the problems are about more or less aggressively courting clients and finally luring them to one's own stall. Here, again, clientelization (Geertz 1978) has some consequences with regard to tensions among traders, most of whom are female. If two merchants come into conflict, the Women's Union, in cooperation with the market management, will try to mediate the problem by inviting the two "adversaries" to talk to each other in the presence of the market management and the Women's Union cadre.

When I spoke with Mrs. Hương, a woman in her fifties trading in straw hats and suitcases, she recounted that her grandmother had traded in chợ Mơ, selling fruit and vegetables, and that her mother, still alive and eighty-eight years old, was also a trader in the same market. Her two daughters do not want to become traders because, as she said, "young people have different ideas." She was optimistic about returning to the newly built chợ Mơ, although the costs, as she argued, will be very high. After the marketplace has been moved back to the old locality, she will have to pay about US$5,000 per year for four square meters. When I mentioned what happened to the Hàng Da market and asked whether she was afraid of losing her business in the near future, she said no, arguing that in the ancient quarter of Hanoi there are too many markets and traders and that this is the reason why the new Hàng Da market is not successful. She was convinced that chợ Mơ will be revitalized after the new opening in the old place, even if vendors will be trading in the basement, making it more difficult for customers to access the stalls.

Unfortunately, Mrs. Hương's expectations have not been realized. In February 2015, I revisited chợ Mơ, which had reopened in 2014. Located in the basement of an empty building of about twenty floors, it became an abandoned place, a ghost market much like the Hàng Da market several years before (see figure 4.2). Traders

Figure 4.2. Chợ Mơ (after relocation), February 2015. Photograph by G. Hüwelmeier.

were very angry because their business crumbled as a result of the loss of nearly all their customers and the burden of high taxes and other costs. One female trader was nearly crying when she told me that she and most of the retailers felt cheated. Others loudly complained about being deceived by the management. A group of traders were waiting for a camera team, who intended to make a movie about the current situation of the marketplace and the disastrous situation of the vendors, whose business virtually collapsed just a few months after the reopening of chợ Mơ. Although traders do not openly resist the policies of local authorities, they organize themselves within the market by consulting with each other about what would be the best solution for each woman in the near future such as giving up business entirely or selling or renting the stall to someone else. They talk about their children's future and most of them agree that the marketplace is no longer a venue for earning good money.

As these ethnographic details have illustrated, clientelization, a central issue, according to Geertz's (1978) analysis of bazaar life, is closely connected with spatial and temporal dimensions. With regard to these dimensions, we have to keep in mind that Hanoi's citizens prefer to visit the market in the early morning to buy fresh fruit, meat, and vegetables and that many of them drive in by motorbike, depending on the marketplace as a drive-through market. If there is no longer a market in the neighborhood, middle-class homemakers will not take the bus or the motorbike to drive several kilometers to buy their goods and to follow their former vendors. Instead, they will look for an alternative place or visit the newly established informal "toad market" (*chợ cóc*) around the corner (Hüwelmeier 2018). In regard to clientelization, moving bazaars challenge the customer-client relationship in two ways: on the one hand, they highlight the potentially fleeting nature of the social relations on which traders' livelihoods depend, while on the other hand, they point to clientelization as being firmly rooted in spatial relations.

Urban renewal, progress, and modernization have become key issues among policy-makers and investors around the world. Within this framework, marketplaces have been rediscovered by government officials and social scientists alike as nodes of economic and social interaction. Marketplaces are a global urban phenomenon and can take various forms, such as open markets on public squares and street markets at crossroads, along rivers, and near bridges. While international scholars in cooperation with local architects were able to put a stop to the urban planning and renovation in Hanoi (Söderström and Geertman 2013), the demolition of traditional markets seems to be on the rise. Indeed, market redevelopment is part of urban renewal and therefore part of urban planners' ideas about creating a "green, clean, and beautiful" city. Although there is no organized opposition, traders and residents question this kind of urban planning and rumors everywhere point to urbanites' awareness about who is making money from the political decisions of the municipal authorities. Likewise, resentment focused, not on whether redevelopment should proceed, but on whether displaced residents had received sufficient compensation for the sacrifice of their property to enable that process (Harms 2016).

In the case of urban redevelopment in contemporary Hanoi, marketplaces can be temporarily moved to other locations. However, markets that are forced to be on the move or are relocated in newly constructed office buildings and shopping malls may become ghost markets, empty and abandoned places, with most of the female traders being priced out from the market with a loss of their livelihood. As many trading connections in Hanoi's marketplaces are based on long-term networks, including kinship ties, and with some of these networks reaching back even to the pre–Đổi mới (economic renovation) period, time and space have a strong influence on the creation and maintenance of sociability in the marketplace. Trading locations are important places for the establishment of long-lasting social and economic relationships between buyers and sellers, in particular when it comes to maintaining regular customers.

Comparisons across markets in Hanoi point to new uncertainties arising from the redevelopment of traditional trading places and threatening to displace and disperse trading communities. Anthropological fieldwork in different marketplaces has illustrated that these sites are not frozen in time and space. We can discern spatial hierarchies among the markets, whereby a market's distance or proximity to the old city center often has a large impact on a site's success. However, even one of the top market sites became a "ghost market" after undergoing renovation, despite its location close to the inner city.

Faced with a decline in business as redevelopment proceeds, some retailers, mostly women in their fifties and sixties, stop their trading activities and give up their "right to return" to the newly constructed selling spaces in the basement of multi-storied shopping malls or commercial centers. Others, predominantly younger women in their forties, have responded to the urban redevelopment by changing their place of business and opening small stores around the sites of former markets.

Many traders invested in a house, where they live with their children and grandchildren, as is usual in urban Hanoi. Some still try to sell or sublet their stall in the renovated marketplaces, but cannot find any tenants or buyers.

Since some of the traditional fresh markets no longer exist, another group of female traders, an increasing number of them living in peri-urban places or the countryside, engage in trading in one of the many *chợ cóc*, informal street markets that have emerged around demolished bazaars and on thousands of corners and alleys in the city, where millions of urbanites are supplied with daily fresh fruit and vegetables. By expanding trading geographies and appropriating urban space, women are not only victims of state policies but also agents of change in an increasingly globalizing Vietnam. Agents on another level are those who still trade in the basements of the "modernized" localities, praying at the newly established market shrines, located on the rooftop of the Hàng Da Galleria or at the new altar erected on the grounds of the Mơ Commercial Center. They ask the spirits of the place, whom they believe to be the legitimate owners of the site, to bring back their regular customers and turn their poor business into prosperous transaction.

Notes

1 I would like to thank Sarah Turner for her inspiring comments as a discussant of my paper that was the origin of this chapter, presented at the "Traders in Motion" conference at the Max Planck Institute for Social Anthropology in Halle. I am grateful to the participants for their stimulating questions and valuable suggestions. Thanks also to Christine Bonnin and Stephanie Geertman for sharing their experiences and views on market redevelopment during my fieldwork in Hanoi, and to the editors and anonymous reviewers for insightful comments and advice.

2 Research was carried out by employing a broad range of ethnographic methods to analyze the reconstruction of Hanoi's markets and their current redevelopment. In order to closely examine the process of transforming traditional marketplaces into new commercial centers, I combined sustained anthropological fieldwork, including participant observation, media analysis, and extensive interviews in Hanoi's marketplaces with petty traders, mobile vendors, market traders, and shop owners operating near the marketplaces, as well as with representatives of the market management and residents living near the trading localities. All names are pseudonyms.

3 First insights of my ethnographic fieldwork on markets in Hanoi were presented at the Euro-SEAS conference in Lisboa in 2013. The essay presented there, "Negotiating Power Relations in Multiethnic (Post) Socialist Bazaars: Vietnam, Eastern Europe, and Beyond," was based on my research project "The Global Bazaar," funded by the German Research Foundation (HU 1019/3–1). Between 2012 and 2015, I conducted ethnographic fieldwork in marketplaces run by transnational Vietnamese in Berlin (Hüwelmeier 2013a, 2013b), Warsaw (Hüwelmeier 2015a), and Prague (Hüwelmeier 2015b). From September 2012 until February 2013, I carried out multisited ethnographic fieldwork in various marketplaces in Hanoi with the help of Vietnamese research assistants. In March and April 2015 and 2016, I revisited some of the marketplaces.

PART II

CIRCUITS OF MOBILITY, IDENTITIES, AND POWER RELATIONS

INTRODUCTION: MOVING AND SHAKING

Erik Harms

Part I of this book focused on the physical transformation of specific markets across Vietnam, many of which are being "civilized" in order to realize new master plans, renovations, beautification projects, and so on. In those examples, the markets themselves often seem to be in motion—and no small amount of commotion—as buildings are upended and traders are moved in and out to accommodate newly conceived spaces. But if marketplaces across Vietnam seem to be moving and shaking at their very foundations, this part reminds us that the traders themselves are even more profoundly on the move: we encounter traders from rural regions who carry goods to different cities for sale, we listen to the stories of men who traveled across the country in their younger days as waste-trading bachelors before eventually getting married and settling down, we learn of itinerant vendors who make ends meet by circulating through the city of Hanoi in response to the loss of land to urbanization, and we also learn of the ways another group of traders cope with government policies that restrict and otherwise police their trading activities. In all these chapters, we learn how migration and movement both shape and are shaped by the identities of these different traders. The world is in motion, which affects the traders, who are themselves in motion, and who in turn affect the way the world moves.

The stories these mobile traders tell speak directly to the central lesson of this book—that Vietnamese "market socialism" is more than a political ideology or a set of abstract economic policies. The market is first and foremost a *social* phenomenon, driven by human beings living in and coping with specific sociocultural, material, economic, and political conditions that constrain, but do not wholly determine, their actions. While important transformations in government policies and actions have certainly affected the lives of Vietnam's traders, these policies are only part of the story. Anthropologists have long understood that "the economy" exists only as a result of the everyday actions and livelihood strategies expressed by the people who make it up (Wilk 1996). These chapters put ethnographic meat on the bones of this anthropological truism and show that we can understand Vietnam's shift to a market economy only by looking closely at how traders live in worlds textured by gender dynamics, spatialized relations of economic inclusion and exclusion, family relations, and other forms of sociocultural interaction. There is no such thing as a market without traders, and the following chapters focus closely on the mobile people who populate "the market" in Vietnam.

In a world of credit cards, e-commerce, electronic payments, and one-click shipping, we often assume that goods simply flow around the globe on their own, without any resistance. But as Anna Tsing has noted, "A study of global connections shows the grip of encounter: friction." Movement and mobility are never purely smooth, and attending to "friction reminds us that heterogeneous and unequal encounters can lead to new arrangements of culture and power" (2005, 5). These chapters take up Tsing's call and also show that the story of emerging market socialism is best told from the ground up, where thousands of feet hit the pavement, and where the real heavy lifting of global circulation takes place. The friction here is real: we encounter men and women carrying goods on their overburdened shoulders to customers across the country, stripping and cleaning waste goods with limited environmental protection, and striving to make a living as they lose land to urban development that is spurred, in part, by the economic growth to which their own labors have contributed but of which they are rarely full beneficiaries.

TRADERS ON THE MOVE

Hy Van Luong's chapter shows the complex history of a far-flung network of itinerant traders, both male and female, from Tịnh Bình village in Quảng Ngãi province. These traders specialize in selling key chains, sunglasses, lighters, wallets, and other trinkets in the cities and towns in the southern portion of Vietnam, the Central Highlands, and even Cambodia, and have developed a specialized niche economy that evolved out of an earlier history selling buffalo horn combs, conical hats, mirrors, saws, woven reed rolls, lottery tickets, and a distinctive sweet mung bean snack. By detailing the ways in which the network is and has been organized and highlighting the ways negotiations and sales play out, as well as the ways in which the traveling vendors mobilize kin networks to raise capital for start-up costs, Luong demonstrates the important role sociocultural factors play in making the economy of mobile trade work. While it is true that the "open door" period following Đổi mới eased restrictions on mobility and changed the landscape of trade, Luong reminds us what these opening doors actually opened onto: a world of traders with their own histories, networks, and social relations, ready to mobilize their own capacities and connections, but also constrained by their own cultural contexts.

State policies may have been important for the way they lifted travel restrictions, but the chapter shows that family circumstances and local gender dynamics also profoundly influence mobility choices. In some cases, vendors with responsibilities to their families often chose to conduct their work in cities closer to home, or even to give up itinerant trade; in other cases, vendors relied on family networks for child care, which enabled married vendors to work together. The gendered expectations of proper male comportment affected traders as well, albeit in sometimes unexpected ways. Although it might have been expected for Vietnamese men to "lose face" when performing the role of submissive trader to potential customers, the fact that their trade took them so far from home at times mitigated the potential sense of shame that trading might bring to Vietnamese men in other contexts. At the same time, the hardship of going off to distant places to engage in trade was seen by some as a way to prove their ability to support their families. Luong also shows how important social networks and social capital are to the success of these male traders, who rely on connections for mustering start-up costs for their trading activities and for persisting in the trade. In sum, the secret to the trade's success was not government policy or intervention but rather sociocultural networks formed by the traders themselves.

Minh T. N. Nguyen's chapter picks up on the importance of gender and other sociocultural frameworks by focusing on ideas of masculinity and how they influence economic behavior over the course of a man's life. The chapter focuses on the lives of male junk traders who come to Hanoi from Spring district in the Red River Delta and who enter and leave the urban junk trade in ways shaped by their changing notions of manhood as experienced over time. Combining rich ethnography with important concepts from the rising field of masculinity studies, Nguyen reminds us that "manhood" is not a fixed concept but a nexus of ideas and practices that are always in a state of emergence and transformation. Manhood has many facets that change over the life course. For example, many of the men emphasized how, in their youth, they expressed a certain kind of rebellion and bravado, which they explicitly cast as a rejection of the more austere style they associated with their fathers. Young male waste traders imagined that they could express their success through cosmopolitan consumption practices, recklessly spending their money, and by gaining sexual experiences. They contrasted these attitudes with their fathers' admonitions to be productive, thrifty, and devoted to family. But as they grew older, many of these men became committed to settling down and began to emphasize their roles as patrilineal "protectors" and heads of households. Over time, they began to renounce the quest for immediate pleasure and focused on marriage, building homes, and establishing a fixed position within the waste-trading community. They started to act like their fathers.

The chapter also shows that the waste trade is gendered through and through. Different aspects of the trade are said to be more profitably pursued by women, while other aspects are seen as part of a man's domain. For example, women are commonly said to be better at cultivating patron-client ties with households in particular parts of the city and to mobilize affect and sympathy in their work of collecting. Furthermore, women are commonly referred to simply as "junk traders" (*đồng nát*), who "go to the market" to sell such junk. The men, by contrast, often stress the "technical" aspect of their work and claim to "go dealing in electrical appliances" (*đi đồ điện*). In other ways, however, male and female labor is seen as complementary, and husbands and wives increasingly develop into entrepreneurial teams as they grow older. Many married couples have collaborated to open up waste depots, which promise them the opportunity to work together and increase their income and capital accumulation. Through the chapter's vivid portraits we see that it is not only traders who are in motion; change is also evident in concepts of gender themselves, which move and transform as they pass through the different stages of a person's life.

Movement begets movement. Nguyễn Thị Thanh Bình's chapter shows how the moving boundaries of a growing city can lead to movement among people on the city's edge—the growth of Hanoi draws many peri-urban residents into petty commodity trade, literally putting them into motion. While the official policies of the Vietnamese central government generally assume that urbanization will lead to industrialization and increasingly formalized employment, this chapter shows that nonindustrial labor has actually increased in the wake of agricultural land conversion in peri-urban Hanoi. Informal petty trade practices proliferate right in the heart of a formerly rural but now urbanized village called Lụa, located on the outskirts of Hanoi, in Hà Đông district. Here the urbanization process has actually stripped many residents of their livelihood strategies, thus forcing them to engage in the informal sector. On the streets of Lụa village, new multistory modern houses have been built using compensation money given to villagers in exchange for their agricultural land. But one sees rows of transport motorbikes and bicycles lined up in front of these new houses, a telltale sign that the occupants are engaged in petty trade, largely organized around the circulation of goods. While members of these households no longer possess agricultural land, few of them have fully transitioned to urban or industrial employment, and many residents rely on "going to market" and carrying goods from market to market as a way to earn a living. At the same time, going to market has itself become increasingly precarious for Lụa villagers, because the same trends supporting the rise of urban order have made the city a precarious place for vendors. Many markets in Hanoi have been upgraded and renovated in ways that exclude petty traders, and roving vendors have become targeted as undesirable elements because they do not fit into the government's conception of what counts as a beautiful and prosperous city.

The chapter by Lisa Barthelmes picks up where the story of Lụa villagers leaves off. Her ethnography focuses on the strategies and tactics street vendors use to engage with the governing practices of Hanoi authorities. Departing from what she considers to be an inadequate model of domination and resistance, Barthelmes carefully traces the connections and interactions among local officials, police, and street vendors to rethink how governmentality is experienced by the street traders themselves. Hanoi authorities, she shows, are simultaneously tolerant of street vendors and oppressive in their tactics for dealing with them. While this might sound like a contradiction, Barthelmes argues that this oscillation between tolerance and oppression actually represents a form of strategic opaqueness that turns the policing of street vendors into something of a guessing game about intent and strategy. Borrowing from the work of Martin Gainsborough (2010, chap. 5), she describes this as an example of "uncertainty as an instrument of rule." Street vendors are left in a perpetual state of uncertainty that pervades their tactics of vending and mobility. Traders are not immobilized by uncertainty, however, and they do not so much "resist" these modes of rule as formulate tactics and strategies to manage uncertainty, and even gain from it. While advocates of legal reform and government transparency might worry that uncertainty allows authorities and police to solicit bribes, we learn here how uncertainty also affords traders opportunities to continue plying their trade. The chapter also shows how traders actively seek to establish relationships and networks with local officials, which are cemented by the collection of "presents" that are given to officers. While these behaviors risk reproducing police power, they also afford traders a sense of control over police actions. Similarly, while vendors sometimes appear compromised by a lack of knowledge about legislation in the city, it is also clear that ignorance of the law might itself actually work as a "strategy" as well, especially since many laws have officially banned street vending in many places in Hanoi. Ignorance of the law, one might say, enables one to ignore the law. In the end, uncertainty cuts both ways: it allows traders to ignore the certainty of laws that would exclude them from Hanoi, while also subjecting them to uncertainty as an instrument of rule.

VALUE IN MOTION

Outside anthropology, the sources used for studying "the market" or "the economy" typically consist of economic indices, largely presented as a series of numbers and charts. While even anthropologists can appreciate a good line graph or bar chart—and who can resist an elegant pie chart?—such visual simplifications make it easy to imagine "the market" as a disembodied concept that exists "up there" in a flighty realm of circulating numbers that rise and fall according to their own volition, like commodity prices, interest rates, inflation, market share, or ever-fluctuating currency exchange rates. Such a perspective may be necessary for the macroeconomic decision making of bankers and economists, but it often obscures the basic fact that goods do not get up and move around of their own accord. Goods must not only be produced but also carried, circulated, purchased, used, disposed of, or recycled. As Vinay Gidwani has noted with his studies on the productive labor of recycling in Delhi, the integration of waste into circuits of value is not only about the value of the "things" being transformed but also depends on the value ascribed to the people doing the work of transformation and circulation, which in turn conditions the very processes through which those things can be converted into objects of value (Gidwani 2010, 2013). All the processes that contribute to the value of commodities, including the process of circulation (which depends, after all, on productive labor), require human labor power, which is necessary not only to make the goods but also to sell them and to bring them to market. Furthermore, the way that labor power is valued in different contexts will depend on the sociocultural setting and human hierarchies within which the laborer is situated—this, of course, is the "socially necessary labor time" that, according to Marxist understandings, determines the value of labor at any given place and time (Marx [1867] 1976, 129). When traders are in motion, however, crossing different social and cultural zones—moving from country to city, shifting from vending on the street to selling in a fixed marketplace, or moving from peri-urban spaces to the urban core—they are also crossing different spaces of value that are themselves central to the economic logic of how value is produced. Value can be realized only once it has been brought into circulation and exchange, and these traders realize the circuit of capital and produce what economists call "the market" by moving things across space.

In short, markets need people to move things in and out of them and things only gain value when people make them, make them circulate, and bring them to market. Things and markets cannot do this work on their own. The people who do this heavy lifting are themselves embedded within social relationships and a web of government regulations, social norms, class, status and gender hierarchies, economic processes, and moral expectations. Furthermore, all these relationships are affected by the physical and symbolic qualities of the good themselves, and different kinds of trade and different kinds of traders will feel the friction (and heat and weight) of commodity circulation in different ways. The chapters that follow show that the work of carrying a shoulder pole heavy with fruit through the city of Hanoi is different from the work of stripping an electric device for valuable components; likewise, a merchant selling silk cloth in a fixed market stall in Hanoi surely experiences "the market economy" in ways quite different from those of a roving key chain seller from central Vietnam, sojourning in Saigon. These differences are material, based on the different demands placed on the specific material qualities of the different objects being circulated; and they are cultural, based on the meanings ascribed to those objects, the normative associations ascribed to people involved with their trade, and the symbolic associations ascribed to both people and things.

CHAPTER FIVE

A MOBILE TRADING NETWORK FROM CENTRAL COASTAL VIETNAM: GROWTH, SOCIAL NETWORK, AND GENDER

Hy Van Luong

Women have played a dominant role in the petty trade of Vietnam (Leshkowich 2011; Luong 2003) and of Southeast Asia in general (Dewey 1962; J. Alexander and Alexander 2001; among others). As early as the seventeenth century, visitors to Vietnam were struck by this phenomenon (Thành Thế Vỹ 1961, 93; Dampier 1906, 608).

This chapter focuses on a rapidly expanding mobile trading network in Vietnam with an equally strong male participation. This trading network began developing in the 1980s from Quảng Ngãi province in the South Central Coast of Vietnam, particularly from Tịnh Bình commune in Sơn Tịnh district of this province (see map on page xi). In 2000, of the active labor force in the 150 surveyed households in this commune, 34 percent were migrants, and 12 percent engaged in itinerant trade. By 2012, these percentages had increased to 50 percent and 24 percent, respectively. Approximately thirteen hundred Tịnh Bình villagers were migrant peddlers in 2012.[1] This itinerant trading network had spread from its earlier concentration in the Ho Chi Minh City–Biên Hòa–Bình Dương area in Southeast Vietnam to all over the southern half of Vietnam and into Cambodia (see map on page xi). About half the migrant peddlers in surveyed households in Tịnh Bình commune in both 2000 and 2012 were male.

In exploring the rapid growth of this trading network and the gender dimension of this itinerant trade, I suggest that our analyses of the growth of this network as well as of Vietnamese gender roles and their malleability in political economy would remain incomplete if we address only the role of the state, no matter whether it is socialist, postsocialist, or neoliberal, and the logic of global capital. We also need to take into account sociocultural dynamics (social capital, deeply rooted gender roles, and moral economy) in our analyses.

THE POLITICAL ECONOMY OF TỊNH BÌNH COMMUNE: AN OVERVIEW

Tịnh Bình was one of the four rural communities, two in Quảng Ngãi province in central Vietnam, and two in Long An province in the southern Mekong Delta, which were chosen in 2000 for research in a large-scale interdisciplinary project on migration and urbanization in Ho Chi Minh City (Luong 2009).[2]

Figure 5.1 Itinerant vendor of sunglasses and key chains in the seaside resort city of Vũng Tàu. Photograph by Hà Thúc Dũng, copyright by H. V. Luong.

Of the two studied migrant-sending communities in Quảng Ngãi, Tịnh Bình was the poorer one. During fieldwork in 2000, I was struck by Tịnh Bình's sandy soil and partly hilly terrain. Hills and forest land occupied 30 percent of Tịnh Bình's surface area of 2,530 hectares. Until the completion of the Thạch Nham dam in 1994, Tịnh Bình villagers had relied primarily on rainwater for its rice cultivation. As rice is a major staple in the Vietnamese diet, many villagers talked painfully about having to mix manioc with rice to fill their stomachs in the difficult days in the two decades after the reunification of Vietnam in 1975, a period characterized by agricultural collectiviza-tion and insufficient irrigation water. During this difficult time, besides growing rice, Tịnh Bình villagers cultivated manioc and sugarcane; raised cattle, pigs, and chicken; and engaged in conical-hat and comb handicraft production in order to supplement rice cultivation.[3]

In 1994, as a part of decollectivization, land began being distributed to cultivators for long-term use and on an egalitarian basis from the central coast to the northern lowlands of Vietnam. In Tịnh Bình, by the late 1990s, each commune member had received about five hundred square meters of cultivable land on a twenty-year arrange-ment between the commune and its households.[4]

By 2000, conical-hat handicraft had disappeared from the Tịnh Bình landscape, and the creation of buffalo horn combs had become barely visible, reportedly because of the meager income from handicraft production and the lack of labor as a result of migration. By 2012, the cattle industry and far-flung trading-and-migrant network had emerged as major income sources for the commune economy. Fifty percent of the people in the active labor force in 199 surveyed households in Tịnh Bình migrated for work for at least a part of the year. During the rainy season (from October to December) along the central coast of Vietnam, a small number of Tịnh Bình villagers worked as seasonal agricultural laborers, cutting sugarcane and picking coffee in the plantations in the Central Highlands.[5] About half the migrant workforce engaged in petty trade and was overwhelmingly concentrated in the itinerant vending of key chains (called *bán móc khóa*), sunglasses, lighters, wallets, and plastic toys for children, among other small items, in cities and many towns in the southern half of Vietnam, as well as in a number of remote Central Highland communes. Some Tịnh Bình peddlers even ventured into Cambodia. The specialization of Tịnh Bình migrants in this trade is a part of the larger pattern in Vietnamese migration; for example, migrants from the coastal Đức Phổ district of Quảng Ngãi, particularly from the commune of Phổ Cường, carved out for themselves the niche of selling noodle soup through home delivery (*bán mì gõ*) in Ho Chi Minh City (Dương Minh Anh 2006). This pattern reflects the powerful force of local social networks in the Vietnamese sociocultural fabric and political economy.

In reunified Vietnam, the Tịnh Bình trading network reportedly started in the early 1980s when despite the command economy, a small number of Tịnh Bình villagers, together with some people in the neighboring Tịnh Thọ commune, engaged in the itinerant vending of locally produced buffalo horn combs, conical hats, and saws, as well as of mirrors and reed rolls (serving as roof panels or paddy-drying panels). The interviewed traders from the 1980s reported that they worked mainly in the South Central Coast of Vietnam, including in ethnic minority villages in Quảng Ngãi highlands.

When the economic renovation policy was implemented and migration control relaxed in the late 1980s and early 1990s, a number of Tịnh Bình villagers began moving to Ho Chi Minh City and the surrounding provinces, selling not only combs, mirrors, and saws but also lottery tickets and glazed mung bean balls (*bánh cam*) to a growing urban population. For female vendors unable to carry a heavy load of saws, the new occupation of selling glazed mung bean balls was a good alternative in the 1990s. Relatively successful peddlers reported to have earned in 1997–98 an average of VNĐ1.8 million a month (around US$145 or four-tenths of a tael of gold). However, by the late 1990s, they seemed to have all switched to the itinerant vending of key chains, lighters, and wallets, among other items.[6]

By the late 1990s, as the comb and saw handicrafts in Tịnh Bình and surrounding communes dwindled, and as quite a few lottery ticket peddlers reported being cheated because of their lack of familiarity with this trade, Tịnh Bình traders had carved out for themselves a niche in Ho Chi Minh City and the nearby cities of Bình Dương and Biên Hòa. They specialized in the itinerant vending of key chains (*móc khóa*), sunglasses, lighters, wallets, and nail clippers, the majority of which were reportedly imported from the People's Republic of China.[7]

In 2000, in Ho Chi Minh City, our research team interviewed five itinerant vendors among Tịnh Bình migrants working there. In 2012, as the Tịnh Bình trading network had spread all over the southern half of Vietnam, and as it was logically challenging and financially costly to interview traders in their numerous destinations, we decided to visit Tịnh Bình for three weeks during the Tết (Lunar New Year) holidays in order to take advantage of most traders' return to their home commune during the biggest holiday season in Vietnam. Selecting half the 199 surveyed households for our migrant interview subsample, and also interviewing some vendors in their destination areas in Ho Chi Minh City and the Central Highlands, in 2013–14, we were able to interview 58 of the 103 Tịnh Bình peddlers of key chains and sunglasses, including three of the five vendors interviewed in Ho Chi Minh City in 2000.[8] In November 2014 and February 2015, we also conducted participant observation of key chain peddlers' behavior in both Ho Chi Minh City and the seaside city of Vũng Tàu (105 kilometers from Ho Chi Minh City), during which additional interviews were carried out with many peddlers from Tịnh Bình.

SOCIAL NETWORK AND THE GROWTH OF AN ITINERANT TRADING NICHE

The trading niche in key chains and the like has rapidly expanded in the past two decades in the southern half of Vietnam. This expansion is underlain by the strong social network among Tịnh Bình villagers. This trade is characterized by low entry costs, a relatively good opportunity for peddlers to move upstream in the commodity chain, and peddlers' great time flexibility and spatial mobility.

According to an early entrant (from household 483) in the aforementioned trading network, the start-up cost (i.e., the cost of carried goods) for a peddler increased from US$40–55 (VNĐ500,000–700,000) in the late 1990s to US$100–250 (VNĐ2–5 million) in 2011 for an average vendor, and to US$350 (VNĐ7 million) for a more experienced and ambitious one carrying higher-quality goods (e.g., real-leather wallets and belts) for customers with more income. Average income increased more modestly, from US$200 (VNĐ3 million) in 2001–3 to US$250–350 in 2011–12 for vendors working in the Saigon–Biên Hòa area, although some reportedly earned as much as US$500 (VNĐ10 million) or more a month.

However, the start-up cost for Tịnh Bình peddlers was negligible because of their social capital. As a common practice, a peddler with direct or indirect social connection to a middleman/-woman received the goods for sale on credit and without interest and paid for them only after sale.[9] Since many middlemen/-women themselves came from Tịnh Bình, a new peddler could easily find a middleman/-woman from the same rural neighborhood, the same kinship network, or another peddler from his or her social network who could introduce him or her to a middleman/-woman for credit extension. Some Tịnh Bình middlemen/-women directly recruited peddlers from their native commune. They routinely offered credit as well as subsidized housing to the latter. As a part of subsidized housing, middlemen/-women normally rented living quarters for their vendors, and charged each only US$4.5–9 a month, mainly or partly to cover utilities. Peddlers usually lived six to ten people in a room, gender segregated, and shared a bathroom. Recruited directly by middlemen/-women and fellow villagers, or introduced to middlemen/-women by their kin and Tịnh Bình neighbors, new peddlers easily entered the trading network with little start-up cost. Tịnh Bình migrants with high school education or less followed one another into this trading network, a network that also included migrants from some neighboring communes such as Tịnh Thọ, Tịnh Hà, Tịnh Hiệp, and Tịnh Sơn.[10] As a reflection of the impact of local social networks, only 3 of the 106 migrants from our 181 surveyed households in the commune of Tịnh Minh, located about eight kilometers from Tịnh Bình, worked as itinerant vendors of key chains in 2012, compared with 103 of the 209 migrants from Tịnh Bình. While we do not have any precise information on the size of the key chain itinerant trade network in the southern half of Vietnam and on the native communes and villages of peddlers, interviewed Tịnh Bình vendors independently reported in 2012–14 that peddlers from their native Sơn Tịnh district made up at least half the peddlers in this network and that Tịnh Bình vendors numerically dominated those from the rest of Sơn Tịnh district.[11]

Many Tịnh Bình migrants entered or settled upon the itinerant trade after having tried other kinds of work. They commented favorably on the time flexibility in itinerant trade in comparison with the strict industrial discipline on factory floors. They reported that they could return to their home village, not only for extended holidays during the Lunar New Year or for the smaller festival on the fifth day of the fifth lunar month, but also for major family events (weddings, funerals, tending to sick family members, taking care of maternal grandchildren for a few months as required of maternal grandmothers by local customs) or for agricultural harvests. A young male migrant (from household 483), having engaged in many kinds of work, when asked about the reason for settling on his itinerant vending occupation, explained, "Having tried many kinds of work, I find factory work tough, too tough. When I worked in a factory, if I wanted to go home for a visit, I had to apply. In one case, it took half a month before the request was granted. As an itinerant vendor, I could go home whenever I wanted. Nobody said anything." A thirty-eight-year-old female peddler (from household 541) similarly remarked, "It is tiresome walking for the whole day as a vendor. Knowing my problem, a younger relative has suggested that I try factory work. But as a factory worker, I can only go home once a year. As a peddler, I can go home to help my family during peak agricultural seasons, and return to my itinerant vending work without any problem." Thus, despite the availability of industrial work with a steadier income, many Tịnh Bình villagers rejected the rigid discipline of industrial capitalism in favor of flexible work patterns in a trading network.

The comment above by a female vendor in household 541 also reflects the fact that in high-density urban areas, peddlers normally traveled by foot up to thirty kilometers round-trip a day, as this facilitated entry into drinking places, restaurants, and crowded areas for sale without having to worry about where to leave their bicycles or motorcycles. Itinerant vendors typically sold their goods in outdoor settings, relatively open drinking places, or restaurants. They had no control over any territory: if two vendors ran into each other at a particular restaurant, one tended to wait for the other to leave before entering. They were constantly on the move. Walking up to thirty kilometers a day in the tropical heat and carrying a load of five to ten kilograms for a workday of ten to sixteen hours required physical stamina. A number of vendors unable or preferring not to walk a great distance chose to sell in very crowded areas (bus stations, theme parks, and beaches on weekends or during school holidays), although in the past few years, itinerant vending has been banned in some of those areas, reportedly because of peddlers' very persistent soliciting and tourists' and travelers' complaints. The three big cities of Danang, Hanoi, and Ho Chi Minh City have banned itinerant trade on selected streets since 2005, 2008, and 2009, respectively.[12] The municipal government in the seaside resort town of Vũng Tàu has also banned itinerant vending on beaches and in certain tourist areas since 2008. Many city governments also ban peddlers at bus and train stations. Some peddlers reported being fined and having their goods seized by the police in the southern coastal tourist city of Vũng Tàu and at a theme park in Ho Chi Minh City following their violation of the ban on itinerant vending there. However, the ban on itinerant vending has not been consistently enforced in Vietnam.[13]

One interviewed female peddler chose busy Saigon street corners or sidewalks to sell her goods although her income was reportedly low with stationary vending, not to mention her violation of the ban on urban sidewalk occupation in effect for Ho Chi Minh City. Another interviewed female vendor in Lâm Đồng province, motivated by her need to care for her small baby, switched from peddling to stationary vending and reported a significant drop in income. Mobility to increase the radiuses of sale areas was thus a vital part of vendors' sale strategy. For this purpose, some vendors took a daily bus from a bigger city for a distance of fifteen to forty kilometers each way and then walked around in smaller towns or displayed their goods in front of industrial zone gates in order to sell to factory workers on the latter's pay days. Only in special circumstances did Tịnh Bình vendors use their own vehicles to move between sale areas. For example, working in the provincial capital of Quy Nhơn (about 175 kilometers south of their own provincial capital of Quảng Ngãi), some vendors rode bicycles between fishing boat docks and bus stops, selling, on the one hand, to fishermen with fresh cash from the sale of fish and, on the other, to bus passengers returning home from more remote areas of the country such as the Central Highlands. In the Central Highlands, some vendors also traveled by motorcycle to more remote communes, populated by mostly ethnic minorities, usually within an eighty-kilometer radius. Some Tịnh Bình vendors, based in their home commune, also rode motorcycles daily, at a distance of up to forty kilometers, to sell garments, nose and mouth covers, and other items, either directly to customers in ethnic communities or to retailers in highland districts (Sơn Hà and Trà Bồng).

On a micro level, once the sale opportunities in an area declined following the increase in the number of peddlers or market saturation, some vendors would move to other areas with more sales opportunities or offering some other advantages such as proximity to their native commune. It was for this reason that the key chain trading network spread gradually from Ho Chi Minh City and the Southeast region to the Mekong Delta, the Central Highlands, and many cities and towns in the South Central Coast of Vietnam.

Comparing the market in Huế with that in Saigon, a fifty-six-year-old male peddler (from household 496), who started his itinerant trade career in 1992 and moved from Saigon to Huế in 2010, reported a much lower volume of sale in smaller cities but more or less the same revenues, thanks to higher selling prices to tourists and customers who were not as familiar with the goods as those in Saigon. Comparing the market in Đà Lạt, a tourist town in the Central Highlands, with that in Saigon, a fifty-six-year-old female vendor (from household 508) similarly provided her reason for staying in Đà Lạt: "In [Ho Chi Minh] City, peddlers have to travel quite a bit but do not make as much profit on a sale item as in Đà Lạt. In Đà Lạt, people come here on vacation, in many cases with their children and other family members. Children want toys, and peddlers can sell more easily and with a higher profit in this context." In the described trading network, Tịnh Bình villagers not only were peddlers. They also occupied upstream positions in the commodity chain, serving as middlemen/-women, wholesale importers of goods from China, or manufacturers. Many vendors who accumulated some capital became middlemen and middlewomen, either in the Ho Chi Minh City region or in new urban sites in the trading network. They either sold their goods to itinerant vendors or used motorcycles to bring their goods to stationary variety retailers (*đi bỏ mối hàng*) within dozens of kilometers.[14] One Tịnh Bình man imported goods from China by the truckload for distribution in the entire trading network. Another had a factory making leather wallets and belts in Ho Chi Minh City and employed many fellow villagers who preferred not to beat the sidewalks in the hot sun in search of customers.[15] The capital required for villagers in upstream operations reportedly reached billions of VNĐ (approximately US$50,000 for one billion VNĐ). However, moving upstream was not always a smooth process. A young male villager who started as an itinerant vendor in 2006, and who became a middleman in a Mekong delta town by 2009, distributing goods to both itinerant vendors and retail stores, reported being caught three times in a year by market inspection teams (*quản lý thị trường*). Buying goods in Ho Chi Minh City for distribution, he could not produce receipts or paid invoices demanded by such a team, whose tasks were to interrupt the flow of smuggled goods and fake manufactured items. His goods were confiscated, and in one year, he lost a half billion VNĐ (around US$25,000), which was the bulk of his capital accumulated from six years of trading. A particular trader's trajectory might encounter turbulence at times. But in the larger picture, in less than two decades, Tịnh Bình villagers succeeded in creating a major trading niche for themselves and a large trading network. Such an occupational niche was fairly common among northern and central coastal Vietnamese villagers, made possible through their strong village-based social networks.[16] And Tịnh Bình villagers' trading network extended into Cambodia; in this network they occupied highly diverse positions in the commodity chain.

In the trading network described above, Tịnh Bình vendors had not only socio-economic but also considerable geographic mobility across different regions in the southern half of Vietnam. The mobility across regions was even organized by middlemen/-women in order to capture seasonal tourist markets and regional variation in weather or to take advantage of region-specific peak income periods in a year. A middlewoman from Tịnh Bình reported moving annually with her fellow villagers-cum-peddlers across three regions in the southern half of Vietnam: Bình Phước in the Southeast during the cashew-harvesting season from February to April, Huế in the South Central Coast from May to September, and the Central Highlands during the coffee harvest season toward the end of the year. Some retail vendors also reported moving back and forth between the Mekong Delta and the Central Highlands, selling to Mekong farmers with after-harvest incomes and to Central Highland farmers and agricultural workers during the coffee harvest season in the last few months of the year and during the cashew and peppercorn harvest seasons from February to May.[17] (For many years Vietnam has been one of the top-two exporters of coffee, cashews, and peppercorn in the world.) Less dependent on seasonality were vendors in the Ho Chi Minh City area and in the shrimp-farming region in the southernmost part of the country (Cà Mau) where shrimps tended to be harvested all year around.[18] But even here, in the rainy season, vendors' earnings tended to drop because they sold mainly to people in outdoor settings and people avoided going out in the rain. However, the daily monsoon rains in the southern third of Vietnam tended to be short (lasting less than an hour daily), affecting itinerant vendors' incomes only slightly. In the South Central Coast, where daily rains tended to last much longer during the rainy season from October to December, many peddlers moved at this time of the year to the Central Highlands, where the weather was dry and people had much more disposable income during the coffee harvest.

Given the spread of the trading network, vendors with family obligations tended to prefer cities and towns closer to their home village in Quảng Ngãi province. Many even gave up itinerant trade to return home to take care of family obligations, obligations that tended to increase with marriage and having children.

Many young migrants, peddlers included, got married after a few years of migration. Once having children, many interviewed itinerant vendors found it quite challenging to combine child care with the itinerant trade for themselves and their spouses. As one income was seldom sufficient to support a family of three or more in a destination with high costs of living, some mothers tried to find some nonmobile and flexible work that allowed them to tend to their children. For example, having learned the basics of the noodle soup trade from a brother-in-law from Mộ Đức district of Quảng Ngãi, a young female migrant in household 508 set up a small noodle soup restaurant in Ho Chi Minh City with the hope that she could take care of her infant daughter and do business at the same time. However, this VNĐ10 million investment of hers did not work out, and she had to entrust her child to her mother at home in order to continue working with her husband in the retailing of sunglasses in Ho Chi Minh City.[19] Her solution was also adopted by many other women, with children being entrusted to grandparents at home. Some parents, especially mothers, in such circumstances reported returning to Tịnh Bình up to seven or eight times a year on average. The home village visits were more frequent during the rainy season in the southern part of Vietnam (May to October) when sales tended to be slower and income tended to drop, except in popular vacation areas such as the coastal city of Vũng Tàu (popular with middle-class people from Ho Chi Minh City). However, many migrant women found it psychologically too difficult to be separated from their children and decided to give up itinerant trade to return to Tịnh Bình. A number of male peddlers interviewed in Ho Chi Minh City in early 2015 supported this, citing their male income-earning responsibility in order to support their families, as well as their concern about their wives' rising expectations about husbands due to the latter's prolonged exposure to and contact with the Ho Chi Minh City life-style and consequently the higher risk of marital discord and divorce. One male peddler elaborated on this point to two of our research team members in a vending context:

> It is also an issue of face [for us men]. We men are family pillars. If a family is poor, it is due to the man. . . . It is a pity [*tội nghiệp*] if my wife has to carry the [fairly heavy] load. It is more appropriate to let her stay home and take care of children. . . . Once both she and I were in this business together. She had the advantage of having a pleading skill [pleading to prospective customers]. She sold more than me. But there are complications regarding women in this environment. They see other women better off, compare themselves to the latter, get sad, and may get into regrettable behavior [such as leaving the family and the marriage for good]. . . . As a man, I take the hardship of this work.

With good incomes earned by the husbands and the low cost of living in the countryside, some women stayed home to take care of the children as well as of household agriculture. Without sufficient income and remittances from husbands, many women entrusted their children to their mothers or mothers-in-law during working hours and found work in garment factories in the Tịnh Phong industrial zone of Sơn Tịnh district (about fourteen kilometers from Tịnh Bình). A number of young fathers in such a context decided to return to Tịnh Bình to be close to their wives and children, with some working at factories, some engaging in itinerant trade in neighboring highland districts, and some who had capital selling footwear, socks, garments, watches, and other items to variety store owners or market retailers in those districts. A number of other fathers continued their itinerant trade but in cities and towns closer to their native province so that they could return home more often. Many vendors working in the smaller cities and towns in the South Central Coast commented favorably on the less hectic pace of life and the lower costs of living, besides the advantage of more affordable and more frequent home visits. If a child did well in school and entered college or university, many parents entered or resumed their itinerant trade so as to provide financial support for the child through college or university.

THE GENDER DIMENSION OF ITINERANT TRADE

Itinerant trade in Vietnam generally requires verbal skills to solicit (*mời*) sales as well as for bargaining purposes. Another important aspect of the key chain itinerant trade is that the majority of prospective customers whom vendors solicit are male. Few women go to beer-drinking places. The majority of customers in coffee shops and restaurants are male. Only on beaches and entertainment parks is gender more balanced.

An essential part of itinerant vending in Vietnam is bargaining. A young and successful male vendor whom I interviewed in May 2014 and who moved from itinerant vending to a middleman position around 2009 explained that as customers usually made an offer at half the asking price, the vendor would normally set the initial price at four to five times the actual cost to him or herself in order to sell it at double the actual cost (i.e., 100 percent profit). The profit margin can be as low as 60 percent in the sale to a regular customer and can be much higher in selling to a customer who seems unfamiliar with the goods and their normal selling prices.[20]

A thirty-eight-year-old female vendor (from household 541) elaborated on the art of bargaining: "If a prospective customer asks about the price, even if a glass costs me five thousand đồng, I say that it costs me seven thousand or eight thousand đồng already. This way, I can sell it for at least ten thousand đồng." By falsely reporting on her cost, this vendor gave the prospective customer an impression of her not-so-high profit and the customer's potentially good deal, as well as indirectly evoked in the customer a sense of pity for her.[21] This female vendor elaborated on the bargaining process:

In the old days, it was possible to start with a high asking price, but nowadays, many customers know the price range already. I start with a somewhat high price, not with a very high one. I also need to solicit the sale [*mời mua*] in a right way, politely and with a stress on sentiment [*tình cảm*], in order to get a sale. Initially, I was shy and did not dare to enter restaurants or drinking places. I stayed outside and just solicited sales from customers sitting outside. Neither did I feel comfortable soliciting at the beginning. I just walked along the street. I did not do well in the trade as a result at the beginning. In the first two or two and a half months, I just earned enough to pay for my own living expenses, and no money for anything else.

Q: How do you think male and female vendors fare in this trade in comparison with each other?
A: Women have an advantage in this trade, but it also depends on individuals and their skills.
Q: Why do women have an advantage?
A: As women, we can deal with the [psychological] hardship in soliciting sales. It is a pity for male vendors to have to deal with that. It is a pity for male vendors to have to approach other men who have a good time in drinking places. Many men have a good time, yet some men as peddlers have to do the hard work. But it also depends on individual skills. Some male vendors are quite successful and can talk better than female ones.

In soliciting and pleading (*năn nỉ*), a vendor puts him- or herself in the vulnerable position of a supplicant, with the risk of being rejected. In the supplicant role and in trying to evoke a sense of pity for him- or herself, the vendor acknowledges his or her hardship and inferiority. In the Vietnamese cultural context, it is more difficult for men to take this, especially in dealing with men of the same age range. It challenges their sense of masculinity more than it does female vendors' sense of femininity, especially among the vendors from Tịnh Bình commune or Sơn Tịnh district of Quảng Ngãi province, where patrilineage halls have been (re)built in a large number in the past decade and a half and where men have taken center stage in public settings. Our research team's participant observation of key chain peddlers in Ho Chi Minh City in early 2015 confirms that female vendors were more patient and persistent in their approach to prospective customers, even when their initial invitations met with negative responses from such customers. In contrast, when encountering initial negative responses, male peddlers tended to move on immediately. A middle-aged male vendor explained clearly that he could not plead with customers, because as a man, he would take prospective customers' words as reflective of firm decisions, and he did not want to plead (*năn nỉ*).

A fifty-year-old Tịnh Bình male peddler in Vũng Tàu, with four years of peddling experience, confirmed the difficulty, especially for men, in dealing with prospective customers' rejection of solicitation: "It was initially not easy to achieve sale success. I properly invited people to buy, but many said all kinds of things. If I persisted, they showed contempt. . . . It was initially difficult and challenging to one's sense of self-respect [*tự trọng*]."

The challenge to male vendors' sense of masculinity is even greater when prospective customers use coarse language or directly insult vendors. A thirty-five-year-old male peddler (from household 524) with over a decade of trade experience and having also engaged in manual labor jobs for many years, acknowledged this challenge as his main hardship in work and migrant life:

> This trade [itinerant vending] has more hardships than any other occupation of mine, although it yields good income. . . . [For example,] in a restaurant, a [difficult] diner whom I invited to buy insulted me: "See that I [pronoun *tao*, implying rudeness and insult] am eating!" . . . I replied: "It is up to *anh* [elder brother] to buy or not. As a peddler, I [*em*, younger sibling] just do my job in inviting." When I replied like that, some difficult diners even threatened to beat me up. I had to swallow [my sense of honor] and to move on. Fuck it. Peddling is like begging. Even worse than begging. . . . But I [have to] do it to earn money. (interview by Nguyễn Công Huy, February 2013)

A fifty-year-old female vendor (from household 478) made a similar point about the greater difficulty for men in dealing with a prospective customer's foul language or rejection:

> For women, if out of thirst, we ask for some free water from people, it is not as pitiful as when men have to do it. . . . The [itinerant trade] work also requires soliciting, and people whom we solicit are different. One person may say no politely, or may wave us away [not so politely]. But another person may respond by saying, "Fuck your mother." As a woman, I will judge the situation first before responding in such a case. If the other person dresses decently enough, I reply in a certain way. But if he looks like a drug addict or a bully, how do I as a woman dare to respond strongly? The other person may hit me, and I will lose face. I have to swallow it. . . . But men are more hot tempered. If the other person uses foul language, if the male vendor says, "Why do you respond with foul language?"

there may be a fight. It is for this reason that I do not want my two sons to enter this trade.

Underlying the hot temper in the preceding remark are face and masculinity. A prospective customer's foul language or even the vendor's request for water with the risk of being rejected (potentially) threatens the face of the person requesting water or soliciting sales. And quite a few female vendors suggested that it was more pitiful or difficult for men than for women to deal with such situations.[22]

Many vendors also suggested that in general, female and older peddlers had an easier sales job than their male counterparts, not only because female peddlers could deal with rejections and insults more easily, but also because prospective customers took more pity on women and older vendors. The male vendor from household 524 stated, "People take pity on peddling women. If I had money, I would do the same to help out. Out of a sense of pity, some people buy from peddlers, but do not use the products in the end. They buy out of a sense of pity for the pleading and miserable-looking female peddler. . . . Female peddlers have an easier time [evoking a sense of pity and] selling." Quite a few vendors, young and old, also reported that many customers had pity for old vendors carrying heavy loads and bought from them as a result. As a fifty-two-year-old male vendor (from household 540) put it, "Many customers took pity [tội nghiệp] on me, on my hardship in carrying a heavy load to earn some money, and bought from me."

Male peddlers adopted different tactics in dealing with the challenge to their masculinity. The previously mentioned fifty-year-old peddler in Vũng Tàu commented on this variation:

Q: Any male-female difference in sale?
A: Women try harder. They try harder in solicitation and pleading.
Q: How about male vendors?
A: It varies. Some try hard and plead to customers. Some, because of face and self-respect, do not. They solicit but do not do any pleading. (Interview by Nguyễn Ngọc Anh in Vũng Tàu, November 2014)

Some male vendors did not even solicit and simply showed their goods in restaurants to prospective customers, as observed by members of our research team in a coffee shop in front of a busy long-distance bus station in Ho Chi Minh City.[23]

Once a prospective customer inquired about the price of an item in the bargaining process, peddlers combined the logic of rationality (quality of goods and savings to a prospective customer) and of sentimentality (feelings in a social relation and even a sense of pity for a hardworking vendor). This is exemplified in the bargaining at a restaurant in front of a busy long-distance bus station between a Tịnh Bình male peddler in his late forties and two members of the research team in their midthirties, one of whom is from Quảng Ngãi province himself and who mentioned to the vendor his previous visits to Tịnh Bình and his knowledge of people in Tịnh Bình. The peddler referred to himself as anh (elder brother) and addressed a researcher as chú (junior uncle to the speaker's children) and occasionally as em (younger sibling):[24]

P [Peddler]:   Would you [junior uncle] buy a wallet to help me [elder brother] out?
R [Researcher]: How much is this wallet? I can afford it only if you sell it pretty cheap.

P:	For these, I sell to you for 250,000 đồng each. If you buy it in a shop, it costs around 400,000–500,000 đồng.
R:	Why do you charge such a high price? I cannot afford it. Would you sell it to me for 100,000 đồng, would you?
P:	No, it is a high-quality wallet. As you see, it is real leather, not fake one. Real leather is not burnt by [a small] fire. If you do not believe it, I can show it. [The male peddler took a lighter and put the flame close to the wallet] I put a fire close to it, and it does not burn.
R:	[If] you charge 250,000 đồng, I cannot afford it.
P:	Well, for the sake of our sibling relation, I lower the price to 200,000 đồng.
R:	I do not have enough money. Would you please lower the price further?
P:	At the price just quoted to you, I do not make any profit. Because you are close, I have lowered the price. In a shop, it costs 400,000–500,000 đồng. If you offer a higher price, I would sell it.
R:	I cannot afford it at 200,000 đồng.
P:	Would you offer a bit more? At 100,000 đồng, I would make no profit.

As the researcher increased his offer to 150,000 đồng, the peddler said that he could not sell it at that price and asked for an increase in the offer. The researcher repeated that he could not afford to pay more: "The vendor held the wallet, thought about it for a short while, and said: 'Well, for our good relation, I [elder brother] sell it to you [younger sibling].' He gave the wallet to me. I paid. He said, 'Thank you'" (Lê Thế Vững, participant observation notes of interaction in a coffee shop in front of a Saigon bus station for buses heading for southeast, central, and northern Vietnam, February 2, 2015).

Some male peddlers went beyond the general appeal to sentiment (*tình cảm*) in a social relation and invoked a sense of pity for themselves in the bargaining process. A thirty-six-year-old male peddler in Ho Chi Minh City (from Tịnh Bình household 497), acknowledging the psychological challenge for him in playing a supplicant role vis-à-vis male customers, highlighted his success when a customer had pity on him:

> [In bargaining] I ask them, "Please, 'elder brother,' please [do not bargain down any more]. It is only a few thousand đồng, which help 'younger sibling' [me] to get an iced tea." [It is out of sentiment that] a customer offering 8,000 đồng [for an item] lets me keep 10,000 đồng. . . .
>
> I have to ask [prospective] customers to help me out with their purchase. [It is] a sales pitch with [the stress on] sentiment. . . . Some think that the price is high, but they still buy it anyway out of sentiment. . . .
>
> At times, [when things do not go well] I feel self-pity . . . I am just like them [the customers] and have to take their not-so-kind words . . . I have to accept the situation.

The use of kinship terms by male and female traders to create social relations with prospective customers and their emphasis on sentiment in bargaining constitute an appeal to a moral framework (see also Leshkowich 2014a, 61–62, 64–65).

Notwithstanding such comments as from the male vendor from household 497, when asked to compare themselves with their female counterparts, the overwhelming majority of interviewed male peddlers emphasized their greater physical stamina and stronger ability to deal with risks in walking through small alleys or in returning after work to sleeping quarters at night. They explained their sale success primarily with those two factors and their bargaining skills. It was an explanation that made no reference to male peddlers' vulnerability and that upheld their *masculine* self-image.

However, male peddlers' masculinity goes beyond physical stamina and the greater ability to deal with physical risks. It also involves a strong sense of face and honor, which are important in Vietnamese social relations in general, and to which any challenge poses a greater problem for men, given the gender hierarchy in Vietnam. While some interviewed Tịnh Bình men opted out of peddling after a short stint because of this challenge to their sense of masculinity, many stayed in this occupation. Among male traders, some just showed their wares without solicitation in order to minimize being rejected. But the overwhelming majority solicited sales and accepted a challenge to their sense of masculinity, although as earlier mentioned, from the observation of our research team, they did so with less persistence than their female counterparts.

In her study of Bến Thành market traders in Ho Chi Minh City, Ann Marie Leshkowich has suggested that men do not engage much in petty trade because petty sale involves status self-deflation, which is unpalatable to men (2011, 283; 2014a, 65–66). The data from the Tịnh Bình trading network suggest that status self-deflation, although more difficult for men, is not unpalatable to Tịnh Bình male petty traders probably because of the context in which they ply their wares. More specifically, this status self-deflation is probably easier for Tịnh Bình male peddlers who operate far from home than it is for the husbands of Bến Thành market petty traders who work in their city of long-term residence and whose status self-deflation in the marketplace may become widely known in their own social networks. Small-scale male traders in Vietnam can deal with status self-deflation more easily because their itinerant trading means that they operate among strangers, rather than in stationary trading in an open market, where status self-deflation takes place in full view of their fellow traders.

Far from home or not, the supplication by many male Tịnh Bình peddlers challenges the essentialization of gender differences that are widespread in Vietnamese discourse, an essentialization that I hypothesize is not simply a result of enframing by the Vietnamese state, but probably has much deeper sociocultural roots. The supplication and status self-deflation by many male Tịnh Bình migrants facilitate their active participation in a far-flung trading network, as active as their female counterparts. However, the supplication does not mean that male peddlers' behavior is completely malleable. Their socioculturally rooted sense of honor and masculinity makes their sale pleas less persistent in comparison with those of their female counterparts. I would suggest that such socioculturally rooted masculinity and femininity are transmitted primarily through socialization within the family and in informal social networks.

Beyond the gender dimension, the growth of the Tịnh Bình trading network highlights the role of social network and social capital in Vietnamese political economy. As part of an informal economy, this network has grown substantially in the past two decades and has a big positive impact on household welfare and the economic trajectory of Tịnh Bình and surrounding communes (see also Luong and Gunewardena 2009; Chen 2012; Luong 2016).

No matter whether we examine gender roles and their malleability in political economy or focus on the impact on household welfare and rural development of a trading network as part of an informal economy, this chapter demonstrates that traders' behaviors and experiences are not simply shaped by top-down processes, such as government policies or the logic of capital. Instead, the experiences of this vast network of Tịnh Bình traders show the crucial role played by long-standing sociocultural dynamics that include dense, multifaceted forms of social capital and rich moral economic frameworks.

NOTES

1 According to official commune sources, Tịnh Bình had 2,599 households and 10,561 officially registered residents in 2012. In 2000, surveyed households were chosen by the random probability sampling method in an interdisciplinary research project on migration and urbanization. The U.S. Social Science Research Council (SSRC) and the Institute of Social Sciences in Ho Chi Minh City (ISSHO) jointly managed this interdisciplinary project, which was funded by the Ford Foundation from 1997 to 2004. I served as the leader of the SSRC expert team in this project. In 2012, with funding from the Social Sciences and Humanities Research Council of Canada, I started a panel study of seven rural communities in Vietnam, three in the south, two in the center, and two in the north. Four of these seven sites were studied in the SSRC-ISSHO project in 2000. The remaining three have been my long-term rural field sites in Vietnam since the late 1980s or early 1990s, all of them restudied in 2000 or early 2000s. This restudy of seven rural sites is an ongoing project on the transformation of sociocultural fabric and political economy in rural Vietnam, with the collaboration of many Vietnamese social scientists and using participant observation and extensive interviews, besides a household and migrant survey. As a part of this restudy in Tịnh Bình, our research team returned to the 150 originally surveyed households and included in the survey additional households comprising members splitting off from the original 150 households.

2 From the first phase of this research project, we learned that outside the Southeast region (surrounding Ho Chi Minh City), Quảng Ngãi and Long An were the two provinces with the largest number of migrants to Ho Chi Minh City. We chose two communes, one in each province, that sent the largest number of migrants to our three studied sites in Ho Chi Minh City. For comparative purposes, we also chose two other communes from the same districts that stood in contrast in poverty/wealth (Luong 2009).

3 The only visible handicrafts in 2012 were those of furniture and door making and the production of rice paper (*bánh tráng*), which over charcoal became rice crackers, regularly eaten for snacks and during meals in Quảng Ngãi.

4 Tịnh Bình commune has three hamlets composed of fairly dispersed twenty-seven residential clusters (*xóm*). The amount of land per commune member varied a bit from one hamlet or even from one residential cluster to another.

5 In 2012, of the 209 migrants from the 199 surveyed households, 5 worked as seasonal agricultural workers in the Central Highlands. As the surveyed population was about 8 percent of the commune population, the number of Tịnh Bình villagers working as seasonal laborers in the Central Highlands is estimated at sixty in 2012.

6 Peddlers reportedly switched from glazed mung bean balls to key chains because the former were perishable and believed to cause some hair loss when carried in a basket on one's head.

7 Most sunglasses are manufactured in Lịch Động village in Thái Bình province in northern Vietnam. The commodities carried by those itinerant vendors might also include leather belts, shoe cream, and ear wax removers, among other items.

8 In an annual cycle, peddlers' income tended to be much higher at Tết time, because of customers' higher disposable incomes at that point and the significantly reduced number of peddlers. Some peddlers with great financial needs continued their trading activities in destination areas at Tết time, given the much higher potential earnings. We interviewed some peddlers not returning to their home village for Tết in order not to miss out on peddlers with great financial needs.

9 A peddler usually used his or her net income after the first few weeks of sale to pay off the credit. After this, the peddler paid for the goods up front. Owning the goods, he or she could move more easily to another city, town, or region that offered more sale opportunities or higher income.

10 The presence of villagers from these four communes and not from Tịnh Minh reflects the stronger marital ties of Tịnh Bình villagers to people in these four communes.

11 A shoeshine man in Ho Chi Minh City, migrating from Thanh Hóa province in north-central Vietnam, informed me in December 2014 that his wife and many other fellow migrants from Thanh Hóa had long engaged in the peddling of key chains, sunglasses, and the like. Further informal interviews by our research team have confirmed that many migrants from Thanh Hóa and Bình Định in central Vietnam have joined this trade, some for over a decade already.

12 Specifically, such trade is banned on five major streets and in three tourist areas in Danang, on sixty-three streets and in forty-eight tourist sites in Hanoi, and on fifteen major streets popular with tourists in Ho Chi Minh City.

13 Instead of banning peddlers, one major long-distance bus station in Ho Chi Minh City sells peddling permits at VNĐ300,000 (about US$14) a month, with vending behavior conditions attached. A violation of conditions will lead to the revocation of the permit, with no return of the money to the peddler. However, the other major long-distance bus station in Ho Chi Minh City continues banning peddlers inside the station compound.

14 In 2012, if an itinerant vendor carried around goods worth VNĐ3–5 million (around US$150–250), a middleman or middlewoman one level upstream had operating capital of around VNĐ70 million to VNĐ100 million (US$3,500–5,000).

15 Tịnh Bình villagers who have moved upstream in the commodity chain include both men and women. However, no systematic data are available on whether more men or more women have succeeded in moving upstream.

16 For example, migrants from the coastal Đức Phổ district of Quảng Ngãi, particularly from the commune of Phổ Cường, carved out for themselves the niche of selling noodle soups through home delivery (*bán mì gõ*) in Ho Chi Minh City (Dương Minh Anh 2006). Similarly, villagers from Lịch Động village in the northern province of Thái Bình dominated the nationwide trade in sunglasses, opening numerous shops selling sunglasses throughout the country (Anh Thu 2005; Hà Thông 2007; Nguyễn Tuấn 2014). A Lịch Động official estimated that more than half of villagers had left Lịch Động to engage in the trade in sunglasses all over Vietnam (Trọng Phú 2005). For another example, the household junk trade in Hanoi and throughout northern Vietnam has also been dominated by migrants from the lower Nam Định province in the Red River Delta (DiGregorio 1994).

17 Interviewed peddlers working in the Mekong Delta have also mentioned slower sales as a result of rising water levels in the Mekong Delta in the last quarter of the year, which has led many to move to the Central Highlands at this time because of the coffee-harvesting season in this latter region. Similarly, a number of peddlers moved from the coastal city of Vũng Tàu to the Central Highlands at the end of the year, because the domestic tourist flow to Vũng Tàu peaked in the summer (a hotter season and a popular vacation time for families, with children out of school).

18 A peddler working in Cà Mau estimated that there were about eighty itinerant vendors from Tịnh Bình selling in that province alone.

19 A grandfather could take care of grandchildren of school age, but a grandmother was normally enlisted to care for a 2- to 3-year-old grandchild.

20 When asked, many also said that despite the significant daily variation in profit, in Ho Chi Minh City, approximately half the revenues went to cover a peddler's cost of goods and the other half was profit.

21 A male itinerant vendor in ethnic minority communities in the highlands of Quảng Ngãi reported that honesty and a long-term cultivation of relations led to referrals and were important for success there. This stands in sharp contrast to the sale practices discussed here for ethnic Vietnamese customers in urban contexts. This issue needs more systematic research (see also Trần Hoài 2013).

22 A female vendor (from household 468) pointed out that a number of Tịnh Bình men reportedly avoided itinerant trade for those reasons. Some male migrants from Tịnh Bình chose some other itinerant jobs, such as knife and scissor sharpening, to avoid individual

solicitation as well as bargaining over commodity prices. They just had to announce their services alley to alley and quoted their rates without much bargaining.

23 Most itinerant vendors in the Western-backpacker quarter in Ho Chi Minh City, whether male or female, did not solicit either, probably because of the language barrier. The solicitation, if at all, was limited to a "hello" and pointing at the goods.

24 The switch in address from *chú* (junior uncle) to *em* (younger sibling) implies lesser formality and slightly more solidarity.

CHAPTER SIX

MONEY, RISK TAKING, AND PLAYING: SHIFTING MASCULINITY IN A WASTE-TRADING COMMUNITY IN THE RED RIVER DELTA

Minh T. N. Nguyen

Spring district, a December evening in 2011. Although it was raining heavily outside, the conversations could not have been livelier, over tea, after a sumptuous meal of dog meat served with fragrant rice wine. Together with my research partner, I listened to the stories of three young men, Nhâm, Dân, and Linh, and Dân's father, Mr. Mạnh, who was my host.[1] Mr. Mạnh's wife, Mrs. Lan, was away in Hanoi working as an itinerant junk trader. Dân and Linh, who had each worked for a couple of years in Ho Chi Minh City, talked excitedly about the great services in Saigon's cafes, where female attendants would stir the coffee for them and stay on for a chat. They declared proudly that they had taken on various Saigon habits, such as drinking coffee at any time—in the morning with a newspaper, or even in the middle of the night. These exchanges prompted Mr. Mạnh to state that coffee drinking in the south is the same as tea drinking in the north. When he had been a manual laborer ten years before in Hanoi, there was a lady who sold such good green tea in Hào Nam that her clients could hardly find a place to get their cup. Her tea in the early morning was the best, as was the Hanoi *phở* that he sometimes allowed himself to indulge in, Mr. Mạnh declared.

The young men, Nhâm, Dân, and Linh, were fellow villagers, remotely related to each other. Nhâm was seventeen, a migrant worker who came home for a break before entering the urban junk trade, guided by his mother, who had been trading junks in Hanoi for more than two decades. Dân, twenty-two, and Linh, thirty, used to work as itinerant junk traders but had both moved on to other occupations. Dân had been working as a hired truck driver in Ho Chi Minh City in the past three years; he returned to prepare for his upcoming wedding, planning to open a waste depot in Hanoi afterward. Linh had been operating his three-wheeled transporter in Hanoi, delivering construction material to building sites, and was now back to oversee the construction of his house. Mr. Mạnh, Dân's father, had never been a junk trader, but in his words, he had been "all over the place" as a migrant laborer until he returned home in the early 1990s so that his wife could leave for work in Hanoi (M. T. N. Nguyen 2014).

This chapter is based on a year of ethnographic fieldwork, between 2011 and 2012, divided between Spring district in the Red River Delta and Hanoi. From such conversations as described above and informal exchanges with male informants in the districts, I started to piece together a picture of the ways in which the men enter and leave the urban junk trade, a predominant migrant occupation in the district (M. T. N. Nguyen 2014). As we shall see, their occupational mobility is shaped by changing notions of manhood, as they make the transition from youth to marriage and fatherhood. During their early youth, they distance themselves from their fathers' ways of life, being influenced by encounters with urban male cultural practices and encouraged by the haphazard opportunities in the urban waste trade. Later, however, normative ideas about appropriate manhood, with emphasis on patrilineal prestige and male protective roles, become more relevant for them. To attain these goals, the young men must start acting in ways similar to those of their fathers, who value hard work, thrift, and moderation, foregoing immediate pleasures for the sake of longer-term goals such as getting married, constructing a house, and, in the district, setting up a waste depot.

The chapter demonstrates the shifting nature of masculinity and how gender identity is central to men's participation in the market, as it is for women. What is normative in the district has been constantly reconfigured in the decades following Đổi mới, especially through the increasing prevalence of female migrants in urban waste trading. With more women migrating for urban work, for instance, these male goals are realized not uncommonly through the income of wives, especially for Mr. Mạnh's generation (M. T. N. Nguyen 2014). The young men's return to "traditional goals" while they actively participated in the urban waste trade is simultaneously a reversal of their fathers' reliance on their mothers' urban income, and a contrast with their fathers in their willingness to take risks, economically and socially. As local people embrace longer distances and more risky transactions, risk taking has become a form of highly masculinized everyday ethics in the waste trade (M. T. N. Nguyen, forthcoming).

Meanwhile, normative male models have undergone a significant shift through broader subject-making processes. These processes produce not only the "desiring subject" who seeks to cast his social relevance through aspirations and desires suitable to the new economy (Rofel 2007) but also the desirable subject able to live up to hegemonic ideas about manhood. What have changed are objects of desires, not just "coffee" in place of "green tea," but a whole new world of consumption, lifestyles, and bodily expressions that shape what it means to be a male person. Yet in their practices, the young men selectively draw on and distance themselves from these ideas, depending on their purposes at certain life stages. Their practices thus push the boundaries of normative manhood and over time help to redefine it, at the same time as they reproduce its symbolic parameters. As such, I do not simply contrast gender ideals with gender practices in relation to class processes (Ong and Peletz 1995) but also show how ideals and practices interact with each other daily to concurrently change and sustain social structures.

Vietnamese Masculinity and Market Trading

Masculinity refers to "approved ways of being an adult male in any given society" (Gilmore 1990, 1); in this definition, what it means to be a man is culturally and socially constructed. Masculinity is necessarily fluid, being constantly defined and redefined within social interactions according to power relations inherent in them. In particular, it is referential to notions of femininity and the expectations that men perceive as coming from others, including women, around them (Cornwall and Lindisfarne 1994; Ford and Lyons 2012). Research on masculinity often starts with the notion of hegemonic masculinity, which categorizes men into dominant and subordinate classes with differential cultural and economic attributes (Connell 2005). The former's social characteristics entertain cultural supremacy over the latter, creating idealized ways of being male that subordinate groups of men often seek to emulate, although not always successfully. More recent masculinity studies also explore the notion of marginalized masculinity in the face of unemployment, female migration, and changing gendered structure of the labor market (Hoang 2014). While these conceptions help us move beyond treating men as a monolithic and universal category, they dichotomize the male types without paying attention to their everyday practices through which they continually readjust their social strategies according to social circumstances and lifecycle stages (Inhorn 2012). They also fail to capture the competing constructions of masculinities that exist not only between groups of men (Hoang 2014) but also as part of the same male person. Following Inhorn (2012), I view masculinity as *emergent*, being part of identity processes foregrounded both by social differences and the ways in which men navigate between social and spatial contexts, between different relationships and social expectations at various points in their lives.

In Vietnam, masculinity has been shaped further by the interplay between multiple historical and cultural forces. First, the peasant patriarch retained varying degrees of influence during state socialism despite socialist interventions in the patrilineal family (Wiegersma 1991) and continues to be an enduring type in social life, albeit with declining power. Second, it is deeply rooted in the Confucian conception of manhood (Song 2004). This centers around a dichotomy between the "gentleman" (*quân tử*), a public-minded and morally superior male person who cares about other people's well-being, and the "small man" (*tiểu nhân*), a self-interested male persona attracted to only private gains and lowly pleasures. Third, similar to the case in China and formerly socialist countries in Eastern Europe (Ashwin 2000; Brownell and Wasserstrom 2002), the socialist construction of manhood during the central planning period, which spanned from the 1950s to the mid-1980s, is key to any understanding of Vietnamese masculinity. Because of the extended wars during this period, ideal manhood was fashioned out of the concept of the productive socialist worker, similar to what occurred in former socialist countries in Eastern Europe (Ashwin 2000) and the idea of a soldier who was ready to sacrifice his life for the nation, as the protector of the nation. Although the Confucian idealization of the cultured and genteel man contradicts the combatant soldier-worker figure during state socialism, what these two models of manhood share is the containment of sexual desires and the subordination of personal interests to collective goals.

Following Đổi mới, these models of manhood have been reshuffled with the greater approval of wealth accumulation, the glorification of entrepreneurship, and the rise of consumerism, as also observed in post-Mao China (see Song 2004). Added to the public sanction of getting rich and consuming lavishly is a tacit endorsement of male consumption of commercial sex for relaxation and for fostering business ties (Horton and Rydstrom 2011; Nguyễn-võ 2008; Vu et al. 2010). To be a highly regarded man today, one no longer needs to refrain from pleasure-seeking activities or shy away from demonstrating that one has and can make money. Money-making power or any kind of power that facilitates wealth generation represents an important post–Đổi mới benchmark for being a man, and the ability to pay for sensual pleasures counts as a privilege of successful men. The hegemonic man is now a successful entrepreneur, who is wealthy and classy in his consumption. Like "the boss" that Harms (2013) analyzes and the wealthy customers of commercial sex that Hoang (2014) portrays, he has a perfect family yet does not refrain from enjoying the pleasures of life outside the home.

Such construction is mutually constituted with the model of the ideal post–Đổi mới woman who is culturally and morally proficient, able to nurture and manage her family in ways that create social distinction for her family and her husband (M. T. N. Nguyen 2015). As for the laboring-class women who must measure up to such a benchmark of womanhood (M. T. N. Nguyen 2015), the male migrant laborers I am discussing in this chapter are subjected to similar hierarchical valuations of personhood prevailing in Vietnamese society today. Many, especially the first generation of male migrants, undergo considerable stress and even a sense of failure in living up to the gendered expectations of the new economy. As we shall see, however, their practices indicate strategic meaning making that serves different purposes in shifting contexts and stages in their life cycle, not unlike how "the boss" selectively displays or makes invisible his wealth and consumption (Harms 2013).

The emergence of new male types does not mean that the former frameworks of masculinity have been erased; rather, they coexist and interact with these emerging ideals of manhood under market socialism. Such coexistence of differing notions of manhood can be observed in, for instance, the differential valuation of male-dominated entrepreneurship (*doanh nhân*) vis-à-vis petty trade (*tiểu thương*) dominated by women. The perceptions of entrepreneurship as requiring modern knowledge, technology, and leadership skills, as opposed to the more intuitive and trifling activities of the female traders suited to their domestic roles (Leshkowich 2011),[2] justifies the Confucian attribution of men as being in the literati, devoted to matters of the mind. A man thus can retain the qualities of a "gentleman" (*quân tử*) when engaging in money making and private gain, as long as he does these in a socially sanctioned manner. This does not rule out the fact that there are female entrepreneurs and male market traders. These perceptions, however, create a situation in which those who transgress the boundaries between gender-appropriate categories of economic activity must justify their action via different means. As successful female entrepreneurs feel obliged to downplay their public success and play up their domestic roles (M. T. N. Nguyen 2015), the male waste traders discussed in this chapter cast their participation in waste trading according to gendered expectations of work and labor.

LOCAL HISTORY OF LABOR MIGRATION AND ITINERANT JUNK TRADING AS A MALE OCCUPATION

Spring district lies in a Red River Delta province, about 130 kilometers from the capital city of Hanoi. The district has nineteen communes, with a population of 180,000 people. Rice cultivation remains important in the district, yet because of the district's high population density, labor migration has always been part of local livelihoods, at least since colonial times (Gourou 1955; Le, Rambo, and Gillogly 1993). This continued, albeit on a smaller scale, during the following four decades of state socialism, despite the state's strict regulation of population mobility (Hardy 2003). The two wars during this period also meant that many adult men and women were absent for extended periods. Since Đổi mới, migration to urban areas has been rising, as elsewhere in the country, alongside the removal of mobility restrictions and rapid urbanization. In Spring district, there are two distinct flows of migrant labor: for waged work and for higher education. The educational migrants often aim to find professional opportunities in Hanoi or return to work as government officials in the district. They largely originate from areas such as administrative centers of the district, where local officials and cadres are concentrated.

Labor migrants from the district, the primary focus of my study, predominantly take up waste trading. Out of a niche that had historical roots dating to colonial times in the waste trade, they have helped develop an extensive recycling economy that employs tens of thousands of people in major cities (C. L. Mitchell 2008, 2009).[3] Spring district people nowadays mainly work as itinerant junk traders (*đồng nát*, or *đi chợ* in the local term) or operators of urban waste depots (*mở bãi*) and transport vehicles (*chạy xe*). Before Đổi mới, men like Mr. Mạnh often went to remote areas to work in gold mines or to the city for manual work, leaving to their female spouses the main tasks of care and household production. Since Đổi mới, the varying forms of waste work embraced by local people have changed the intrahousehold care dynamics. Either the woman leaves to work as an itinerant junk trader and her husband stays home to do agricultural work and assume care duties, reversing the previous arrangement, as in Mr. Mạnh's household, or the married couple migrate together to operate a waste depot, leaving their children in the country with grandparents or other relatives.

The work of itinerant trading is also gendered. Only a fifth of the itinerant junk traders are male. Although both men and women do basically the same activity—buying recyclable wastes from businesses and households and reselling them to waste depots or recyclers—there is a clear distinction between the two genders' work. In local terms, the women are called *đồng nát* (junk traders), and their urban work is designated as *đi chợ* (going to the market); the men are said to *đi đồ điện* (deal in electrical appliances). The men often emphasize the technical knowledge and market know-how that is necessary for their trade in used electronic appliances, in comparison with the abilities of female junk traders, who in the men's opinion can deal in only trivial household waste. Unlike the female junk traders who cultivate personalistic ties with households in particular urban neighborhoods, especially through their interactions with urban women, the male traders cover a wider urban geography and are more connected to the male-dominated repair-and-remaking sector.[4] The young male itinerant traders in this chapter like to emphasize the financially risky "deals" they are able to make and the social risks they are ready to take in relationships, even if that might involve pushing certain moral boundaries.

Whereas itinerant junk trading is an individual activity performed predominantly by women, operating a waste depot, in addition to requiring significant financial investment, requires the joint labor of more than one member of the household. For this reason, the married couple usually migrate together. Depot operation, furthermore, is much riskier than itinerant trading. The ambiguity of waste categories and market booms and busts aside, one needs to be prepared for tricky transactions in the waste economy and maintain precarious patron-client relationships with state agents (M. T. N. Nguyen, forthcoming). To open a waste depot, therefore, involves a significant level of risk taking. Since men are supposed to deal more with the dangers of the outside world, they tend to be in charge, especially if the household owns a transport vehicle.

The trading practices of male traders indicate their efforts to disassociate themselves not only from the social implications of dirt and waste that are part of waste trading, but also from being a market trader, an occupation considered to be in the provenance of women. They also suggest that to be ready and able to take risk have become important qualities of manliness in a masculinized economy that glorifies the risk-taking of the male entrepreneur.

"I Was Fed Up with Going Places"—Mr. Mạnh's Stories of Injured Masculinity

Over tea after dinner, Dân's father, Mr. Mạnh, many times told us about the old days when he went away to seek livelihood opportunities. He recounted in great detail his gold-digging trips in the early 1980s together with other male villagers, which left him with painful memories. In order to undertake these gold-digging trips, he and his wife had to borrow from many people to pool together one or two taels of gold for each trip, in the hope that he would make a fortune at the gold-digging sites. These trips usually lasted about three to six months, during which time the family did not hear a word from him. The work was arduous and dangerous: there was robbery on the site, many gold diggers took opium (drug addiction later became a problem in the district, although not only because of this past), and they did not eat or sleep properly. Most of the time that he did not spend working in the pit was spent searching for food in the forest or in ethnic villages nearby. It was so harsh that sometimes, as he was lying on top of a gold pit for a break, he thought that it would have been a welcome end to all his ordeals if the pit would suddenly collapse.

Yet the financial returns of such work were minimal: occasionally he came home with one or two taels of gold, enough to pay pack the debt; other times, he came back with empty hands and a deep sense of failure and shame, a feeling that he was disappointing his wife and children. The prospects were not improved when he started to work in Hanoi as a bike transporter (*xe thồ*) in the mid-1980s. His income was small, barely enough for saving, and the work and living conditions were wretched. On top of that was the sense of social inferiority that he experienced as a migrant laborer in the capital, where he felt looked down upon as an urban outcast: "They called you *thằng này thằng kia* [derogatory terms used as a belittling form of address for men, both second and third person]. They did not regard you as a being of any worth." These experiences with poverty and indignity culminated in his becoming "fed up with going places" (*chán chả muốn đi đâu nữa*). Such disenchantment with migrant livelihoods partly explained why he was ready to stay home with the two children, Dân and his younger sister, so that his wife, Mrs. Lan, could leave for waste work in Hanoi in the early 1990s, when Dân was barely a year old.

Mr. Mạnh is now in his early fifties. His stories are by no means unique in Spring district; they are common narratives from men of his generation. Several related themes emerge from these narratives. First of all, these men's early livelihood ventures beyond the village took place in the final years of state socialism, when the economy was in disarray and there were few local opportunities for the men to make significant changes to their household economy. Second, their urban work in the mid- and late 1980s, aside from the poor conditions and remuneration, was characterized by a deep sense of lost status. Most of the men of this generation had been in the army—they had been the defenders of the nation, the heroic and strong men, adored and admired by the people, until they returned home and were faced with the reality of making a living in a declining and isolated economy. Because earning cash income for the family is not necessarily a primary role of the "traditional" man, they could ease into caring roles at home, so that their wives could migrate to earn money. While not rewarding in monetary gain, life and work in the countryside do not subject the men to the indignities of migrant life in the city. On the contrary, the women's later entry into the urban junk trade benefited from greater urban consumption and a more thriving economy, and women are not as affected by such contradictory evaluations of personhood when engaging in urban waste trading. After all, women not only are associated with petty trading but also are constructed to embody the disorder and pollution of the urban space (Leshkowich 2005).

Perhaps because of his past experiences with scarcity and difficulty, Mr. Mạnh is thrifty and works hard. He wakes up before five o'clock every morning to feed the pigs and go to work in the field. He hardly ever buys food from the market for himself—almost all the vegetables, fish, and rice, plus the occasional meat consumed by the family—are products from the family's garden, pond, and field. Except for his daily amount of cheap green tea, unrolled tobacco, and, less regularly, rice wine, his daily expenditures are limited to the most basic necessities. He often reproaches his son Dân for his spending behavior, which he considers excessive, especially that when Dân was still making good money as an itinerant junk trader in Hanoi some years ago. One night Dân came back heavily drunk from a karaoke session in the district center with his friends to celebrate the purchase of a friend's motorbike (or to "wash the new motorbike," as they say). The next morning, his father scolded him, again saying that if Dân had enough sense to save the money he had earned, he would have made his parents' life easier. Dân, now seeming guilty over what had happened the night before, weakly protested, "As a youngster it is normal to play. Whoever does not have his time of playing and destroying in life? [*Thanh niên thì chơi tí có gì đâu. Đời ai mà chả có lúc chơi bời phá phách?*]," a statement that he often makes more emphatically on other occasions.

ITINERANT JUNK TRADING AS URBAN ADVENTURES: YOUNG MEN'S STORIES OF MONEY MAKING, RISK TAKING, AND PLAYING

At other times, however, Mr. Mạnh often listens with appreciation to Dân's vivid stories about his years of "going electrical appliances" (*đi đồ điện*), starting about five years ago when Dân was sixteen years old. Although Dân was first brought to Hanoi by his junk-trading mother, he did not live with her in the same lodgings but teamed up with Hưng, a friend a few years older from another village, who was skilled in identifying valuable goods and negotiating with customers. Hưng could easily make deadpan statements about certain items' lack of value to convince people to sell them their scraps at giveaway prices. They then lived together with about thirty people, men and women from the same district, in a rented house in Hoàng Cầu, an area that used to be slum-like, with poor infrastructure and a concentration of cheap migrant lodgings, but now has been transformed into a middle-class neighborhood of upmarket villas and private houses. Each of them occupied a sleeping space in a joint makeshift bed. In contrast to the poor lodgings they live in, their operations were "so very professional," in Dân's words. Dân describes their ways of working as superior to how female junk traders operate: "One needs to know how to do things in the right ways. If we had done things like the female junk traders [*các bà đồng nát*], going after little amounts of discarded stuff, it would just be enough for a hand-to-mouth existence [*vừa đủ đút miệng*]."

A male university student from the district helped them to put an advertisement on the Internet, describing them as a trading company dealing in recyclable waste from offices and companies. This worked well; many people called, wanting to sell loads of used computers and other kinds of scrap to them. Sometimes they had more telephone calls than they could deal with and had to pass purchases on to other traders. Like other male electrical appliance dealers, Dân emphasizes that such transactions require the trader to know people's psychology, to be able to spot their weaknesses and act indifferent, not showing too much interest in the goods. Thus some people would not sell their scrap to other traders at a higher price but in the end would sell it to Dân and his partner "as cheaply as mud."

Their income was boosted by their specialty in antique electrical appliances (*đồ cổ*). In the 2000s, wealthy people started to favor restored items from earlier times—televisions, radios, and especially fans—in home decor. Specialized restorers turn discarded electrical items into pricey, sought-after collectibles. In fact, old electrical goods still sell very well (although there are relatively good brand-new imitation products); a retouched early ceiling fan can fetch hundreds of million đồng, and the price restorers pay for the original item can amount to several tens of millions.[5] In particular, Marelli fans in different varieties are of great value, with their classical elegance and rarity. Hưng had a keen eye for these items and their value, a skill that Dân also learned quickly. As soon as they saw such an item, they would gear up their negotiation skills. One time they were called in by an elderly woman who wanted to exchange her old ceiling fan with a new one costing VNĐ 400,000 (US$19). After promptly buying her the new fan, they removed the ceiling fan and left right away. They were not far away from the elderly woman's house when her son caught up with them and wanted it back, saying that it was a family keepsake. They told him that they had bought it from another trader for four million đồng (about US$190), and if he wanted it back, he could have it for five million, to which the son had to agree in the end. Another time, the two of them saw a female junk trader intending to chop up a Marelli standing fan to obtain the copper parts for sale to the waste depot, and it took them no time to seize the opportunity:

> Most of the junk trader ladies [*các bà đồng nát*] do not know what an antique fan looks like. As I saw her about to do it, I said, "Why are you chopping it up like that? I can buy it whole from you. I'll pay more than what you would get from the waste depot for the copper." After some haggling, the lady sold it to me for 220,000 (about US$10), and we made five million (US$240) from it that day. After selling it to the restorer in Hàng Gai, we went together to Bờ Hồ to have a session of German draught beer that evening.

In their conversations about waste trading, Dân and the others highlight not only their skills and knowledge about the goods they trade but also their boldness in quickly identifying and seizing opportunity—daring to take the risks of either overpaying for an item or running into confrontations with urban people. In their narrative, not only is the money they could make important; they also stress what they do with the money. Unlike their fathers, or their wives and mothers, who would rather save or urge them to keep their earnings for their future families, the young men did not hesitate to spend money. Whenever they made a good profit from a transaction, Dân and Hưng were ready to go after pleasures that are often available to urban middle-class men, such as drinking foreign draught beer or having an expensive meal with imported alcohol. The significance of their going to a bar serving German beer in downtown Hanoi cannot be overstated. What they emphasize, to two middle-class urban female researchers, is, rather than just their having some ephemeral fun, is their ability to claim their belonging to the urban social space through an act of consumption. According to Erik Harms (2009), the Vietnamese urban space has been increasingly appropriated by the urban elite and middle class for their exclusive consumption as an expression of social status. The fact that migrant laborers like Dân and Hưng occasionally avail themselves of spaces frequented by middle-class men suggests a certain level of contestation of such processes of exclusivity. It signals, however, the hegemonic power of this class-based model of consumption.

Fitting in with and living up to the male model of the new economy (Nguyễn-võ 2008) also mean that one needs to demonstrate a level of mastery over relationships with women and sexual encounters. While they do not explicitly mention experiences with commercial sex, the men like to boast about their sexual encounters, often saying to Nhâm, the youngest man, with meaningful winks that also carry authority and weight, "Your skills with girls are still very low! [*Cái trình của các chú với gái còn kém lắm!*]" Once Linh had a bet with another young man about "conquering" a young woman within a week and won the bet. Other times he flirted with beautiful women from mountainous regions who were allegedly very easygoing. He had often been to bars, and had even met with homosexual men—"They are very particular, you have to know how to deal with them and once you have won their trust, they are very easygoing [*thoải mái*]. They are rich and would treat you to a good meal without thinking much about it," he said. Replicating the consumption patterns of the urban middle-class male through consuming, spending, and the ability to gain sexual experiences was indeed central to how the young men defined their manhood, and they were able to capitalize on the hidden profits of the waste trade in order to achieve this. Like their fathers, they remained part of the urban laboring class, with inferior social status. Yet unlike their fathers, they consciously compensated for such experiences of marginalization through the ability to occasionally afford the same goods and services consumed by urban middle-class men with the money they made from urban waste.

Coming of Age: "Straightening Up" and "Settling Down"?

There are, however, limits to the men's consumption and ability to participate in urban social space. First, the money did not always come easily, and in Dân's words, "one cannot play forever." He and Hưng stopped waste trading about three years ago, partly because antique goods became less available. Although the male dealers of electric appliances then had more opportunities with the greater urban consumption of e-waste such as computers or mobile phones, these did not bring in as much profit as the antiques that they had specialized in. Further, Hưng was into gambling, and he lost not only his own money but also his father's savings. In the end, his father almost forced him to return home to get married. Without his partner and friend, Dân then went to Ho Chi Minh City to join Linh, who had left waste trading in Hanoi several years earlier, to work as a hired truck driver for a private transport company. Linh afterward returned to the north to get married; Dân stayed on and had been living a less adventurous life there with a stable monthly wage until his return some years later.

Second, they must also face up to other kinds of social pressure: to realize their "traditional" life-cycle goals of getting married and starting a family. Starting their working life much earlier than their peers, leaving school early while others went on to higher education, these men have the autonomy to explore adventure in ways that the others cannot, when remaining within the boundaries of their parental home. Yet the local expectation is also that they will start their adult life earlier than their college-attending peers; in the district, men commonly get married in their early twenties and women in their late teens. When Linh was in the south, his father had said to him, with such finality that there was no point in arguing, "You can play as much as you want, but you must get married now. Otherwise my mind cannot be at peace." His father had identified the woman he should marry, a younger woman in the neighboring village, well brought up, hardworking, and, in his words, decent looking (*trông cũng được*). After several meetings, he thought that it was a good choice and that they would be compatible as a couple. Rather than just out of obedience to his father, however, he also considered marriage at this point to be sensible, something one is bound to do as a grown man.

In these younger men's narratives, the departure from their work as itinerant waste traders was presented as a move to a different life stage, when they started to be more forward looking rather than just living for the moment. For instance, they started saving more of their monthly income and sending money to their parents—Dân often complained to me that he had sent money to his parents so that they could buy a refrigerator and a flat-screen television, but the parents just saved the money. The period of migrant waged work in the south set the scene for Linh's and Dân's later transition into marriage and family life, and indeed for their subsequent reentry into the waste trade. Linh had thought that he would get married just to please his father, who wanted him to settle down closer to the family, yet he has since experienced a consequential change in his attitude to life: "In the past I played a lot and would go to any places that interested me. But since I got married and then my son was born, I have not felt the need to go out to eat and drink or try things out as much. I don't know why, I just do not feel like doing it so much anymore. Perhaps I am at a stage when I have straightened up [*tu*—the word he used can mean 'straighten up,' as in *tu tỉnh*, or 'be a monk,' as in being self-controlled in terms of sensual pleasure]."

Linh's wife had been working as an itinerant junk trader in Hanoi, and their son lived at home with Linh's father, whose current wife, Linh's stepmother, also did the same work in Hanoi. His wife was a lucky trader (*đi chợ có lộc*), as they say in the district; she made a good income from her junk-trading work in combination with cleaning by the hour for urban households. With his own three-wheeled transport vehicle, Linh also had steady income, as long as his vehicle could still operate in Hanoi without being fined by the traffic police. Their combined income amounted to ten million to fifteen million đồng (US$500–700) a month, depending on their luck. Linh no longer felt the need to engage in costly spending habits, and his money was now managed by his wife, a frugal woman, meaning that the possibility for saving was greater. Therefore, they could start building their relatively large house on the land his parents had given him. They had to take loans from relatives, and the full completion of the house may take years, but Linh was positive about their capacity to repay the debts in the near future. When the house is completed, and if the opportunity arises, they might consider opening a waste depot in Hanoi to improve their chance of earning a better income. In the village, younger men admired Linh for his experience and success, while older people praised him for being able to build his house when he was barely thirty.

Like Linh, Dân had had a girlfriend, who was a college student, for some time. The reason they split up was because, as he said, "I am a peasants' child [*con nhà nông dân*] and should get married to someone with the same circumstances." He was pleased that he had found his soon-to-be wife, a younger woman from another commune in Spring district, the daughter of a waste-trading family. He was visibly excited about the prospects of getting married and becoming the head of a family. In his discussions with the other men, he liked to talk about the various wedding expenses, and the topic of what his future wife would or should do—stay home or go to Hanoi with him—often came up. It was in his parents' plan that the two of them would open a waste depot in Hanoi, and the parents are prepared to give them significant financial support to do so. For Dân, it seemed natural that he would do that at the next stage of his life; his experience of driving in the south would make things easy should they later procure a vehicle for the depot, he said. If they succeeded with the waste depot, they would realize a goal that has eluded his parents. As a depot operator, he would have a different position in the waste trade and would have to be more strategic in his trading activities than previously. Waste depot operations require greater investment and skills in dealing with all sorts of dangers, from cheaters and gangsters to uncertain rental tenure and price fluctuations (M. T. N. Nguyen 2016). It remained to be seen whether he would achieve the goal, yet Dân was confident that his past experience and knowledge would facilitate their plan; as expected of him, he was ready to take the risks.

In short, while the men like to portray a male identity somewhat similar to that of Latin American machismo (Horton and Rydstrom 2011), highlighting life experiences revolving around sensual pleasures as male privilege and their "upper hand" in relationship with women, they are no longer the younger men they talked about. Hưng has now become the father of two children (his gambling habit seems to have been brought under control). Linh is also a father, while Dân is ready to become a husband, and soon-to-be father. Instead of "playing and destroying," as Dân said, they now try to live up to the role of being the head of the family; money for them is no longer merely a means to achieve immediate pleasures, but more to attain their male prestige through building a house or investing in future livelihoods. They do not talk about their wives the way they talk about the women they had met; the wives are to be "feared" and their opinions are to be taken seriously. In daily life, they do not shy away from domestic duties, including caring for their children, cooking, or washing up when their wives are not around. As soon as the women return from their migrant work in Hanoi or whenever the couple live together, however, these tasks are automatically retransferred to the women. As such, these men's behavior is similar to that of their fathers, when their mothers had been away working in the city (M. T. N. Nguyen 2014). Yet unburdened by the legacies of the previous eras and emboldened by their past heady urban adventures, they are more ready to take their chances beyond the village and perhaps less likely to stay home than their fathers; in other words, they are more likely to take risks. Although they now choose to temper the adventure and "playing" that they allowed themselves as youths for the sake of longer-term goals, consumption and sensual pleasures for them remain worthy male pursuits.

MASCULINITY, LIFE CYCLE, AND HYBRIDITY

This chapter has demonstrated the shifting ideas and practices of masculinity of young men from Spring district, whose occupational mobility centers on the urban waste trade, a popular form of migrant livelihood in the district. These ideas and practices change over time as the men transition from youth to their adult life, and they are related to the varying degrees of distance they wanted to create between them and their fathers, especially through the ways in which they make money, spend it, and take risks. The previous generation's economic roles were hampered by the lack of opportunities and their exposure to dramatic changes in social values around Đổi mới. The older men's low-status existence in the city as migrant laborers after a period in which men were constructed as protectors and builders of the nation inflicted injury on their masculinity. Thus they were ready to temporarily swap gender roles with the women, staying within the safe boundaries of the home and the village so that they did not have to face the indignities of urban life. Their sons, born around the time of Đổi mới, have not confronted such issues, and thus have adapted more easily to the new social conditions, being more daring in their actions. Although their urban life and work as labor migrants remain precarious (M. T. N. Nguyen and Locke 2014), they are ready to emulate hegemonic ideas and practices of masculinity that center on money making, risk-taking, and sensual pleasures. These ideas, however, appeal more to them as youths, and less so when they become husbands and fathers, when the ideas embraced by their fathers turn out to be equally influential for them.

Such generational and life-cycle dynamics are crucial to how men participate in the urban junk trade, although how they do so is also strongly shaped by the constructed difference between them and the female waste traders, potentially their mothers or wives. These evolving ideas and practices suggest a masculinity framework that is not only shifting and relational (Cornwall and Lindisfarne 1994; Ford and Lyons 2012) but also increasingly hybrid. They encompass multiple ideas about what it means to be a man in Vietnam today, both as desiring and as desirable subjects, as their lives bridge rural and urban life-worlds on a daily basis.

Notes

1 I would like to thank Tạ Thị Tâm for her research assistance. All the local and personal names in the paper are pseudonyms, except for the provincial name.
2 These two categories are of course located in different social classes. While they may have differing relations to men and women of the same class, their actions are governed by the same gendered processes.
3 One former villager was the director of the colonial Hanoi Sanitation Company (DiGregorio 1994; C. L. Mitchell 2008). Under his patronage, a number of male villagers were recruited to work in the company, bringing along their wives and children, who first worked in the municipal dumps of Hanoi and later established their niche in urban waste trading.
4 The female junk traders predominantly take up cleaning by the hour for urban households on their itineraries, which is also a way for them to gain access to household waste and build connections to the households in the neighborhoods they frequent.
5 The current exchange rate is VNĐ21,000 to US$1.

CHAPTER SEVEN

"STRIVE TO MAKE A LIVING" IN THE ERA OF URBANIZATION AND MODERNIZATION: THE STORY OF PETTY TRADERS IN A HANOI PERI-URBAN COMMUNITY

Nguyễn Thị Thanh Bình

Oanh is a forty-two-year-old woman who has been living in Lụa village for twenty years.[1] She was born in a neighboring village, and after finishing high school she married a Lụa man who worked for a construction labor group in the village. In 1996, after giving birth to her first child, Oanh joined the movement of "going to the market" and became a mobile vendor in Hanoi. At that time, her family income mainly derived from growing rice and vegetables on three hundred square meters of agricultural land that her husband had been allocated in 1993. Her income was also supplemented by small trading and her husband's hired work. In those first decades of the Đổi mới reform era, her trading practice was somehow spontaneous and relaxed. Since the early 2000s, the government's efforts to beautify and civilize the city have forced more and more Lụa vendors to quit their work in Hanoi's city center. In 2008, when Lụa village suddenly became part of an urban administrative unit, the government appropriated virtually all agricultural land for mega-projects. Some Lụa mobile vendors transformed their livelihood thanks to land compensation or the capital they received by selling a part of their residential land. However, Oanh and many other mobile vendors in Lụa village had no choice but to continue their work. They are mostly middle-aged women who have little or no savings, while their children are of school age. They cannot change this heavy work for other hired work that would be more stable but offer a lower income. Their petty trading has become the main income source to cover the everyday expenses of the family. Processes of urbanization in Lụa village have turned Oanh and other vendors into the most marginalized group.

Oanh's story reflects the dynamics of the marketplace in Hanoi and the processes of urbanization and modernization that are taking place as peri-urban communities are incorporated into the city proper. Following the Vietnamese government agenda to develop the urban system (Thủ Tướng Chính Phủ 1998, 2009), Hanoi city continuously expanded its administrative boundary since the end of the 1980s. In 2008, the city of

Hanoi alone expanded by more than two thousand square kilometers and by nearly three million people. This was a kind of urbanization by administrative integration at the greatest pace in the history of the city (Trần Thị Hồng Yến 2013). In practice, from 2000 to 2004, Hanoi converted 5,496 hectares of land for 957 projects, and this has had critical consequences for the life and work of 138,291 households, among them 41,000 classified as agricultural households (Hồng Minh 2005). For many among those peri-urban villagers who used to rely on both agriculture and petty trade for their living, not only did they suffer the shock of losing their agricultural land for urban projects, but they also had to face challenges in transforming their occupations. Additionally, they encountered difficulties in continued participation in small trading activities in the urban area.

In the effort to develop Hanoi "to be prosperous, beautiful, civilized, modern, and typical of the country," the municipal government issued various regulations that forbade mobile vendors in many roads and streets.[2] This made the life of street vendors much more difficult. Also, since the early 2000s, new policies were issued in the areas of distribution network planning; general market regulations and management issues; and the privatization of market construction, renovation, and upgrading (Chính Phủ 2003; Bộ Công Thương 2007). The renovation and rearrangement of most markets in Hanoi reduced the income of market vendors and even dispossessed them of their livelihood (Endres 2014a).

This chapter explores how the processes of urbanization and modernization have affected citizens like Oanh in Lụa village, Hà Đông district, which was incorporated into greater Hanoi in 2008. By examining the role of petty trade in the livelihoods of these peri-urban villagers during the process of urbanization and modernization, the research aims to better understand the continuity of trade practices among a considerable number of those villagers under the new circumstances and the new patterns they have adopted to strive for a living. This chapter argues that the pattern of rapid urbanization through the top-down urban integration of Hanoi and other places in Vietnam has had the unintended effect of pushing people into the informal economy. As this model of urbanization does not create much development in the industrial or service sectors, many peri-urban villagers and rural-to-urban migrants have no choice but to practice small trade in the city. Meanwhile, urban modernizing efforts focusing on the privatization of public marketplaces and on cleaning up the streets have rendered small-scale traders and poor urban dwellers who strive for a living more vulnerable. The story of Lụa petty traders shows how urbanization in Vietnam has impacted their identities and social status in that transitional community.

Drawing on material from fieldwork in Lụa village in 2014, this chapter explores the dynamics of petty trade in this community under the impact of urbanization and modernization.[3] The research was carried out using both quantitative and qualitative research methodologies. For the quantitative component, two hundred households were surveyed to determine the socioeconomic situations of households. In this chapter, the quantitative survey results are not presented and are used only to understand the social context of the village. For the qualitative component, which represents the core of this chapter, sixty semi-structured interviews were conducted with individuals in the village. The interviews included open-ended questions on informants' personal information and their families' socioeconomic situation. Villagers were free to share their opinions, feelings, and thoughts on urbanization and its impact on their lives and their community. Interviews and observation with traders were conducted at both the village and marketplaces in Hanoi where people are engaged in their work.

PERI-URBAN URBANIZATION AND INFORMAL ECONOMY

Urbanization is a process that is often seen as a consequence of economic development. This in turn causes a higher proportion of the total population to live in cities and towns. Some decades before, urbanization and urban growth were regarded as an indicator of modernization and progress (Evers 1975, 775). Today, these processes are more and more dependent on the expansion of the global economy, and they occur more rapidly in developing countries (Cohen 2004, 27). The rapid growth of cities in the developing world, especially in Asia, has produced several distinct forms of urbanization. From locations surrounded by regions of densely agricultural populations, many large Asian cities have experienced an explosive growth, evolving into megacities that exceed ten million, such as Bangkok, Jakarta, and Manila (34; Demographia 2017).[4] Rapid modernization and redevelopment have shaped the extension of these cities, together with massive urbanization of their peripheries resulting from residential development and the search for low-cost sites for factory production (Scott, Agnew, Soja, and Storper 2001). As a city grows, it spreads farther into the countryside. In this context, the urban edge surrounding large cities—the so-called peri-urban—has become a zone of encounter, conflict, and transformation (Friedmann 2011, 426). The process of peri-urban modernization is often marked by growing pains and sometimes difficult experiences, but it can also promise a better life. The peri-urban zone therefore is considered a terrestrial space where the drama of the urban transition is played out (429).

The informal economy—composed of workers who have no security of employment, receive few or no benefits, and are often unprotected by labor laws—has grown dramatically worldwide in developing countries since the 1970s (Huang 2009, 405). Contrary to the experience of developed countries, informal activities did not decline with industrialization in developing countries, but remained essentially constant during the past few decades (Castells and Portes 1989, 16). In many Asian countries, the number of street vendors in fact increased further after the financial crisis of 1998, as Sharit Bhowmik notes: "One does find that there was a sharp rise in street vendors in Thailand, Singapore and Philippines" (2005, 2256). In the course of the restructuring of the global economy, even in developed and newly industrialized countries, workers who lost their jobs in the formal sector have also taken up informal activities as a livelihood (Lyons and Snoxell 2005, 1301). Evidence from China suggests that the increase of the informal sector may be particularly marked in the transition from socialism to a market economy. In 1978, there were only an insignificant 15,000 employees outside the formal sector in China; by 2006, that figure had exploded to 168 million, out of a total urban labor force of 283 million, to make up 59.4 percent of the total. Most of the 168 million employees of the urban informal economy come from the 120 million-odd *nongmingong* (peasant-workers) working in the cities in two primary sectors: 36.4 million (30.3 percent) in manufacturing and 27.5 million (22.8 percent) in construction, for a total of almost 64 million (53.1 percent) in urban "secondary industry." Fifty-six million *nongmingong* work in the "tertiary industry," mostly providing services, a category that includes employment in hotels or eateries (8 million, or 6.7 percent); domestic work, security, garbage collection, delivery, and street cleaning (12.5 million, or 10.4 percent); and small-scale wholesale and retail trade (5.5 million, or 4.6 percent) (Huang 2009, 407–8).

Like many other developing countries in Asia, Vietnam did not have a strong industrial base, and since the old days the country's urban forces have been mainly engaged in the informal sector (Bhowmik 2005, 2256). An estimate includes 1,450 "craft villages" across the whole country employing 1.4 million people (DiGregorio 2001, 25), but the handicraft and cottage industry in Vietnam is still an imperfect supplementation for agriculture. Not many "craft villages" (*làng nghề*) can develop and form industrial zones (Bùi Xuân Đính 2009). In fact, a case study of Hòa Mục village in Hanoi city has shown that during the late French colonial era (1920–40), and under the socialist revolution's industrial development, local people in this village had embraced industrialization by taking advantage of being close to the city. This process had transformed some of the village population from farmers to artisans and workers. In this way, a kind of early in situ urbanization process emerged in this peri-urban village even prior to the 1986 economic reform (Labbé 2014). According to Labbé, only under the administrative integration process since the 1990s, and as a result of urban transformations initiated by developers and authorities, have villagers complained about negative impacts on their livelihoods (154).

Like Labbé (2014), other researchers on urbanization in Vietnam also affirm that local government and private investors do not keep their promises to create jobs for local people after taking away their agricultural land (Nguyễn Văn Sửu 2014; Trần Thị Hồng Yến 2013; Vu Hong Phong 2006). As a result, many have to return to agriculture or develop petty trade. Statistics from the Ministry of Agriculture and Rural Development indicate that only about 13 percent of farmers have stable jobs after land appropriation (Lưu Đức Khải, Hà Huy Ngọc 2008, 18). The results of other surveys show that in various provinces of Vietnam, the number of people engaging in business or small trade increased from 9.7 percent (before land appropriation) to

Figure 7.1 A street vendor on her way home to Lụa village through the new urban area that once was the village's rice fields. Photograph by Nguyễn T. T. Bình.

20.8 percent. This number is much higher in the Hanoi area, where it increased from 12.5 to 31.3 percent (Cục Việc Làm 2013, 154). However, thus far few studies have paid attention to how these activities play out in the urban transition, especially in peri-urbanization.

URBANIZATION AT LỤA VILLAGE

Located in the west of Hanoi, Lụa village is about sixteen kilometers from the center of the city. Despite experiencing various administrative changes in the late colonial and revolutionary period, before 2009 Lụa village basically belonged to one of the lowest administrative units (a commune) of Hoài Đức district, Hà Tây province. As an ancient village in the area of Hà Đông silk production, rice cultivation and silk weaving were the two main livelihoods of villagers since the old days.[5] Their silk products were sold at the village market and along the roadside by traders, or sold directly in the town. After the August Revolution of 1945, this practice of traditional weaving disappeared. During the socialist period of a subsidized economy (from the late 1950s to 1986), the cooperative of Lụa village developed weaving products for export to Eastern Europe. After Đổi mới, some families restored weaving and dyeing on a large scale. They bought machines and materials from southern Vietnam and established workshops in the village to produce and dye cloth.

Immediately after decollectivization in the late 1980s, Lụa people diversified their economic activities because of their geographical proximity to Hanoi. Prior to 2009, approximately 70 percent of over two thousand households in the village were agricultural households, their incomes supplemented by petty trade, hired labor, food processing, or small service industries. During harvest times, both men and women usually worked in the rice fields. In the off season, men grew cash crops, vegetables, and flowering peach trees or worked as hired labor, while women went to the market or to the city to sell their farm products and ply their petty trade. Thirty percent of households were nonagricultural households. Members of most of these were traders and entrepreneurs who no longer cultivated rice. Of these households, about two hundred had stalls at Đồng Xuân market and some other markets in Hanoi. Almost one hundred households owned weaving and cloth-dyeing workshops at the village. The remainder ran different kinds of businesses, ranging from wood workshops and garment workshops to tobacco trade, food shops, and the like. The dynamics of Lụa village trade can be seen as a continuation of the craft village tradition. According to many interviewees, the 30 percent of households involved in trading and craft were ranked as being wealthy in the village. The other 70 percent of households, by intensifying their cash crops, flowering peach trees, and petty trade, had a relatively stable livelihood.

Under the urban growth policy in the region, on March 1, 2006, the commune to which Lụa village belonged was assigned to Hà Đông town (Hà Tây province). In 2009, soon after Hà Tây merged with Hanoi, Lụa village became an urban administrative unit belonging to Hà Đông district. The urbanization of Hà Đông district took place rapidly after two major roads cutting across Lụa village were opened in 2006 and 2007. In early 2008, most Lụa villagers were shocked when more than three hundred hectares of agricultural land belonging to their village and another village in the same ward to which they both belong (about 90 percent of the total agricultural land of the whole village) were taken for thirteen housing projects, shopping centers, hotels, offices, high-end housing, and a hospital.

In response to this sudden change, the majority of the villagers (especially the agricultural residents) disagreed with the compensation policy. As with most complaints related to land clearance for development projects all over the country, Lụa people complained that the compensation was too low (Harms 2016, 211) and considered offers to provide jobs as replacement for the loss of land to be vague. In March 2008, a protest formed against land appropriation and lasted for over one year. Only toward the end of 2009, under a variety of pressures from the city government and tactics by property developers, did most villagers accept the compensation and cease protesting (Nguyen Thi Thanh Binh 2017).

The majority of Lụa villagers moved from a feeling of anxiety to the impression that they were "floating on air" (*bồng bềnh*) after they received a large amount of compensation. Also, from 2009 to 2012, all areas of Hanoi and many cities in Vietnam experienced a period of land fever. With compensation, together with money from selling their "service land," Lụa villagers enjoyed some prosperous years.[6] The village became a construction site, as so many families built new multistoried houses. People could spend more money on food and buy new household items. However, since 2012, with the real estate market of the city declining and with their compensation funds gradually dwindling, local people began to face challenges, especially difficulties in their livelihood transformation.

As opposed to peri-urban villages (which are closer to the center) where most households can earn money from lodging for hire, running shops, and providing services along the village roads (Nguyễn Văn Sửu 2014; Trần Thị Hồng Yến 2013), very few households in Lụa village offer lodging, and only 13 percent of two hundred households surveyed are engaging in trade and services in the village.[7] Thus, as with some villages in Thanh Trì district, there has been a phenomenon of reintensifying agriculture in this village (van den Berg, van Wijk, and Pham 2003). After losing land, many Lụa people (mostly men) continued growing peach trees on the land they rented from neighboring villages and expanded that cash crop.[8] Other men were unable to find a job one or two years after losing land, and so looked for land to rent in surrounding villages to grow peach trees and vegetables. Women in these households often grow vegetables under the peach trees to sell in the market or practice small trade. Fifty percent of the two hundred households in the village who were invited to participate in the survey have at least one member engaging in petty trade (both in the village and outside). Compared with the situation before urbanization, there is a slight change in the number of small traders in the village, as some villagers switched from doing agriculture and mobile vending in the city to doing service or petty trade within the village. These are mostly people who received compensation for their large area of cultivated land or could sell a part of their residential land. Those who have no choice but to continue small trade, particularly mobile vending in the city, now practice this work in a new dynamic situation and with a new social status.

DYNAMICS OF PETTY TRADE UNDER THE URBANIZATION AND MODERNIZATION PROCESS

MOBILE VENDORS

Although petty trade had always been a source of additional income for peasants in the Red River Delta, this practice was limited during the subsidized economic period. Only since Đổi mới have mobile street vendors become an integral part of everyday urban life in Hanoi (Barthelmes 2014). Research on seasonal migration has shown that rural migrants began to move to Hanoi during the early 1990s (Nguyen Van Chinh 2013). Given their proximity to Hanoi, Lụa villagers have practiced their petty trade in Hanoi since the 1980s. It is not difficult to find elderly women in the village who have been employed in petty trade for thirty years in Hanoi, selling such items as vegetables, fruit, or recycling materials. Beginning in the 1990s, the practice of street vending also became popular in Lụa village. There was a particular movement in the village at that time where many young and middle-aged women, and some men, carried vegetables and fruit on two big baskets hung on their bikes to sell at the market and on the streets of Hà Đông town and Hanoi.

During the 1990s, mobile vendors of Lụa village were present at most markets and on main roads of Hà Đông town, Thanh Xuân district, and Đống Đa district. In the late afternoon, it was common to encounter many long lines of bicycles with two big baskets of vegetables and fruits along main roads. A forty-year-old woman, Mrs. Duyên, recalled her experience: "At the time when we were growing up, we didn't go to high school so did not know what to do except go to work at the market. There was a kind of 'army of two baskets' [*đội quân hai sọt*] in the village. It was crowded and cheerful, as we often hung around in groups with each other the whole day surrounding markets, offices, and on the pavement. I met my husband when we both went to the market."

The number of practicing street vendors in Lụa village began to decline only in the early 2000s. The period from 2008 to 2009 was a time of restrictions for mobile vendors on many streets because of several official regulations. In reality this activity had already been curtailed through various policies put in place by the city intended to promote civilized trading streets, urban order, or sidewalk order.[9] In other words, the new regulation was just an upgrade of the general policy Hanoi city had implemented previously in order to build a prosperous, beautiful, and civilized capital (Kiều Minh 2008). Our interviews show that street vendors were dismissed when practicing their work in the late 1990s, especially in the central areas. However, it is only since 2003 that they did not dare to cross the Ngã Tư Sở roundabout with their bicycles and large baskets, as that was considered the limit of the inner urban area where mobile vendors with bulky goods are strictly forbidden. Since then, street vendors in Lụa village have withdrawn to Thanh Xuân and Hà Đông district—two newly created urban districts of Hanoi. The work in these areas is also not so easy. They can no longer sell on the street. Instead, they have to hang around markets or look for a place at temporary markets (*chợ tạm*), "toad markets" (*chợ cóc*) or the head of lanes (*đầu ngõ*).

These kinds of temporary markets are not officially recognized by local government and are still a target to be dismissed during each campaign of the city to reestablish urban order.[10] In many cases, interviews with mobile vendors show that these forms of markets result from residents' fights with their local government. Elderly and retired people often raised their voices in meetings with local authorities, arguing that they are not healthy enough to go to distant markets. They also do not have enough money to go to supermarkets, and so they really need these places to buy their daily food. In such cases, the ward officials often let leaders of the residential groups (*tổ trưởng tổ dân phố*) or some other individuals administer these markets. When mobile vendors go to look for a place in these markets, they have to approach representatives of the residential groups or individuals who have the power to arrange a place for them. If a vendor starts searching early and is lucky, she or he can obtain a good place. Others who start looking too late might not gain a place or, if it is possible to do so, may be able to secure a place only at the end of the market, an inconvenient location for customer access.

Vendors selling in these markets group together in a certain area of a street or at the head of a big lane. They either stand along the street or sit in front of a house there. Each month, the mobile vendors standing in these places have to pay VNĐ200,000 (about US$10), not including a daily market fee of VNĐ10,000 (about US$0.5). Vendors who rent the pavement in front of houses along the temporary market often pay about one million đồng [US$50] to sit in front of a house. However, it is not easy to find these places to rent as there are limited numbers of places available. Mobile vendors in Lụa village who successfully found a place to sit are considered self-starters and dynamic. They have good speaking skills and know how to get along well with local residents there.[11] After a long period practicing in that area, mobile vendors could trust and share the same sentiments with local residents. By paying to sit at the gate of the street-front houses in the temporary markets, vendors can have a small space to hide their goods whenever the police implement their cleanup campaigns.[12] By following "the law" set up by representatives of the local residential group or individuals who administer the temporary market, the mobile vendors are informed of cleanup campaigns or are overlooked during these campaigns.

Given the above dynamics of the market in Hanoi, many Lụa vendors had to quit their jobs, as they could not find a place to stand: "Street vending also needs a consistent place and to have regular customers who are familiar with us. As we were dismissed so often we could not make sales. I felt discouraged when I could not earn well. It was difficult to find a stable place to stand so I decided to stay at home to grow vegetables, peach trees, and flowers with my husband" (Quang, thirty-five-year-old woman who used to be a mobile vendor). Selling vegetables, fruits, and meat at the village market or selling clothes, miscellaneous goods, or food along the village road have become other choices for the petty vendors. Hundreds of Lụa mobile vendors withdrew to their village market and main road despite the fact that they earn less there than in the city.

As a majority of the 70 percent of peasant households in Lụa village spent their land compensation for building new houses and on daily expenditure, very few people invested their compensation to purchase a stall at a market of the city. The main reason is the new dynamics of the market:

Very few of us bought a stall at the market, because if we cannot sell well after spending a big amount of money to buy a stall, we will be impatient. It is better to go on being mobile. We might catch customers being mobile better than sitting in a place. (Quang, thirty-five-year-old woman who used to be a mobile vendor)

Someone suggested to me to rent a stall at Vồ market [Hà Đông district] at the price of three million đồng [about US$150] per month to sell fruits, but I do not dare. Because I am afraid that if I pay a big amount of money to rent a place to buy expensive first-grade fruits but cannot sell, I will lose [*lỗ*]. I do not like this and cannot sit in one place. I am used to going and standing in my position. I have familiar customers. I know exactly the time workers finish their jobs, the day they get payment to buy more fruits from me. I know the way the police go on patrol there. I survive thanks to [*sống nhờ*] workers of the factory where I often stand around. (Xuân, a forty-two-year-old mobile vendor)

For more than one hundred Lụa women who are still practicing mobile vendors in Hanoi, there is no choice but to continue to move. Many women in the village withdrew to the village market and transformed their livelihood thanks to their family's economic improvement after compensation. Others vendors simply returned to the village because they could not withstand the new dynamics of the market. These mobile vendors often have less agricultural land for compensation, while their children are of school age (and so need money for daily food and education).[13] In many cases, they are marginalized women whose husbands are sick, or a member of their family is engaged in inappropriate activities such as gambling or alcohol or drug abuse. Therefore, only by going to the market can they afford the daily living costs for the family. If they stop for even a few days, they have to borrow money to spend:

> When we had cultivated land, we rarely borrowed money to spend. With two *sào* of rice fields, we had enough rice to eat, one *sào* of vegetable farmland to sell vegetables for money every day, and some *sào* of peach trees (both from our own land and rented from a neighboring village) to get some savings at the end of the year.[14] Thus, I went to the market just to have an additional income. Whenever I take off one or more days from the market, I had work to do at home. Now in the days I am tired or having few customers, I hesitate to take time off. (Hồng, a thirty-eight-year-old mobile vendor)

> I think people here feel something missing after land appropriation. Before we had a more stable life as there was a combination of agriculture and small trade. There was a diversity of income sources. Nowadays we only concentrate on flowering peach trees and going to the market. After losing land, everyone goes to the market so work is more difficult and earnings are less. People now "strive to make a living," the market pressure means that what they earn that day, they spend that day. Thus, at night, many sleep with worries. The future for many people is so far away and dark. (Mr. Sinh, a fifty-eight-year-old retired local cadre)

Not only did the consequence of urban transformation create pressures on those female vendors; the new dynamics of the market also pushed them to work harder:

> Recently there are more and more vendors so we accept less profit, ranging from only two thousand to five thousand đồng [US$0.1–0.4] per kilogram of vegetables or fruits. Instead, we have to increase the amount of goods. Vendors with bicycles often carry seventy to eighty kilos to make sure that they can earn over one hundred thousand đồng [US$5] per day. As I rent a place, I have to carry double (150 kilograms) by motorbike. If I cannot sell all the vegetables in the morning, I must stay the whole day in the market. If I finish early, I return home and grow vegetables to earn some additional income. (Thủy, a thirty-six-year-old vendor who could rent a place in a temporary market)

Vendors at Markets

Besides selling vegetables and fruits, Lụa villagers used to be key suppliers of poultry for the markets of Hà Đông, Thanh Xuân, and Đống Đa districts in Hanoi. In the late 1980s when bicycles were the main means of transportation, Lụa vendors often bought poultry in Ngã Tư Sở wholesale market to sell in other markets in those above-mentioned areas. Since the early 1990s, many of them could buy motorbikes and go to Sơn Tây town (about sixty kilometers from Hanoi) to buy chickens and ducks directly from farmers there. This resulted in more than one hundred

Lụa poultry vendors going into poultry wholesale in the Hà Đông area or becoming poultry retailers in Hanoi markets. However, beginning in 2003, the number of Lụa poultry vendors began to decrease. People felt they could not earn enough, given the continuous problems with disease in poultry and the resulting decline in consumer demand. Besides this, the market restructuring scheme of the city also had an impact on their livelihood. In the precincts of urban public markets before the 2000s, for example, Ngã Tư Sở, Thanh Xuân Bắc, or Phùng Khoang markets, Lụa poultry vendors could sit freely after paying the daily market fees. Since the early 2000s, some of these markets, such as Thanh Xuân Bắc or Ngã Tư Sở market, were demolished in order to be rebuilt. In these restructured markets, vendors had to pay twenty million đồng [about US$1,000] a year (in advance) if they wanted to rent a stall (Trần Cường 2006). This form of market restructuring aggravated the unstable position of traders in many Hanoi markets even further (Endres 2014a, 106). This was the main reason why between 2006 and 2007 about thirty poultry vendors from Lụa village ceased their retail trade in Hanoi.

Approximately thirty Lụa people are still working as poultry wholesale vendors and are mostly concentrated in a new market near their village. Although this wholesale market was formed on a fallow area of land in Hà Đông district and managed by someone unknown to the individual traders, vendors still have to pay fifteen million đồng [US$680] for a three-square-meter stall for an uncertain duration (because of the absence of a formal rental agreement). Usually, a poultry vendor has to rent three stalls to have enough space for presenting his or her goods. It was therefore quite a substantial and vulnerable investment for the vendors, but they had no choice other than to accept the manager's conditions.

Another group of Lụa poultry vendors continued their trade by selling chickens and ducks in small markets in the Hà Đông area. Thúy, a vendor, has been selling poultry for over thirty years in several markets in Hanoi but withdrew to the village market given her poor health situation. She affirms, "Even if my health was strong I would not dare to rent a stall at the new market because it is so expensive, over one million đồng [US$50] a month, while it is difficult to compete with the long-established vendors at the market." In total, over the past decade about fifty vendors have quit their poultry trade in Hanoi and now sell poultry in the village market, grow peach trees, or pursue other jobs.

In comparison with those petty traders mentioned above who were easily excluded from their places at the markets, given that they had no rental agreement with the market management board based on legal stipulations, about two hundred Lụa vendors who are stallholders at roofed market halls such as Đồng Xuân market have experienced different market dynamics. Since the end of the 1980s, about ten Lụa villagers started buying and selling cloth between Saigon, Hà Đông town, and Đồng Xuân market. In the early 1990s, those first ten cloth traders in Lụa village began to rent stalls at Đồng Xuân market. However, at that time none of them could make a direct rental agreement with the market management board. Instead, they all had to rent stalls from the previous owners.[15] Gradually, more Lụa vendors came to the market to trade. Usually, after some years assisting a relative at the market, a vendor could learn trading and rent a stall for him- or herself. Since 1994, some Lụa traders have adopted new textile production technologies and reinvigorated the traditional village craft of producing textiles. By 2000, there were about thirty workshops engaged in weaving and dyeing cloth in Lụa village. The workshop owners also rented stalls at Đồng Xuân market to sell and market their products. This brought the total number of stalls owned by Lụa vendors at Đồng Xuân market to about 200, of a total of 260 cloth and clothing stalls there.

In the eyes of villagers at home, their co-villagers who own stalls at Đồng Xuân market are rich people. At the time of writing, a stall in the cloth section of Đồng Xuân market was worth one billion to two billion đồng (approximately US$44,000–88,000).[16] As these vendors are no longer engaged in agriculture, the land appropriation did not have an impact upon their livelihood. In contrast, the peri-urban infrastructure improvement after urbanization had linked villagers with the city better and made it easier for traders to commute. In the wave of upgrading old markets in the city (Endres 2014a), the rebuilding of Đồng Xuân market is currently under discussion, but for the time being it is still maintained as the biggest traditional wholesale market in northern Vietnam and an ancient historical place of Hanoi (Ngọc Ngọc 2016). However, many Lụa stallholders complain that the high competition in the market and the economic downturn in the 2010s have made their businesses more difficult than before. Moreover, traders in this market fear that, like traders in other "upgraded" markets, they will suffer from higher fees and a decrease in income if the city decides to rebuild the market.

The story of Lụa petty traders shows how they have been affected by an assemblage of urbanization and modernization policies. From being a rural village where most households earned their living by combining agriculture with petty trade and other activities, Lụa has become a part of an urban administrative unit after an administrative decision was issued. Combined with the city's decision to take away the cultivated land of villagers for mega-projects, this form of urbanization has had the unintended effect of turning the majority of villagers from farmers into members of the informal economy. After having undergone the transitional experience of pain and anxiety, 70 percent of the two hundred peasant households surveyed in Lụa village spent most of their land compensation on building new houses. For them, the compensation money was almost akin to receiving cooked food when they were hungry. If they did not build new permanent houses, they might have spent all their compensation money on their daily needs and household items. Meanwhile, it is not easy to find an opportunity for investing their compensation to transform their livelihood in a context of the contemporary highly competitive market. This is why in front of many new multistoried houses in the village, there are bicycles and motorbikes with baskets and racks to carry goods—the preferred means of transportation for mobile vendors and petty traders.

Many villagers, especially the middle aged who find it difficult to transform their livelihood in the urbanization process, have taken petty trade both in the village and in the city as their job. Among those, a group of village women "strive to make a living" in the streets and marketplaces of Hanoi. As the breadwinners of their families, they have no choice but to find a place and a way to circumvent the city government's regulations to work as mobile vendors. From being an additional job that supplemented their earnings, "going to market" has become one of the main sources of income in their households. Both urbanization at home and the modernization of the city have lowered these women's informal status so they have become even more vulnerable.

NOTES

1   This is a pseudonym to protect my sources.
2   Regulation No. 46/2009/QĐ-UBND had replaced Decision No. 02/2008/QĐ-UBND on January 9, 2008, "Regulation on Managing Mobile Vendors in Hanoi City."

3 This chapter is drawn from my individual research project on urbanization and sustainable development in Hanoi's peri-urban communities, funded by the International Foundation for Science. I would like to express my gratitude to the foundation for financially supporting my research, and to colleagues at the Institute of Anthropology, VASS, for supporting my fieldwork, especially Nguyễn Thu Quỳnh and Lê Thị Mùi. Alasdair Paterson kindly helped me in editing this paper.

4 Projections in the early 2000s indicated that by 2015, of the world's thirty largest cities, eighteen would be in Asia, six in Latin America, three in Africa, and three in the rest of the world (Cohen 2004, 34). These projections turned out to be basically accurate. By 2016, seventeen of the world's thirty largest urban areas were in Asia, with the top eight all in Asia (Demographia 2017, 18).

5 According to the oral history of local people, the village belongs to the system of "seven La villages, three Mỗ villages," which are considered ancient villages, formed in the Hùng king period. In reality, the earliest historical document kept in one of Lụa village's pagodas was written in the sixteenth century.

6 In addition to providing financial compensation, the province allowed farmers to retain 10 percent of the reclassified land, referred to as service land, for use or sale. Our survey and interview results show that 50 percent of households in Lụa village sold their service land to obtain money for building new houses and spending on other purposes.

7 It is difficult to count exactly the number of migrants who rent houses to live in this village, as the number is not stable. In 2014 about two hundred to three hundred migrants were living in lodging houses of about thirty households in the village.

8 Interview results show that households often grow five to ten *sào* (one *sào* equals 360 square meters) of peach trees. Most of these areas are rented from surrounding villages that have not been appropriated yet.

9 For instance, Government Decree No. 36/CP of May 29, 1995, on ensuring traffic order and safety on roads and in urban centers (Chính Phủ 1995).

10 Such markets are not mentioned in government documents (Sở Công Thương Hà Nội 2012).

11 Some mobile vendors shared with us that they gained the sentiment of the local residents surrounding the market by selling good products at good prices. Sometimes, they give some vegetables or fruits from their own home garden as gifts to them. Knowing how to relate to them is also very significant.

12 The vendors are not sure where this money goes.

13 In many cases, if the wives are not original villagers and married after 1993 (the year of land allocation), only the husband in the family received allocated land and received compensation in 2009. Meanwhile, some families may have more than four portions of agricultural land if the couples are original villagers and their children were born before 1993.

14 One *sào* equals 360 square meters.

15 According to Endres (2014a), traders in Vietnam's state-run markets do not own their stalls but have rental agreements with the market management board based on legal stipulations. With this rental agreement, they have a right to operate the stall. This right is transferable; thus, the vendor can also "sell" or sublet the stall to someone else.

16 The real rental price that the market management board takes from each stall each year is VNĐ700,000 (over US$30) at the moment. This price can change when contracts are renewed every five years.

CHAPTER EIGHT

DEALING WITH UNCERTAINTY: ITINERANT STREET VENDORS AND LOCAL OFFICIALS IN HANOI

Lisa Barthelmes

> *Thieves steal by night, officials steal by day.*
> (Cướp đêm là giặc, cướp ngày là quan.)
> —Vietnamese saying

In the context of reconfiguring the urban landscape to make way for a free, socialist-oriented market economy, the notion of "civilization" (*văn minh*) assumes great significance in the propaganda rhetoric of the Vietnamese state. Aside from undertaking infrastructural and market redevelopment projects, the state also regulates the use of streets in an effort to "civilize" them (Harms 2011, 216). As a result, streets are increasingly falling under the domain of the state. Against this backdrop of overall reform and modernization, itinerant street vendors are considered backward, nonproductive, and obstacles to traffic, representing the "remnants of an undesirable past" (Leshkowich 2005, 188) of a regressive Vietnam. In a state effort to control informal economic practices and regulate sidewalk activities, itinerant vendors have increasingly become the target of state policies that impose various restrictions on their businesses. State policies against street vending date back to the pre-reform era, when peddlers were considered counterproductive to the socialist planned economy.[1] Legislation passed in 2008 essentially sought to ban street vendors from a total of sixty-two selected streets and forty-eight public spaces in Hanoi (Turner and Schoenberger 2012, 3; UBND TP Hà Nội 2008). These measures have generated random police controls, which often result in the imposition of fines on the itinerant street vendors and the confiscation of their merchandise. Despite these hostile state policies, itinerant vendors continue to trade in large numbers on the streets of Hanoi by developing mechanisms and strategies to anticipate and circumvent police controls. The perseverance of the itinerant street traders shows that despite its deep commitment to the modernization project, the Vietnamese state practices a certain degree of permissiveness when enforcing laws and regulations.

This chapter examines the paradoxical dynamics of urban governing practices in the Vietnamese capital by using the theoretical framework of uncertainty. Uncertainty, defined as a general lack of being able to predict the future, may refer to different aspects of human life: economic survival, existential issues such as food security, or political instability. In the case of Hanoi's itinerant street vendors the uncertainty is of a particular kind, one that evolves only in the context of urban governing practices. Uncertainty is inherent to human life and social action, "a generic feature . . . of the human condition in general" (Jenkins, Jessen, and Steffen 2005, 12). Arbitrarily shifting between two parameters—tolerating and fining itinerant street vendors, condoning on the one hand and imposing fines on the other—allows local officials to define the boundaries of what is legal and what is illegal on a case-by-case basis. These governing practices, wherein enforcement measures are ultimately also contingent upon the discretion of local officials, create uncertainty about the outcome of police controls and render the laws on sidewalk vendors illegible. Instead of applying the rather dichotomous framework of power and resistance, I describe the tactics and strategies that Hanoi's itinerant street vendors employ to deal with uncertainty. These tactics and strategies range from evasion techniques, complicity in corruption, and moral claims to performing "ruralness."

The ethnographic data for this chapter were collected during sixteen months of fieldwork between July 2012 and November 2013. I conducted in-depth interviews with a total of thirty-nine vendors. Whenever possible, I also visited their families in their hometowns and interviewed their spouses, children, parents, and parents-in-law. I also did a survey with Hanoi residents to find out how itinerant street vendors are perceived in the urban environment. In addition, I conducted semi-structured interviews with investors, government officials, and social scientists regarding their vision of urban planning and their perceptions of itinerant street vendors. Finally, I draw on media sources such as local newspapers, government resolutions, and other legal documents in order to scrutinize the state's perception of itinerant street vendors.

BETWEEN TOLERANCE AND DISCIPLINE—URBAN GOVERNING PRACTICES IN HANOI

As a police car drives down the street on the east coast of Westlake in Hanoi, the officer at the back of the pickup truck shouts into a megaphone, "All stores tidy up your bikes, tables, and chairs! Make more space on the pavement! Street vendors go away!"[2] But his words are swallowed up by the din of the surrounding traffic. The itinerant street vendors who sell fruit around the famous Trấn Quốc pagoda understand nevertheless (see figure 8.1). They hurriedly pack up their goods, lift their shoulder poles, and start pushing their bicycles loaded with bananas, water chestnuts, and lychees to escape police control. A pineapple falls off the basket of a shoulder pole and rolls along the sidewalk. There is no time to collect it; everyone is too busy rushing to hide behind the next corner. When the police car reaches the pagoda, all itinerant street vendors are already well on their way.

This cat-and-mouse game can be observed on a daily basis on Hanoi's streets. As soon as a police car approaches, itinerant street vendors start to hastily pack up their goods and move a few meters up the street or retreat into a back alley, only to resume work immediately after the police car is gone. Vendors who aren't fast enough might be fined, and the officer in charge might even confiscate their goods. "They are always chasing us, we need to be careful. It is hard to work under these conditions," Thương, a thirty-five-year-old pineapple vendor, explains, echoing what many vendors' stories reiterate, namely, that itinerant street vendors have little bargaining power.[3] For example, Tâm, a forty-five-year-old pillow vendor, recounts, "I used to have a small

Figure 8.1 Street vendor selling water chestnuts on the edge of
Westlake, Hanoi. Photograph by L. Barthelmes.

bike and went around selling oranges on it. I was often fined by the police. Once, they
even confiscated all my belongings, including the bike. They only returned them once
I paid the penalty" (interview, August 22, 2013). Although routinized, always immi-
nent police controls and the possibility that their goods might be confiscated are the
most stressful and antagonizing aspects in a street vendor's life.[4]

To understand this paradoxical practice of simultaneously fining and tolerating
itinerant street vendors, one has to take a closer look at Vietnam's political system.
The socialist state in Vietnam has an extensive administrative apparatus that is characterized by network politics, personal relationships, and nested hierarchies (Gainsborough 2010, 178).[5] Thus a police officer may be in a dominant position when fining
a vendor but is in a subordinate position when interacting with his or her superior.[6]
Caroline Humphrey has shown for socialist Mongolia that "domination resides in
a series of equivalent positions in nesting hierarchies, such that a similar domination may be exercised at each level" (1994, 24). This also applies to Vietnam, where
a dualistic, clear-cut dominant-subordinate structure is not present. The resulting
clientelistic politics are in general characterized by reciprocity and exchange of gifts.[7]
Maintaining one's position within the networks of power through gifts and favors
is inevitable. This systematic corruption dates back to ancient times and persisted
throughout colonial rule and the so-called subsidy period (Endres 2014b, 614).

Extracting charges from below in order to advance within the networks of power
is a common practice in contemporary Vietnam. Itinerant street vendors are easy to
integrate into these networks because of their ambiguous legal status. In Hanoi, vending laws are implemented at the lowest level of local government, the ward (*phường*).
When implementing laws, ward officials might consider the needs of local residents

and at the same time pursue their own personal interests (Koh 2004, 2006). In contrast to the arbitrary fines imposed on street vendors, a "user fee" may be negotiated with the ward officials by Hanoians selling food on the streets. Yến, for example, has been selling sticky rice at the exact same spot on Châu Long Street for over thirteen years and pays a monthly user fee to the ward officials. Itinerant street vendors might be more flexible in their movements but are usually less successful in establishing stable networks with state officials. Fines for itinerant street vendors vary and often include new fees, as officials seek ways to supplement their own personal income (Leshkowich 2005). In this context, the boundary between self-interest and leniency becomes blurred, as the lax responses of local officials to "illegal" or "informal" practices commonly serve to further their own economic interests.

Police raids and fines in the context of itinerant street vending have to be analyzed against this backdrop. Tolerating, but at the same time fining, itinerant street vendors provides local officials with the means to maintain their position within a clientelistic system. Itinerant street vendors thus contribute to the financial transactions that keep this system running—even if only locally and marginally. Furthermore, police controls and confiscations are effective as spectacles of state power. The harassing of itinerant vendors signals to the local population both the willingness and the ability of the police to crack down on any form of unwanted public behavior. In this sense, itinerant street vendors have become an effective scapegoat when the legitimacy of state authority has been subject to question.[8]

The oscillation between tolerance and discipline is possible because both modes of governmentality are simultaneously legitimate and justifiable. Fining itinerant street vendors and keeping them in check is legitimate, as they allegedly are obstacles to smooth traffic flow and violate laws concerning the use of sidewalks and street vending. Moreover, in media reports, itinerant street vendors are portrayed as harassing and cheating tourists, distributing spoiled food, and engaging in "uncivilized" behavior (Anonymous 2012). Thus, through crackdowns on the street vendors the government signals that it cares about modernizing its capital and national progress. Tolerating itinerant street vendors is equally justifiable because they constitute an essential part of Hanoi's goods distribution system and the demand for their cheap products is high. By conveniently delivering fruits, vegetables, household wares, and ready-made food to the doorsteps of Hanoians, itinerant vendors fill in the gaps of an otherwise inefficient urban infrastructure. Many Hanoians enjoy the presence of the itinerant street vendors and consider them part of the capital's street culture. At the same time, residents often also complain about chaotic street life, which they see as an indicator of Hanoi's lack of development. The random and halfhearted fining of itinerant street vendors then results in a situation in which traders are allowed to practice their trade in recognition of their ability to meet otherwise unmet demands, while they are publicly depicted as undesirable and illicit. In other words, even though itinerant street vendors are undeniably an essential part of the urban infrastructure, they are decried as an obstacle to the country's modernization. Both the discourse on the "uncivilized" itinerant vendors and the paradoxical treatment meted out to them on a daily basis by local officials produce a range of ambivalences associated with street vending. For example, it is common that the very police officers who roam around fining vendors will then have lunch at street food restaurants or buy flowers and fruits from itinerant vendors when off duty.

Ironically, the same political and economic logic that gives rise to itinerant vendors on Hanoi's streets also deems them uncivilized and unmodern. Privatization, industrialization, and other neoliberal processes caused by the 1986 Đổi mới reforms created an opening for itinerant street vendors as an occupational group. As in other countries of the Global South, reforms and structural adjustment programs imposed by the World Bank and the International Monetary Fund resulted in deregulation and privatization processes in the 1990s. In most postcolonial and postsocialist societies embracing a market economy, privatization of health care systems, introduction of school fees, and gradual withdrawal of state services led to high rural-urban migration. As a consequence, the demand for cash in rural areas increased significantly. Households were forced to adapt to these new circumstances by diversifying their income. More and more people migrated to cities in pursuit of additional income opportunities, such as petty trade. Soon, sidewalk vending reemerged on Hanoi's streets as itinerant vendors gradually appeared on corners and intersections, which resulted in "an unprecedented revival of small-scale female-dominated trade" (Endres 2014a, 100). The very existence of itinerant street vendors is thus a function of a specific configuration in which national policies, exogenous capitalist forces, the conditions of the postcolonial state, and sociocultural dynamics conflate.

At the same time, images of clean urban space and modern indoor shopping facilities constitute the ideological underpinnings for rational economic development in which itinerant street vending should be regulated and, at best, eradicated. Whereas itinerant street vendors have become an integral part of Hanoi's street life, discursively they constitute "matter out of place" (Douglas 1966); underpinned by the rationale of a state-propelled logic of development, they symbolize backwardness. Both realities are effects of the same project that aims to create a developed, modern nation. This ideological project of the state is inextricably linked to material governing practices that manifest themselves in unpredictable police controls and the arbitrary fining of vendors. To better understand these state effects (Trouillot 2001), I will now analyze how concrete governing practices are experienced and talked about "from below," that is, from the perspective of itinerant street vendors.

Uncertainty

As transparent information about the legal framework is absent and outcomes of police controls are incoherent, itinerant street vendors operate in a political environment that is characterized by uncertainty, albeit not of a general, all-encompassing kind. Traders are aware that the police are just around the corner and react in the routinized manner described above; namely, they pack up their goods and vanish from the scene. The uncertainty is also not existential, since the income of an itinerant vendor is relatively stable and amounts to approximately VNĐ3,000,000 (about US$150 at the time of research) per month. Rather, it is an uncertainty that evolves in the context of the urban governing practices. Because of the inconsistent implementation of regulations and a lack of information, local officials produce an uncertain political environment. The illegibility of vending laws further perpetuates this uncertainty about what is actually "legal" and "illegal." In Hanoi, police controls neither are consistent with the legal framework nor follow a logical pattern.[9] "Sometimes they [police] come in the afternoon, sometimes in the morning. Sometimes they don't do controls for a couple of days," Thương once complained to me (interview, May 14, 2013). Martin Gainsborough, who has analyzed uncertainty as an instrument of rule in Vietnam, argues that keeping people in the unknown about what they are allowed to do and what not is an effective way to exert power. He states that "from the perspective of workers, this means they can never be sure what the consequences of their actions will be" (2010, 182).

Resolution 20/2008/QĐ-UBND, which regulates street vending, identifies designated streets and places, such as intersections, spiritual places, and traffic points, where street vending is officially forbidden (UBND TP Hà Nội 2008). However, police controls occur all over the city, independent of the parameters stipulated in the official legal framework. This results in the spatial illegibility of vending laws. When asked where they were not allowed to sell, my informants could not give a clear answer. Many assumed that they were operating illegally everywhere. One vendor thought street vending was allowed only in the morning when demand is high: "It is okay for us to gather around the market in the morning and sell to customers, but in the afternoon we have to be careful" (interview, August 18, 2013). Even though street vending laws clearly specify where and when they were allowed to work, my informants had incomplete or no knowledge about them. The vendors' information deficit serves the interest of police and ward officials, as they can make money from uneven enforcement of "laws" that may or may not in fact exist. This shows that uncertainty about the existing rules on street vending, and not impartial and clear regulations, resides at the core of how the state relates to itinerant street vendors.

Unclear jurisdictions further perpetuate this uncertainty. At least five branches within the state apparatus are responsible for surveillance, crowd control, security, and policing in Hanoi. These include *đội tự quản* (ward-level "self-management security"), *công an* (public security), *cảnh sát giao thông* (traffic police), *thanh tra giao thông* (traffic inspectors), and *cảnh sát cơ động* (mobile police, or "fast response" team) (Turner and Schoenberger 2012, 1035). Officially, only the *công an* have the right to fine street vendors. However, *đội tự quản* can often be seen participating in raids and chasing after vendors alongside *công an*. Even though the *đội tự quản* are (theoretically) not allowed to fine vendors, they nevertheless do so when patrolling Hanoi's streets (1035). "Yes, both *công an* and *đội tự quản* chase us," said Tâm in our discussions about police interventions. "I don't know if they are allowed to do so, what can I do?" (interview, March 30, 2013).

The consequences of confiscation also vary depending on which branch of the police is enforcing them. Sometimes the respective vendor can pay the fine immediately. Other times, the officers stipulate a time and date for the confiscated goods to be collected at the police station. If brought to the police station, fresh goods often either rot or are consumed by officers. "Once I could only get my goods back after three days. By that time most of the fruit was rotten," Ngân, a thirty-year-old fruit vendor from Hưng Yên, recalled (interview, May 21, 2013). Fines also vary depending on the officer on duty and can often also include extra fees. During my research, the official fines ranged from VNĐ50,000 to VNĐ100,000 (between US$2.50 and US$5.00 at the time of research) but the actual fines were more arbitrary and varied between VNĐ50,000 and VNĐ500,000 (between US$2.50 and US$25 at the time of research) depending on the actual situation and the officer in charge. Fines and confiscations are also determined by the area of operation. In the Old Quarter, law enforcement is stricter because of the pressures of tourism, and street vendors face harsher harassment by the police there than elsewhere in the city.[10] "They are always chasing us, we need to be careful. It is hard to work under these conditions," Liên, a peanut vendor, told me in front of St. Joseph's Cathedral, located at the heart of the Old Quarter (interview, May 14, 2013). The scope of the practices of spatial governing is directly related to the image the city government is trying to produce for its visitors: a clean, modern, well-regulated capital. In other areas, itinerant street vendors do not get chased and are thus not forced to navigate police controls as much as their counterparts in the sightseeing areas.

The lack of information and the illegibility of the manner of enforcement of vending laws are the prime causes of excessive reliance on and the proliferation of rumors about changes in legislation or future scenarios. When asked if they had heard about the plan to completely ban street vending in Hanoi, traders commonly told me something along these lines: "Yes, I've heard they want to ban street vendors everywhere in Hanoi, but I am not sure if it is true." The outcome is a feeling of powerlessness and being at the mercy of local officials. This uncertainty is reflected in a dialogue occurring between two fruit vendors about the state and its policies:

Vendor 1:   What do the people know, the "above" make the call, the "below" just follow.
Vendor 2:   Yeah, how can we know about the government's decision?
Vendor 1:   People are merely people. (interview, May 17, 2013)

The question "How can we know about the government's decision?" hints at a lack of information transparency from the state, which leaves vendors in the dark about the legal situation. Ananya Roy has shown for Calcutta that local officials apply specific "regulatory techniques" to manage the constant relocation of the informal economy by withholding information (2004, 154–55). These governing practices co-produce the aforementioned uncertainty about regulations as well as the outcome of the encounter. Uncertainty as an instrument of rule thus perpetuates a culture of bribery, informal understandings, and other forms of corruption, as local officers interpret and enforce the law according to their needs (Smart and Zerilli 2014, 232).

Moreover, in the context of governmentality, particular discourses and practices are used to calculate uncertainties and manage threats by assigning them to categories of the population, through which governments define certain behaviors as ir/rational, un/desirable and un/safe (O'Malley 2008, 63). The discourse on itinerant street vendors as obstacles to the flow of traffic, or as premodern and backward, provides local officials with the legitimacy to implement ambiguous practices. Hence, even though the state's will to legibility (J. C. Scott 1998) is present in the violence of police raids and fining, inconsistencies in law enforcement and arbitrary fining underscore the illegibility of state laws and the uncertainty about the outcome of an encounter. It is exactly this environment of uncertainty that allows local officials to operate with a significant level of flexibility, in which they shift between tolerance and discipline.

Uncertainty as a tool of governmentality has to be analyzed in the wider context of Vietnam's exposure to global capitalism. Although the neoliberal project in Vietnam is uneven, exceptional, and highly problematic, it has affected various fields of governmentality (Schwenkel and Leshkowich 2012). For example, Hanoi's urban landscape is increasingly shaped by foreign investments, which go hand in hand with a deregulation of urban space and the undermining of local governance capacities, especially in the field of housing and infrastructure projects (Labbé 2014). Simultaneously, authoritarian surveillance and uncertainty are increasingly employed to circumvent the neoliberal logic of accountability and transparency (Bui Hai Thiem 2015, 96). In the case of Hanoi's street vendors "the state" does not rule from afar but in a very present and real manner. As mentioned above, public police controls are a powerful display of state control—and local officials signal the presence of "the state" and its ability to govern by harassing street vendors.

At the same time, the presence and persistence of itinerant vendors on Hanoi's streets hint at the impact of the neoliberal processes in Vietnam. One key feature of the neoliberal logic is the production of self-reliant and self-managing individuals who take matters into their own hands after the state has withdrawn from providing basic services (Rose 2000; Ong 2006). Itinerant street vendors are self-reliant citizens in the literal sense, as they generate the income to pay formerly state-subsidized tuition and health care fees. However, they are denied urban citizenship by a discriminatory household registration system (*hộ khẩu*)—a tool of governmentality that stems from the socialist period. The example of itinerant street vendors thus vividly shows how surveillance-based, authoritarian governing practices that draw on socialist legacies converge and coexist with neoliberal-influenced state effects in contemporary Vietnam.

TACTICS AND STRATEGIES

How do itinerant vendors respond to these governing practices? How do they deal with the instrument of uncertainty in their daily lives? Many scholars have conceptualized the persistence and resilience of small-scale trade and street vending in the context of hostile state policies by using the framework of "everyday resistance" (J. C. Scott 1985,1990)—both in Vietnam and elsewhere.[11] I find this approach not as useful, as the dichotomy between power and resistance that is often suggested in resistance studies does not leave room for ambiguity and contradictory behavior.

In fact, very early on in my stay in Hanoi, I had the impression that everybody was actually "resisting the state"—be that during random traffic controls, in informal understandings with local policemen, or through alternative discourses about the state.[12] Many people I met mentioned the transactions involving informal payments and presents via personal networks. My landlord, a wealthy man in his fifties, complained about the extensive (and never ending) fees he had to pay to the authorities in order to renovate his house. "We have this saying in Vietnamese: 'Build a bridge if you want to cross.' You need to have connections to get things done here."[13] Social capital and links to people in powerful positions are crucial—not only for social upward mobility but also for getting by on a daily basis. If everyone is evading the corrupt state apparatus and working around legislation (some are able to do so more successfully than others), describing street vendors' everyday acts as "resistance" does then not say much about their everyday politics (Kerkvliet 2005, 2009) or the complexity of their experiences.

As I have shown, local officials' oscillation between tolerance and discipline creates an ambiguous political arena in which uncertainty flourishes. Instead of merely "resisting" these governing practices, street vendors employ a range of tactics and strategies that are partly contradictory. Pat O'Malley points out that all attempts to control and govern the future involve calculation (2004, 72, 73). In this sense, not only governments but also ordinary people calculate the future and intentional options while dealing with uncertainties by "applying rules of thumb, ordinary foresight, collecting information, relying on past experiences and so on" (Calkins 2014, 48). Tactics are spontaneous maneuvers, whereas strategies are planned, long-term practices. In contrast to Michel de Certeau (1984), who ascribes strategies to those in power and tactics to the subordinates, I conceive of both strategies and tactics as a set of practices that people at large, regardless of social strata, use in order to get by.

Tactics of itinerant street vendors in Hanoi involve mostly evasion and avoidance, both spatially and temporally. As mentioned above, itinerant street vendors try to elude police controls by retreating into back alleys and avoiding certain areas. "In the afternoon I go back to the market since the police often come to the pagoda," Ngân explained to me when I asked her about her daily routine (interview, March 2, 2013). Another tactic is to simply "move around the corner" when a police car approaches. In Hanoi, itinerant street vendors tend to decide spontaneously which avoidance strategy best fits the situation at hand and then react accordingly.

Itinerant street vendors in Hanoi do not form a homogenous group but are highly diversified in terms of products, vending strategies, places of origin, and areas of operation. There are semi-mobile vendors who display their products on the street, as well as itinerant vendors who use pushcarts, bicycles, or shoulder poles and have established routes of business. Aside from the means of transportation they use, they differ in the merchandise they sell, which ranges from fruits and vegetables to shoes, clothes, and cheap consumer items. Some are quite successful in their trade, while others earn very little because of physical constraints or lack of bargaining skills. This high fragmentation of itinerant street vendors contributes to the differences in their experiences with local officials. For example, the ability to avoid confiscations depends on the type of product a street vendor sells. Hà, a fifty-four-year-old itinerant street vendor who sells watermelons and oranges from a basket strapped to the back of a bicycle, explained to me, "If you only have a basket, running is easy. Having lots of fruits with you, plus a bike, is difficult though" (interview, May 30, 2013). Hà thus has a harder time evading the police than do her counterparts with lighter loads.

Many of the street vendors with whom I spoke were conscious of how the political system works. When I asked about why the police control street vending, Thương simply said, "The police need money like everybody needs money. Everything is getting more and more expensive lately" (interview, October 27, 2012). Instead of arguing over violation of the law, she clearly hinted at the corrupt practices of the people working for the state and beyond. Negotiating fines and trying to evade controls then becomes part of a system where "everybody needs money."

One long-term strategy in this context is establishing informal networks with local officials, as Kirsten Endres (2014b) has shown for petty traders at the Vietnam-China border. Naturally, my informants did not like to speak about the practice of advance bribing and it took a long time for me to actually gain enough trust before they were willing to share the following information with me. One of my informants told me that she and other itinerant street vendors do give "presents" to the police in advance—unrelated to the actual fines. One vendor with close relations to the police would collect money from the vendors and hand it over to an officer. Those involved in these informal interactions consider themselves lucky to be able to influence their profits in this way. A vendor participating in these informal transactions told me she would still face police controls but was convinced that there were not as many as before (interview, July 23, 2013). Some of my informants thus actively took part in advance bribing. In this particular example, itinerant street vendors actively reproduce state hegemony and power by playing along with the rules. That cooperation as a strategy prevails next to tactics of evasion and avoidance might seem paradoxical and contradictory, but they are both part of the available strategies to negotiate the tension between the local state's permissiveness and authority.

Another tactic that itinerant street vendors employ to deal with uncertainty is to refer to discourses of the moral economy (Thompson 1971; J. C. Scott 1976). Even though many of my informants stated, "There is nothing we can do about it, we have to accept it," when asked about police controls, they in fact still "do something about it." Their perceived powerlessness is true only to a certain extent, as moral claims are often employed to negotiate fines. "When they catch me, I try to explain and tell them about my family's background and hope they don't fine me," one pineapple vendor told me (interview, May 12, 2013). Another flower vendor said, "They [police] only want money. But we are hardworking people, it is simply unfair that we are always fined, I have children I need to provide for" (interview, June 20, 2013). Thus in their dealings with the police, itinerant street vendors are aware of and motivated by the necessity of providing for their families. Necessity, hard work, and low earnings serve as moral justifications for the semi-legality and moral ambiguity of small-scale traders (Endres 2014b, 618).

These moral justifications are behind tactics street vendors employ that are meant to evoke "compassionate complicity" (617) from officers who might lower the fee or turn a blind eye. However, this strategy does not always lead to the intended outcome: "Well, I try to ask for mercy. If they do not agree and bring my goods to the police station, I have to go to the station to pay the fine," Thương explains (interview, June 4, 2013). The respective officer is the one who has the final say in the matter of fining and confiscation.

That street vendors use their "smallness" to their advantage can also be observed during interactions with customers. Here, itinerant street vendors often mention their rural background and family context. During the bargaining process, claims such as "I can't sell it that cheap, believe me; my profit is marginal anyway; help me to send my children to school" or "I need to provide for my family" are common.

It is in this context that the appearance of itinerant street vendors has to be analyzed. When working in the city most vendors wear simple clothes that are in a poor state. When I asked one of my main informants why she always wears the same old clothes to work, she replied: "It is dirty in Hanoi, why should I wear my good clothes" (interview, August 22, 2013). This explanation seemed perfectly plausible, but I soon noticed that practicality is only one aspect of a more complex phenomenon. For example, when I asked my informants why they don't wear proper shoes, many responded, "We are poor people from the countryside, we can't afford nice expensive shoes" (interview, August 22, 2013). That this was not true became obvious when I visited their houses in the countryside: Besides proper shoes, my informants all wore "fashionable" shirts and drove motorcycles.

Moreover, as shown in the photo on this volume's cover, most itinerant street vendors wear the *nón lá* (conical hat) when working in the city. Again, the purpose of this typical accessory is twofold: First, it protects the face from sun and rain. Second, it is *the* symbol of the Vietnamese peasant, thus marking itinerant street vendors as "rural" and distinguishing them from urbanites. However, I have observed that vendors usually took off their *nón lá* when they were not working, that is, when they took a break or returned to their dormitories. In their hometowns, my informants virtually never wore the *nón lá*, except when they had to work in the fields.

Regina Abrami (2002a) has shown that identifying oneself as "poor peasant" was an important strategy for itinerant street vendors to make a living in the city during the 1990s.[14] Today, itinerant street vendors continue to perform their "ruralness" by maintaining a consistent dress code and signaling the necessity of earning a living in order to evoke pity from urban customers and local officials. While making moral claims can be seen as a tactic that is employed spontaneously, performing the rural peasant is a long-term strategy itinerant street vendors use to improve their livelihoods.

My informants—and this applies to other migrant workers as well—have internalized the discourse of their inferiority. Itinerant street vendors in Hanoi use both the dress code and their claim to being poor when referring to themselves. This strategy to invoke pity plays on the discourse of the backward, poor, working migrant. Here, Confucianist notions of traders as cheaters and socialist ideologies of trading as a capitalist activity enmesh with contemporary ideologies of the "civilized" urban and the "uncivilized" rural. Moreover, claims of being "small" and supporting a family are deeply gendered, as they are typically more credible when a woman voices them, as Ann Marie Leshkowich (2014a) has shown for female traders at Saigon's Bến Thành market. By amplifying their marginality, itinerant vendors reinforce and reproduce their marginality in urban settings.

Confronted with uncertainty as the primary instrument of rule, itinerant street vendors also engage with and thus reproduce those corrupt practices as well as their own ambiguous status in the urban environment. They continue to be both an essential part and a symbol of failure of urban infrastructure. They are self-reliant citizens but are denied urban citizenship. Their performance of ruralness is both an obstacle and an asset. Their livelihoods are the result of a specific economic-political configuration, which also deems them undesirable.

By shifting between permissiveness and oppression, local officials keep street trade in check, demonstrate state power, and generate extra income. In a culture of arbitrary fining, itinerant street vendors participate in an ambiguous, unregulated system that ultimately underpins the ability of local officers to maintain their positions within a clientelistic political system. Combined with unclear jurisdictions and the lack of information transparency, these governing practices include the production of uncertainty as a potent instrument of rule. Rather than merely resisting the state, itinerant street vendors employ a range of tactics and strategies to deal with this uncertainty. In addition to using avoidance techniques and moral claims and performing "ruralness," itinerant street vendors also seek to establish informal networks with police officers.

In the context of Vietnam's integration into the global capitalist system, the existence of itinerant street vendors is a direct result of the intersection of national state policies, international capital, and local governing practices. These neoliberal effects conflate with socialist modes of urban governmentality, which rely on surveillance techniques, oppression, and uncertainty. The case of itinerant street vendors bears parallels to Goethe's poem "The Sorcerer's Apprentice," in which a young wizard loses control over his own magical spell and soon the whole house is flooded with water. Not being able to reverse the repercussions of his own words, the apprentice cries out, "The spirits that I've summoned, my demands ignore!" Similarly, the Vietnamese government is unable to reverse the self-made "problem" of street vending. These vendors were summoned into being by particular economic and political conditions but are now perceived as undesirable by the same underlying logic—on both an ideological and material level.

NOTES

1 See Drummond 1993, 2000; Pettus 2003; Leshkowich 2005; Harms 2009; Turner and Schoenberger 2012.
2 Public service announcements like these are quite common in Hanoi. During the war period in the 1960s and 1970s, public loudspeakers disseminated evacuation information. Today, news and other information about garbage collection are distributed via these public

speakers in every ward. The mobile announcements by policemen on the streets are supposed to evoke an image of strong law enforcement, whereas information dissemination through public speakers is more subtle in its control mechanism.

3 Pseudonyms have been used to protect the identity of my informants.

4 A vendor is typically fined once or twice a month, depending on the success of evasion as well as on the frequency of controls.

5 The Vietnam party-state has an administrative machinery that at its lowest level organizes a so-called ward (*phường*) for about every ten thousand residents, one party cell for about every five hundred, and one state agent for every one hundred people in Hanoi (Koh 2008, 146).

6 Hanoi municipality is divided into twelve urban districts (*quận*) and seventeen suburban districts (*huyện*). Urban districts are further divided into wards (*phường*), which constitute the lowest political and administrative level within the city.

7 Clientelism is often seen as a relationship between a single patron and his or her client. However, in many cities state agents and governments constitute the most important patrons (Smart and Zerilli 2014, 235).

8 Economic downturn, rent-seeking practices, clientelism, and a growing discrepancy between rich and poor, among other factors, have contributed to increased criticism of the Communist Party of Vietnam.

9 Police controls need to be random in order to be effective; however, the police controls I am talking about lack an inherent logic and are characteristically despotic.

10 The tourist-induced commodification of street vending seen elsewhere in Vietnam (particularly Hội An) has not yet emerged in Hanoi.

11 Turner and Schoenberger (2012) apply the concept of "everyday resistance" to Hanoi's street vendors. Kurfürst (2012) and Drummond (2000) study resistance in the context of public space in Hanoi. For locales other than Vietnam, see, for example, Milgram 2014; K.T. Hansen, Little, and Milgram 2013; Bhowmik 2010; Crossa 2009; Cross and Morales 2007; Zlolniski 2006.

12 Such as jokes and stories.

13 An informal chat, February 12, 2013.

14 Abrami (2002a, 2002b) conducted fieldwork in China and Vietnam in 1997 and focused on the moral claims of street vendors, which were still shaped by a socialist rhetoric at the time of her research. Socialist ideology favoring peasants and workers played an important role in the self-understanding of the itinerant street vendors in Hanoi. The vendors claimed to be "just peasants," as if to hint at the smallness of the scale of their trade and their noncapitalist activities.

PART III

BORDERWORK

INTRODUCTION: CONSTRUCTING, MAINTAINING, AND NAVIGATING BOUNDARIES

Chris Gregory

The four chapters in this part take us from the dangerous and hazardous cross-border trade over the Beilun River, where morality and law are almost nonexistent, to Ho Chi Minh City, where police raids on gold shops strive to ensure that the value of the state's most precious asset—its money—is kept tightly under its control. Along the way we follow a coal briquetting chain as it wends its way into the outdoor kitchens of the urban poor, blackening the social status of all those who are forced to handle this "bad" commodity as it makes its journey. Only in the ancient trading village of Ninh Hiệp, which has become a hypermarket for Chinese apparel, are prices said to be "right" and haggling almost nonexistent. Morality and legality are matters of judgment, but when the state is the judge then citizens have to find ways of coping with the problematic powers of the state if they are to assert their own values. These chapters reveal how consumers and traders do precisely that by situating the voices of interlocutors in the concrete social, geographical, and historical context of Vietnam today.

Vietnam's border with China has a long and troubled history of invasions and military conflict, the last incidence being in 1979. The border was subsequently closed. Markets were disrupted but not extinguished as merchants moved into illicit underground trade. The official reopening of the border in 1991 enabled trade to boom once again in the open. Caroline Grillot's chapter, based on original fieldwork with smugglers, traders, transporters, and others in the cities on both sides of the border, explores the dynamics of this cross-border trade—a form of trade that, she rightly notes, relies on extensive bribery. The dangerous and hazardous nature of this trade is aptly captured by a Vietnamese trader who likens it to holding a knife: "The Chinese hold the handle and we hold the blade." Presumably the Chinese don't share this image because, as a state agent told her, when the mafia come to solve disputes between traders and clients they may threaten the Chinese with knives. The author's decision to liken the organization of small-scale cross-border trade to arbitrage is an apt one. The "salaries" and other payments needed to bribe state officials are the costs necessary to secure profits. An important finding of Grillot's chapter is how the political tensions between China and Vietnam have colored the moral sentiments and valuations of consumers. As one trader told her, many Vietnamese customers refuse to buy any product that shows a Chinese character on it.

If boundaries define the territorial limits of a state then the coins and paper money it issues define its internal limits. Vietnam, by this definition, is a relatively weak state because the Vietnamese đồng struggles to assert its dominance over the two global standards of value: gold and the U.S. dollar. Hyperinflation in Vietnam in the 1980s and 1990s debased the đồng relative to gold and the U.S. dollar. Like people everywhere, the Vietnamese prefer to be paid in a transnational currency whose value is rising rather than a national currency whose value is falling. This has led to a national economy that has three spheres of exchange (gold, U.S. dollars, and đồng) instead of one (đồng): gold is used for real estate and other transactions involving relatively large amounts of money; the đồng is used for petty market transactions involving food and everyday items; and the U.S. dollar is often used for middling transactions, especially those involving foreign tourists. The Vietnamese government has sought to bring this situation under control by developing prudent monetary policies to control inflation and by introducing laws to outlaw trade in gold and foreign currencies. Allison Truitt's chapter, which tells the tale of a police raid on a gold shop in Ho Chi Minh City in April 2014, captures a dramatic moment in the modern economic history of the Vietnamese state. Gold, as she notes, is viewed one way by the state and another by the citizens, for whom it is often a family heirloom in the form of jewelry as well as an instrument of exchange. Rival cognitions of this kind create a problem for the state as it strives to develop laws, because ambiguities in them are artfully exploited by those accused of breaking a law. Such was the case with the law that banned the buying and selling of gold as money but enabled citizens to possess gold in the form of jewelry. Thus the family whose shop was raided could claim that the gold the police found was a family heirloom, not capital of the business. In this case, the moral values of the family challenged the legal values of the state. The court of public opinion came down heavily on the side of the family. This fascinating case illustrates the fact that a family business is now a family, now a business, depending on the circumstances, and that interpretation is a political act that varies with the point of view of the interpreter.

Rich shopkeepers have much greater control over the moral valuation of "good" commodities like gold than poor householders have over "bad" commodities like coal briquettes. The principles of contagious magic mean that the virtuous qualities of good commodities attach to its handlers in the same way that the vicious qualities of bad commodities pollute their handlers. Users of black, dirty, ugly coal briquettes in the urban areas of Vietnam find themselves at the wrong end of "green, clean, and beautiful" government policies of urban development. Ambiguity in this context, as Annuska Derks reveals in her chapter, works against the users and traders of coal in moral terms even though it might yield economic benefits in lower costs or higher profits. Coal cookers are cheaper than gas cookers but the technological differences have social implications. Coal cookers are slow, require the attention of someone not otherwise employed, need to be used outside, and pollute the neighborhood; but they can also create good neighborly relations based on sharing and conviviality. The vendors who supply the coal have greater freedom than a wage earner, but Buddhist values equate black with bad luck, especially on the first and fifteenth days of the lunar calendar.

If Derks's chapter illustrates the thesis that immoral economy (in the eyes of the rich and powerful) is the theory of the inauspicious commodity, then Esther Horat's chapter provides yet another exemplar of the ancient and widespread idea that moral economy is the theory of the "just" price, or the "right" price, as they say in Ninh Hiệp. Given the widespread notion of this conception of morality, Horat's thesis that this has not changed much despite the revolution in state ideology should, perhaps, come as no surprise. Nationalist ideologies on border regions may shape moral sentiments, as Grillot's chapter shows, but short-term changes in the ideology of state power often don't, however much the state might want it to be the case that they do. When the high-socialist period ended, and the Vietnamese state no longer valorized workers in the sphere of production, the dawning of the new era created new dilemmas for the merchants in Ninh Hiệp's booming cloth market. The first was that of how to reconcile "wealthy" with "good"; the second was how to do this by selling Chinese cloth when state policies declared that the buying and selling of Vietnamese products was good. The contradictions mount for Horat's interlocutors because they promote the ideal of the virtuous farmer while employing laborers to run their farms so that they can concentrate on their urban businesses.

The construction and maintenance of the legal boundaries of commerce is the work of the state. It erects territorial boundaries vis-à-vis other states within which it defines the limits of the circulation of its legal tender among its citizens; it also defines the legal limits of good commodities. Statecraft is an imperfect art that varies across place and time as these four chapters on Vietnamese statecraft brilliantly illustrate. But more important, they illustrate that the construction and maintenance of the *moral* boundaries of commerce is the work of buyers and sellers situated concretely in time and place. Commercial morality is the art of trading together well in pursuit of the common good. This, too, is an imperfect art that excites value judgments that reflect the point of view of a participant, be it as buyer, seller, official observer, or unofficial observer. Morality and law, for their part, have ill-defined boundaries that provide the scope for vice to flourish, as these chapters demonstrate. But vice is defined by virtue and Horat's report that "Ninh Hiệp is known as a place where no or only little bargaining is done and goods are sold at the 'right price' [*đúng giá*]" serves to remind us of this important fact. This is a Vietnamese expression of a moral sentiment that is transnational and transhistorical. The sign "just price" was carved in stone at the gateways to the ancient Babylonian markets. Today the mark "Fairtrade" can be found on certain products that meet the standards of Fairtrade International, an organization established in 2009. "Not all trade is fair!" its website (http://www.fairtrade. net) declares. "Farmers and workers at the beginning of the chain don't always get a fair share of the benefits of trade. Fairtrade enables consumers to put this right." Be it called a "right price," "just price," or "fair price," the meaning is the same everywhere: if it does not describe what is the case then the expression prescribes what should be the case. If marketing is, as Geertz notes, "more than another demonstration of the truth that, under whatever skies, men prefer to buy cheap and sell dear" (1978, 29), it is also a demonstration of the truth that traders would also prefer to do it fairly.

Chapter Nine

Regulations and Raids, or the Precarious Place of Gold Shops in Vietnam

Allison Truitt

On an unremarkable afternoon in April 2014, the owner of a gold shop in Ho Chi Minh City stepped outside, leaving a trusted employee to handle any inquiries. The shop occupied the ground level of a four-story building on a street clogged with motorbikes and cars. A large digital board flashing the buying and selling price for gold vied for the attention of passersby while inside glass display counters filled with sets of wedding jewelry in red velvet boxes beckoned consumers. But as residents in Ho Chi Minh City knew, gold shops offered to buy and sell more than gold; they were venues for quick currency transactions.

Since the 1990s, gold shops have operated as venues for converting value across the three major currencies in circulation—Vietnamese đồng, gold, and U.S. dollars. Open early and closing late, the shops kept time with the city's boisterous cash economy and provided an alternative to the staid banks where guards stood watch and gates were pulled shut during the noon hour. While I was conducting fieldwork in Vietnam in 2000–2002 and for subsequent stays, I also relied on nearby shops to exchange my dollars into đồng. The transactions were quick, the rates decent, and no paperwork was required. I later learned the transactions were also illegal. Spot transactions such as mine were restricted to licensed credit institutions registered with the State Bank of Vietnam, yet many residents continued to rely on shops for occasional conversions, which set the stage for conflicts over currency circulation. While the Vietnamese state restricted foreign exchange transactions, including in gold bars, residents had the right to *possess* currencies, a right paradoxically reaffirmed by the same ordinances that sought to restrict transactions to licensed credit institutions. Regulating foreign exchange transactions thus exemplified what anthropologist Arjun Appadurai has called "tournaments of value," in which state officials and citizens contested the proper place of these currencies in society (1988, 21).

What happened on that day in April shocked not only the owner but also seemingly the entire city. Just after the owner left, a young man entered the shop to convert a hundred dollar bill into Vietnamese đồng. As soon as the young man left the store, several police officers entered and demanded to search the shop. They searched not only the bottom floor where the owner conducted business but also the upper floors, which were her personal residence. After several hours, they confiscated US$1,400 and some Thai baht and impounded 559 SJC gold bars. Reports of the raid generated a flurry of media attention, spurred by journalists and bloggers who were becoming increasingly vocal in criticizing what they viewed as excessive use of state power (Thayer 2014, 354). Newspapers, including *Tuổi Trẻ* and *Thanh Niên*, published interviews of police officers, lawyers, and other gold shop owners. Several days later, *Dân Làm Báo*, a website well known for its biting commentary on corruption among government officials, uploaded a video of the raid, which was then widely disseminated by Facebook users. The raid had gone global.[1]

Urban residents were accustomed to police seizing goods of roving street vendors or extracting payments from market traders (Endres 2014b; Jensen, Peppard, and Vũ 2013; Leshkowich 2014a). But gold in Vietnam was no ordinary good. It also circulated as a quasi-official currency in the form of domino-sized bars measured in tael units of 37.5 grams. Gold shops served as crucial nodes in the country's circulation of currency by maintaining the social liquidity of gold and converting value across other currencies, namely U.S. dollars and Vietnamese đồng. The raid thus exposed the role of the Vietnamese state not just in regulating trade but also controlling the pathways of currency circulation (Guyer 2004, 30).

In this chapter, I examine the clash between the official justification for the raid and the owner's strategy for reclaiming the confiscated gold and currencies as a tournament of value. From a state-centric perspective, the police raided the gold shop for allegedly engaging in the once common but now illegal practice of buying and selling foreign exchange, which included gold. In addition to ordinances restricting foreign exchange to licensed credit institutions, in 2012 the Vietnamese government had just passed Decree No. 24/2012/NĐ-CP, the intent of which was to demonetize gold. Decree 24 banned small gold shops such as the one described above from selling gold bars, although it reaffirmed that citizens still had the right to *possess* foreign currencies and gold. And here is the twist. The owner of the gold shop provided documents that the currency and bars were possessions bequeathed by her parents and gifted by her children. The raid sparked fears among residents, especially in Ho Chi Minh City, that the police would confiscate their gold and foreign currency as well. My interest in the raid is in the disappearing act, that is to say, how the resolution to the raid required erasing the role of the small trader in maintaining gold's social liquidity.

By way of setting the stage for this argument, I first refute a popular claim that people's reliance on gold as currency marks a traditional orientation toward money. I instead emphasize how gold's transformation into currency was propelled by state-led market-oriented reforms that initially authorized the Saigon Jewelry Company to manufacture standardized bars measured in taels and later encouraged domestic banks to offer attractive interest rates on gold deposits. By 2001, as the price of gold began to rise on world markets, its role as a unit of account in Vietnamese real estate markets contributed to price instability. Gold imports also generated trade imbalances as the price for gold continued to climb. Decree No. 24/2012/NĐ-CP, or Decree 24 for short, was passed as a mechanism to tame the country's gold markets (Chính Phủ 2012). But the legislation failed to address how many citizens regarded the place of gold in their own economic lives, particularly as the raid stoked lingering fears among residents that their personal and household wealth might once again be seized by state officials. By way of conclusion, I address how gold shops in Vietnam are caught then by the changing regulations over gold's circulation as well as consumer preferences, both of which may reshape the social liquidity of gold in Vietnam.

TURNING GOLD INTO MONEY

On August 15, 1971, President Richard Nixon officially closed the "gold window," which severed the last link between the U.S. dollar and gold. Until that day, the U.S. government had pledged that the U.S. Treasury would convert U.S. dollar holdings by other central banks into gold bullion at the fixed rate of thirty-five dollars to one ounce of gold. This pledge was made during the Bretton Woods Conference in 1944, when the United States controlled nearly two-thirds of the world's gold. By the 1960s, the country's domestic expenditures and military expansion in Vietnam eroded its credibility among the world's major industrial states, who converted foreign-held dollars for gold.

The end of the Bretton Woods era of the convertible dollar marked a shift to fiat money, in which paper currency was not redeemable for anything. Anthropologist C. A. Gregory has argued that closing the gold window signaled "a decline in the power of the State to tame the forces of the market and a growing distrust among citizens of the world in the capacity of the State to act morally" (Gregory 1997, 1). As institutional interest in holding bullion waned in the subsequent decades, the price for gold on world markets declined. After the September 11, 2001, terrorist attacks, the price began to rise once again and then after the financial crisis in 2008, its price on world markets quickly escalated as central bankers, institutional investors, and even ordinary citizens saw gold as a safe haven and a reserve asset.

Today gold no longer anchors the value of any state-issued currency. Yet it has retained its luster because of its historic role as coinage and later a monetary standard. European banknotes issued by private banks in the nineteenth century had liquidity because they were redeemable for bullion. This practice was later enshrined by central banks and then hardened into an ideology of "practical metallism," or the belief that "the monetary unit 'should' be kept firmly linked to, and freely interchangeable with, a given quantity of some commodity" (Schumpeter 2006, 288). But this belief cannot explain why gold circulated as a quasi-currency in Vietnam after 1975. People held gold not because it anchored the state's monetary unit but precisely because it did not. Moreover, both state officials and ordinary citizens were agents in widening the circulation of gold (Elyachar 2003, 576). In southern Vietnam, the failure of socialist projects contributed to the informalization of trade and commerce (Freeman 1996), which involved side-stepping or evading state-sanctioned pathways of circulation. Traders who participated in informal systems of exchange required a monetary instrument that both condensed value and conjured trust, something the state-issued VNÐ did not. In southern Vietnam, citizens had lived through not one but three currency reforms—in 1976 a provisional currency was swapped for the former regime's in southern Vietnam, in 1978 a new national currency was introduced, and finally in 1985 as part of a price-wage-currency adjustment, the entire physical stock of currency was replaced. These reforms replaced the physical stock of currency with newly designed bills, and citizens were permitted to swap their old currency for the newly issued one but only in fixed and limited amounts. By the mid-1980s, hyperinflation reinforced the value of gold and U.S. dollars as hedges against economic and political instability within Vietnam. Gold in particular embodied an alternative currency, one whose value was priced on world markets and not by the communist government.

Gold and U.S. dollars were both ideal alternatives to the state-issued currency—easily concealed and widely accepted. People transacted with a range of gold objects, from simple bands to gold foil or thinly pressed sheets of gold leaf impressed with the name of Kim Thành, a reputable gold manufacturer in Saigon. But gold differed from state-issued currency or U.S. dollars because its value was ostensibly anchored in its physical properties of purity and weight, which could be verified. In Ho Chi Minh City in the 1980s not even the widely circulated bars manufactured by Kim Thành were taken at face value. The thinly pressed sheets of gold leaf could be easily "clipped" or cut with kitchen shears. So within this context of informal trade and profound distrust of the government's management of the economy, small-scale gold shops served as intermediaries for the monetization of gold.

It is worth reflecting on how the widespread circulation of gold in Vietnam challenges scholarly understandings of money. State theories of credit presume government officials authorize and verify currency. But in the streets of Ho Chi Minh City, it was gold traders who operated as intermediaries in settling payments. Other theorists emphasize how the state puts currency into circulation through payments to soldiers and administrators, which in turn create markets. State officials in Vietnam, however, demanded payments not in state-issued currency, but in gold, from potential migrants seeking to flee the country. Migrants outside Vietnam would tuck gold jewelry or rings in packages to their nonmigrant family members still in Vietnam, endowing gold with meaning as a transnational currency linking stretched families.

By the late 1980s, the municipal authority in Ho Chi Minh City recognized the need to authorize a new payment instrument in gold that might circulate alongside U.S. dollars and Vietnamese đồng. If gold offered Vietnamese citizens a way to "shield themselves from the intrusions of government" (Maurer, Nelms, and Swartz 2013, 264), by the late 1980s, this shield was tacitly approved by city officials in an effort to regularize gold markets in Ho Chi Minh City. In 1988, the Ho Chi Minh City People's Committee created the Saigon Jewelry Company (SJC) in an attempt to address the city's turbulent gold market (Nguyễn Hữu Định 1996). The following year, SJC introduced a new product, a gold bar measured in taels (37.5 grams) and smaller units (chi, or one-tenth of a tael). Unlike sheets of gold leaf that required a set of three to make a tael, the SJC bars were thick and solid. Their design drew on authorizing devices of state-issued currencies, including holograms on the plastic coverings and individual serial numbers. Even the company's name in English anchored their worth, not in the aesthetics of the nation-state but in the global marketplace. Today, more than twenty million SJC bars of gold are estimated to have been produced for the Vietnamese market, or over 90 percent of the total number in circulation.

Small-scale gold shops were crucial nodes in Vietnam's expanding currency circulation. These shops maintained the social structure of liquidity, especially in SJC bars, by posting the prices and providing a ready market of buyers. By the 1990s, some gold shops were licensed as foreign currency exchanges; the logo of banks affirmed their place as intermediaries between the informal economy and financial institutions. Unlike banks, gold shops were also participants in the sidewalk economy of Ho Chi Minh City (Kim 2015). Placards with the day's buying and selling prices advertised the buying and selling prices of different forms of gold, and at the top of these lists was the SJC tael. While these small shops did not manufacture the actual bars in circulation, they ensured a visible and imminently realizable price for the taels.

Gold's place in the domestic economy as a currency was formalized when the State Bank of Vietnam authorized banks to mobilize the gold and dollar savings of citizens. By the mid-1990s, retail banks were recruiting customers to deposit their dollars and gold bars in interest-bearing savings accounts with enticing interest rates. The banks then used their new capital base for loans, fueling the country's securities and real estate markets. Gold, once held by ordinary citizens as a hedge against political and economic uncertainty, became the basis of a new speculative economy. Eventually, the sharp increase in the price of gold after the 2008 financial crisis exposed the fault lines of gold's monetization in Vietnam. Borrowers were unable to repay loans denominated in gold, while buyers were increasingly reluctant to negotiate contracts, especially for houses, in SJC taels for fear the price of gold would suddenly jump. Ultimately, the volatility of gold transformed what had been regarded as a safe asset into a speculative instrument and unreliable measure of value. Just as the investors sought more reliable means of pricing real estate and settling debts, the Vietnamese government imposed new controls over gold markets under the banner of Decree 24. This decree recognized SJC taels as the exclusive national brand, prohibited banks from mobilizing gold savings, and banned small-scale gold shops like Hoàng Mai from buying and selling gold bars. And it is this background that set the stage for the raid of Hoàng Mai gold shop on April 24, 2014.

Gold as Good, Gold as Commodity

Hoàng Mai was one of an estimated ten thousand privately owned shops in operation throughout Vietnam. On April 24, 2014, the police raided the entire building in response to the shop's alleged violation of buying and selling foreign exchange without state authorization. After searching both the shop and the owner's personal residence, the police seized fourteen hundred U.S. dollars, Thai baht, and a computer and impounded 559 taels of gold. News of the raid rapidly spread over official news channels and social media. The state-run press hinted at other violations, including a report mentioning that customers had been shortchanged when exchanging dollars for Vietnamese đồng and that there had been a disagreement with Japanese tourists (Gia Minh 2014a). But a few days later, *Dân Làm Báo* uploaded a video of the raid that showed the gold shop owner vigorously demanding to see evidence of the alleged violation, which turned attention on the raid itself.

Scenes of police confiscating the goods of small-scale traders are a common sight in Vietnam. But this raid was not met with the usual indifference of the urban middle class, who largely approved restrictions on roving street vendors (Jensen, Peppard, and Vũ 2013, 112). The public outrage targeted the "excessive power" of the police. The legality of the search warrant was questioned, for the warrant was dated April 23, 2014, the day before the raid occurred, sparking concern that the violation itself had been manufactured (Gia Minh 2014b). Readers also demanded to know why the police had impounded the gold bars if the alleged violation was the unauthorized sale of U.S. dollars. In response, State Bank of Vietnam officials invoked Decree 24 and reminded readers that because gold shops were no longer licensed to trade gold bars (*mua bán vàng miếng*) or exchange foreign currency, doing so could incur substantial fines (A. H. 2014). The officer who conducted the raid explained that the shop owner did not have a receipt attesting to how she had come to possess the gold, given that it was no longer legal for gold shops to trade SJC bars.

The newspaper *Tuổi Trẻ* responded with commentary by other experts regarding the legality of the search (Gia Minh 2014c). Lawyer Võ Xuân Trung of the Ho Chi Minh City Lawyer Association noted that neither the gold bars nor U.S. dollars were "material evidence" (*tang vật*) of the alleged violation and so their seizure was excessive (*lạm quyền*). Moreover, he added, holding foreign currency and gold was not in itself illegal. And because the owner's shop was also her personal residence, she had the right to her property, thus setting up another iteration in conflicts over the recognition of property rights and the marketization of those rights (Tai and Sidel 2012, 2).

The raid dramatized the tournament of value over the legally sanctioned and culturally defined pathways of gold circulation in Ho Chi Minh City. Decree 24 restricted buying and selling those bars to financial institutions as part of a larger set of regulations intended to control who could manufacture and trade gold bars that had long served as a quasi-official currency. At the same time, the government was wary of sparking popular unrest and so had affirmed the right of people to *possess* gold and foreign currency. What was at stake was not merely gold's classification as money or commodity, but its pathways of circulation.

The raid on Hoàng Mai gold shop made visible the contentious politics over gold's role as currency. While citizens retained the right to possess foreign currency and gold, the Vietnamese government restricted transactions of gold bars (e.g., *vàng miếng*) to financial institutions, effectively outlawing gold shops as venues for buying and selling bars. The raid, however, exposed how this classification scheme depended on a spatial separation between the house and the shop. By raiding the entire building, the police demonstrated there was no separation between the household where gold bars could be stored and the shop where gold bars could no longer be traded.

Ultimately, the shop owner did not challenge the state's classification scheme. She instead asserted her rights to the foreign currency and gold, not as a trader but as a mother and daughter. She produced documents attesting that the bars had been passed down by her parents and the foreign currency was a gift from her children. Her claim reclassified the goods from tradable commodities into valuable gifts. By asserting her rights as daughter and mother, the owner drew on a common strategy of couching economic behavior in terms of kin-based relations among traders, especially in southern Vietnam (Leshkowich 2014a). Traders invoke these relations not to claim "some essentialized core of Vietnamese-ness" but rather to respond pragmatically to economic and political circumstances both under socialism and within market-socialist regimes (79). This strategy, as Leshkowich argues, has its roots in socialist policies that restricted trade when gold and U.S. currency were classified as contraband and subject to confiscation by state agents. By framing their economic activities within the idiom of the family, traders appeared to endorse rather than challenge state-promoted ideals. As Leshkowich argues, "Familism was a key tool in traders' ongoing efforts to manage the shifting political economy of appearances surrounding their enterprises" (85). In this case the discourse of familism transformed gold from an alternative to the state-issued currency to a ceremonial gift and form of inheritance.

The raid on Hoàng Mai gold shop invoked the state-led separation between tradable goods and money. By drawing on familism, the owner conflated the commodity and gift (Gregory 1982, 1997; Carrier 2005). While gold was an indisputable "good" (Gregory 1997, 74) insofar as the owner justified her possession within terms of consanguinity, any good, as Gregory reminds his readers, can be converted into a "commodity" through various switching strategies. Traders were switch points in which gold as a good was converted into gold as money. But even switch points could be switched. By claiming that the gold and currency were "goods"—intergenerational wealth that should not have been subject to seizure— the owner switched her own gendered subjectivity from wayward trader to daughter and mother. While her strategy was successful, her claim of having inherited the gold triggered anxieties among ordinary citizens over the legitimacy of gold in Ho Chi Minh City's money economy.

GOLD AS MONEY

The raid on Hoàng Mai gold shop provided a stark reminder of the postwar years when people transacted with a devalued state-issued currency. Gold served as an asset or valuable with which people could hedge against the political and economic uncertainty in the 1980s. What spurred people's fears was not just the confusion over gold's classification as money or commodity but also that residents could be dispossessed of their gold. One commentator warned, "Don't even bother wearing gold because [you] could be questioned any time by the police" (Gia Minh 2014b). Here the commentator elides the state's classification scheme by insisting that wearing gold in public would leave one vulnerable to state-led dispossession.

Also at issue was documentation. The owner of the gold shop presented documents that attested to her inheritance. Most people who purchased gold did so without any formal receipt. The value of the gold, after all, was presumed to be in the physical properties of the bar itself, a value that could objectively be measured, tested, and weighed for verification. To be sure, each SJC bar carried a serial number that could allow its circulation to be traced, yet the bars wrapped in their plastic sleeves circulated as high-value coins, akin to U.S. hundred-dollar bills and five-hundred-thousand-đồng notes even though their price followed the spot markets in London and New York.

Despite gold's volatility on world markets, most people assigned its meaning through their acts of saving, not spending. One commentator attributed the newly implemented decree as burdening those savers who bought gold before the regulations were implemented: "My wife and I saved several months to buy two-tenths of a tael in case we fell ill or for our child's wedding. We didn't receive a receipt because at that time the state allowed people to freely trade [gold]. . . . Why do I have to produce evidence for property [*tài sản*] produced from my own sweat and blood in order for it not to be confiscated?" (Gia Minh 2014b). In this comment, the man described gold as a hedge to protect his family in the face of economic uncertainty and a financial instrument to pay for the wedding of his child. He decried the capriciousness of the new decree by pointing out that the new legislation retrospectively criminalized acts that had once been completely legal. Finally, he made a moral claim that the gold symbolized his "own sweat and blood," and so for the state to confiscate his gold would be a criminal act. What this comment and others left unexamined was the importance of gold shops like Hoàng Mai, which ensured the liquidity of even the smallest amounts of gold like his two-tenths of a tael.

It is not surprising that most commentators identified with the owner of the gold shop as an ordinary citizen and not as a trader. One commentator asked rhetorically, "Who does the money in my pocket belong to?" thus reinforcing the widespread perception that the raid exposed more than the state's management of the economy—it also revealed the state's power to seize people's property. The commentator then mused, "So some day the police can search my pockets, then force me to provide evidence that what's in my pocket is mine or else they confiscate it?" (A. H. 2014). The metaphor of carrying money in one's pocket has its origins in Karl Marx's ruminations about the social power of money. In Ho Chi Minh City, the image of state officials searching the pockets of citizens resurrected memories of the state's role after 1975 when houses were searched and property confiscated. Only later were gold and dollars elevated into quasi-official currencies as part of the state's market-oriented reforms, reaffirming the private power ascribed to money by Marx. The legal ban on holding dollars was lifted in 1988, and just three years later, banks began to mobilize people's savings by offering time deposits denominated in the foreign currency (Kovsted, Rand, and Tarp 2005, 23). Although state officials couched their justifications for the raid in the newly passed Decree 24, the raid triggered memories of dispossession associated with the city's postwar years, as attested by the viral spread of the video across Facebook and other social media immediately upon its posting.

Once the two domains of shop and household were conflated, commentators perceived their own vulnerability to having their wealth or assets seized. As one commentator noted, "It's really unreasonable, people keep gold in the house and suddenly, without permission, it's impounded and they become suspects, it doesn't make any sense if anyone who keeps gold in their house could become an object of inspection and suspicion, now does it?" (Gia Minh 2014b). Another commentator posed a series of rhetorical questions: "So all of the sudden I have to have proof that the money kept at home is mine, then what kind of proof? If I don't have proof, then the state can confiscate everything? If a car or house has paperwork, then what proof does money or gold have because Vietnamese people have long hoarded gold. This problem affects every gold shop and family" (Nguyễn Sa Linh 2014). Here the commentator juxtaposes cars and houses against gold and money, pointing out that ownership of the former is transferred through state-sanctioned documents but not of the latter. The fact that gold circulates but is not "registered" as property reinforces how its value resides in its exchange value. Its circulation facilitates economic transactions, standing apart from other commodities as (M) or "money" in Karl Marx's formula by which commodities and money are distinguished. But the commentator attributes the value of gold not to exchange but tradition: "Vietnamese people have long hoarded gold." The commentator notes that hoarding gold is a social practice that has led Vietnamese families to depend on gold shops, which provide the infrastructure of gold's social liquidity. By searching both the shop and the owner's residence, the police conflated these two spaces, allowing people to "see" the raid not as a means of enforcing regulations over foreign exchange but instead as encroaching on where people stored wealth: inside the household.

Not all the commentary focused on the vulnerability of ordinary citizens. Some remarks instead centered on how the widespread use of gold bars and foreign currency signaled the country's backwardness. One commentator wrote, "Acting this way is 'old' already," and expressed approval for Thailand, where foreign currency could not be used because it would corrupt the national body. To drive home the point, the commentator added, "Vietnam men just use 100 dollar bills to booze it up." This perspective could be identified as "state-centric," insofar as Decree 24 was promoted as a way of governing the country's money economy by ensuring that foreign currency and gold bars were confined to financial institutions rather than gold shops where they could corrupt society.

Let us return then to the strategy employed by the gold shop owner. She asserted her right to possess the gold bars and foreign currency by providing proof that these goods were handed down from her parents and gifted by her children, thereby anchoring her claims in her role as daughter and mother and domesticating gold within family relations rather than the marketplace. In doing so, she also erased her own role as trader, highlighting the precarious role of small-scale gold shops in Ho Chi Minh City but also engendering fears that any family who kept gold would be vulnerable to having its wealth confiscated. What did this raid portend for the thousands of gold shops around the country, whose operations followed the rhythms of daily life of ordinary citizens?

Precarious Traders

The raid on Hoàng Mai's gold shop made visible to Vietnamese audiences around the world that gold's status as a currency beyond the state's reach was under threat. Decree 24 attempted to demonetize gold by defining two distinct spheres in which gold would be bought and sold. The first sphere defined the circulation of gold bars (*vàng miếng*) to banks and several large gold producers, including the Saigon Jewelry Company. The second sphere, by contrast, was not authorized to sell SJC bars but was permitted to sell jewelry and other forms of adornment. These two spheres were spatially and conceptually separated insofar as gold of different forms would be bought and sold. Within the financial sphere, gold would be bought and sold as an investment asset, that is, something to be stored but no longer capitalized, whereas in the consumption sphere, gold would be bought and sold as adornment.

Yet the thrust of commentary about the raid focused on not the gold shops but rather the status of gold as a valuable or form of wealth. Gold in this light signified what anthropologist Jane Guyer has called "future transactional possibilities," whereby people preferred stores of value "that had greater longevity and security than the currencies themselves" (2004, 30). Decree 24 interrupted the very transactional pathways on which many Vietnamese savers had come to rely by exposing the precarious switch point of gold shops in the circulation of multiple currencies.

Shops like Hoàng Mai were being legislatively defined as outside or external to the country's payment infrastructure even though they had ensured the liquidity of gold in whatever form a seller possessed since the late 1980s. Gold was being reclassified from a highly liquid coin or money into a treasured good to be passed down over generations, a shift reinforced by the successful petition of the owner of Hoàng Mai gold shop to reclaim the currency and gold bars that had been seized. Her very success incited people's anxieties over how they could shield their possessions from state agents.

What was largely overlooked in the public discussion of the raid was the future of the country's loose network of ten thousand gold shops that maintained the social liquidity of gold. Economists, by contrast, had already cautioned that the new legislation would put upward pressure on the price of gold in Vietnamese markets. SJC bars were in hot demand as people holding non-SJC bars sought to exchange them for SJC bars. Banks, in turn, were required to return gold deposits. Even the manufacturing of SJC bars was slowed by the newly imposed regulation that the company had to solicit approval from the State Bank of Vietnam to import gold bullion. The domestic price for SJC bars in 2012–14 surpassed the world price of gold by as much as 20 percent.

Gold shops faced other pressures, including the changing preferences of Vietnamese consumers. As the price of gold on world markets surged, people shifted their demand from elaborate handcrafted jewelry sets made of pure gold to sets made of gold-plated jewelry wrapped around plastic tubing. Young adults no longer purchased jewelry made of 24-karat gold or the "four nine's," but "Italian jewelry," made by machines and costume jewelry that could be swapped out like ready-to-wear clothing. The decline in consumer demand contributed as well to a decrease in the number of young men who attended a vocational school in Ho Chi Minh City to learn the trade of goldsmithing. Not only were privately owned gold shops facing the changing preferences of Vietnamese consumers, but they also could no longer support the skilled artisans who would etch and cut finely wrought designs into soft pliable metal. In the face of these uncertainties over heightened state regulation, changing consumer tastes, and the volatility of the price of gold on world markets, it was not surprising that Nguyễn Thị Thanh Mai, the owner of the Hoàng Mai gold shop, announced that she would be closing her business for the rest of the year. She described her shock at the way the police conducted the raid: "They took all the property that my parents and my family had accumulated for so many years, so when they demanded to take it, I was unbelievably angry. Finally, they forced me to sign a report but meanwhile there was no information about the person who traded the dollars, so I filled out the documents and signed my name. Now I'm in a terrible state. I have already sent paperwork to the Tax Department of Bình Thạnh District informing them I will stop doing business through the end of 2014" (Gia Minh 2014c).

The raid on the gold shop demonstrated the vulnerability of gold traders, many of whom had accumulated their capital base over years of doing business in what had formerly been their legal position as intermediaries in the monetary ecosystem of Vietnam. When the owner of Hoàng Mai gold shop claimed, "They took all the property that my parents and my family had accumulated for so many years," she invoked the classical concept of a "good," or valuable that families withhold from circulation as an object that defines their social identities. Yet the property to which she referred was so highly valued because of its convertibility in the currency pathways of Ho Chi Minh City and despite her claim it was what she had been bequeathed and gifted, not what she had bought and sold (Gia Minh 2014c).

As we have seen, the owner invoked the logic of familism, which shielded her actions from being seen in purely entrepreneurial and commercial terms as a trader. But the raid had implications far wider than for her gold shop on a busy thoroughfare in Ho Chi Minh City. Rather, the raid exposed a reordering in the circulation of currency in which gold was no longer a quasi-currency but once again a good or valuable to be preserved and passed down as inheritance. While there is some evidence that suggests small gold shops and large manufacturers such as PNJ are producing gold rings as substitutes for bars, these objects do not have the ready-made exchange value embodied by the SJC tael that had been so effectively monetized. Still, by producing other objects, these gold companies resisted what was at stake in the government's regulations—that gold would no longer shield Vietnamese citizens from the state's control over managing money.

The state's hand in managing money cannot be fully understood outside the unexpected success of the SJC tael as an instrument of exchange, an investment asset, and even a pricing mechanism. It was not small-scale gold traders who put the wildly popular gold bars into circulation but the Ho Chi Minh City People's Committee that authorized the creation of SJC. As people throughout the country relied on these bars to price real estate and settle debts, Vietnam's money supply encompassed both formal financial institutions and informal ones. Gold shops, as we have seen, played a crucial role as payment intermediaries by providing liquidity and converting value initially under the auspices of credit institutions authorized by the State Bank of Vietnam. Eventually, gold as a pricing mechanism and as financial capital made the domestic economy highly vulnerable to the fluctuations of value on world markets. Even buyers eventually shunned gold bars as a means of pricing and settling debts because of its price instability. Decree 24 was the state's legislative attempt to constrain the power of gold by reducing its circulation and street-side convertibility into U.S. dollars and Vietnamese đồng.

The raid on Hoàng Mai gold shop offers a case study for understanding the policing of small-scale trade even though the changing place of SJC bars in the city's

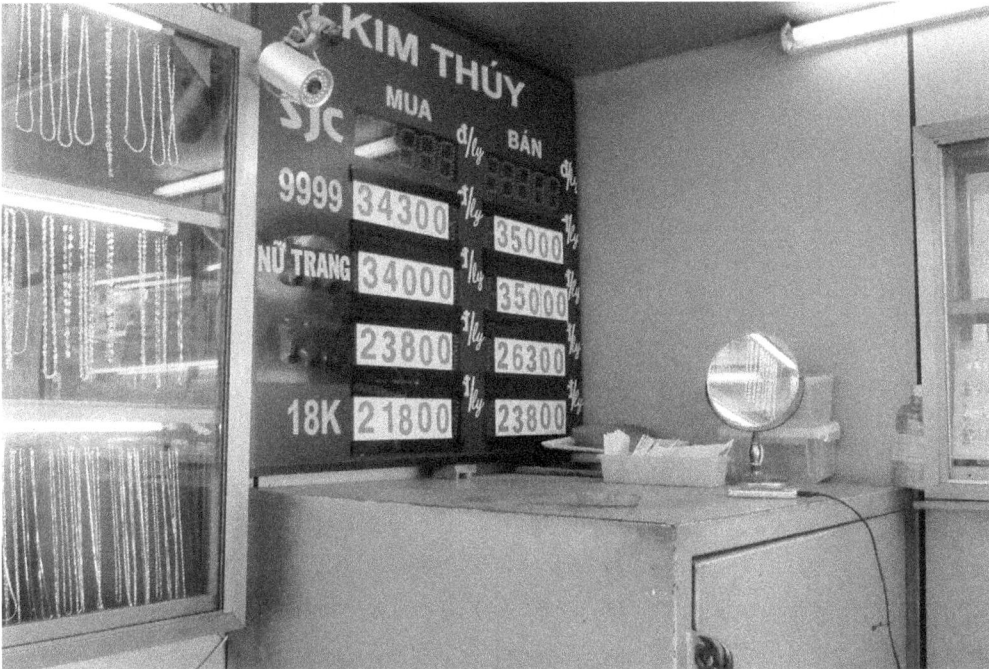

Figure 9.1 The buying and selling price for SJC bars (gold) is left blank on this list in a shop in District 5, Ho Chi Minh City, June 2013. Photograph by A. Truitt.

currency circulation was evident well before the raid. In the summer of 2013, price boards outside gold shops in Ho Chi Minh City advertised SJC bars, but the price was left blank as if their market value had momentarily been suspended (figure 9.1). It was still possible to purchase those bars in local gold shops, provided one asked the right person or inquired in the right way. By restricting gold shops from buying and selling these bars, the Vietnamese state effectively curtained the circulation of currency and restricted the social liquidity of both gold and dollars. And by doing so, the raid reminded ordinary citizens in Ho Chi Minh City that the state still controlled the pathways of gold's circulation.

NOTE

1 In summer 2013, I returned to Ho Chi Minh City in order to understand the effects of Decree 24 by interviewing the owners of small gold shops and residents. I was alerted to the raid by its posting on people's Facebook pages and subsequently collected articles about the raid in Vietnamese-language sources. For purposes of this analysis, I have not included the extensive comments posted about the video of the raid itself but rather those comments posted in response to the newspaper articles, which I argue serve as an imperfect proxy for responses to the raid by the urban middle class in Ho Chi Minh City.

CHAPTER TEN

MORALITIES OF COMMERCE IN A NORTHERN VIETNAMESE TRADING COMMUNITY

Esther Horat

It is almost a general rule that wherever we find agreeable manners, there commerce flourishes; and that wherever there is commerce, there we meet with agreeable manners.

—Montesquieu, *The Spirit of Laws*

Instead of being lauded for its booming clothing market, which has contributed to a strong local economy since 2002, the ancient Vietnamese trading village of Ninh Hiệp has been consistently vilified in media reports and become a symbolic target for journalists writing about the corrupting influence of money on society.[1] Traders from the village have been subject to criticism by the national press for what is seen as their rapid, and somewhat unearned, financial success, which is attributed to dishonest business practices. The traders have also come under fire for adopting spending patterns that do not always align with the state's preferred consumption practices. For instance, *Lao Động* (Vietnamese for "Labor"), a leading daily in the country, caused a considerable stir in Ninh Hiệp when two of its journalists decried the discarding of small bills of money by local children and the rampant demand for consumer goods such as smartphones, while education concerns had been neglected (An Nhiên and Nguyễn Trang 2013).[2] In short, traders in Ninh Hiệp are portrayed as money hungry, privileging the market over the pursuit of knowledge and higher education. Reinforced by proliferating media reports, this image of Ninh Hiệp is widely shared and reproduced in neighboring villages and in Hanoi.

The denigration of petty traders in the media and by scholars is not a new phenomenon in Vietnam. Traders, most of whom are women, have often been represented as uneducated and uncivilized as well as careless and greedy (see Leshkowich 2014a, 11–13, 81–82). One additional reason why traders across Vietnam have been vilified is that much of their merchandise (edible and nonedible) originates in China. These wares are usually cheaper than those produced in Vietnam and are said to not always meet Vietnam's safety regulations. Thus traders not only are able to make more profit with food and other goods of Chinese origin but also are perceived as threatening the domestic economy as well as the health of Vietnamese citizens. The fact that Ninh Hiệp traders are among the most vigorous in boosting Chinese imports is among several reasons for the negative attention they received in the media.

Although traders in Ninh Hiệp are deemed in state-owned media to be immoral, for them, morality (*đạo đức*), as a shared understanding about how things ought to be done, forms a core element of their actions. During my research, I came to understand the crucial role morality played in interactions among traders as well as between traders and customers. From an anthropological point of view, markets are not only sites of economic exchange but also social institutions in which moral evaluations and power relations are deeply embedded. As Roy Dilley contends, "The market represents a contested field of power and the moral evaluations attached to the agents and relations of exchange are a consequence of the processes of contestation" (1992, 4).

That morality and power relations are tightly enmeshed, as the preceding quote indicates, is also evident in the Vietnamese context. Traders in Vietnam were confronted with the issue of morality especially during the high socialist period (1954–86), as trade was considered unproductive and therefore an immoral activity. The seeming contradiction between the portrayals in newspaper articles of the Ninh Hiệp traders as being money oriented and their own perceptions of their having a strong moral fiber epitomizes this contestation.

This chapter sheds light on the complex intertwining of the economic and moral processes of transformation in Vietnam. While the emerging market opportunities in the aftermath of Đổi mới are widely embraced, an undertone of anxiety is present in daily conversations and media reports on the negative consequences of new capitalist relations, such as the corruption scandals of leading politicians or the rise of "social evils," ranging from drugs, gambling, and prostitution to theft and violence. Anxiety is primarily provoked not by the steep rise in wealth or its unequal distribution but by uncertainties about "how to be at once wealthy and good" (Jellema 2005, 235).

These concerns are vibrantly present in Ninh Hiệp, where traders responded rapidly to the new incentives of the socialist-oriented market economy. While they were often able to make a decent living pursuing commerce, they were also among the first to be cast as morally dubious. In the context of the state-led discourse that denigrates traders as immoral and undeservedly wealthy, Ninh Hiệp traders developed a specific set of moral values around which they produced their own local discourses and social practices. Declarations stressing that they sold at "fair price" did not just aim to counter state-propelled discourses that throw a bad light on them; they constitute a performance of very specific local identities. In this chapter, I examine the articulations of small-scale entrepreneurial morality in Ninh Hiệp. While building on earlier studies on moral subjectivities of petty traders in northern and southern Vietnam, I contribute to this topic by providing fresh empirical data on a contemporary peri-urban trading community in northern Vietnam. Interestingly, the research I conducted, almost thirty years after Đổi mới was first implemented, shows that the moral identities of petty traders had not changed much in spite of the country's socioeconomic transformation. Often, causality is assumed between a liberal economy and the freedom to make choices in production and consumption. Yet the downplaying of one's commercial activities as well as the moralizing about consumption practices to be found in Ninh Hiệp suggest a more complex relation between economic and moral change. Using the research data I collected over a twelve-month period (from October 2012 to September 2013) during my ethnographic fieldwork in Ninh Hiệp, I will discuss three local moral discourses—about honesty, patriotism, and peasantry—that are central in shaping traders' identities. These discourses are mainly a response to the media's criticism and are expressed toward customers in an attempt to restore their reputation. Presenting themselves as honest, traders emphasize their good business practices, for instance, by selling at a fair price so as to establish and maintain a reputation for trustworthiness. Traders echo the broader patriotic discourse of the "Buy Vietnamese" campaign, which aims to reduce dependency on other countries, particularly China. Finally, values typically associated with the peasantry, such as hard work, modesty, and community spirit, as well as a strong emphasis on agriculture, are subsumed under a "peasant discourse." Following Nguyễn-võ Thu-hương's (2008, xiv) argument that techniques of governance in Vietnam consist of the promotion of market freedom, on the one hand, and the employment of measures of repression, on the other, I analyze traders' performance of moral identities as a way of dealing with the ambiguous economic and political situation in which they find themselves.

The Village in the Market

As one approaches the Ninh Hiệp commune after an eighteen-kilometer ride on the main road from Hanoi to Bắc Ninh province and then takes a smaller road that runs along paddy fields and leads to the village, one easily recognizes the rural character of the place. Lining both sides of the road approaching the village gate are clothing shops displaying the latest fashion trends. This road leads straight to the old market in the center of the village. The closer one gets, the more crowded and noisier it becomes, especially at the front and side of the old market, where vendors and customers on motorbikes jam the narrow streets. The old market, also known as Nành market, used to be an aggregation of temporary stalls selling fabric before it was turned into a permanent market after extensive renovation in 2001 and 2002. In addition, the old market was enlarged when a second market hall was built adjoining it and took on a different character when the stalls in the original section of the market hall were given canopies after their absorption into the market building. In the original section, the aisles are like mazes and the roof is low, making it unbearably hot during the summer months. The other, newer part is much more spacious, with a higher roof and aisles running parallel to one another. In both sections, the stalls are tiny and offer just enough space for vendors to sit on their merchandise or on small plastic chairs in front of their stall. At the time I conducted my research, the old market accommodated 1,125 stalls all together. Opposite the old market are two privately owned, multistory markets that were established in 2011. Although there is some market activity there, they are not as busy as the old market. The stalls here are bigger than the ones in the old market and have enough room for customers to be invited in. Instead of the merchandise lying in a pile, clothes are displayed on mannequins or hung on hangers to attract potential customers. Since these stalls have iron shutters, the stalls can be locked at night. The aisles between the stalls are large enough for transport carts to deliver the merchandise directly to the stalls. Many traders in Ninh Hiệp agree that the new markets seem modern, and some say that they are beautiful and convenient, but almost all of them fault the new markets for lacking the usual hustle and bustle of customers.

Even though Ninh Hiệp has been famous for its cloth trade for centuries, the decades following Đổi mới, and especially the last few years, have contributed much to its reputation as a center for textiles. Since the expansion of the marketplace in 2002, it became the biggest wholesale fabric market in northern Vietnam and one of the main suppliers of textiles nationwide. Trade flourishes not only in Ninh Hiệp but across the whole of Vietnam. This is partly a result of the state's efforts to encourage the development of marketplaces. The renovation and "upgrade" of markets has become as common in rural as in urban areas. In the face of this enormous marketization process, traders are confronted with two main challenges. First, they are often faced with the risk of losing their source of income when markets undergo transformations that are geared toward privatization and, second, traders have to reconcile conflicting ideas about (relative) wealth and morality. These concerns are also present in Ninh Hiệp, where most traders are enjoying a significantly higher standard of living than they were just a few years ago, thanks to the growth of the local economy, which, again, makes the place very attractive for new private market projects. The moral discourses of Ninh Hiệp traders can be seen as a way of addressing these tensions and dealing with an environment riddled with economic and moral uncertainties.

SMALL-SCALE ENTREPRENEURIAL MORALITY IN VIETNAM

During her research in Ninh Hiệp in the 1990s, just as trade was mushrooming as a consequence of the economic opening, Regina Abrami (2002a) noticed a rhetorical insistence by merchants on downplaying the magnitude of their commercial transactions and their connection to trade and commerce, as they instead preferred to continually refer to themselves as peasants. As she points to traders' emphasis on their small scale and the economic insignificance of their businesses, she wonders why the economic transformation did not result in a change of identity. She then analyzes this phenomenon in light of the legacy of socialism, suggesting that traders use the norms of a socialist economy to make moral claims upon the state. By adopting the label *small traders*, merchants hope to keep the state regulators at a distance, in order to be able to accumulate wealth. Ann Marie Leshkowich (2014a), who conducted ethnographic research among small-scale traders in Bến Thành market in Ho Chi Minh City in the 1990s, made similar observations about merchants' tendency to highlight the small scale of their businesses. Struck by the traders' adoption of an essentialist notion of petty trade as insignificant, marginal, and backward, Leshkowich set out to understand how particular forms of essentialism may be meaningful for creating certain identities and making room for agency. She thus argues that female stallholders strategically use these essentialist depictions of the petty trader to develop their businesses away from the gaze of the state. As she explains, trade in Vietnam in the 1990s was "an act of speculation" (20–21), because the development of market socialism was in its early stages and traders were not sure if they would need protection when engaging in commerce. Therefore, narrating and performing an identity that resembled the official stereotype was a strategy to avoid attracting attention while making considerable profit. Interestingly, as traders in the Bến Thành market played down the issue of how wealth was produced, their consumption practices were aimed at upgrading their lifestyles and buttressing their ability to belong to the middle class. Ashley Pettus elaborates on the ethics of small-scale traders, simply referring to them as having a "*buôn bán* ethic" (2003, 186–89).[3] She differentiates moral subjectivities between two generations of women merchants in Hanoi: while elderly traders portrayed themselves as the bearers of the authentic *buôn bán* ethic—the most important of which is to be honest and trustworthy—younger generations of women strategically used the *buôn bán* ethic with customers, but they admitted to the researcher that if they were honest, they would not be able to make a profit. Pettus also found that older generations of traders tended to emphasize the economic insignificance of trade and referred to it as an extension of their domestic responsibilities. Younger women, in contrast, did not define their selling activities as unimportant but rather stressed

Figure 10.1 Market bustle close to Ninh Hiệp´s old market. Photograph by E. Horat.

the challenge of meeting the contesting demands of family and business, especially their duty to support the family financially.

Comparing these three accounts from different marketplaces in Vietnam, it is striking that all three authors emphasize petty traders' attempts to create a moral identity as a "business strategy" that often included playing down the economic relevance of trade. Interestingly, Ninh Hiệp traders also stress the importance of moral principles when doing business and portray themselves as "small people." However, as the accounts below demonstrate, their moral identity is shaped partly by local notions of what it means to be a good person and partly by pragmatic business considerations.

Discourse of the Honest Trader

To start with, Ninh Hiệp is known as a place where bargaining is rarely practiced, and goods are sold at the "right price" (*giá đúng*). Traders emphasize this to potential customers at every opportunity and declare they are honest (*thật thà*) and upright. What the right price is, that is, how much profit is legitimate, is a crucial, yet highly complex question.[4] In political economic literature, a just price is often viewed in relation to the labor and costs involved in the production process, as in Marx's labor theory of value, while in capitalist societies prices are usually set in relation to demand. In the present context, a just price seems to imply that it is enough to make a living but not necessarily to enrich oneself. As Richard Tawney (1961, 44) noted long ago, a level of wealth acquired to sustain one's livelihood was legitimate, but more than that pointed to avarice.

One day in Ninh Hiệp, as I was talking to an elderly villager about attitudes toward wealth, he recited the maxim written on one of the pillars of the old market gate to stress the importance of virtue and morality.[5] More than once, he used the term "civilized commerce" (*thương nghiệp văn minh*) in this context: "By selling at a fair price and delivering goods reliably, Ninh Hiệp traders create trust and prestige. This reputation [of civilized trade] is one decisive reason why Ninh Hiệp market is able to attract so many customers from all over Vietnam" (interview, June 13, 2013).

To sell at the right price is relevant not only in situations involving customers from outside the community but also in deals made among traders within the community. When I asked a young trader from whom she usually buys cloth for her production site, she answered, "I buy the kind of fabrics I like [patterns, colors], it doesn't matter from whom. It's the same price everywhere. I know the prices. If it's different, I don't buy it" (informal conversation, March 3, 2013). Thus, "the right price" represents a careful balance between what is considered appropriate by both customers and other traders. Customers should not be excessively overcharged, and it is also important to respect what the majority of traders in the community perceive to be the right price, so that as stall neighbors they do not engage in price wars and instead adjust to the dynamics of competition in the marketplace. Stealing each other's customers is not considered appropriate behavior.

In fact, forging and maintaining relationships underpinned by shared sentiments (*quan hệ tình cảm*) is very important for traders, especially for those in nearby stalls and for those who interact on a daily basis. Often in the afternoon, when business is not that brisk, they sit together and chat, play cards, share food and drinks, and help each other prepare vegetables for dinner. The popular Vietnamese saying "*Buôn có bạn, bán có phường*" (Trading is done among a group of friends) serves as an instructive reminder that trade is as much an economic activity as it is a social practice that is deeply woven into the web of community life. In the conviviality of the group, traders share information and support one another. Conflicts or tensions do not figure prominently in the marketplace or are prevented from spilling into it. The few conflicts I encountered broke out between traders and customers when the latter tried to steal something or between traders when one had copied the other's clothing designs. An elderly trader used the metaphor of a bowl of rice for the market (*chợ như bát cơm*). With that she meant that the market had to feed everybody and served as a means of subsistence for the whole community, thereby implying that a strong sense of fairness and equality persisted among traders.[6]

Inherent in this discourse is the belief that the "morally good" begets what can be considered "economically good."[7] The wife of the villager I cited at the beginning of this section shared her experiences from the time when she was a trader: "It is important for traders to remain true to their skills [*bản lĩnh*], abilities [*khả năng*] and level of knowledge [*trình độ hiểu biết*] instead of copying others. In Ninh Hiệp, unlike other villages, insiders and outsiders are not differentiated.[8] Everybody can come and do business. If one is serious-minded [*đứng đắn*] and does business in a true [*chân chính*] and legitimate [*chính đáng*] way, the business will be successful. If one is not serious, the business will fail. We have seen both cases here many times" (interview, June 19, 2013).

Acting in accordance with and respecting moral values is perceived as enhancing one's trustworthiness, which then becomes the basis for generating the kind of individual success the trading community desires. It is not my intention to invoke the myth of a perfectly harmonious moral community but to put forth the idea that sharing and self-interest are both part of actual community solidarity.[9] In this sense, morality helps traders navigate between competition and cooperation. The following statement, made by the same trader as above, explains its value and wisdom: "It is not that traders are just gentle, but they imitate each other in the way they do business. Customers don't buy from hot-tempered and sharp-tongued vendors but from the ones who treat them in a nice way" (interview, July 11, 2013).

Ninh Hiệp traders explained that it was as important to be trustworthy as it was to be gentle and serious. In their perception, the market could have expanded in that measure only because people in the community trusted each other and lent money to one another. To borrow money from the bank is complicated and inefficient, whereas the informal banking system in the community is able to respond quickly to the needs of traders. However, this system works only as long as traders treat each other fairly and repay their debts, because such transactions cannot be legally enforced. Assurances of honesty thus serve as important business strategies not only with customers but also with other traders as assurances that all can get fair portions from the bowl of rice that is the marketplace.

The Patriotic Trader

Stimulated by the increasing political tensions between China and Vietnam, the image of the patriotic trader has taken on immense importance in the moral discourse. In the early years of socialism, petty traders were categorized as patriotic laborers and organized into commercial cooperatives in line with the state's aim to use their contribution to "serve production" by providing supply inputs through state purchasing channels (Abrami 2002a, 95–96). Even if the situation has changed considerably with Đổi mới, as private trade is allowed and traders no longer work for a commercial cooperative, traders continue to identify with patriotic values on many levels, such as acting for the good of a collective at the local level or contributing to the national cause by selling domestic instead of foreign products. Propelling this discourse is also the so-called Buy Vietnamese campaign, launched by the Ministry of Industry and Trade together with the Ministry of Information and Communications in 2009 (Ly 2014). As the name suggests, Vietnamese products have to be given preference over foreign, especially Chinese, goods. In addition to quality concerns (particularly safety when it comes to food), the campaign has clear economic and political intentions, which are to strengthen the domestic economy and reduce dependence on imports. Sometimes, the campaign is referred to as "Be Vietnamese Buy Vietnamese"—a clear hint that the campaign is also morally charged, in that buying and selling Vietnamese products is considered "good," while giving preference to Chinese goods symbolizes betrayal of the Vietnamese nation. The impact of the campaign on the shopping habits of consumers should not be underestimated, at least when domestically produced goods are available and affordable. For example, in June 2014, buyers boycotted Ninh Hiệp traders for several days as a way to penalize them for selling Chinese instead of Vietnamese clothes.[10]

Ninh Hiệp's markets have the reputation of being dominated by made-in-China clothes—so much so that collectively they are referred to as the "hypermarket for Chinese apparel" (*đại siêu thị may mặc Trung Quốc*). This is not without reason, as the majority of clothes are cheap, low-quality imports from Guangzhou. The association between Ninh Hiệp's markets and Chinese goods was evident in my own personal interactions while conducting fieldwork. On one occasion, after having explained to a Vietnamese friend that my research was devoted to Ninh Hiệp's traditional cloth market, she suggested in a somewhat chastising manner that I should go to China instead if I was interested in Chinese trade. This was by no means an isolated incident during my time in Vietnam outside the village. Nearly all my interlocutors in Hanoi knew about Ninh Hiệp's wholesale market, and almost everybody mentioned, at least as a side note or an afterthought, the visible predominance of Chinese goods. Yet in light of the complicated and emotionally charged relationship with China in the past, as well as today, these are not neutral and casual comments but, rather, harsh criticism. Therefore, political propaganda and the heightened awareness of the readiness of the people and the traders to adapt to these requests (or at least pretending to do so) have supported the emergence of the discourse of the patriotic trader.

This discourse is also linked to the discourse of the honest trader, in that traders are expected to provide clear information about the country of origin of their merchandise. Even though the campaign has already been in full swing for a few years now, only the recent rise in the popularity of made-in-Vietnam clothes has had a decisive impact on Ninh Hiệp traders to prioritize home production.[11] Some traders take this step very seriously and invite potential customers to their production site in order to provide proof of the country of origin of their garments. However, not everybody owns production facilities. And for traders who do not have the means to improve their economic strategy, the "right to survive" weighs more heavily than does their patriotic duty to comply with the motto "Buy and Sell Vietnamese." Driven by its own moral logic, the "right to survive" may challenge the discourse of the patriotic trader.

This discourse touches upon two important points. One is the dilemma of navigating conflicting demands and choosing between contrasting moral values, epitomized here by the decision to make a living for oneself and one's family or being a "good citizen" and supporting the national cause. The other point, going back to the introductory section of this chapter, is that morality is a core aspect of state-led campaigns.

THE PEASANT TRADER

In addition to these two specific trade-related discourses, there is a third, more general moral discourse related to images of the peasantry. Many traders speak of farming as their main occupation and trading as an ancillary activity. This statement may seem paradoxical at first glance, in view of the fact that most traders use hired help to work their fields and, in turn, dedicate most of their time to trade, which is their main source of income.

This rhetorical insistence on magnifying one's agricultural roots instead of aligning with one's trading pursuits falls in line with what Regina Abrami (2002a, 102) encountered while conducting her fieldwork in this very village in the late 1990s. Based on her own observations, she argues that this narrative is part of the socialist legacy of production and virtuous labor. By framing trading activities as tangential to an agricultural household, the focus is shifted to productivity rather than gain. Abrami explains traders' continuous emphasis on the smallness of their businesses by pointing to the fact that ideas of the socialist economy have not completely disappeared, and that wealth as such is not glorified in Vietnam, as if to preserve social unity.

A crucial yet seemingly oppositional dimension of this rhetoric is to refer to trade as the traditional occupation of the village (*nghề truyền thống của làng*) in order to emphasize stability and continuity and, at the same time, to render it legitimate. Yet the rhetoric of continuing the village tradition of selling at the market conceals the actual extent and form of contemporary trade, the major part of which is dealing with Chinese textiles and garments for wholesale.

Another aspect of manifesting historicity—which is typical for long-standing craft and trading villages—lies in the way people in Ninh Hiệp highlight the rich history and culture of their village. Not only have a multitude of officially recognized historical sites been maintained until the present day, villagers also remember a number of famous scholars from the village, whose names are inscribed on the steles at the Temple of Literature in Hanoi.[12] The appreciation for Ninh Hiệp's culture is expressed in poems and songs composed by the local villagers. Similarly, education is highly valued, as demonstrated by the initiative taken by some elderly people to teach Nôm to children, but also by an incident that transpired in January 2014, when the plan to launch a privately funded market project on the secondary school premises at the village center was announced.[13] As the project required the school to be relocated to the periphery of the village to make space for the construction of yet another market, hundreds of villagers appeared before the commune's People's Committee in protest.[14] That the planned market would displace the school was perceived as unacceptable, because it openly degraded education and privileged private over public interests. This event contradicts the concerns generally voiced by journalists, since the planned market project clearly does not reflect the villagers' but rather the state's interest in furthering the marketization process in the commune.

The emphasis on hard work and making "just enough" to make ends meet is also part of this discourse. A sentiment I often heard from traders was that "trading makes just enough money for the daily vegetables and fish sauce" (*buôn bán thế này chỉ đủ tiền rau mắm hàng ngày thôi*). As for their external appearance, an inconspicuous style is seen as appropriate. Wearing dresses, high heels, makeup, and jewelry at the village marketplace is frowned upon and therefore never, or only very rarely, found there.

Finally, villagers strongly emphasize Ninh Hiệp's rural character by contrasting it with that of Hanoi, although Ninh Hiệp is located in Gia Lâm district and thus formally belongs to Hanoi. For instance, villagers often stress the importance of social relations and solidarity, as in the following statement made by an elderly villager: "This is the countryside. Activities are still carried out with community spirit [*tính cộng đồng*], unlike in urban centers, where 'nobody cares when the neighbor's house burns down' [*cháy nhà hàng xóm thì bình chân như vại*]. It's not like this in the countryside. If something happens, people gather to ask and care for each other. The community relations [*quan hệ cộng đồng*] are tighter [than in cities]" (interview, June 13, 2013).

Even though Ninh Hiệp is a trading village, its reference point is the capital city of Hanoi, which is perceived as urban and modern, while Ninh Hiệp is considered "not modern" (*không hiện đại*). A young woman trader in the old market said, "People in Ninh Hiệp think about money in a traditional way, they don't know how to spend it. Most villagers don't like to go to a café because they consider it a waste [of time and money]." She then continued by pointing to the discrepancy, as she perceived it, between money and modernity in the village: "Although iPhones are common nowadays, we still wear jeans, not dresses [*nhưng mà làm gì có iphone mặc váy, vẫn iphone mặc quần bò*]" (interview, June 25, 2013), referring to the different dress codes in the city and the countryside.

The tension between gaining wealth and simultaneously maintaining traditional customs was an issue often raised in my conversations with the villagers. While young people tended to be more concerned with consumption and modernity, like the trader just mentioned, elderly people often brought up the question of values and the meaning of a good society. Moral anxiety and the fear of bad habits indirectly framed these conversations, as in the statement of an elderly villager: "The economy is developing too fast, society has no time to accommodate these changes" (*kinh tế phát triển quá nhanh, xã hội không có kịp theo*). Danièle Bélanger, Lisa B. Welch Drummond, and Van Nguyen-Marshall have noted that "middle classness seems to have become very effectively normalized as simply 'modern,' and takes in a wide swathe of urban citizens" (2012, 9). Constructing a "traditional" village identity that relies heavily on community relations—as is the case in Ninh Hiệp—signals a rejection of urban middle-class consumerism, which traders deem immoral because it contradicts some of their basic values. Thus, drawing an ideological, and ultimately moral, demarcation line between one's own village and the perceived Other remains a common modality for self-identification. The discourse of the peasant trader illustrates this point by revealing contrasting juxtapositions—agriculture versus commerce, rural versus urban, solidarity versus anonymity, and tradition versus modernity. Like the two discourses described above, this discourse is also built into everyday encounters between traders and other village inhabitants yet gains in importance in the exchanges between traders and customers or other people from outside the village.

MORAL MODERNITIES

Abrami (2002a) makes a valid point when acknowledging the powerful legacy of ideas of the socialist economy. Yet in addition to the legacy of the past, the paradox of the current configuration of a market economy under the guidance of a socialist state evokes confusion about how to be wealthy and moral at the same time. As Helle Rydstrøm has observed, this leads to the creation of "new moral in-between spaces" (2009, 118). In a similar vein, Elizabeth Vann pointed out that the lines between moral and immoral behavior have become less clear in the Đổi mới era (2012, 164). Nguyễn-võ Thu-hương takes the argument one step further, suggesting that this moral uncertainty, provoked by the "government's simultaneous use of freedom and tradition," is a contemporary way of governing (2008, xx).

In the case of Ninh Hiệp, a similar line of reasoning is palpable. By claiming the moral authority to publicly criticize certain people or groups of people as immoral, state representatives seek to render their own actions legitimate. Framed as enhancing the process of "modernity" and "civilization," market projects come under the banner of promoting a "good life." However, the rhetorical praise for the market projects conceals an awareness of the fact that they may strengthen social inequalities and even undermine other publicly celebrated values, such as education in the case of Ninh Hiệp. Furthermore, the aforementioned market project also heavily works to the detriment of the local people, as not only the school was going to be relocated, but also the parking lot of the old market. Traders at the old market worry that if customers cannot park their motorbikes next to the market but are forced to park them more than one kilometer away, they will stop coming to the old market and instead go to a market with a parking lot. Therefore, the relocation of the parking lot is expected to result in a decline in the number of customers and eventually might cause the old market to close down.

This case also reflects the various ideas and perceptions of modernity in a trading community in northern Vietnam. While elderly people display fear of change and associate "modernity" with commodification and a possible loss of meaningful social relations, young people tend to emphasize new opportunities, an enhanced standard of living, and freedom of choice. From the state's perspective, modernity is captured in the official slogan "Wealthy people, strong country, equal and civilized society." In practice, this implies a broad range of measures to develop and "civilize" the country, the primary focus of which is not poverty alleviation or sustainably securing livelihoods, but, rather, creating, tapping into, and satisfying the demands of emerging middle- and upper-middle-class consumers. While Ninh Hiệp was celebrated as a success shortly after Đổi mới because of the rapid growth of its local economy, it is now faulted for not being modern enough. Privately invested market projects—some planned for the near future, others already realized in the past few years—are thus envisioned as a means to transform Ninh Hiệp into a "civilized" place of commerce. Here again, perceptions of the local people and the state differ: while villagers speak of "civilized trade" as a particular set of business moralities, for the state it is a stage in the development process that is related to ideas of orderliness and cleanliness.

In contrast to the Bến Thành market traders in Leshkowich's (2014a) study, Ninh Hiệp traders rejected middle-class consumer practices and instead chose to reproduce the same peasant discourse that Abrami (2002a) observed in the 1990s. While the peasant discourse is distinctly strong among elderly traders, young people also contribute to it, but with a slight resentment, because for them, rather than connote the perils of corruption or bad social behavior, modern life brings the promise of new opportunities and a lifestyle many find desirable. Living in Ninh Hiệp and working at the market, they find themselves deprived of fully participating in what they consider a "modern life." Thus, the notion of generation-specific moral subjectivities that Pettus (2003) suggested seems highly relevant to the case of Ninh Hiệp. Furthermore, the strategic use of a particular moral identity, as suggested by Leshkowich as well as by Abrami and Pettus, is also a crucial feature I observed in my research. While Ninh Hiệp traders adopt parts of the essentialist notions of a petty trader in their self-representation, insisting that commercial pursuits were insignificant and only a side occupation of a household, they reject the idea that they are dishonest and immoral. By being—or appearing to be—honest, patriotic traders who uphold the values of the peasantry, Ninh Hiệp traders strive to create a good reputation so as to attract customers as well as to navigate their way around the inquiring gaze of the state. In certain moments, for example, when plans for new private market projects are announced, this identity is used as a strategy to make moral claims upon the state by invoking the right to make a living.

The similarity in the moral discourses and performances of identity among traders between the 1990s and 2010s is striking, considering the thorough socioeconomic transformation Vietnam has undergone in the past three decades. However, instead of understanding these discourses as part of the socialist legacy, I suggest seeing traders' emphasis on honesty, patriotism, and peasantry as an appropriate strategic response to a current political economic context that creates situations of moral uncertainty. A close look at the status of trade then and now shows that trade went from being a risky activity, or "an act of speculation," as Leshkowich (2014a, 20–21) referred to it, to an activity that in most of its forms does not conform to the state's vision of development and modernity. Although commerce is one of the most common ways to earn a living in Vietnam, it does not enjoy a high standing, except in its professionalized— and more easily controllable—form of an enterprise. As I have shown, morality is also an important element of governance and is sometimes used ambiguously. While state media condemn Ninh Hiệp villagers for what is perceived as immoral behavior and for their corruptibility, the marketization process in the commune, evinced by the emergence of new market projects, proceeds. Thus, morality remains a core matter of national and local concern and is the sum of coexisting, but also contesting and ambivalent, norms and practices.

NOTES

This chapter is based on chapter 8 of my book, *Trading in Uncertainty: Entrepreneurship, Morality, and Trust in a Vietnamese Textile-Handling Village* (Cham, Switzerland: Springer International, 2017). Reproduced with permission of Palgrave Macmillan.

1 All print and broadcast media of Vietnam—radio, television and newspapers—are state owned, and thus opinions expressed are considered to represent state entities.

2 The journalists also write that civil servants are not respected because they don't earn as much as traders and that sometimes there was a shortage of teachers, because they sold at the market, too. As a final remark they write that men only eat and play with their friends and that never in their life had they seen men as disengaged as in Ninh Hiệp.

3 *Buôn bán* means "trading," usually in the form of small-scale trade. When using the term *buôn bán*, Pettus emphasizes its cultural meaning, implying that it refers to informal "women's work" (180).

4 Paul Alexander (1992, 91) put forth the point that a fair price is difficult to calculate because the notion of cost is also culturally constituted. Examinations of the "just price" have a long history, beginning with Aristotle and continuing on with Thomas Aquinas, Karl Marx, E. P. Thompson, and newer proponents of the moral economy approach. As Chris Gregory stated, "The theory of moral economy is the theory of the just price" (2012, 394).

5 Originally: "*Nhi tác nhi tức ẩm hòa thực đức, dư túc dư bố dịch vụ thông công*" (Working and resting, eating and drinking, is all done virtuously; trading and farming, buying and selling, of which the essence is fairness) (author's translation).

6 This bears a close resemblance to Cristina Szanton Blanc's (1972) findings at a fish market in the Philippines, where she came across a strong emphasis on the "right to survive," in the sense that every vendor had to be able to make a living.

7 This is reminiscent of the "gentleman's path" that Richard Lufrano (1997, 113–26) describes in his study on merchants in late imperial China. Instruction manuals written for merchants emphasized the value of acting virtuously and morally. Traders should prove to be reliable and hospitable as well as flexible, generous, trustworthy, and confidential. Kirsten Endres (2015b) makes a similar point in the context of contemporary Vietnam, arguing that economic success among small-scale traders is seen as the result of fate, fortune, and self-cultivation. In a similar vein, Ann Marie Leshkowich (2012, 101–3) stresses the importance of the concept of Buddhist fate among traders, who must use their individual skills and talents to cultivate virtue in order to achieve business success.

8 Usually, Vietnamese villages differentiate between resident population (*dân bản địa, dân gốc*) and migrant population ((*dân nhập cư, dân ngụ cư*), or, as Hy Van Luong suggested, between "insiders" (*nội tịch*) and "outsiders" (*ngoại tịch*)). After three generations, people who came as migrants can claim residential status and are thereby granted all rights and duties of the residential population (Luong 2010).

9 According to James Ferguson (2014, 119), "communal solidarity" is built neither solely on altruism nor on asocial calculation but consists of a range of differently motived acts.

10 This boycott must be seen in light of the particularly tense relationship between Vietnam and China resulting from the territorial dispute that was very intense during those weeks.

11 It should be mentioned that the bulk of cloth used to sew clothes in the village is also imported from China, with only a minor segment imported from other countries, such as Thailand, Korea, and Japan, and sometimes, from southern Vietnam.

12 The Temple of Literature (Văn Miếu), established in 1076, contains the Imperial Academy (Quốc Tử Giám), the first university in Vietnam.

13 Nôm is the Vietnamese language based on Chinese characters preceding the usage of the Latin script.

14 Because the Hanoi's People Committee advocates the project, the commune's People's Committee cannot defy the decision. The project was scheduled for completion in 2016. For more information, see Phương Sơn 2014; Tuấn Hợp 2014.

CHAPTER ELEVEN

FUEL TRADE: PEOPLE, PLACES, AND TRANSFORMATIONS ALONG THE COAL BRIQUETTING CHAIN

Annuska Derks

One of the challenging things in anthropological research is to make sense of the experiences of encounters, observations, or activities that, at first sight, do not seem to make sense, that demand explanation. It is through this search for explanations that we try to come to "insights into the world behind everyday appearances" (O'Connor 2011, 2). In my research on an ordinary, everyday cooking fuel, the beehive coal briquette (*than tổ ong*), I encountered such experience when visiting a People's Committee of an urban district of Hanoi. After I introduced the topic of my research and my intention to conduct research in this particular district, the vice chairman's first reaction was that the residents of this district do not use the coal briquette anymore because they do not consider it to be a convenient fuel for urban life. He explained that people stopped using the coal briquette because of the lack of space in new urban housing, because neighbors may complain about the smell and pollution, and because people have now the means to use other fuels. There had not been any particular regulations prohibiting the use of coal briquettes, but social forces had pushed the coal briquette out of the city to the outskirts. I already feared that the vice chairman actually meant to tell me that it would be no use—and that he would therefore not agree—to conduct research on the beehive coal briquette in this part of the city. Yet, to my surprise, he turned to the other delegates in the room and asked how they could support my research. A week later, I was brought to half a dozen coal briquette production sites and introduced to several food stall owners and users in that district—all of which revealed to me the prevalence of the coal briquette in this part of town.

Why is it that the coal briquette is so obviously present and at the same time denied as being there? This small anecdote illustrates how the beehive coal briquette is, on the one hand, omnipresent in the back alleys, at food stalls, on the back of the (motor)bikes of vendors, and in production sites distributed all over town and, on the other hand, considered to be something out of place—an object that should not be there anymore. The latter is above all related to the idea that the beehive coal briquette does not go well with the image of Hanoi as a modern city that is, as is written in billboards all over town, *xanh, sạch, đẹp* (green, clean, beautiful). In fact, it embodies the very opposite, namely, an outmoded fuel that is black, dirty, and ugly (Derks 2015a, 343). So where does this put those who continue to make, sell, and use coal briquettes?

In this chapter, I focus on the trade chain of this everyday, but increasingly shunned, cooking fuel. I am particularly interested in the interlinkages between people, things, and places in the coal briquette chain. Cooking on coal requires some kind of outdoor place, distributing briquettes involves movement between places, while producing coal briquettes entails a constant struggle to keep one's place, physically as well as in the market for cooking fuels—thus leading to questions about the use of urban space and the networks of people in different places. In contrast to what occurs in most commodity chain studies, here I will trace the journey of the coal briquette backward, from the kitchens in which it is used, to the trolley in which it is

Figure 11.1. "Out of place?" A vendor delivers beehive coal briquettes in Hanoi. Photograph by A. Derks.

transported, and to the production site in which it is made, highlighting the contestations over spaces in which the coal briquette is made, transported, sold, and used. The example of the trajectory of this particular commodity illustrates well how the dynamics and networks of small-scale commercial activities are inherently linked to the changing uses and meanings of place and space in urban Vietnam. By analyzing how an object and its trade have come to be seen as out of place, this chapter at the same time sheds light on the everyday practices and perceptions underlying social inequalities in contemporary Vietnamese society.

PEOPLE, THINGS, AND PLACES

The stove in front of a house, the bicycle or trolley with briquettes weaving through the streets, the briquetting press in a workshop, all invoke images of things in particular spaces and to particular uses of that space, or what Lefebvre referred to as social space. Lefebvre (1991) famously proposed that space is socially produced and affects everyday practices and perceptions. Space, as Gottdiener argues, is "an important concept because the built environment, including both production and consumption spaces, is critical to the transformation of everyday life" (1994, xv).

I examine these tangled linkages between the transformation of everyday life and the transformation of (the uses of) space through a study of the chain of production, distribution, and consumption of an ordinary cooking fuel. Starting in the kitchen, I ask: What is considered to be an appropriate place to cook? How does this affect the choice of fuel? How does the fuel arrive in the kitchen? By what means and routes? And where does the briquette come from? Where is it produced and by whom? Answering these questions requires a consideration of how the trajectory of coal briquettes is connected to specific places as well as to the networks of people who make, transport, and use the briquettes.

The tracing of the trajectory of a product from its origins, through production, retailing, and final consumption has been the hallmark of various strands of commodity chain studies (Leslie and Reimer 1999, 404). By focusing on the circulation of commodities, commodity chain studies reveal hidden connections between production and consumption regimes in places widely separated by distance and culture (Collins 2000, 98). Yet, as Leslie and Reimer (1999, 402) argue, commodity chain studies should focus not only on how commodities move through space but also on how their production, distribution, and consumption are shaped by and produce space and place.

While there has been quite some attention to the production of space in the Vietnamese context, most studies relate to housing projects and commercial, leisure, or monumental spaces in an urban context (Thomas 2002; Waibel 2006; Labbé and Boudreau 2011). These studies describe how urbanites have, after introduction of the market-oriented reforms in the late 1980s, increasingly occupied urban space for commercial and leisure activities. In the process, boundaries between public and private have, as Drummond (2000, 2383) points out, blurred as urbanites perform in public spaces some of the most basic and intimate activities, such as eating, cooking, bathing, sleeping, and, for young couples at night time, cuddling. At the same time, there is also a tendency to try to control and regulate urban space according to notions of a modern, "beautiful, breathable, and orderly city" (Harms 2012, 735). In this context, certain things and activities are now considered to be out of place.

One of these things is the beehive coal briquette. The beehive coal briquette was introduced in Vietnam in the mid-1980s as an alternative to wood fuel. While initiated and promoted by the state sector, the beehive coal briquette became an immensely popular household cooking fuel in the 1990s because of the growing number of private producers and their vendors, who literally brought the briquettes into the kitchens of its users. This was particularly the case in urban areas like Hanoi, where the coal briquette came to replace kerosene and electricity as a main cooking fuel. Electricity used to be highly subsidized up until the 1980s. When these subsidies fell away with the economic reforms, electricity became too expensive for most households and the coal briquette took over as a cheap and convenient cooking fuel. This popularity of this cooking fuel declined, however, in the early 2000s. While it remains up to now the main cooking fuel at small food stalls and street side restaurants in Hanoi, the coal briquette stove plays only a secondary role in urban households that have increasingly turned to gas (Derks 2015a, 341). Indeed, with rapid economic development, urbanization, and changing household organization, and the focus on the greening and beautification of the city, cooking with coal as well as the production and distribution of the coal briquette have increasingly been relegated, literally as well as symbolically, to the margins of city life.

By exploring the changing place of coal in the city, I intend to shed light on the articulations of networks, space, and urban transformation along the coal briquetting chain. This chapter is based on two years of ethnographic research on the briquette during which I followed the thing from its source in the coal mines of Quảng Ninh province and its transport as raw coal, to its production and distribution as coal briquettes in Hanoi, to its use as fuel in households and at food stalls, and to its final form as a waste product.[1] Throughout this journey, I conducted more than one hundred interviews with coal miners, traders, shippers, producers, vendors, users, waste collectors, local authorities, and religious experts. I observed informants as they collected coal from mines, made coal briquettes, prayed for profits, went on selling rounds, and cooked food. I engaged informants in pile-sorting exercises and conducted a quantitative survey on cooking fuel use and cooking practices among four hundred households in Hanoi. I furthermore collected reports and online resources on the coal briquette and related issues in order to explore developments and discourse regarding the coal briquetting chain (see also Derks 2015a, 2015b).

Cooking on Coal

Squatting next to the coal briquette stove, my neighbor Hương was preparing lunch when my assistant and I arrived. The smell of braised fish with cabbage filled our noses as we looked in the pan. Putting the lid back on, Ms. Hương left the pan on the stove in the courtyard and invited us inside her house. She explained how practical the coal briquette stove is. There is no need to sit next to it, which means that she can leave the food simmering outside while she continues to do chores inside. She added: "We have both, a gas cooker and coal briquette stove, but we cook more on the coal briquette stove. We have children, so we need to cook many types of food, porridge, stew, and water. Only when we are in a hurry, I use the gas stove. As we have a yard, we can leave the stove outside and cook with the coal briquette stove. If we didn't have a yard, we wouldn't use coal briquette." Ms. Hương has two children and lives with her husband and mother-in-law in a three-story house in a back alley of an upmarket neighborhood. She shares her yard and stove with the family of her sister-in-law living next door. Her sister-in-law goes out for work during the day, but cooks dinner for her family on the same coal briquette stove. Ms. Hương keeps the stove burning the whole day, also to prepare hot water for both families and her mother-in-law. She uses about one hundred briquettes per month, amounting to VNĐ250,000 (US$12.50). She calculated that if she used gas instead, it would cost her about VNĐ500,000 (US$25) per month.

The economics of cooking on coal may be clear. Yet Ms. Hương's example illustrates other important aspects in the use of the coal briquette stove, namely, space and time. Cooking on a coal briquette stove, as I was often told, entails a particular way of cooking. Unlike with a gas stove that one can easily turn on and off, it takes time to ignite the coal briquette and once it burns it has to burn completely, which may take three to four hours. This means that cooking with the coal briquette requires someone to stay at home to occasionally watch the stove. This makes the coal briquette hardly a suitable fuel for busy, modern urban families (Derks 2015a, 342).

Also, as the example of Ms. Hương illustrated, the coal briquette stove is used outside the house, either in the courtyard or on the street in front of the house, in order to prevent harmful emissions from entering the living area. This separation of cooking and living spaces can also be observed with the design of traditional Vietnamese houses, in which the kitchen was located in a building separated from the main house. Yet with increasing urbanization and ongoing construction there is less space available to put a stove outside the house. Moreover, modern architecture has driven the kitchen increasingly into the house. This is most obviously the case for the new apartments in the high-rise buildings that have come to dominate the city skyline. These apartments often come equipped with standard kitchens and with strict safety regulations prohibiting the use of the coal briquette stove on balconies and in corridors (Derks 2015a, 343). While most studies on urban change tend to emphasize the connections between lifestyle changes and the new *public* spaces for consumption, traffic, and leisure (Drummond, 2012, 90–91), I found that a major change is actually happening right at the hearth of the home (Derks 2015a, 343).

The place of cooking affects not only the dynamics of cooking within the home but also interactions with neighbors. Used outside, the coal briquette stove offers a lot of potential for collective practices as well as disputes. Ms. Hương shares her coal briquette stove with her sister-in-law. After she has finished cooking her meal, any neighbor can put on a kettle to heat water for tea or washing. This sharing of the stove, of the food prepared on the stove, and also of a single burning coal briquette, is a recurrent practice at different places throughout the city. One can observe how, after lunch hour, neighbors make use of the burning stoves at food stalls to cook water or prepare a soup. One may also observe someone walking with a burning coal briquette along the street, bringing it from one stove to another. Not only the stove or the burning briquette but also the waste product of the coal briquette may be shared. The neighbor living opposite Ms. Hương gladly makes use of the burned briquettes for the litter box of her cat, as ground, fully burned coal briquettes apparently absorb moisture and odor very well.

Other neighbors, however, are not as happy with Ms. Hương's daily use of the coal briquette. They complain about the fumes and find it dangerous to leave a burning stove outside while the children are around. Complaints about the smell, about the hot stoves blocking alleyways, and about how the smoke of the coal briquette caused iron gates to rust repeatedly came up in discussions I had about the beehive coal briquette with friends, colleagues, and informants. And when reading Internet forums and online newspapers, I could clearly see that these complaints had gone viral. One woman posting a complaint about those who "use the coal briquette and place the stove in front of the neighbor's house" wrote that she is "very upset. In the morning, the first breath of the day I have is coal briquette smell" (Anonymous 2010). She added that because she was pregnant, she had offered her neighbors money to use another kind of fuel, but they refused and told her, "Our children also breathe [the fumes] and they are okay." She kept her windows tightly shut for four months. Also, newspapers regularly warn about the dangerous beehive coal stove in the streets of Hanoi—particularly after an increase in gas prices—with descriptions of how "poisonous fumes spread throughout the day, especially in the morning when people ignite their stoves and the fumes spiral up right along the road and in the alleyways" (Anonymous 2013).

The problem, as Ms. Hương's mother-in-law argued, is that there are now "more people and less space" in the city. She remembered how she would collect leaves and firewood as cooking fuel when she was young. But "now they cut all the trees to build houses and schools." She argued that since "society is growing, the people should actually not use coal briquette any more. It pollutes the environment and also affects your health. It is very dirty, but because of our economic situation we have to use it." Ms. Hương added: "I know it is toxic, but actually it is a matter of economy. For people like us, it is like that. We think of saving money first and we don't care much about the consequence in the future."

This indicates that fuel use, and related to that the place of cooking, has become an important indicator for rising inequalities within a rapidly urbanizing environment. It shows how broader societal changes are experienced in the kitchen as well as how the tensions and contestations related to the use of the coal briquette are intimately linked to the disparities between those with modern kitchens and those with stoves outside (Derks 2015a, 345).

SELLING BLACKNESS THAT TURNS INTO RED FLAMES

Tay	Hands
Chân	feet
Mặt	face
Nhọ nhem	all smeared
Bán cái đen	Selling blackness
Thành lửa đỏ	that turns into red flames
Bán lặng lẽ	Selling silence
Cho bập bùng bếp reo!	to make the flickering stove sing!
Chiếc xe thồ gieo neo	With towering baskets
Len phố phường, ngõ ngách	the bicycle weaves through streets and alleys
Lửa đỏ đã sạch	The red flame has been cleansed
Người bán hàng	The seller
Đạp xe về	pedals back home
Đầy sọt	The baskets
Gió đông!	full with winter wind!

Phạm Đức, "Người bán than tổ ong"
(The Beehive Coal Briquette Seller)[2]

The poet Phạm Đức wrote a rare ode to the coal briquette vendor, pedaling through the dense traffic on his way to deliver the blackness that turns into red flames. Selling coal briquettes is not normally considered to be the most poetic profession, though. As one vendor described, "There are not many people who want to sell coal briquette. They say that selling coal briquettes is hard and dirty. But for me, I don't have any other job, so I sell coal briquettes."

This does not mean, however, that it is easy to start working as a coal briquette vendor. Almost all vendors I met told me how they either painstakingly built up a network of customers or took over a network of customers from a relative or friend. This was different twenty years ago, when finding customers was much easier and, as a vendor noted, "the people needed [briquettes] to use for cooking. Before people used them a lot. In Hanoi, about 80 percent of the people used coal briquettes." As noted before, the coal briquette was a commonly used cooking fuel in Hanoi in the 1990s. Vendors would walk along the streets and sell their briquettes to any household that called them in. This changed when households increasingly turned to gas as their primary cooking fuel and the beehive coal briquette lost its place as the main fuel in Hanoian households. Vendors are now struggling to keep their place in the urban fuel market. In order to survive, they need to be able to serve a network of fixed customers who give them a call whenever they need a new stock of briquettes.

Ms. Hương is such a regular customer. She buys her briquettes from a vendor who is attached to a production site behind the Flower Market. There are in total seven vendors, two of them women, at this coal briquette production site. On a gray afternoon in December 2011, I accompanied one of the vendors, Ms. Thu, on her selling round. After she had packed her trolley with two hundred briquettes and provided me with a conical hat and gloves to wear, we pushed the heavy trolley along the dirt road to the main route along which her customers were located. The sight of a foreign woman pushing a trolley with briquettes got quite some attention. As I joked with people along the road, trying to entice them to buy briquettes, Thu remarked that she also used to talk with people this way when she had just started selling briquettes. In order to attract customers, she said, it is important to "talk in a polite way, have a friendly attitude, and speak with a sweet voice in order to convince them to buy." Moreover, she added, "I always make sure to clean the place where I put the briquettes for them." She now has her regular customers. Two of them had called her earlier that day: one food shop preparing duck soup ordered fifty briquettes and another food shop specializing in dog and goose meat ordered one hundred pieces. On our way, one customer called Thu over, buying twenty briquettes. I helped Thu to pierce the holes in the briquette, put them in a bag, and bring them inside. After delivering the briquettes to the food stalls, we continued our tour into a small back alley. We halted at the house of an elderly woman who kept a coal briquette stove in the alley in front of her house. While she uses a gas stove to cook food, she also keeps the coal briquette stove to prepare hot water. She had not called in advance, but Thu knew that it was time to restock. Indeed, the woman had only one briquette left and bought the last thirty pieces. With our trolley now empty, we returned to the production site.

Vendors like Ms. Thu are linked to one production site, where they often also live. They are not paid employees but independent traders who earn according to their capacity to sell. Ms. Thu, for example, was able to sell about three hundred to four hundred briquettes a day. Buying the briquettes for VNĐ2,000 (US$0.10) apiece from the briquetting plant, she would sell them for VNĐ2,500 (US$0.12).[3] Other sellers attached to the same plant can sell five hundred to six hundred briquettes a day. One of the more prolific vendors is Mr. Tân. His parents-in-law are the neighbors of Mr. Phú, the owner of the briquetting plant. During one of their visits back to the village,

Mr. Phú and his wife, Ms. Nhài, had told them about their business and asked his wife to work as a vendor. As they could use the extra money, the wife of Mr. Tân decided to give it a try while Mr. Tân stayed in the village to raise pigs and work as a mechanic and take care of their, at that time, one-year-old daughter. Last year, however, Mr. Tân's wife had an accident. A car crashed into her from the back while she was selling briquettes. She hurt her leg and could not walk. As Mr. Tân said, "We could not just leave all our customers which she had worked very hard to find. That's why I decided to work for her." Hence, his wife went back to the village to recuperate, take care of their child, and, once her leg was healed, take up a job in a nearby electronics factory, while Mr. Tân started selling briquettes. He noted: "Selling coal briquettes is like going fishing: on some days I can earn more and on other days, I earn less. When I was working as a mechanic, I had a stable income. But selling coal briquette gives me more freedom. So, when I am sick or tired, I can take a day off. And if I work hard, I can have a higher income than with mechanic work." Mr. Tân added that he could earn about VNĐ100,000 (US$5) a day as a mechanic in the village, as opposed to VNĐ250,000 to 300,000 (US$15) a day as a coal briquette vendor. Moreover, he added, he can earn more than his wife because "I am stronger. I can travel a longer way than her." It is, however, not only strength, but also the means of transport that determines the distances that can be traveled. Mr. Tân uses his motorbike to deliver orders of coal briquettes to customers located far away, or who call him for an immediate delivery. Ms. Thu cannot ride a bike or motorbike and therefore continues to push her trolley to deliver briquettes, which limits the radius of her trading route.

Whatever their means of transport, beehive coal briquette vendors are necessarily mobile. They navigate the dense traffic with bicycles, trolleys, or motorbikes, which are packed with piles of coal briquettes to deliver the cooking fuel into households and at food stalls. In that sense, they are not different from other itinerant traders who move from place to place to provide customers with vegetables, fruit, or flowers— albeit without the "aesthetic appeal" of the female vendors with their conical hats and colorful products wandering along the streets of Hanoi (Lincoln 2008, 264). And they are subject to the same regulations regarding street vending. One coal briquette vendor in Thanh Xuân complained to me about the fact that the use of the cyclo for the transport of coal briquettes had been banned.[4] Although several vendors keep using the cyclo on the smaller streets, he started using the pushcart after the police caught him several times and confiscated his cyclo and briquettes, which—he heard later—were donated to an orphanage.

Several authors have written about the everyday struggle of street vendors in the informal sector in Hanoi (Turner and Schoenberger 2012; Lincoln 2008; Jensen and Peppard 2003; Higgs 2003). With the capital's "drive towards modernity" (Turner and Schoenberger 2012, 1029), the authorities seek to constrain street traders' access to and use of urban space. Street vending, as Lincoln claims, makes authorities uncomfortable because it "is associated with premodern, undisciplined urban commercial patterns" (2008, 263). Accordingly, a decree put into force in 2008 banned street vendors from sixty-two streets and forty-eight public places in the city's urban core (Turner and Schoenberger 2012, 1029). In a newspaper article on the ban on street vending, a coal briquette vendor laments, "I don't understand, is my coal trolley also classified as hawking, creating chaos and traffic disorder or not. . . . As I see it, most hawkers are already in a situation close to outcast. When they ban street vending with trolleys and baskets, they will immediately be down and out" (Công Thanh and Phạm Hải 2008).

As vendors of a product that is regarded as black and dirty, coal briquette traders are particularly aware of their use of space, avoiding times and places that are prone to traffic jams and making sure that they put their bicycle or trolley in a safe place before they deliver the coal to customers. One of the greatest worries, as one vendor confided, is having an accident in which the bicycle with towering briquettes falls down on the street. This would result in not only the loss of a coal load, a fine by the police, and traffic congestion, but also the scorn of wealthy urbanites who have long abandoned coal fuel.

Coal briquette vendors' mobility, however, relates not only to the daily travels through the streets of Hanoi to sell their product but also to their movements between the city and the countryside where they originate. The coal briquetting trade is a typical migrant trade. The vendors at the briquetting plant behind the Flower Market all come from the same native place (*cùng quê hương*) in Hải Dương and are relatives, neighbors, or friends of the owners, Mr. Phú and Ms. Nhài.

The movements between the city and the native place are regulated along with the rhythm of the lunar calendar. This is because customers avoid buying coal briquettes on the first (and sometimes also the fifteenth) of the lunar month (Derks 2015b). Mr. Tân, for example, noted, "I go home twice a month, on the first and fifteenth of lunar calendar . . . because customers *kiêng* [lit. abstain]. They don't buy coal as it is black and people who follow the Buddha say that it brings bad luck to their house if they buy black coal briquette at the beginning of the month. . . . [And since] we work hard all month, it is also an opportunity for us to relax." This shows how beliefs regarding what to do and what to avoid on particular days of the lunar calendar have a direct impact on consumer behavior, work routines, and commuting patterns in the coal briquetting trade (Derks 2015b).

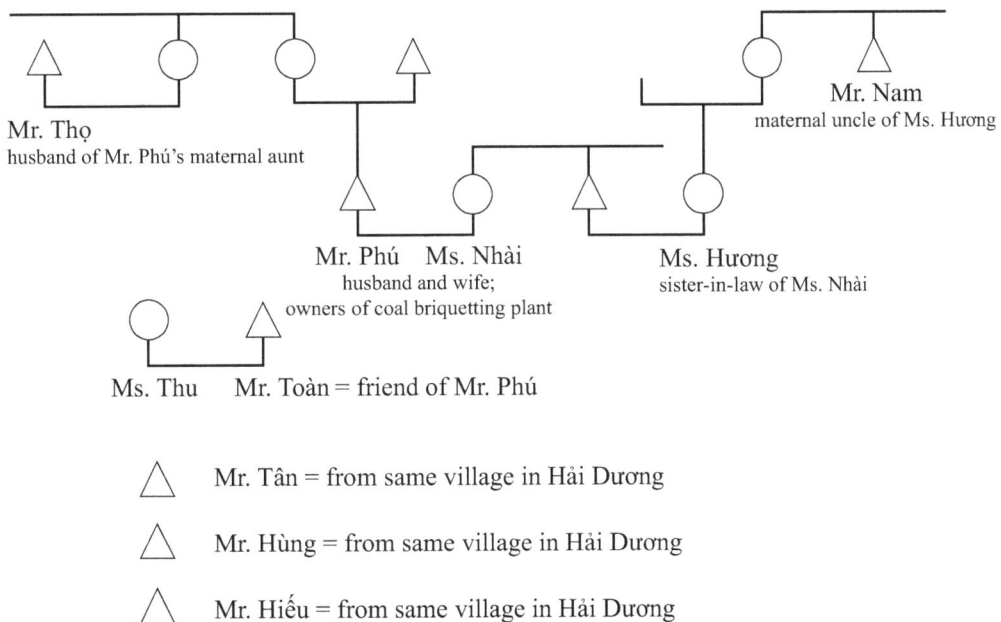

Figure 11.2. Vendors at Mr. Phú and Ms. Nhài's briquetting site.

It is thus not only the use of coal briquette but also its trade that are linked in very particular ways to time and space—as well as to inherently social and cultural processes and practices. Moving from place to place, coal briquette vendors are subject to changing notions of urban space in general and of the domestic space of their urban customers in particular, as these changing notions of space influence how, how much, and where they sell their briquettes. Moreover, while located in the city, the coal briquette trade is intimately linked to people and needs in the native place, allowing vendors like Ms. Thu and Mr. Tân to bridge spaces and places.

RIDING THE HORSE ONE HAS MOUNTED

> I work [in this business] already, so people say that when you already mounted the horse, you have to ride it. But actually I don't like this work at all. I am very tired of this business, it provides no good income.

Sitting at the small table, next to the space that served as the kitchen, in a corner of the coal briquette production site, Ms. Nhài went on about the difficulties of the beehive coal briquette business. It was 10:00 a.m. and unusually quiet at the workshop, as the workers who normally operate the briquetting press had gone back to their villages. Ms. Nhài was dressed in her usual working clothes: black pants, checkered shirt, scarf to cover her hair, rubber boots, and plastic gloves that have become black from the coal. She looks older than her thirty-two years, which she blames on the hard work in the briquetting plant. She is indeed a hardworking woman: whenever I came to her production plant, I saw her carrying coal in a wheelbarrow from the pile of coal on the other side of the road into the workshop, stacking coal briquettes, or assisting her husband with the repair of the briquetting machine.

Ms. Nhài got involved in the coal briquetting trade because of her husband, Mr. Phú. Coming from a large family with little land, Mr. Phú moved to Hanoi in 1991 to find work. He first tried various odd jobs and then found a job at a coal briquetting workshop. At that time, the briquettes were still made by hand with a mold, involving hard and tedious work. Mr. Phú soon found out, however, that those working as vendors had a lighter job and earned more. So he changed to become a beehive coal briquette vendor. After they got married in 2001, Ms. Nhài joined her husband to sell coal briquettes. In 2007, they decided to start their own briquetting business. They borrowed money from the bank, relatives, and friends to buy a piece of land, a briquetting press, and a stack of dust and mud coal. However, it was not easy to make good coal briquettes. Ms. Nhài remembered:

> During the first year, we met a lot of trouble. We did not know how to make a good coal briquette. . . . It is not a matter of money or talent. You need to have many years of experience before you know what percentage of dust coal and how much mud coal you need. And each time you buy coal, it is different. . . . Many people who invested millions of đồng only made briquettes for a few months and then lost everything and had to move on to another business because their briquettes did not burn well. Customers would only buy from them once or twice and then stopped buying from them. When you lose your customers, you must close your business. We also had problems like that before, but we know how to correct our mistakes, so we still keep our customers. But many failed.

The coal briquetting business comprises networks of people, capital, and raw materials. Coal is an important link in the chain of production, distribution, and consumption. Good-quality coal is important for producers to be able to make the briquettes that vendors can sell their customers. Producers who have the capital and space to buy and store large amounts of coal therefore have a competitive advantage over small, mostly family-run production plants.

Ms. Nhài's plant is an example of the latter type. It is located on the outskirts of the city, along the river basin of the Red River, an area that is mostly dedicated to the cultivation of flowers and kumquat and peach trees. The workshop is an open shack made out of corrugated material and bricks. Everything is blackened by coal—the unpaved floor, the walls of piled coal briquettes, the machine surrounded by heaps of coal. Right next to the workshop is the open kitchen, with several coal briquette stoves surrounded by coal briquettes and a small table with plastic stools. At night, Ms. Nhài and her husband, daughter, and mother-in-law stay in a room that can be sealed with a sliding door, while the workers and vendors stay in a dormitory above the workshop. In front of the workshop lie heaps of dust coal and mud coal covered with plastic sheeting as well as finished coal briquettes drying in the sun. Talking about her site, Ms. Nhài said, "Of course, it is better in the countryside where there is a lot of space and where the air is fresh and clean. That is different here. Yet, we have to accept, because we do business. And if we compare our site with some other production sites, ours has more space."

Yet space has become increasingly sparse and regulated in urban Vietnam. Several studies have shown how urban residents have had to give up their way of life and houses in order to make way for the construction of what is considered to be a modern, beautiful, breathable city (Harms 2012, 737; Labbé and Boudreau 2011; Waibel 2006; Thomas 2002). Visions of such a modern, beautiful, and breathable city definitely do not go well with the presence of dusty, black, and loud coal briquetting workshops. Many briquetting plants therefore have been relocated out of areas of high population density. The bigger production plants moved to dedicated zones sites with coal storage areas along the Red River and the Đuống River. The environmental departments of the local People's Committees undertake regular inspections to keep air and water pollution under control.

Ms. Khánh, for example, used to have a briquetting plant in a small but busy street, but was told that "the coal briquette is too dirty for the city." She had to move her site to Thanh Trì, southeast of Hanoi and close to the place where ships arrive with coal from Quảng Ninh. She now produces the briquettes at her production site in Thanh Trì and then brings them to a distribution site in a more residential area. While the production of coal briquettes may be relocated to the outskirts, for vendors location remains important. Proximity to customers defines the travel distance of vendors, and with it their capacity to sell briquettes. When a briquetting plant moves to another site, vendors may lose touch with their network of customers, who are usually located within a specific area.

In this context of cleaning and beautifying the city, coal briquette producers are increasingly moved around or pushed out of the city. Producers are well aware that their product is becoming increasingly unpopular. Some producers, in an effort to retain a place in the urban fuel market, have engaged in the "greening" of the black coal briquette. Whether by adding a secret mixture of herbs or by dipping briquettes in a bath of lime, the production of so-called clean coal briquettes has increased markedly over the past few years. These efforts to create a cleaner image of the coal briquette are not limited to the making of briquettes but also extend to their distribution. Special brands of clean coal briquettes are now packaged in carton boxes and transported on the back of motorbikes to ensure a fast and clean delivery. Hence, in an effort to resist being displaced, entrepreneurs are trying out a reinvention of the coal briquette in compliance with visions of a green, clean, and beautiful urban space.

Following the trajectory of an ordinary cooking fuel backward, from consumption to distribution to production, means moving between the kitchens, the streets, and the briquetting plants. As I have tried to show, these are not neutral places, but infused with meanings and intentions. The anecdote in the introduction of this chapter made clear that the coal briquette is a common cooking fuel, and yet out of place. While, on the one hand, considered to be "too dirty for the city," the coal briquette is, on the other hand, a bare necessity of daily life for those urbanites and urban migrants who depend on it to cook their food or earn a living. As a young female representative at the People's Committee of suburban district of Hanoi argued, these contradictions are related to the fact that "Vietnam is divided between the rich and the poor. Of course, young people like us will not use [the coal briquette] but the poor people still use. . . . They only use coal briquettes. They cannot use gas. It is only when the government imposes a ban, then no one would be able use coal briquette anymore."

The coal briquette, in other words, is seen as one of the tangible manifestations of the uneven developments and rising inequalities that have characterized post–Đổi mới Vietnam. The market-oriented reforms have created new opportunities for entrepreneurs, including those in the briquetting trade who have sprouted up all over town to provide users with a daily cooking fuel. Some of them made high profits, as one producer noted: "It looks very dirty, but one can earn a lot of money." Yet, as we have seen, the golden days of the black fuel are over. Urbanization, modernization, and visions of a green, beautiful, and breathable city have shaped notions of how and where to cook, causing the coal briquette and its business to be regarded as something that should not be there anymore. And that puts those who make, distribute, and use coal briquettes in an awkward position—being everywhere but at the same time denied being there, shunned but also tolerated for their efforts to keep stoves burning.

As I have shown, this awkward position of those at the different nodes in the commodity chain is inherently linked to the shift in the classification of places—the place of the kitchen in urban housing, the place of peddlers in urban space, the place of manufacturing in the city landscape. These discourses about, and the actual reordering of, physical space and spatial relations function to impose order and control in the city—or even in urban housing—in which certain things (fuels) have no more place. In this context, it remains to be seen whether efforts to reinvent the beehive coal briquette as clean and green will eventually be successful to help vendors like Ms. Thu and Mr. Tân and producers like Ms. Nhài and Ms. Khánh retain a place in the urban fuel market.

Notes

1   The research was financially supported by the Swiss National Science Foundation and hosted by the Faculty of Sociology at the University of Social Sciences and Humanities at the Vietnam National University. I am very grateful for the support of Nguyễn Tuấn Anh and other colleagues at the USSH and for the wonderful research assistance of Ngô Thúy Hạnh.

2 My translation with the help of Nguyễn Phan Quế Mai.
3 In the meantime, the price for a coal briquette has risen to VNĐ3,000 (US$0.15) per piece.
4 The Vietnamese government officially banned cyclo, or bicycle rickshaw, transport as part of Decision 12/2001/QĐ-UB in 2001. The ban was meant to counter traffic congestion and concerned in particular the transport of heavy goods. Cyclos are still used, however, for taking tourists on sightseeing rides in a limited area of the city (V. Nguyen 2016).

CHAPTER TWELVE

ARBITRAGE OVER THE BEILUN/KALONG RIVER: CHINESE ADJUSTMENTS TO BORDER TRADE PRACTICES IN VIETNAM

Caroline Grillot

Any mention of the Sino-Vietnamese frontier generally evokes images of mountainous landscapes, diverse ethnic groups, key historical events, and memories of past invasions and military conflicts. The last conflict, which occurred in 1979, continued to disturb border life until the early 1980s and left its profound marks on the landscape and the memories of the locals (Chan 2013; Endres 2015a; Womack 2006; J. Zhang 2011). Over the following decade, the area was slowly reconstructed. With no authorization to cross the border, alternative routes were forged to rebuild informal trade relationships across borders. The official reopening of the border in 1991 brought life back into the borderland villages and markets and changed previous perceptions. Cross-border trade between Vietnamese and Chinese traders was built on the underground petty trade dating back to the early 1980s, while more recent trade entrants, migrants in search of opportunities, have expanded its scope. Since the 1990s, market-oriented economic reforms, Đổi mới in Vietnam (1986–present) and the *gaige kaifang* (economic reform) in China (1978–present), signaled an encouraging trend for larger-scale cross-border trade. Despite these efforts at normalization, the delicate issue of sovereignty over the maritime territories of the Spratly and Paracel Islands continues to be a formidable impediment. Far from its being an anecdotal development, traders regularly experience this geopolitical issue as a cause for palpable animosity on the ground and as an issue that takes on various forms depending on individual sensitivities and the degree of exposure to political rhetoric. While some are very much influenced by propaganda discourses and are suspicious about their neighbors' day-to-day actions, others stay pragmatic and focus on grasping trade opportunities rather than on diplomatic issues. Nevertheless, as this chapter demonstrates, the idea of harmonic cooperation and friendship, praised by both Chinese and Vietnamese officials, is yet to become a reality for cross-border trade.

The adjacent border cities of Móng Cái (Quảng Ninh province) and Dongxing (Guangxi province), located at the last border gate in the extreme northeast of Vietnam, are part of an international economic zone that allows free trade between China and ASEAN countries, according to an agreement that went into effect in 2010. With increasing volume of trade contributing to the development of the region in the past two decades, Móng Cái, the largest border trade zone of northern Vietnam, is now officially recognized for its success.[1] Chinese traders dominate the trade as investors in merchandise and resources, as well as infrastructure. Most trading and shopping centers there are designed, built, and managed by the Chinese, who produce and export most commodities on the market (Nguyen Van Chinh 2013).

The long shipping barges of the Beilun/Kalong River, which separates Móng Cái from Dongxing in the Chinese province of Guangxi, endlessly transport goods and people along the numerous ports on both sides. The official and illegal ports (some even privately owned) are meant to handle transportation of licit or illicit goods, through the official and controlled, or illegal and informal, import-export channels. A vast network of logistics and transportation companies takes care of the cross-border trade shipment. However, smuggling is neither necessarily intended to facilitate trafficking of restricted or prohibited items (such as wild animals) nor hidden from the border officers' scrutiny. As Bruns and Miggelbrink (2012, 11) remind us, the "status of il(legality) qualifies a relation between a trading activity and a state's law" more than it qualifies the object of exchange itself. Therefore, some goods (garments, for instance) are authorized but are smuggled on a daily basis to avoid customs clearance and high taxes. Each morning, hundreds of Chinese traders cross the border carrying one big pack of merchandise in order to supply their wholesale shops in Móng Cái's various markets. Importing large quantities of clothes, mobile phones, or medicine through formal routes is expensive, whereas paying the customs duties charged for each bag (without necessarily checking its content) at the border along informal routes is ultimately cheaper. These routinized activities show that by circumventing legality, the configuration and feasibility of cross-border trade, which has largely transformed the region and allowed thousands of entrepreneurs and workers to benefit from its opportunities and play an active part in local development, is in jeopardy in the long term. Móng Cái's ambition to become an efficient international trade node is undercut by its failure to consistently meet standardized trade practices and its vulnerability to tensions in the Sino-Vietnamese relationship.

The modalities of the Chinese and Vietnamese cross-border trade in the Sino-Vietnamese borderlands and the complex interplay of politics, history, economic crisis, and business praxis were central to my inquiries in the several months of fieldwork I conducted in both Móng Cái and Dongxing. Relying on a network previously established and lately extended in both cities and with the help of a Vietnamese research assistant, I used the snowball method to meet informants: individual traders, managers, transporters, and smugglers from both countries in the adjacent cities of Móng Cái and Dongxing. They were either long-term residents or newly settled entrepreneurs at the borderland. Interviews were conducted mostly in Chinese and sometimes in Vietnamese during regular business hours in the shops or during leisure time.

I explored four major markets of this border trade zone, but for the purpose of this study I focus primarily on the most active one in Móng Cái. The city's largest market is officially named Chợ Trung Tâm Móng Cái (Móng Cái Central Market) and colloquially named Móng Cái's Market number one, and it comprises about 870 spaces dedicated to shops, packaging areas, and warehouses on four floors, including an underground level. Constructed with state funds in 1991 and renovated in 2004, the market symbolizes the city's commercial prowess. Initially, investors bought stall use rights to either start businesses or rent them to Chinese traders. According to the informants, most stallholders now lease their shops to newcomers at an increasingly lower price, indicating a decline in this economy. The tenants include petty and small-scale traders from China, who become cross-border wholesalers so as to take advantage of the demand for scarce commodities in Vietnam. Based on a concept introduced by Elmar Altvater (1998), Allan Williams and Vladimir Baláž identify such trade patterns—also characteristic of postsocialist countries in Eastern Europe after their opening—as a form of arbitrage "understood as the exploitation of differences in prices and exchange rates over time and space via circulation activities" (2002, 323).

At first, many cross-border traders find that wholesaling manufactured goods and natural products through informal channels is less constraining, more flexible, and more appealing than formal import-export trade. But doing so in a context charged with remnants of political conflict requires maintaining a network of reliable partners to overcome structural obstacles. In this chapter, I argue that the traders' relationships at the ground level mirror and are increasingly shaped by the tense Sino-Vietnamese diplomatic relations. To support this argument, I first analyze the practices of Chinese and Vietnamese small-scale traders in terms of their similarities with arbitrage, an economic activity that in this particular case involves a wide range of mobile actors who operate under hazardous conditions. After describing the specific context for cross-border trade in this region, I introduce the spatial and temporal dimensions of commodities shipment, drawing on the ethnographies of two main objects of cross-border trade: Vietnamese seafood and Chinese garments. I demonstrate how traders on both sides struggle to sustain their collaborative projects by constantly adjusting their expectations of partners whose behavior suggests divergent interpretations of business ethics. The last part of the chapter examines the governance of arbitrage through information, documentation, and corruption.

Figure 12.1. Móng Cái Central Market, 2013. Photograph by C. Grillot.

THE VAGARIES OF POLITICS AND THEIR EFFECTS ON TRADE

In May 2014, escalating tensions in Chinese-Vietnamese diplomatic relations led to demonstrations in southern Vietnam, where thousands protested against China in light of the never-ending question of sovereignty over the Paracel Islands. This unprecedented expression of anger and frustration in an organized protest culminated in violence and led to a large-scale departure of Chinese businesses from Ho Chi Minh City. Only a month earlier, I had inquired about the current state of small-scale trade and its complex logistics in Móng Cái, where the tension was already palpable and seemed to prefigure the upcoming crisis.

On the day I arrived in the town, shots had been fired to prevent a group of Chinese migrants from crossing the border to enter Vietnam illegally in what media reports described as an attempt to make their way to a third country. According to official reports, two Vietnamese border guards and five Chinese migrants had been fatally shot, while others had been deported to China (see Anonymous 2014; Pham 2014; Tang 2014). Only two weeks earlier a journalistic report broadcast on national TV had focused on illegal border trade involving Chinese border guards in the same city. There was recurrent and unwanted focus on local affairs, including the possibility of entering into informal arrangements at the national frontier, and on the obscure rules of cross-border trade. As a result, Vietnamese officials increased their scrutiny of the border and more strictly enforced their control over the flow of goods over the Beilun/Kalong River. These measures directly affected the illegal trade modality and contributed to the tense atmosphere in the markets of Móng Cái.

The Vietnamese state intervened even more decisively in local affairs in 2010, after Nguyễn Tiến Phương, one of the most influential snakeheads of Móng Cái's mafia network, had been apprehended and sentenced to death after his trial in 2012 (Nghĩa Hiếu 2012). The state action further disrupted local cross-border trade. Chinese shop-keepers of Móng Cái became reluctant to comment on these events and the situation they co-created, as they experienced losses on a daily basis and the transportation of their goods from China had been affected.

The regular recurrence of these events undermines the stability of traders in the local economy. But given the ensuing violent demonstrations in southern Vietnam immediately thereafter (May 2014) against the economic aspirations of the Chinese, an end to the border-trade crisis is not foreseeable in the short term. According to local informants, Móng Cái had not become a venue for border chaos resulting from more anti-Chinese demonstrations because "the Vietnamese government had successfully intervened and made the necessary arrests of would-be protestors." Notwithstanding that, as reported in July 2014 by A Bo, a Chinese wholesaler from Dongxing who cited unofficial figures, about seventy thousand Chinese involved in cross-border trade had left Móng Cái and Dongxing over the past year, reducing the local population by almost one half. Many shops have closed, entire districts are empty, and the new complex intended for hundreds of shops and the attached new long-distance station is empty, too. Luckily for him, A Bo rents a shop in Dongxing's People International Wholesale Market, which most tourists visit: "I mostly rely on old customers from China who come to buy my imported Indian incense. It's enough to maintain my business; in a way, I am luckier than others who face bankruptcy."

Dealing with different customers, A Qiu is a trader who was born in Vietnam to a Chinese father and fled to China in 1978. Selling bathroom fittings in a different area of the city, he describes how tricky his business has become since the outbreak of the latest political conflict. He mentions that his customers have become so sensitive that they now refuse to buy any item that displays a Chinese character on it. Meeting customers' requirements is just one among a series of complications in conducting border trade in 2013. Customs authorities on both sides of the border have raised taxes, enforced stricter control on illegal shipping, limited exports, and imposed longer processing times for import-export companies. Like cross-border trade, tourism, one of the most flourishing sectors in Dongxing, is also clearly changing. Up to 2014, Chinese tourists wanting to explore the city of Móng Cái could obtain a one- to three-day Vietnamese visa with just an identity card. Now, a regular passport bearing a tourist visa (from a Vietnamese consulate in China) is necessary. Those without such a document visit Dongxing to simply enjoy what Vietnam has to offer along the shore of the Beilun River and purchase a little souvenir of their neighboring country at one of the Vietnamese street vendors' stalls or in the People's International Wholesale Market: (fake) perfume, (fake or smuggled) tobacco, precious wood bracelets, traditional medicine oil, rubber shoes, and other items.

With most sectors affected by the developments in the Sino-Vietnamese diplomatic conflict, a large proportion of the Chinese shops in Móng Cái have closed and many Chinese traders have declared bankruptcy. Despite the construction of impressive skyscrapers and residential areas in and around it, Dongxing remains rather empty. Shops along the once bustling fashion streets are now competing with attractive promotional deals, new districts remain empty, development projects are left pending, and existing traders struggle to avoid bankruptcy. Import-export companies must comply with stricter conditions for running their businesses according to international regulations, whereas small-scale traders must rely more than ever on informal channels. Fragile, but crucial to maintain, the traders' partnerships at the ground level are marked by the ups and downs of China and Vietnam's bilateral relationship. Chinese traders who manage to survive have the ability to comply with more complex conditions and have established a long-term agreement with their customers and networks. The following section will analyze two cases demonstrating how border-trade actors constantly adjust to unpredictable working conditions and remain active in an apparently chaotic trading environment.

SPACE AND TEMPORALITY OF ARBITRAGE: MÓNG CÁI'S IN-AND-OUT

A typical working day in the lives of many Chinese traders living in Dongxing's residential complexes begins when they cross the border at 8:00 a.m. (Chinese time) with their lunchbox, their handbag, and one big bag of goods. Because of restrictions, many choose this temporary route to carry their goods to the Vietnamese market: phones, clothes, and accessories bought from the wholesale markets and factories that supply the Zhejiang and Cantonese region. Carrying small quantities every day allows them to avoid cross-border scrutiny and maintain a minimum required inventory in the shops. They also ask some local Vietnamese (mostly women) to carry their goods the same way once or twice a day to avoid restrictions on amounts per person, per crossing, and per day.

Upon reaching Móng Cái some time after 7:00 a.m. (Vietnamese time), Chinese traders hurry to open their shop at one of the big markets of Móng Cái and begin a seemingly monotonous daily routine, involving ordering goods from factories, receiving deliveries from transporters and shipping them to clients, negotiating new deals, contacting indebted clients, and so on. Even in a fast-moving economy where competition is fierce and solidarity is rare, basic material requirements are needed; among these are a shop, possibly a warehouse, a smartphone (with QQ or WeChat software, sometimes with two phone numbers, Chinese and Vietnamese), a few notebooks, and a calculator.[2] But to enjoy a sustainable business, most important, traders need a network of reliable collaborators (carriers, transporters, translators, money changers) and the ability to anticipate new market trends and needs.

Cross-border trade is increasingly difficult to sustain and bankruptcies are legion, but newcomers still endeavor to participate in the borderland economy. When asked why such a difficult context does not prevent new courageous traders from going into business, A Xiu, a middle-aged man who opened a clothing shop in Móng Cái two years ago, answers: "People come here with ambition, but they don't trust each other and must learn the tricks of cross-border trade by themselves. No one dares to give advice; otherwise, there would always be someone to blame if a business turns bad. Nothing is sustainable in border trade; you never know how things will turn out. So better to keep your mouth shut and avoid giving too many details. You don't want to take the responsibility for somebody else's failure of success that may affect your own business, right?"

About 2:00 p.m., all Chinese shopkeepers and businesspeople at Móng Cái's Central Market count their money, put away their cards and tea sets (sometimes embroidery), close their shops, meet with the woman who exchanges currency and loans out money, and prepare to return to China. At the border gate, even as they cross the Beilun River to start the second part of their day in Dongxing, which mostly involves noncommercial activities, the phones continue to ring and business activity is never really suspended. While traders return to China, their goods continue to be shipped day and night from factories in Zhejiang and Guangdong provinces to various parts of Vietnam.

This routine is characterized by fragility. The commercial transactions transpiring between China and Vietnam involve not just business partners (sellers, buyers, negotiators/intermediaries) but also other key actors such as logistics agents (truck, boat, and bus drivers and warehouse owners), financial agents (bank, money changers, intermediaries), and state and law-enforcement officers (customs officers, border guards, checkpoint security officers, and traffic controllers). Every link in the chain is closely bound with others through agreements, tacit understandings, and financial arrangements, which all serve the sole purpose of making money by taking risks and responsibility for one or several sections of freight shipping. The failure of one of these links to respect the terms of an agreement affects the balance of the chain. This is true of many economic environments, but as far as border economy and informal trade in this particular region are concerned, the viability and reliability of business partners are paramount.

SHIPPING FROM CHINA TO VIETNAM

To illustrate how the current Sino-Chinese border trade is structurally fragile, let us examine the logistics of producing ordinary goods in a factory in the Cantonese region to be transported to a retailer in provincial Vietnam. Because of the import-tax imposed by the Vietnamese state, Chinese traders who do not deal with significant quantities of goods avoid using the onerous official import-export channels reserved for companies. Informal shipping is faster, cheaper, and tax free. Therefore, many prefer to accept the risks that using these channels entails, rather than subjecting themselves to an arduous and time-consuming process.

Vietnamese retailers in Haiphong seeking goods that Chinese wholesalers are presumably selling in Móng Cái would ask an acquaintance to act as a go-between and look for the requested items there. Communication tools, such as smartphones, support the search. Pictures sent instantly allow the client to take a more active part in the final choice. Once the appropriate item is located, negotiations with the wholesaler on behalf of the Haiphong client ensue. Prices, quantities, and financial procedures are discussed. If the client and the seller have had previous business relations and have not encountered difficulties in the past, the seller might be willing to accept only a small amount in advance payment or a simple oral agreement as a guarantee before ordering the requested stock at the factory. If not, the seller might require a sizable or full advance payment before accepting the order. This wholesaler then pays a percentage of the order to the factory that prepares the goods for shipping, at which time the rest of the payment is requested and the goods leave the factory for Dongxing via a truck belonging to a transport company paid by the wholesaler. Once the goods arrive in Dongxing, they are stocked in a warehouse, another link in the logistical chain. The warehouse then informs the wholesaler about the receipt of the order, and that wholesaler then contacts a local shipping agent to take charge of the border crossing. This *laoda* (leader or protector in the informal sector) is usually a Vietnamese intermediary who has good relations with border guards on both sides of the border. The support of intermediaries is essential to all traders who intend to establish business at the border. This intermediary may also be the owner of the barges that technically transport the boxes, bags, or furniture, but he may also use private boats and laborers to organize the river crossing to bring the goods safely to Móng Cái.[3] If goods are lost, damaged, or confiscated, the intermediary will provide compensation or a full reimbursement will be made to the wholesaler established in Móng Cái.

The next phase of the shipping is then handed over to another Vietnamese middleperson, an employee at the import-export company or an independent logistics agent, who takes on the riskiest part of the shipping process to bring the goods from the border to the retailer client in Haiphong. All along, the transporter and his team (truck drivers) will have to face various law enforcement agents whose duty is to regulate the shipping of the goods. This includes the border police, the traffic and transport police, the environmental police, the anti-smuggling agents, product quality inspectors, tax officers, and others. The commission that the intermediary gets (per box of goods) to organize the passage usually includes fees for the border customs agents, salary for carriers, and his own share.

Upon the safe arrival of the goods at their final destination, the client pays the transporter, who had advanced a large percentage of the cost. The client will not lose much of his investment in case the goods happen to get lost on the way. The exact apportionment of the shipping costs depends mainly on the degree of acquaintance-ship and trust between these two persons, but also according to the risk undertaken for each specific order.

It is difficult to obtain accurate information on the different channels used by smugglers to transport legal and illegal goods. However, according to the description offered by a few informants, the use of one or the other route for transporting specific goods over water and land also depends on how strictly border controls are enforced at any given time. Hence, what is deemed a regular—undeclared but tolerated—mode of transportation for a standard commodity through a border gate may at a different time be deemed illegal, equivalent to smuggling or trafficking of foreign products through a mountain path. In such a case, all intermediaries and main actors involved in the arbitrage activity can be penalized for criminal activity. As Altvater notes, "Arbitrage is not necessarily criminal, but the step from pure profit making by trading legal goods or services to criminal activities, such as smuggling and trafficking in illegal goods, is small" (1998, 602). But lowering the shipping costs is not the primary motivation for arbitrage traders when using informal channels, despite the risks and unpredictability. In seafood trade, temporality poses a crucial problem.

SEAFOOD: THE TEMPORALITY OF ARBITRAGE BETWEEN
VIETNAM AND CHINA

Certain categories of entrepreneurs in Vietnam benefit from the large supply of natural resources that are in high demand in China. Mrs. An, a Vietnamese trader in seafood, undertakes several tasks previously mentioned, while also functioning as the direct negotiator with Vietnamese fishermen. This mother of two teenagers is an extremely busy woman with a good reputation trading in Vietnamese oysters despite the challenges: time is a crucial factor when the trading routine revolves around keeping the product fresh. Delay in the transportation inevitably leads to the loss of the whole harvest. Mrs. An described this problem with a metaphor:

> Trading with China is like holding a knife: the Chinese hold the handle and we hold the blade. Whatever happens, a client always enjoys the advantage of controlling a sale, and I need to satisfy him over myself; seafood can't wait for another offer. I'd rather throw away boxes of oysters, but I would not risk losing a client with whom I have established a long-term partnership by insisting that he buy the oysters, if he estimates they are unsuitable for consumption. I need to evaluate his sincerity; I have no other option but to trust him.

Experienced Vietnamese traders view their Chinese business partners as controlling and powerful. Trading with them demands patience and accommodation of the volatile Chinese markets, diverse customers' tastes and demands, and borderland governmentality. Mr. Trung, an old Vietnamese trader in his eighties, had participated in trade with China in the early days of the reform era. While he considers the Chinese to be opportunistic and clever, he also blames their unpredictability for the vulnerability experienced by Vietnamese traders in cross-border trade. To avoid losing fresh products because of the volatility of the seafood market or the capriciousness of the Chinese customers, Mrs. An has learned to appreciate and maintain their loyalty: "One of the most delicate parts of my work is to estimate . . . the demands of my clients and the offers of my suppliers . . . and to figure out how to satisfy both sides. That means that I also have to accept the fishermen's conditions [price] no matter for what price I will be able to sell their oysters to Chinese clients. . . . We all depend on each other to make money."

Once traders gain a degree of respectability, they must cast their eyes on the long-term benefits, at times foregoing short-term gains, and respect each other's word in terms of financial transactions. But navigating the interstices of state regulations on border trade also requires flexibility. Mrs. An continues:

> Vietnam does not limit the exportation of some of its natural resources; there is no export tax on seafood, for example, but China taxes the imports. Lately, the cost is two to three times higher than usual. . . . But the consumers' demands

remain the same, so I fulfill their orders by using the barges routes to ship the oysters, and I manage to make about 70,000 đồng [US$3.23, May 2014] profit per box this way. Using the official way would entail nearly the same costs, but the procedure is much more complicated and long . . . and oysters can't wait!

Because Mrs. An is constantly connected to her clients and suppliers on her mobile phone, her fast access to price information gives her the ability to take advantage of profitable opportunities: "It is the ability of the entrepreneur to subjectively perceive and exploit opportunities for arbitrage, based on information not available to everyone else in the economy, that generates the entrepreneur's profits" (Landa 1994, 25). Although Mrs. An generates a daily income of close to 5 million đồng (US$46, May 2014) and is considered successful, she still shows signs of exhaustion. To her, the key to success resides in managing good relations with her suppliers and clients through compromising negotiations, as well as with her transporter associates, to whom she delegates the task of handling border crossing. And this demands full commitment and the ability to constantly improve human resources management skills to solve logistical issues along the chain connecting a Vietnamese fisherman to a Chinese restaurant's customer.

THE GATEKEEPERS AND THE OPERATORS: THE GOVERNANCE OF ARBITRAGE

In seeking to develop peripheral regions, China and Vietnam have often focused on the Sino-Vietnamese borderlands to introduce specific forms of governmentality that encourage investment and trading initiatives. Aihwa Ong labels these processes "graduated sovereignty": "an effect of states moving from being administrators of a watertight national entity to regulators of diverse spaces and populations that link with global markets" (2006, 78). Border trade and arbitrage activities among small-scale traders, as in other borderlands, are a combination of formal governance frameworks (e.g., control of border gates and shores) and informal agreements that benefit each party. Móng Cái is a known trading center where lots of commodities—be they licit or illicit—are transported through informal, sometimes illegal channels, whether for big investors with means and connections or for a modest small-scale trader dealing with invisible partners. Avoiding state offices is not always a realistic option for logistics and shipping companies, which are forced to develop strategies to enhance their potential profit while avoiding being detected as serious legal offenders.

At the customs gate from Dongxing to Móng Cái, Chinese wholesalers and their carriers must comply with import-export regulations and practices. Once the bridge between Dongxing and China is crossed, they present their travel pass to Vietnamese customs and pay a fee of 5,000–10,000 đồng (US$0.23–0.46, May 2014) to enter Vietnam with their bag and a stamp on their border pass. Mr. Tang, who sells garments at the Móng Cái Central Market, explains that discrepancies in trade policies lead to illicit practices: "Chinese customs don't prevent us from taking many goods out of the country, but the Vietnamese authorities are protectionists and corrupt. Before, we had to put money inconspicuously inside the officers' hat that they would place near the window. They would take off their name tag to prevent identification. There was no proof. But they changed the system after a journalist reported on the trick. With a receipt, that looks more official now." This fee is paid in return for being allowed to carry Chinese goods into Móng Cái despite the official import-export regulations.

Adjusting to Bribery

Informal channels of transportation are well organized, but they involve many state agents who receive monthly financial rewards to allow border crossings to transport goods across the Beilun River. Besides this monthly "salary," the guard also receives commissions in varying amounts depending on the nature of the goods and their weight, value, and size.

Informal routes, while well organized, are always accompanied by the risk of being apprehended. Shipping agents mostly negotiate over the phone and in face-to-face meetings at significant hot spots along the trading path between China and Vietnam. Responsible for the physical movement of goods, they constantly oscillate between uncertainties, valuing the benefit of experience and sustainable, trustful relationships with the different actors of border trade and enhancing their skill of predicting impending upheavals in the border trade environment to keep the costs low. Cross-border trade stresses the logistical importance of intermediaries and their difficulty to guarantee smooth economic exchange in an uncertain and changing environment.

Chinese border guards tend to hold short-term positions, and the employee turnover in the customs department is high, so that agreements between officials at the state agencies and the transporters who operate on the Beilun River and in the hill paths around are difficult to sustain. In addition, any sudden change in national politics could increase the transportation costs or make it impossible to bribe. Officers are subject to regular scrutiny within their hierarchy and must always remain vigilant. The common perception among Chinese and Vietnamese local traders is that the Vietnamese border guards are easier to corrupt than their Chinese counterparts, whose national pride can trump all other economic considerations. In practice, one must admit that the corruption level in Vietnam reaches a critical point when it comes to border smuggling and traffic (Endres 2014b). While law enforcement officers in both countries share responsibility for policing irregularities in border trade, their attitude toward the long-term effects of tax evasion upon regional and national economic development differ. Differences in the level of development in Dongxing and Móng Cái (e.g., infrastructure, city planning, market management) demonstrate the damaging effects of the "flexibility" of local authorities in controlling exchanges and crossings.

Both Chinese and Vietnamese local traders acknowledge their own responsibility in participating in, adjusting to, taking advantage of, and renewing every aspect of this uneven, risky, yet efficient mechanism. All are equally eager to comment on the lack of responsibility of the Vietnamese authorities. Local-level Vietnamese officials express the difficulties of implementing regular, fair, and realistic policies under the current conditions, albeit in hushed tones. Mr. Tuần works in the Economic Affairs office of the Móng Cái city People's Committee. He is a young officer who speaks fluent Chinese and fairly good English, learned during his graduate studies in Taiwan. He acknowledges the lack of experience and resources available to many Vietnamese traders. During an informal conversation over a bowl of grilled pork with noodles in a street restaurant, he offered me his perspective on how state directives at the local level empower entrepreneurs who struggle with the vagaries of intense competition and the pressure imposed by international business and financial institutions' rules:

> We try to help local entrepreneurs who lack the investment capacity to borrow money from the bank to establish their business or invest in a new project. But

banks demand high levels of guarantees to lend money: lots of paperwork, a guarantor, property proof, et cetera. Companies also lack expertise and professional accountants. With the reluctance of banks to offer loans, companies and private entrepreneurs borrow from private lenders, which is riskier and at higher interest rates. We try to smooth the dialogue between actors for the benefit of local development and trade regulations.

This illustrates what Aihwa Ong and Li Zhang call "socialism from afar," in which "state controls continue to regulate from a distance the fullest expression of self-interest. The interplay between the power of the state and powers of the self is crystallizing a national environment of great diversity and contingency" (2008, 3). Many state agents in the borderlands endorse this specific role of maintaining the equilibrium between national and local policies, private stakeholders and entrepreneurs' sensibilities, with more or less ease.

SECURITY AND TRUST AT THE CORE OF COMMERCIAL PARTNERSHIP ISSUES

Most informants, Vietnamese or Chinese, who are willing to share their experience as actors in the bustling commercial life in Móng Cái's markets emphasize two concerns: security and trust. Mr. Tu is a Vietnamese state agent who has been on the management board of Móng Cái's Central Market for years. His obligations to different parties are onerous. Because of commercial inactivity in 2014, Móng Cái has witnessed the worrisome departure of many Chinese traders. Mr. Tu was charged with reversing the trend, attracting greater investment from traders to open new shops as well as persuading those who remained to stay on. His response reveals that security issues are affected by the need to sustain a delicate balance in public space:

> Our staff must be fair to traders of both nationalities, but when a fight occurs in the market, some employees become emotional and sympathize with the Vietnamese over the Chinese. When the mafia intervenes to solve disputes between traders and clients, they use knives to threaten the Chinese, who blame us for refraining from intervening. We used to have real guns but now we only carry nonlethal weapons. In case of violent conflict, we must call the police . . . who take their own time to come. The mafia threatens us, too, even though we represent the law!

Despite the familiar daily bustle outside, quiet reigns inside the edifice in the way power holders cautiously negotiate in interactions charged with tension. Both Mr. Tuần and Mr. Tu stress that law enforcement depends largely on flexibility and adjustment to border trade's well-established practices and on acknowledging the power hierarchy. The general impression that the organization of border trade in Móng Cái and Dongxing is a parallel entity still remains at a far remove from the highly praised, but still only imagined, collaboration that Vietnamese and Chinese provincial and national governments advocate.

The difficulties experienced by Vietnamese state agents in navigating between policy implementation and the realities on the ground find an echo in the narratives from the Chinese traders, who stress the need to make constant efforts to make the imagined project a reality, while facing sensitive and hardly debatable concerns. For instance, one major structural obstacle to operating a Chinese business smoothly in Móng Cái lies in the number of administrative procedures. Residence permits, visas, and various taxes are complex issues that traders need to handle with the opening of a simple shop. Representing the most direct interface between the Vietnamese state and traders, the management of Móng Cái's Central Market provides unsatisfied Chinese traders a site to complain about the lack of justice to which they fall victim. State policies implemented for managing the market are recurrently interrogated. Mr. Tang has been selling garments on the second floor for six years. He bemoans a lack of security, the indifference of the management until disputes reach a tipping point, and management's focus on enhancing their own income. All this makes the market a chaotic place lacking in trust: "This market is slowly deteriorating despite all the taxes we pay. It doesn't benefit the Vietnamese state and the city's development to do anything about it. If they invested in simple repair, the place would at least look more attractive. Last year we were asked to pay an extra tax to fix the floor near the elevator. The repair was of such poor quality that holes have already appeared on the floor. How can we trust these offices?"

Several other traders I met in the oldest market of the city, which is in a state of utter disrepair, discussed a related issue. Stall owners were regularly required to pay an amount toward repairs and maintenance that was excessively high. While some traders acquiesced, others refused, explaining that the maintenance tax they paid sufficed. The situation had remained unresolved ever since the renovation plan was introduced to stall owners a few years prior to this study, and the building has been slowly dilapidating. There was distrust of traders—Chinese and Vietnamese—in state agencies charged with maintenance of the trade infrastructure and with planning of local economic development. The general mood of despair signaled to Chinese entrepreneurs that the Vietnamese government aimed to limit the influence of Chinese economic power and projects in Vietnam, an attitude that generally met with a lack of understanding among Chinese entrepreneurs. Even though China's administration is also regularly blamed for pressuring Chinese citizens with endless regulations and taxes that raise the costs of living, their predictability and internal logic seems more acceptable than the apparent lack of rationale behind the Vietnamese policies and practices.

Chinese comments on market management in Móng Cái highlight their own vulnerability as foreign investors, traders, and taxpayers, as well as their exclusion from the logic of circuit capital in Vietnam. They complain not just about the incoherence of the local management but also that they do not have ready access in Vietnam to the same informal rules that regulate business operations in China. Yuk Wah Chan has emphasized in her analysis of Vietnamese-Chinese relationships in trade that both security and trust matters affect the cultivation of familiarity and connections. While *guanxi* (relations) "refers to relations and connections to people in power, such as officials and cadres" (2013, 55), the concept of *shuren* (familiarity) "involves state agents, private sectors and codes of social interactions and sociality within daily economic settings" (54). But building networks of familiarity in border trade demands the skills of sociability; patience; understanding; and compliance with the codes the exercise implies, including bribery or tacit agreements with state agents' practices.

With such complaints from the Chinese side about the "unscrupulous" Other, a blind eye is turned to similar impediments within the Chinese networks and marketplaces, and to the failure of the Chinese to develop commercial projects in a challenging foreign environment. Conducting successful business in a border environment requires more than financial means, good business flair, and reliable trade partners. It also demands a degree of familiarity with and acceptance of disorienting forms of complicity with local gatekeepers.

In his overview of scholarship on brokers, Johan Lindquist reminds us that the intermediary generally figures as an "actor whose primary commitment appears as maximizing individual gain and is therefore deemed untrustworthy" (2015, 873). In this particular border context, many factors that underline the relationships between traders and intermediaries—misunderstandings, lack of communication, contradictory mutual perceptions, and different strategies for circumventing regulation—combine to breed a mistrust born of insecurity. Many Chinese admit that they constantly feel at risk in the Vietnamese environment. They believe Móng Cái to be a dangerous city at night (there are rumors about Chinese people being mugged on the street), consider the entire country backward, and complain about their unease with traveling in Vietnam, where they also hardly trust their closest collaborators.[4] Chinese businesspeople stress the differences in business practice: in China, once a network is settled, it does not need extra care, while in Vietnam, nothing seems sustainable, because of the lack of trust. Therefore, they must ensure on a daily basis that their networks facilitating the passage of their goods across the Beilun River and from Móng Cái to other cities in Vietnam remain reliable all through. Still, the possibility persists of incurring losses, in higher shipping fees and bribes, goods lost en route, controls, extra taxes, and so on.

Some Chinese experience the prospects of having to establish a sustainable trade partnership with Vietnam as being akin to a long expedition. Success in terms of customers' diversity, trade volume (both total and in each transaction), and net earnings—no small feat under any circumstances—may allow traders to switch from private business to an import-export company. The main difference is that a company may use official channels of border trade and still make sufficient profit. Very few of the hundreds of traders who cross the bridge over the Beilun River each day manage to attain that level of success, and many choose to either move on with another project elsewhere or sustain a modest level of ambition.

In their edited volume dedicated to border activities in a globalized world, Itty Abraham and Willem van Schendel have emphasized how "we need to approach flows of goods and people as visible manifestations of power configurations that weave in and out of legality, in and out of states, and in and out of individuals' lives, as socially embedded, sometimes long-term processes of production, exchange, consumption, and representation" (2005, 9). Informed by their approach, this chapter describes what occurs every day in the Sino-Vietnamese border towns of Móng Cái and Dongxing. The informal economy is an integral part of borderland life, an economy in which the roles various actors play seem to have been redistributed for the whole system to function. Cross-border trade relies on various informal commercial exchanges that resort to mobile networks and extensive bribery. Arbitrage represents a large part of this multilayered economy, involving an extensive range of actors using complex tactics to adjust to or circumvent the regulations of the Vietnamese and Chinese states, as well as the (in)formal rules established by local power holders. The current system responds to a call for a liberalized economy, which has garnered praise from the local and national governments and has encouraged investors and entrepreneurs to cooperate as a strategy of development in a globalized environment. But such movements and activities are clearly built on the conflicts of an old historical and cultural setting that oils and impedes trade dynamics. As Christina Schwenkel and Ann Marie Leshkowich remind us, "neoliberalism travels precisely because it resonates with preexisting logics and cultural values and hence can be reconfigured in service of diverse agendas" (2012, 385).

By exploring the dynamics of shipping in small-scale trade, this chapter has illustrated how this boundary was technically created and maintained throughout economic transactions. Drawing from specific cases and narratives, it also shows the risks of undertaking Sino-Vietnamese cross-border trade and the fragile links between local economic actors that are regularly reshaped by global economic crisis, fast-changing markets, and disparate political attitudes. What occurs at a diplomatic level affects law enforcement at the ground level, where agents endeavor—although differentially—to implement strict regulations without disturbing the mechanism that maintains the dynamics of cross-border trading.

Such adjustments challenge the routines followed by Chinese traders, who claim the superiority of Chinese business practices and express annoyance at what they perceive as resistance and the uncompromising attitudes of the Vietnamese, the main obstacles to a successful, mutually beneficial business partnership. Arbitrage opportunities may offer appealing perspectives, but ambitious Chinese entrepreneurs find they have to learn to overcome structural obstacles and adjust to unexpected challenges, because of perceived differences in business ethics, practices, and values between them and their Vietnamese partners.

Local traders and officers who have observed and participated in cross-border trade reveal some concerns about anticipated drastic changes on the ground level in the configuration of Sino-Vietnamese economic relations. Vietnamese now pay more attention to the quality of Chinese goods. Vietnamese consumers turn to either imported goods from other countries or an expanded offering of national products. Many Chinese entrepreneurs have now chosen to open factories directly in Vietnam rather than import Chinese goods. The importance of the railway line between Nanning and Hanoi also allowed trade to circumvent the wholesalers' network of the Móng Cái markets to supply Chinese goods to the capital. Many experienced Vietnamese retailers have learned to deal directly with Chinese suppliers in the Cantonese region (factories and wholesale markets) and avoid intermediaries in the borderland markets (see chapter 10 in this volume). All these changes prefigure a serious metamorphosis of trade features in this region, redistribution of economic roles, and competition in development planning. For instance, Dongxing has seen a tremendous transformation of its urban space with the opening of large but empty commercial districts and similarly extended residential towers in its periphery. These changes arouse the suspicion of the local population, as exemplified by these comments: "useless investments," "inadequate development policies," "stricter migration policies," and so forth. Obviously, these are calls for adjustment of state policies in order to strengthen the specificities of the Móng Cái and Dongxing nodes caught in the turmoil of a global dynamic that challenges the long-established customary system of commercial exchanges.

NOTES

1 See various reports on the official website of Móng Cái city: http://www.mongcai.gov.vn.
2 The instant-messaging programs QQ and WeChat are currently very popular in China, including among businesspeople. They allow sending pictures and voice messages. They are also time-saving tools that fit the needs and demands of trading partners, especially when it comes to communicating in languages that many master only orally.
3 Trade in redwood furniture is the latest trend in Sino-Vietnamese border trade.

4 Several young Vietnamese interpreters who work in Chinese shops and deal with most aspects of commercial negotiation have explained to me how their commitment did not prevent them from being cheated by their Chinese employers. Despite their effort in satisfying their bosses' requirement by being their guide during business trips in Vietnam, for instance, they have been blamed for cheating and betrayal. Some of them lost their jobs on the grounds of mutual mistrust.

AFTERWORD

Gracia Clark

The excellent chapters collected here provide a fascinating and comprehensive overview of the diversity and historical complexity of informal trading relations in Vietnam. Broad geographical and topical coverage serves to introduce those less familiar with Vietnam to the range of scholarship extant and ongoing. These chapters integrate an evidently coherent and theoretically sophisticated body of knowledge in which local and expatriate Vietnamese and foreign researchers from many countries clearly respect and build upon each others' published work. Their obvious familiarity with classic and contemporary work on trade and traders from Asia and farther afield means their collective effort directly addresses many global research and policy concerns. The central issues resonate in particular with many studies of African trade and markets published by historians, ethnographers, geographers, and archaeologists. Vietnam's distinctive experience also offers instructive, even corrective contributions to those lively discussions.

LOCALIZING GLOBALIZATION

Globalization shows its power once again as a fruitful organizing concept, enabling these authors to approach economic change and development programs from many sides while highlighting their relevance to each other. With detailed ethnographic research, several of them explore the intricately local configurations through which global dynamics always manifest themselves. These cases continue and extend an Africanist discourse pioneered by Charles Piot's *Remotely Global* (1999), James Ferguson's *Expectations of Modernity* (1999), and Karen Tranberg Hansen's *Salaula* (2000), among many others. Piot and Ferguson both construct broader regional or global models in later books, while Hansen places her theoretical analyses in comparative regional perspective through her several edited volumes (K. T. Hansen 2005; K. T. Hansen and Vaa 2004). The excellent specific studies in this volume could profitably be expanded in either manner to explore regional or national patterns of trade.

The Togolese ethnic group Piot describes chose their remote mountain homeland as a refuge from slave raiders. They became known for their devotion to the annual rituals held there, even after the majority migrated to regions with better farmland and one of their members became head of state. These ceremonies incorporated globalized material culture, ranging from plastic dolls to television cameras. Significant distortions accommodated migration and political aims yet did not prevent the ceremony from remaining effective in marking and generating ethnic commitment.

By contrast, Ferguson looks at urban miners and clerks in Zambia's Copper Belt towns who embraced their new identities as modern sophisticates. Many intended to reside permanently in town, and so they neglected to play the role of generous, loyal son with their kin left farming in their home villages. Mines cut back and closed when the global price of copper fell, but moving back to farm villages was not as easy as colonial planners had assumed. Without the cultural credibility, relationships, and farming skills needed to reintegrate into a rural community, some faced a chilly reception on their return.

K. T. Hansen's pioneering commodity chain study follows the trail of secondhand clothing from the local to the global level and back again. Consumption and value receive as much attention as commercial practices in a remarkably thorough treatment of each stage: clothes donated to Western charities, resale and consignment shops in Western communities, multinational wholesalers bulking and baling, Africa-based importers, and the myriad small retailers in urban and rural Zambia.

These three exemplary studies of the interpenetration of historical changes in economic and cultural trends at the local and global levels find their closest parallel in this volume with Hy Van Luong's account of the international and national trading networks that have long attracted migrant traders from the villages of Tịnh Bình on the southern-central coast. He integrates documentary and statistical material and individual life histories to trace the expansion and contraction of various forms of labor migration and the laborious construction of new trading networks. His thorough analysis shows in meticulous detail historical and contemporary participation in these networks by both women and men, explaining how and why their roles have changed dramatically at several historical moments in response to shifting opportunity structures.

He starts with their earliest migration to more remote highland areas within Vietnam for agricultural labor, establishing useful ties with villagers for selling them imports and manufactured items at their specific harvest times for shrimp, coffee, cashews, and peppercorns destined for export. Forays by later Tịnh Bình cohorts into military service, factory work, lottery ticket sales, and transport also carried instructive lessons for those who followed. Their stories of successes and failures trace the changing patterns of opportunity and repression over many decades in relation to national and international events. Their contemporary specialization in key chain vending leaves many alternatives open, as individuals and families try different strategies of ambulatory and settled vending, sending women and men of specific ages near and far or choosing other options that keep kin or married couples closer together.

Africa and western Asia furnish interesting comparative examples of ethnic groups long famous for trading who sustained extensive diasporas using relations of kinship, clientship, and religion. Strengthening their capacity for partnerships, credit arrangements and consignments of goods enabled these networks to adjust their geographical reach and the commodities they carried rapidly and efficiently, remaining viable despite dramatic political and economic reconfigurations. The well-known Swahili-Yemeni coalition in East Africa linked up with Armenian and Gujarati networks to the west and east. In West Africa, Igbo trade networks extended across Nigeria to Ghana and England, switching commodities from slaves and palm oil to bicycle parts and secondhand clothes over time (Abimbola 2012; Abu-Lughod 1987; Eades 1994). Hausa ethnic networks reached from northern Nigeria along the western Sahel long before colonial conquest, and they are now expanding footholds in Paris and New York (MacGaffey and Bazenguissa-Ganga 2000; Stoller 2002).

Likewise, the stereotypically isolated uplands or hill tribes in fact participated in long-standing trading networks that supported their awareness of current conditions and opportunities in the metropolitan areas of Vietnam or other parts of Southeast Asia. Highlanders historically attended periodic markets and practiced seasonal street vending in small upland towns. Sarah Turner reports that official policies presumed that subsistence farmers lack experience with trade and these policies have consequently threatened this important element stabilizing their dispersed communities. When these crowded marketplaces were repeatedly improved and relocated, officials displaced experienced upland vendors in favor of lowland immigrants who resided permanently in town. Those pushed out of the markets remain active traders, responding creatively to the increasing demand for upland handicrafts by following tourists around the town center, dodging anticongestion enforcement near the central square, and supplying Hmong wholesalers at a periodic dawn rendezvous.

The upland towns in Christine Bonnin's regional study had thriving self-organized markets in rural produce since the 1700s, yet their new official markets stand empty or half empty. High rents and small stalls presume that traders will do the same business every day of the year. The facilities fail to accommodate the upland farming season and household needs, paradoxically pushing rural minorities backward into more informal street vending. Dorothy Hodgson (2001) has documented a parallel contradiction through British colonial officers' complaints about the East African Maasai. While some explained that Maasai herders failed to patronize their newly established cattle markets in district capitals because they did not understand cattle as a commodity, others reported the same Maasai clandestinely selling cattle regularly to Somali traders, who visited their nomadic cattle camps at the appropriate season.

Trade in Border Areas

The distinctive characteristics of international borders and their markets have received special attention from a considerable body of scholarship referenced here by Caroline Grillot. In West Africa, the Ghana-Togo and Nigeria-Benin border areas have generated detailed studies, the first by Paul Nugent (2002) and Brenda Chalfin (2010) and the second by Donna Flynn (1997). In East Africa, cattle smuggling and raiding in the Kenya-Ethiopia-Somalia borderland and the Uganda-Sudan-Ethiopia borderland have drawn notice because of their connection to communal violence (Fleisher 2000; Little 1992). Refugees and arms flow from one to the other and back again as unrest ebbs and flows across long distances. Researchers in both regions have argued for considering the territory on both sides of such international borders to be a semi-autonomous border zone, with its own interactional conventions and cultural identity that center upon the border itself as an economic asset.

Grillot shows how northern Vietnamese traders use their flexibility and long-standing commercial relationships to circumvent the ebb and flow of official policies on cross-border trade with China. The remote land routes and barges that cross the Beilun River to China offer a lucrative niche to the highlanders most familiar with their geography. Sophisticated trading relations based on highly mobile rural networks enable traders to respond sensitively to shifts in international political tensions and in national policy. Traders from both countries constantly adjust their practices to keep goods flowing through twin border cities despite mutual distrust and fluctuating legal status. While this rapid response reflects an intimate connection to global dynamics, it also allows more effective detachment from national and international control.

On the one hand, the China trade appears to be hypermodern, featuring cosmopolitan manufactures, such as sex toys and jeans, which qualify perhaps as icons of modernity in their own right. Corruption among traders in these goods is common and reminds Kirsten Endres's informants of the murky dealings in the criminal underworld. Chalfin (2010) analyzes the dominance of such personalized relations within the ultramodern context of Ghana's international airport. On the other hand, the participants and practices of Vietnamese border trade seem to qualify as bastions of ancient tradition or backwardness. Luong documents a long history of villagers in the southern lowlands taking itinerant long-distance trade across national borders within Indochina.

On the border with China, Grillot finds that freight trucks, readily available on a modern highway, have not displaced foot traffic entirely. Trucks regularly unload their goods on one side of the bridge and hire individuals to walk them across piecemeal. A niche remains for those willing to carry over small quantities of goods, if they can pass as poor peasants bringing goods for their personal and family use. Taking on this persona manipulates ideological contradictions among those who draft national regulations and contradictory ideologies among customs agents themselves. Trucks may look more efficient in technical and economic calculations, but they are less efficient for managing patronage relations with customs agents, more important in actual practice.

RELATIONS WITH GOVERNMENT

Many of the chapters here focus on the distinctive politics of engagement by local and national governments with informal trade. Border areas again reveal particularly sharp contradictions within policy and practice. Using remote rural routes and hand carriage of goods obviously constitute strategies to avoid state intervention as much as possible. While smuggling in any form seems a clear indication of weak central government control, successful smuggling requires closer relationships than many legal occupations with national government employees, particularly customs agents and border guards. Corruption and the visibility of informal trade reveal and perpetuate the inadequacy of state institutions while requiring frequent and skillful interaction with them.

Smuggled supplies serve as a vital lifeline for state functionaries as well as ordinary citizens when civil war or state fragility interrupt legal channels, for example, in Biafra and Zaire (Nwapa [1980] 1992; MacGaffey 1991). K. T. Hansen (1989) has analyzed the theoretical implications of de facto mutual interdependence between the state and illegal economic institutions. Endres shows here how the communicative channel of bureaucratic reports by urban market officials erects a protective barrier between higher and lower authorities. The lucrative trade in smuggled goods, thus sustained, both underwrites local officialdom and preserves the precious illusion of national coherence. The dense network of relationships with customs agents and market officials that is shown suggests that relations with these state actors are as dominant in shaping trade here as in Hanoi, where Gertrud Hüwelmeier and Lisa Barthelmes describe daily raids on street vendors.

Nguyễn Thị Thanh Bình and Barthelmes provide fine-grained analyses of interventions by Hanoi's municipal planners to eliminate street vending and illegal markets. Hostile policies toward street vendors follow the forms of prohibitive licensing and violent street clearances all too familiar to vendors on many continents (Clark 1988; Lindell 2010b). Rigorous enforcement preceding international conferences and diplomatic visits, as elsewhere, makes one of the more ironic statements about global-ization's repressive effect on local livelihoods. Barthelmes stresses the unpredictability of enforcement, in which patronage ties with local authorities and tax collectors govern more reliably than written regulations. Nguyễn Thị Thanh Bình follows the polariz-ing effect of metropolitan zoning that confiscates farmland in a peri-urban village and pushes many villagers into the illegal streets. Few can afford stalls at high rents in the official markets or to rent farmland in adjacent villages still classified as rural.

Hüwelmeier explores the development of new markets in Hanoi despite official city rhetoric promoting supermarkets and commercial centers. As in the upland regions, constructive engagement leads more often to expensive modern "ghost markets" than to increased incomes or employment for traders.[1] The lack of consultation, unfortu-nately common in too many arenas worldwide, leads to poor design and choice of locations and distorts market organization and stall allocation. Relocated or rebuilt markets often fail to thrive, but effectively displace former stallholders into temporary "toad" markets with tenuous legal status. Hüwelmeier proves that most traders cannot survive the poor economic conditions in their allotted temporary location, while the new market only promises them a basement with limited access.

The private gold shops described here by Allison Truitt are another instructive special case. The theme of avoiding nonfunctional formal institutions carries over, in this case to a national currency rendered worthless by reforms in 1976 and 1985. Com-parative studies of economic responses to unstable currencies in colonial West Africa show how often such strategies have been needed (see Berry 1995; Ekejuiba 1995; Law 1995). One could even argue that the resort to gold in Vietnam for both local and international transactions served to conceal or divert attention from the collapse of the official currency, by stepping in to fulfill so many of its usual economic functions.

Shifts in government policy toward and regulation of gold shops reflect this con-tradiction. They prove to be as volatile as enforcement of sanctions against illegal marketplaces and street vendors, triggering some of the same effects and responses. Truitt focuses on the raid on a single shop, a case that was very widely publicized and discussed. Her clear exposition of the national policy timeline balances any narrow-ness in her argument. A remarkably rapid series of reversals ranged from official rec-ognition and investment in gold shops and gold bar manufacture, through mandating their incorporation into the formal banking system, all the way to limiting them to the buying and selling of gold jewelry. The very unpredictability of enforcement, not its effectiveness, destabilized gold as a means of payment and savings. Police confiscation of gold and foreign currency from the shop owner's home above her shop left ordinary citizens nervous about even owning gold jewelry.

IDEOLOGY IN THE MARKET

Many fascinating ideological contests emerge within these case studies, entan-gling socialist and neoliberal aspirations to modernity with diverging invocations of traditional peasant culture. Esther Horat's peri-urban villagers cling to their rural image to protect their thriving market against private competition while it shifts from traditional cloth to industrial textiles and ready-to-wear clothing. Annuska Derks like-wise lays out the tenacity of both urban and rural connections for producers, traders, and consumers of charcoal briquettes, supposedly extinct in modern "green and clean" Hanoi. In the public debate over gold that Truitt documents, ideological arguments both condemned and defended gold shops as not modern, as a part of Vietnamese traditional culture and family legacy, as parasitic intermediaries, and as exemplars of the new economic policy defending private property and wealth accumulation.

The neoliberal free-market ideology that is currently dominant globally offers traders in general some space under the rubric of entrepreneurship, but it gives market and street vendors only a contingent reprieve. Still not fully modern, this sector supposedly has no future despite its evident and persistent growth. Socialist modernization programs retain more suspicions about bourgeois capitalism but share underlying evolutionary assumptions. Capitalism is set to disappear less imminently than the feudal relics of petty trade, though it is still ultimately doomed. Such contradictions resonate in the many postsocialist countries on every continent. Particularly detailed explorations of Tanzania by Aili Mari Tripp (1997) and of then Zaire by Janet MacGaffey (1987) focus on the portrayal of traders as parasitic intermediaries inimical to both frameworks (see also Clark 2001).

The resulting ideological juggling creates some intriguing incongruities in Vietnamese government policy toward marketplaces. For example, in the "backward" highlands (see Bonnin and Turner in this volume) daily marketplaces are promoted as a step forward from periodic markets and itinerant peddlers or collectors. Intended to integrate supposedly isolated hill tribes into the market economy, these new markets end up dominated by immigrants from lowland ethnic groups. These regions promote tourism, so the intersection of such policies raises the irony of tourist attractions inaccessible to tourists. In Vietnam's largest cities, planners aspire to more formally organized corporate or public-sector institutions and condemn open marketplaces as backward relics with no potential future. City governments literally marginalize their largest markets to peripheral locations that are not economically viable, intending to transform them into the type of wholesale produce market found on the edges of many Western European cities (Hüwelmeier, this volume). Another alternative planning policy rebuilds centrally located markets as Western-style shopping centers, priced out of the reach of original market traders or customers as happened in Ghana after the demolition of Accra's famed Makola No. 1 market (Robertson 1983; Clark 1988).

Traders themselves energetically invoke pro-peasant Marxist ideology in various settings (see Turner, Barthelmes, and Horat, this volume). They claim protection or tolerance as poor peasants, deserving special consideration by a government that has not delivered their promised prosperity. Older vendors who are demonstrably poor, especially if they are war veterans or widows, often succeed in escaping arrest. They reinforce nationalist sentiments with surviving Confucian household ideals built on respect for the elderly to generate guilt when they confront police and officials. Performing these identities can also serve as an effective bargaining strategy (see Luong and Minh T. N. Nguyen, this volume) in immediate transactions. In the larger context these strategies are self-limiting, because they rely on pity and work only while the performer remains visibly poor. The one case that seems to dodge this constraint is Horat's peri-urban community. Residents determinedly foster their image as an egalitarian farming community with traditional noncapitalist values, despite hiring farm workers and hiding their wealth.

Marxist and traditionalist nationalisms also overlap in the vilification of foreign traders, primarily Chinese, while Chinese traders (and Chinese goods) are also currently attracting hostility across Africa. Xenophobic violence sparked the epic exodus of East African Asian populations soon after independence. There has been repeated targeting of Lebanese in West Africa and in South Africa of immigrants from Zimbabwe, Mozambique, and Nigeria in the urban informal sector. A reverse dynamic still attracts newcomers to identify with ethnic groups known for their successful trading—the Hausa, the Creole, and the Swahili.

TRADING IN GENDER

Another key unifying theme in the ideological and material struggles analyzed here is gender ideology and practice. Even though gender was not highlighted in the conceptual outline of the volume, the cases themselves provide a gratifying demonstration of gender as an economic variable. For both men and women, gender has been a major and often the deciding factor in their choices of economic specializations. For Minh Nguyen and Hy Van Luong, their interviews with traders clearly show men and women consciously pondering whether or how gender roles condition individual success in various trading strategies.

These two case studies also trace changes in the content and expression of gender ideals as men and women's economic options shrink and expand in particular directions, serving as excellent examples of the historical construction of gender. The authors show gender being fully inflected by class and ethnicity as these identities also change in response to economic shifts. Jon Holtzman (2003) makes a similar case for Samburu young men in Mombasa, weaving together stints as security guards or beach boys in place of their iconic years away at the cattle camps. Individuals reconstruct and redefine valid gender identities for themselves and their peers by adopting and assigning meaning to new activities when they no longer expect to fulfill outdated gender standards. Young Vietnamese men take up beer and cigarettes for adventure, while young women take up peddling to care for their children.

Luong presents a particularly detailed account of historical change, working backward from his villages' current concentration in hawking key chains and other small consumer items. The reality of gender stereotypes emerges separately from internal and external perceptions, when men and women admit that women have better luck appealing to a predominantly male retail clientele in bars and cafes. Customers buy these items more out of pity than need, so the transaction thus reinforces the buyer's masculinity and self-esteem. Women peddlers also are more used to taking advantage of this inferior stance in other arenas of life; they find it easier and perhaps have better skill in modulating their performances to their audience's reaction. Male traders find it psychologically unpleasant to take this inferior stance and male customers find their performances less credible. They must step outside the rhetorical frame of gender and into that of kinship, petitioning for solidarity by addressing their potential customers as uncles or brothers. The marital bond is also highly valued and treated as somewhat vulnerable to personal strategies. Both men and women worry that spouses who spend too long away from them in the city can easily pick up bad habits, showing weaker economic or sexual commitment. The contested meanings of urban or even transnational migration, as Paul Stoller (2002) explores for Africans in New York, range from selfishness to self-sacrifice and from achieving adulthood to running away from its demands (see also Buggenhagen 2011).

Minh Nguyen's chapter is particularly strong in showing the overt and covert contestation of gender roles over several generations of economic and cultural change. Starting well beyond the idea of masculinity and femininity as homogenous variables, she portrays both men and women making sometimes difficult choices as the opportunities for fulfilling gender ideals or expectations ebb and flow. She follows individuals and families as they protect, transgress, and redefine the demands of gender adequacy.

One option is to take advantage of ideological alternatives and redefine the criteria for fulfilling the ideal. She paints a poignant picture of older men, once respected as soldiers and liberators, retreating to the multigenerational household. They take on domestic tasks usually coded feminine (cooking and child care) to remain in a context where their status as household head gives prestige. In many cases these older men relied on their wives, who migrated to the city, for cash income. Women of this older cohort found it easier and more gender appropriate to combine collecting discarded goods for resale or recycling with cleaning urban houses.

Younger men struggling to marry or build houses find urban definitions of masculinity that stress individual autonomy and conspicuous consumption more attainable. They boast of personal coups in identifying valuable antiques, and combine their collection efforts with repairing electronics and appliances rather than housecleaning. In this context dirt and cleaning are coded female, while cleaner modern technology is coded male. Although young men manage to maintain this self-image despite limited incomes, the pull of family-based respectability remains strong enough to induce many to work closer to home as they marry or their families mature. Earning less income that way, they endorse the older virtues of thrift and unselfishness. More fortunate men set up wholesale recycling depots that can employ their wives and children, reuniting the household in the city.

Younger women can more easily draw on gender solidarity to build a client network of homemakers, an asset that husbands recognize and respect. One husband tried to retain his wife's network by taking over himself, since she had built up a large enough clientele to dispense with housecleaning. Wives' incomes also justify compromise over domestic duties. A couple often agrees to leave their young children in the village with grandparents. Mothers and wives visit their village homes frequently to show their loyalty, performing the cooking and child care when at home. They tend to play down their economic success rather than bragging as men do. However, young women can also draw upon the socialist ideal of the new woman, who works hard and manages her household successfully while still preserving its cultural and moral integrity. In West Africa, men and women also juggle multiple gender ideals: the Akan maternal provider, the Christian joint marriage, the Islamic husband supporting his wife, and the admired independent "male" woman.

Gender validity appears as an important factor to protect or debate in other chapters throughout this volume. Derks's lively chapter on coal briquettes traces a parallel interpenetration of considerations of age and youth, modernity and tradition with gender. Clean and dirty have an ambiguous relation to gender in the context of official environmental campaigns that deny the continuing use of charcoal for cooking. Dirty cooking and cleaning work seems more appropriate for women, while dirty work making and selling briquettes falls to men. Older women feel entitled to keep their coal fires burning despite official prohibitions. Younger working women who have more expensive gas stoves feel entitled to protect their children and themselves from noxious fumes, fulfilling mandates of tradition as well as meeting their aspirations to be new women and modern consumers. They also work outside the home, making it more convenient to cook quickly on kerosene or gas than to monitor a smoldering coal stove.

In several chapters, traders invoke their special needs as women to claim tolerance for their continued activity in occupations classified as backward or traditional. Turner, Hüwelmeier, and Barthelmes studied predominantly female populations of market traders or street vendors who played this card for all it was worth. It apparently had some effect in their public demonstrations over market relocations and street clearances and helped even more often in their individual confrontations with police and local officials. In Ghana, women traders legitimize their incomes through their traditional responsibility for feeding their children, expanding it to cover school fees, clothing, and other paternal responsibilities and dodging or confronting the stereotype of the greedy wife (Clark 2001).

In Horat's thriving peri-urban market, women traders face even more pressure than men traders to deny their profit motivation, though both adapt commercial practices to respect moral principles, for example, by avoiding open price bargaining or competition. The male stereotype of "civilized trade" leaves more room for personal consumption, whether in drinking, gambling, or housebuilding. Women's moral (and sexual) reputations are more vulnerable to immediate challenge if they appear "obsessed with money." References to women gold traders and money changers appear in Grillot and Truitt, although not part of their main discussion. Truitt does chronicle a public debate that raised a gender issue, remarking that Vietnamese cultural tradition required daughters to inherit gold instead of land, which was reserved for sons.

Gender emerges from this collection as a salient dynamic within globalization not simply because contemporary scholars have been trained to look for it, but because it interpenetrates all the other aspects of globalization. Globalization is no more a homogenous category than gender, and it is constructed not only in opposition to the local, or even the glocal. Gender need not be an equally central issue for every research question. This volume shows the reader how globalization is significantly inflected also by national policy history and by ethnic experience. In Vietnam the divide between upland and lowland peoples, a divide deserving regional analysis across Southeast Asia, carries the weights of colonialism, class, and other dominations. Cohort effects mark both gender and global contestations, where men and women a few decades later face different challenges and opportunities than their parents at the same age (cf. Nigeria in Guyer 1997).

Gender does not offer an alternative or competing focus to globalization, so much as a complementary one. Along with other complementary principles of inequality just mentioned and more, it requires attention for the purpose of understanding how globalization is ever enacted. By explicitly mapping and analyzing these inflections, the authors of these chapters throw light on the process of mutual construction and continual renegotiation through which each of these dominations is actually realized and reproduced, that is, in terms of the others. Such a holistic analysis draws upon a historical strength of anthropology without resurrecting the specter of structural functionalism. Rather than producing a bland and repetitive catalog of traits to classify each local configuration, ethnographers now must consciously interrogate each of these arenas of life in relation to the others. As seen here, this very productive approach yields lively and realistic portrayals of personal and collective strategies as these unfold.

NOTE

1 An example from Ghana is Accra's Kaneshie market, which was slow to take off. South Africa's Durban, a relatively pro-market city, provides another example (Lindell 2010b; Skinner 2008).

REFERENCES

A. H. 2014. "Nhiều Tiệm Vàng Tăng 'Phòng Thủ' Sau Vụ Niêm Phong Vàng [Many Gold Shops Increase Their 'Defenses' after the Impounding Gold Affair]." *Tuổi Trẻ*, April 27. http://tuoitre.vn/Kinh-te/604759/nhieu-tiem-vang-tang-phong-thu-sau-vu-niem-phong-vang.html.

Abimbola, Olumide. 2012. "The International Trade in Secondhand Clothing: Managing Information Asymmetry between West African and British Traders." *Textile* 10 (2): 184–99.

Abraham, Itty, and Willem van Schendel. 2005. "Introduction: The Making of Illicitness." In *Illicit Flows and Criminal Things: States, Borders, and the Other Side of Globalization*, edited by Willem van Schendel and Itty Abraham, 1–37. Bloomington: Indiana University Press.

Abram, Simone, and Gisa Weszkalnys. 2013. "Elusive Promises: Planning in the Contemporary World: An Introduction." In *Elusive Promises: Planning in the Contemporary World*, edited by Simone Abram and Gisa Weszkalnys, 1–33. New York: Berghahn.

Abrami, Regina M. 2002a. "Just a Peasant: Economy and Legacy in Northern Vietnam." In *Post-socialist Peasant? Rural and Urban Constructions of Identity in Eastern Europe, East Asia, and the Former Soviet Union*, edited by Pamela Leonard and Deema Kaneff, 94–116. Houndmills, UK: Palgrave.

——. 2002b. "Self-Making, Class Struggle, and Labor Autarky: The Political Origins of Private Entrepreneurship in Vietnam and China." PhD diss., University of California, Berkeley.

Abrams, Philip. 1988. "Notes on the Difficulty of Studying the State (1977)." *Journal of Historical Sociology* 1 (1): 58–89.

Abu-Lughod, Janet. 1987. "The Shape of the World System in the Thirteenth Century." *Studies in Comparative International Developments* 22 (4): 3–25.

Agergaard, Jytte, and Vu Thi Thao. 2011. "Mobile, Flexible, and Adaptable: Female Migrants in Hanoi's Informal Sector." *Population, Space and Place* 17 (5): 407–20.

Agnew, Jean-Christophe. 1986. *Worlds Apart: The Market and the Theater in Anglo-American Thought, 1550–1750*. Cambridge, UK: Cambridge University Press.

Albrecht, David, Hervé Hocquard, and Philippe Papin. 2010. *Urban Development in Vietnam: The Rise of Local Authorities: Resources, Limits, and Evolution of Local Governance*. Focales Report #5, Agence Française de Développement. http://librairie.afd.fr/urban-development-in-vietnam-the-rise-of-local-authorities-resources-limits-and-evolution-of-local-governance/.

Alexander, Jennifer, and Paul Alexander. 2001. "Markets as Gendered Domains: The Javanese *Pasar*." In *Women Traders in Cross-Cultural Perspective*, edited by Linda J. Seligmann, 47–69. Stanford, CA: Stanford University Press.

Alexander, Paul. 1992. "What's in a Price? Trade Practices in Peasant (and Other) Markets." In *Contesting Markets: Analyses of Ideology, Discourse, and Practice*, edited by Roy Dilley, 79–96. Edinburgh: Edinburgh University Press.

Altvater, Elmar. 1998. "Theoretical Deliberations on Time and Space in Post-socialist Transformation." *Regional Studies* 32 (7): 591–605.

An Nhiên and Nguyễn Trang. 2013. "Ninh Hiệp—Bạc Tỉ Và Sự Thụt Lùi Của Tri Thức [Riches and the Decline of Knowledge]." *Lao Động Online*, April 3. http://laodong.com.vn/phong-su/ninh-hiep-bac-ti-va-su-thut-lui-cua-tri-thuc-109018.bld#.

Anh Thu. 2005. "Làng Kính [Eyeglass Village]." *Hà Nội Mới*, February 20. http://hanoimoi.com.vn/Ban-in/Phong-su-Ky-su/38044/lang-kinh.

Anjaria, Jonathan S. 2011. "Ordinary States: Everyday Corruption and the Politics of Space in Mumbai." *American Ethnologist* 38 (1): 58–72.

Anonymous. 2010. "Than Tổ Ong [Beehive Coal Briquettes]." August 20. http://like2chat.blogspot.com/2010/08/than-to-ong.html.

Anonymous. 2012. "Tourists Ripped Off by Vendors in Hanoi's Old Quarter." VietnamNet, August 14. http://english.vietnamnet.vn/fms/travel/25663/tourists-ripped-off-by-vendors-in-hanoi-s-old-quarter.html.

Anonymous. 2013. "Hiểm họa từ những lò than tổ ong giữa thủ đô [Hazards from the Beehive Coal Briquette Ovens in the Capital]." June 17. http://www.thiennhien.net/2013/06/17/hiem-hoa-tu-nhung-lo-than-to-ong-giua-thu-do/.

Anonymous. 2014. "21 Chinese Migrants Arrested Elsewhere on Day of Fatal Gunfight in Vietnam." *Thanh Nien News*, April 20. http://www.thanhniennews.com/politics/21-chinese-migrants-arrested-elsewhere-on-day-of-fatal-gunfight-in-vietnam-25532.html.

Appadurai, Arjun. 1988. "Introduction: Commodities and the Politics of Value." In *The Social Life of Things: Commodities in Cultural Perspective*, edited by Arjun Appadurai, 3–63. New York: Cambridge University Press.

Applbaum, Kalman. 2005. "The Anthropology of Markets." In *A Handbook of Economic Anthropology*, edited by James G. Carrier, 275–89. Cheltenham, UK: Edward Elgar.

Ashwin, Sarah, ed. 2000. *Gender, State, and Society in Soviet and Post-Soviet Russia*. New York: Routledge.

Atkinson, Paul, and Amanda Coffey. 2004. "Analysing Documentary Realities." In *Qualitative Research: Theory, Method, and Practice*. 2nd ed. edited by David Silverman, 56–75. London: Sage.

Babb, Florence. (1989) 1998. *Between Field and Cooking Pot: The Political Economy of Marketwomen in Peru*. Revised edition. Austin: University of Texas Press.

Báo Cáo. 2010. Báo Cáo Thành Tích. Đề Nghị Tặng Thưởng Danh Hiệu Tập Thể Lao Động Tiên Tiến [Performance Report. Application for Award of the Title "Advanced Labor Collective"]. Unpublished document issued by the Lào Cai Central Market Management Board, December 13.

Báo Lào Cai. 1996. "Khánh Thành Hai Chợ Bắc Hà và Cốc Lếu Đưa Vào Sử Dụng [Inauguration and Turnover of Bắc Hà Market and Cốc Lếu Market]." *Báo Lào Cai*, December 5, 267.

Barth, Fredrik, ed. 1969. *Ethnic Groups and Boundaries: The Social Organization of Culture Difference*. Boston: Little, Brown.

Barthelmes, Lisa. 2013. "'Dort gibt es nichts zu sehen'—Shoppingmalls, Supermärkte und Stadtplanung in Hanoi." *Südostasien* 1:8–10.

——. 2014. "Những Người Bán Hàng Rong Tại Hà Nội: Những Nét Đặc Trưng và Tính Năng Động Của Một Nhóm Kinh Tế-Xã Hội Riêng Biệt [Mobile Street Vendors in Hanoi: Features and Dynamics of a Distinct Socioeconomic Group]." *Tạp chí Dân tộc học* 3 (186): 50–60.

Bayly, Susan. 2009. "Vietnamese Narratives of Tradition, Exchange, and Friendship in the Worlds of the Global Socialist Ecumene." In *Enduring Socialism: Explorations of Revolution and Transformation, Restoration and Continuation*, edited by Harry G. West and Parvathi Raman, 125–47. New York: Berghahn.

Bear, Laura. 2011. "Making a River of Gold: Speculative State Planning, Informality, and Neoliberal Governance on the Hooghly." *Focaal: Journal of Global and Historical Anthropology* 61:46–60.

Bélanger, Danièle, Lisa B. Welch Drummond, and Van Nguyen-Marshall. 2012. "Introduction: Who Are the Urban Middle Class in Vietnam?" In *The Reinvention of Distinction: Modernity and the Middle Class in Urban Vietnam*, edited by Van Nguyen-Marshall, Lisa B. Welch Drummond, and Danièle Bélanger, 1–17. Dordrecht, the Netherlands: Springer.

Beresford, Melanie. 2008. "*Doi Moi* in Review: The Challenges of Building Market Socialism in Vietnam." *Journal of Contemporary Asia* 38 (2): 221–43.

Berry, Sara. 1995. "Stable Prices, Unstable Values: Some Thoughts on Monetization and the Meaning of Transaction in West African Economies." In *Money Matters: Instability, Values, and Social Payments in the Modern History of West African Communities*, edited by Jane I. Guyer, 299–313. Portsmouth, NH: Heinemann.

Bhowmik, Sharit K. 2005. "Street Vendors in Asia: A Review." *Economic and Political Weekly*, May 28–June 4, 2256–64.

——, ed. 2010. *Street Vendors in the Global Urban Economy*. New Delhi: Routledge.

Bierschenk, Thomas, and Jean-Pierre Olivier de Sardan, eds. 2014. *States at Work. Dynamics of African Bureaucracies*. Leiden, the Netherlands: Brill.

Bộ Công Thương (Ministry of Industry and Commerce). 2007. "Quyết Định Số 012/2007/QĐ-BCT Ngày 26 Tháng 12 Năm 2007, Phê Duyệt Quy Hoạch Tổng Thể Phát Triển Mạng Lưới Chợ Trên Phạm Vi Toàn Quốc Đến Năm 2010 và Định Hướng Đến Năm 2020 [Decision 012/2007/QĐ-BCT of December 26, 2007, Approving the Master Plan of Developing the Nationwide Market Network up to 2010, with Orientations toward 2020]." http://vanban.chinhphu.vn/portal/page/portal/chinhphu/hethongvanban?class_id=1&mode=detail&document_id=52836.

——. 2014. "Dự Thảo Báo Cáo Tổng Hợp. Qui Hoạch Tổng Thể Phát Triển Mạng Lưới Chợ Toàn Quốc Đến Năm 2025, Tầm Nhìn Đến Năm 2035 [Draft Synthesis Report. Master Plan of Developing the Nationwide Market Network up to 2025, with Orientations toward 2035]." http://www.moit.gov.vn/vn/tin-tuc/4198/du-thao-bao-cao-tong-hop-quy-hoach-tong-the-phat-trien-mang-luoi-cho-toan-quoc.aspx.

——. 2015. "Quyết Định Số 6481/QĐ-BCT Ngày 26 Tháng 6 Năm 2015, Phê Duyệt Quy Hoạch Tổng Thể Phát Triển Mạng Lưới Chợ Toàn Quốc Đến Năm 2025, Tầm Nhìn Đến Năm 2035 [Decision 6481/QĐ-BCT of June 26, 2015, Approving the Master Plan of Developing the Nationwide Market Network up to 2025, with a Vision toward 2035]." https://thuvienphapluat.vn/van-ban/Thuong-mai/Quyet-dinh-6481-QD-BCT-2015-Quy-hoach-tong-the-phat-trien-mang-luoi-cho-toan-quoc-den-2025-280779.aspx.

Bộ Thương Mại (Ministry of Trade). 1996. "Thông Tư Của Bộ Thương Mại Số 15/TM-CSTTTN Ngày 16 Tháng 10 Năm 1996 Hướng Dẫn Về Tổ Chức và Quản Lý Chợ [Circular nr. 15/TM-CSTTTN of the Ministry of Trade, October 16, 1996, Providing Guidance on the Organization and Management of Markets]." https://thuvienphapluat.vn/van-ban/Thuong-mai/Thong-tu-15-TM-CSTTTN-huong-dan-to-chuc-quan-ly-cho-40162.aspx.

Bonnin, Christine. 2012. "Markets in the Mountains: Upland Trade-Scapes, Trader Livelihoods, and State Development Agendas in Northern Vietnam." PhD diss., McGill University.

——. 2013. "Doing Fieldwork and Making Friends in Upland Northern Vietnam: Entanglements of the Professional, Personal and Political." In *Red Stamps and Gold Stars: Fieldwork Dilemmas in Upland Socialist Asia*, edited by Sarah Turner, 121–42. Vancouver: UBC Press.

——. 2018. "Cultivating Consumer Markets: Ethnic Minority Traders and the Refashioning of Cultural Commodities in the Sino-Vietnamese Border Uplands." In *The Routledge Handbook of Asian Borderlands,* edited by Alexander Horstmann, Martin Saxer, and Alessandro Rippa. London: Routledge.

Bonnin, Christine, and Sarah Turner. 2012. "At What Price Rice? Food Security, Livelihood Vulnerability, and State Interventions in Upland Northern Vietnam." *Geoforum* 43 (1): 95–105.

——. 2014. "Remaking Markets in the Mountains: Integration, Trader Agency, and Resistance in Upland Northern Vietnam." *Journal of Peasant Studies* 41 (3): 321–42.

Brenner, Neil. 2000. "The Urban Question as a Scale Question: Reflections on Henri Lefebvre, Urban Theory, and the Politics of Scale." *International Journal of Urban and Regional Research* 24 (2): 361–78.

Brenner, Neil, Jamie Peck, and Nik Theodore. 2010. "Variegated Neoliberalization: Geographies, Modalities, Pathways." *Global Networks* 10 (2): 182–222.

Bromley, Ray. 2000. "Street Vending and Public Policy: A Global Review." *The International Journal of Sociology and Social Policy* 20 (1–2): 1–28.

Brown, Alison, ed. 2006. *Contested Space: Street Trading, Public Space, and Livelihoods in Developing Cities*. Warwickshire, UK: ITDG.

Brown, Alison, Michal Lyons, and Ibrahima Dankoco. 2010. "Street Traders and the Emerging Spaces for Urban Voice and Citizenship in African Cities." *Urban Studies* 47 (3): 666–83.

Brownell, Susan, and Jeffrey N. Wasserstrom, eds. 2002. *Chinese Femininities, Chinese Masculinities: A Reader*. Berkeley: University of California Press.

Bruns, Bettina, and Judith Miggelbrink. 2012. Introduction to *Subverting Borders: Doing Research on Smuggling and Small-Scale Trade*, edited by Bettina Bruns and Judith Miggelbrink, 11–19. Wiesbaden, Germany: VS Verlag.

Buggenhagen, Beth. 2011. "Are Births Just 'Women's Business'? Gift Exchange, Value, and Global Volatility in Muslim Senegal." *American Ethnologist* 38 (4): 714–32.

Bui Hai Thiem. 2015. "In Search of a Post-socialist Mode of Governmentality: The Double Movement of Accommodating and Resisting Neo-liberalism in Vietnam." *Asian Journal of Social Science* 43 (1/2): 80–102.

Bùi Xuân Đính, ed. 2009. *Làng Nghề Thủ Công Huyện Thanh Oai (Hà Nội): Truyền Thống và Biến Đổi* [*Craft Villages of Thanh Oai District: Tradition and Changes*]. Hanoi: Social Sciences Publishing House.

Calkins, Sandra. 2014. "Survival at the Margins. Processing Uncertainties in North-Eastern Sudan." PhD diss., University of Leipzig.

Carrier, James G. 2005. *Gifts and Commodities: Exchange and Western Capitalism since 1700*. New York: Routledge.

Castells, Manuel, and Alejandro Portes. 1989. "World Underneath: The Origins, Dynamics, and Effects of the Informal Economy." In *The Informal Economy: Studies in Advanced and Less Developed Countries*, edited by Alejandro Portes, Manuel Castells, and Lauren A. Benton, 11–37. Baltimore: Johns Hopkins University Press.

Chalfin, Brenda. 2010. *Neoliberal Frontiers: An Ethnography of Sovereignty in West Africa*. Chicago: University of Chicago Press.

Chambers, Robert, and Gordon R. Conway. 1991. "Sustainable Rural Livelihoods: Practical Concepts for the 21st Century." *Institute of Development Studies (IDS)* Discussion Paper 296:1–29.

Chan, Yuk Wah. 2013. *Vietnamese-Chinese Relationships at the Borderlands: Trade, Tourism, and Cultural Politics*. New York: Routledge.

Chen, Martha Alter. 2012. "The Informal Economy in Comparative Perspective." In *A Handbook of Economic Anthropology*, edited by James G. Carrier, 485–500. Cheltenham, UK and Northampton, MA: Edward Elgar.

Chính Phủ (Government). 1995. "Nghị Định Của Chính Phủ Số 36-CP Ngày 29 Tháng 5 Năm 1995 Về Bảo Đảm An Toàn Giao Thông Đường Bộ và Trật Tự An Toàn Giao Thông Đô Thị [Government Decree Number 36-CP of May 29, 1995, on Ensuring Traffic Order and Safety on Roads and in Urban Centers]." https://thuvienphapluat.vn/van-ban/Giao-thong-Van-tai/Nghi-dinh-36-CP-bao-dam-an-toan-giao-thong-duong-bo-va-trat-tu-an-toan-giao-thong-do-thi-39155.aspx.

——. 2003. "Nghị Định 02/2003/NĐ-CP Ngày 14 Tháng 1 Năm 2003 về Phát Triển và Quản Lý Chợ [Government Decree Number 02/2003/NĐ-CP of January 14, 2003, on the Development and Management of Marketplaces]." http://www.moj.gov.vn/vbpq/lists/vn%20bn%20php%20lut/view_detail.aspx?itemid=20570.

——. 2004. "Quyết Định Số 559/QĐ-TTG Ngày 31 Tháng 5 Năm 2004. Chương Trình Phát Triển Chợ Đến 2010 [Prime Minister's Decision Number 559/QĐ-TTG of May 31, 2004, Approving the Program on the Development of Marketplaces until 2010]." https://thuvienphapluat.vn/van-ban/Thuong-mai/Quyet-dinh-559-QĐ-TTg-Chuong-trinh-phat-trien-cho-den-2010-52119.aspx.

——. 2008. "Quyết Định Số 46/2008/QĐ-TTG Ngày 31 Tháng 3 Năm 2008. Phê Duyệt Quy Hoạch Tổng Thể Phát Triển Kinh Tế—Xã Hội Tỉnh Lào Cai Đến Năm 2020 [Prime Minister's Decision Number 46/2008 SRV/QĐ-TTg of March 31,

2008, Approving the Master Plan on Socio-economic Development of Lào Cai Province until 2020].” http://vanban.chinhphu.vn/portal/page/portal/chinhphu/hethongvanban?class_id=1&mode=detail&document_id=62783.

——. 2009. “Nghị Định 114/2009/NĐ-CP Ngày 23 Tháng 12 Năm 2009, Sửa đổi, Bổ Sung Một Số Điều Của Nghị Định 02/2003/NĐ-CP Ngày 14 Tháng 1 Năm 2003 Về Phát Triển Và Quản Lý Chợ [Government Decree 114/2009/NĐ-CP of December 23, 2009, Amendments and Supplement to Government Decree No. 02/2003/NĐ-CP of January 14, 2003, on the Development and Management of Marketplaces].” http://vanban.chinhphu.vn/portal/page/portal/chinhphu/hethongvanban?class_id=1&mode=detail&document_id=92355.

——. 2012. “Nghị Định Số 24/2012/NĐ-CP Ngày 03 Tháng 4 Năm 2012 Về Quản Lý Hoạt Động Kinh Doanh Vàng [Government Decree Number 24/2012/NĐ-CP of April 03, 2012 of the Government on Gold Business Activities].” http://vanban.chinhphu.vn/portal/page/portal/chinhphu/hethongvanban?class_id=1&mode=detail&document_id=157073.

Chio, Jenny. 2014. *A Landscape of Travel: The Work of Tourism in Rural Ethnic China.* Seattle: University of Washington Press.

Chu, Julie Y. 2010. *Cosmologies of Credit: Transnational Mobility and the Politics of Destination in China.* Durham, NC: Duke University Press.

Clark, Gracia, ed. 1988. *Traders versus the State: Anthropological Approaches to Unofficial Economies.* Boulder, CO: Westview Press.

——. 1994. *Onions Are My Husband: Survival and Accumulation by West African Women.* Chicago: University of Chicago Press.

——. 2001. “Gender and Profiteering: Ghana’s Market Women as Devoted Mothers and ‘Human Vampire Bats.’” In *“Wicked” Women and the Reconfiguration of Gender in Africa*, edited by Dorothy L. Hodgson and Sheryl A. McCurdy, 293–311. Portsmouth, NH: Heinemann.

Cohen, Barney. 2004. “Urban Growth in Developing Countries: A Review of Current Trends and a Caution Regarding Existing Forecasts.” *World Development* 32 (1): 23–51.

Collins, Jane L. 1988. *Unseasonal Migrations: The Effects of Rural Labor Scarcity in Peru.* Princeton, NJ: Princeton University Press.

——. 2000. “Tracing Social Relations in Commodity Chains: The Case of Grapes in Brazil.” In *Commodities and Globalization: Anthropological Perspectives*, edited by Angelique Haugerud, M. Priscilla Stone, and Peter D. Little, 97–109. Lanham, MD: Rowman and Littlefield.

Công Thanh and Phạm Hải. 2008. “Hàng Rong Hà Nội Vái Lạy: ‘Cho Tôi Kiếm Cơm!’ [Hanoi Street Vendor Invocation: ‘Let Me Make a Living!’].” http://vietbao.vn/Xa-hoi/Hang-rong-Ha-Noi-vai-lay-Cho-toi-kiem-com/20764099/157/.

Connell, R. W. 2005. *Masculinities.* 2nd ed. Berkeley: University of California Press.

Cornwall, Andrea, and Nancy Lindisfarne. 1994. *Dislocating Masculinity: Comparative Ethnographies.* New York: Routledge.

Coulthart, Alan, Quang Nguyen, and Henry Sharpe. 2006. *Vietnam’s Infrastructure Challenge—Urban Development Strategy: Meeting the Challenges of Rapid Urbanization and the Transition to a Market Oriented Economy.* Washington, DC: World Bank.

http://documents.worldbank.org/curated/en/2006/06/7037447/vietnams-infrastructure-challenge-urban-development-strategy-meeting-challenges-rapid-urbanization-transition-market-oriented-economy.

Cresswell, Tim. 2010. "Towards a Politics of Mobility." *Environment and Planning D: Society and Space* 28:17–31.

Cross, John C. 1998. *Informal Politics: Street Vendors and the State in Mexico City*. Stanford, CA: Stanford University Press.

Cross, John C., and Alfonso Morales, eds. 2007. *Street Entrepreneurs: People, Place, and Politics in Local and Global Perspectives*. New York: Routledge.

Crossa, Veronica. 2009. "Resisting the Entrepreneurial City: Street Vendors' Struggle in Mexico City's Historic Center." *International Journal of Urban and Regional Research* 33 (1): 43–63.

Cục Việc Làm; Bộ Lao Động, Thương Binh và Xã Hội (Department of Employment; Ministry of Labour, Invalids and Social Affairs). 2013. "Tình Hình Di Chuyển Lao Động Từ Nông Thôn Ra Thành Thị Và Các Khu Công Nghiệp Trong Bối Cảnh Việt Nam Gia Nhập WTO. Báo Cáo Tổng Thể [The Situation of Labor Migration from Rural to Urban and Industrial Areas in the Context of Vietnam's WTO Accession. General Project Report]." Hanoi.

Dampier, William. 1906. *Dampier's Voyages*. Edited by John Masefield. London: E. Grant Richards.

Das, Veena, and Deborah Poole. 2004. "State and Its Margins: Comparative Ethnographies." In *Anthropology in the Margins of the State*, edited by Veena Das and Deborah Poole, 3–34. Santa Fe, NM: School of American Research Press.

de Certeau, Michel. 1984. *The Practice of Everyday Life*. Berkeley: University of California Press.

de Haan, Leo, and Annelies Zoomers. 2005. "Exploring the Frontier of Livelihoods Research." *Development and Change* 36 (1): 27–47.

Demographia. 2017. *Demographia World Urban Areas*. 13th annual edition. http://demographia.com/db-worldua.pdf.

Derks, Annuska. 2015a. "Fuelling Change: A Biography of the Beehive Coal Briquette in Post-*Đổi Mới* Vietnam." *Journal of Material Culture* 20 (3): 331–49.

——. 2015b. "Stars, Spirits, and Coal: Materiality and Immateriality in Northern Vietnam." *The Asia Pacific Journal of Anthropology* 16 (1): 1–16.

Dery, David. 1998. "'Papereality' and Learning in Bureaucratic Organizations." *Administration and Society* 29:677–89.

Dewey, Alice G. 1962. *Peasant Marketing in Java*. New York: Free Press of Glencoe.

DiGregorio, Michael R. 1994. "Urban Harvest: Recycling as a Peasant Industry in Northern Vietnam." *East-West Center Occasional Papers*, Environment Series, no. 17 (September).

——. 2001. "Iron Works: Excavating Alternative Futures in a Northern Vietnamese Craft Village." PhD diss., University of California, Los Angeles.

——. 2011. "Into the Land Rush: Facing the Urban Transition in Hanoi's Western Suburbs." *International Development Planning Review* 33 (3): 293–319.

——. 2012. "Hanoi Public Market." Hanoi: Redbridge TV & Film Production.

DiGregorio, Michael, A. Terry Rambo, and Masayuki Yanagisawa. 2003. "Clean, Green, and Beautiful: Environment and Development under the Renovation Economy." In *Postwar Vietnam: Dynamics of a Transforming Society*, edited by Hy V. Luong, 171–99. Singapore: Institute of Southeast Asian Studies / Lanham, MD: Rowman and Littlefield.

Dilley, Roy. 1992. "Contesting Markets: A General Introduction to Market Ideology, Imagery, and Discourse." In *Contesting Markets: Analyses of Ideology, Discourse, and Practice*, edited by Roy Dilley, 1–34. Edinburgh: Edinburgh University Press.

Douglas, Mary. 1966. *Purity and Danger: An Analysis of the Concepts of Pollution and Taboo*. London: Routledge.

Drummond, Lisa B. W. 1993. "Women, the Household Economy, and the Informal Sector in Hanoi." Master's thesis, University of British Columbia.

——. 2000. "Street Scenes: Practices of Public and Private Space in Urban Vietnam." *Urban Studies* 37 (12): 2377–91.

——. 2012. "Middle Class Landscapes in a Transforming City: Hanoi in the 21st Century." In *The Reinvention of Distinction: Modernity and the Middle Class in Urban Vietnam*, edited by Van Nguyen-Marshall, Lisa B. Welch Drummond, and Danièle Bélanger, 79–95. Dordrecht, the Netherlands: Springer.

Dương Minh Anh. 2006. "Theo Dấu Mì Gõ [Tracing Noodle Soup]." *Sài Gòn Giải Phóng Online*, June 26. http://www.sggp.org.vn/theo-dau-mi-go-98881.html.

Eades, Jeremy. 1994. *Strangers and Traders*. Trenton, NJ: Africa World Press.

Eakin, Hallie, Catherine Tucker, and Edwin Castellanos. 2006. "Responding to the Coffee Crisis: A Pilot Study of Farmers' Adaptations in Mexico, Guatemala, and Honduras." *Geographical Journal* 172 (2): 156–71.

Eder, Klaus. 2006. "Europe's Borders: The Narrative Construction of the Boundaries of Europe." *European Journal of Social Theory* 9 (2): 255–71.

Eidse, Noelani, and Sarah Turner. 2014. "Doing Resistance Their Own Way: Counter-narratives of Street Vending in Hanoi, Vietnam through Solicited Journaling." *Area* 46 (3): 242–48.

Ekejiuba, Felicia. 1995. "Currency Instability and Social Payments among the Igbo of Eastern Nigeria, 1890–1990." In *Money Matters: Instability, Values, and Social Payments in the Modern History of West African Communities*, edited by Jane I. Guyer, 133–61. Portsmouth, NH: Heinemann.

Ellis, Frank. 1998. "Household Strategies and Rural Livelihood Diversification." *Journal of Development Studies* 35 (1): 1–38.

——. 2000. *Rural Livelihoods and Diversity in Developing Countries*. Oxford: Oxford University Press.

Elyachar, Julia. 2003. "Mappings of Power: The State, NGOs, and International Organizations in the Informal Economy of Cairo." *Comparative Studies in Society and History* 45 (3): 571–605.

Endres, Kirsten W. 2014a. "Downgraded by Upgrading: Small-Scale Traders, Urban Transformation, and Spatial Reconfiguration in Post-reform Vietnam." *Cambridge Anthropology* 32 (2): 97–111.

——. 2014b. "Making Law: Small-Scale Trade and Corrupt Exceptions at the Vietnam-China Border." *American Anthropologist* 116 (3): 611–25.

——. 2015a. "Constructing the Neighbourly 'Other': Trade Relations and Mutual Perceptions across the Vietnam-China Border." *SOJOURN: Journal of Social Issues in Southeast Asia* 30 (3): 710–41.

——. 2015b. "'*Lộc* Bestowed by Heaven': Fate, Fortune, and Morality in the Vietnamese Marketplace." *The Asia Pacific Journal of Anthropology* 16 (3): 227–43.

Espeland, Wendy. 1993. "Power, Policy and Paperwork: The Bureaucratic Representation of Interests." *Qualitative Sociology* 16 (3): 297–317.

Evers, Hans-Dieter. 1975. "Urbanization and Urban Conflict in Southeast Asia." *Asian Survey* 15 (9): 775–85.

Fadiman, Anne. 1997. *The Spirit Catches You and You Fall Down: A Hmong Child, Her American Doctors, and the Collision of Two Cultures*. New York: Farrar, Straus, and Giroux.

Fassin, Didier. 2011. "Policing Borders, Producing Boundaries. The Governmentality of Immigration in Dark Times." *Annual Review of Anthropology* 40:213–26.

Ferguson, James. 1999. *Expectations of Modernity: Myths and Meanings of Urban Life on the Zambian Copperbelt*. Berkeley: University of California Press.

——. 2012. "Structures of Responsibility." *Ethnography* 13 (4): 558–62.

——. 2014. "The Social Life of 'Cash Payment': Money, Markets, and the Mutualities of Poverty." In *Cash on the Table: Markets, Values, and Moral Economies*, edited by Edward F. Fischer, 113–31. Santa Fe, NM: School for Advanced Research Press.

Ferguson, James, and Akhil Gupta. 2002. "Spatializing States: Toward an Ethnography of Neoliberal Governmentality." *American Ethnologist* 29 (4): 981–1002.

Fleisher, Michael L. 2000. *Kuria Cattle Raiders: Violence and Vigilantism on the Tanzania/Kenya Frontier*. Ann Arbor: University of Michigan Press.

Flynn, Donna K. 1997. "'We Are the Border': Identity, Exchange, and the State along the Bénin-Nigeria Border." *American Ethnologist* 24 (2): 311–30.

Ford, Michele, and Lenore Lyons, eds. 2012. *Men and Masculinities in Southeast Asia*. New York: Routledge.

Freeman, Donald B. 1996. "Doi Moi Policy and the Small-Enterprise Boom in Ho Chi Minh City, Vietnam." *Geographical Review* 86 (2): 178–97.

Friedmann, John. 2011. "Becoming Urban: Periurban Dynamics in Vietnam and China. Introduction." *Pacific Affairs* 84 (3): 425–34.

Gainsborough, Martin. 2010. *Vietnam: Rethinking the State*. New York: Zed Books.

Geertman, Stephanie. 2011. "Chợ Dân Sinh: Lối Sống và Sức Khỏe Cộng Đồng bị Đe Dọa [Disappearing Fresh markets: Public Health and Happiness under threat in Hanoi]." *Tạp chí Quy hoạch Đô thị* [Vietnamese Journal of Urban Planning] (4): 28–32.

Geertz, Clifford. 1978. "The Bazaar Economy: Information and Search in Peasant Marketing." *American Economic Review* 68 (2): 28–32.

General Statistics Office (GSO). 2010. *The 2009 Vietnam Population and Housing Census: Completed Results*. Hanoi: Central Population and Housing Census Steering Committee.

Gia Minh. 2014a. "Giải Tỏa 559 Lượng Vàng Bị Niêm Phong [Releasing the 559 Impounded Taels]." *Tuổi Trẻ*, April 27. http://tuoitre.vn/Chinh-tri-xa-hoi/Phap-luat/604715/giai-toa%C2%A0559-luong-vang-bi-niem-phong.html.

———. 2014b. "Niêm Phong 559 Lượng Vàng: Có Dấu Hiệu Lạm Quyền? [Impounding 559 Gold Taels: A Symptom of an Abuse of Power?]" *Tuổi Trẻ*, April 28. http://tuoitre.vn/Ban-doc/604768/niem-phong-559-luong-vang-co-dau-hieu-lam-quyen.html.

———. 2014c. "Vụ 559 Lượng Vàng: Trả Lại Tài Sản Tạm Giữ [The 559 Tael Affair: Returning the Impounded Property]." *Tuổi Trẻ*, April 30. http://tuoitre.vn/Chinh-tri-xa-hoi/Phap-luat/605141/vu-559-luong-vang-tra-lai-tai-san-tam-giu.html.

Gidwani, Vinay. 2010. "Remaindered Things and Remaindered Lives: Travelling with Delhi's Waste." In *Finding Delhi: Loss and Renewal in the Megacity*, edited by Bharati Chaturvedi, 37–54. New Delhi: Penguin Books India.

———. 2013. "Value Struggles: Waste Work and Urban Ecology in Delhi." In *Ecologies of Urbanism in India: Metropolitan Civility and Sustainability*, edited by Anne Rademacher and K. Sivaramakrishnan, 169–200. Hong Kong: Hong Kong University Press.

Gillespie, John. 2009. "The Juridification of Administrative Complaints and Review in Vietnam." In *Administrative Law and Governance in Asia: Comparative Perspectives*, edited by Tom Ginsburg and Albert H. Y. Chen, 205–29. New York: Routledge.

Gilmore, David D. 1990. *Manhood in the Making: Cultural Concepts of Masculinity*. New Haven, CT: Yale University Press.

Gottdiener, Mark. 1994. *The Social Production of Urban Space*. 2nd ed. Austin: University of Texas Press.

Gourou, Pierre. 1955. *The Peasants of the Tonkin Delta: A Study of Human Geography*. New Haven, CT: Human Relations Area Files.

Graaff, Kristina, and Noa Ha, eds. 2015. *Street Vending in the Neoliberal City: A Global Perspective on the Practices and Policies of a Marginalized Economy*. New York: Berghahn Books.

Gregory, Chris A. 1982. *Gifts and Commodities*. Studies in Political Economy. New York: Academic Press.

———. 1997. *Savage Money: The Anthropology and Politics of Commodity Exchange*. Amsterdam: Harwood Academic.

———. 2012. "On Money Debt and Morality: Some Reflections on the Contribution of Economic Anthropology." *Social Anthropology* 20 (4): 380–96.

Guide Alphabetique Taupin. 1937. *Guide Touristique Générale de l'Indochine*. Hanoi: Édition G. Taupin & Cie.

Gupta, Akhil. 1995. "Blurred Boundaries: The Discourse of Corruption, the Culture of Politics, and the Imagined State." *American Ethnologist* 22 (2): 375–402.

———. 2012. *Red Tape: Bureaucracy, Structural Violence, and Poverty in India*. Durham, NC: Duke University Press.

Guyer, Jane I. 1997. *An African Niche Economy: Farming to Feed Ibadan, 1968–88*. Edinburgh: Edinburgh University Press.

———. 2004. *Marginal Gains: Monetary Transactions in Atlantic Africa*. Chicago: University of Chicago Press.

Hà Thông. 2007. "Cả Làng Đua Nhau Làm . . . Hàng Giả [The Entire Village Competes to Make . . . Fake Goods]." *Dân trí,* December 18. http://dantri.com.vn/xa-hoi/ca-lang-dua-nhau-lam-hang-gia-1198072551.htm.

Hansen, Karen Tranberg. 1989. "The Black Market and Women Traders in Lusaka, Zambia." In *Women and the State in Africa,* edited by Jane L. Parpart and Kathleeen A. Staudt, 143–60. Boulder, CO: Lynne Rienner.

——. 2000. *Salaula: The World of Secondhand Clothing and Zambia.* Chicago: University of Chicago Press.

——. 2004. "Who Rules the Streets? The Politics of Vending Space in Lusaka." In *Reconsidering Informality: Perspectives from Urban Africa,* edited by Karen Tranberg Hansen and Mariken Vaa, 62–80. Uppsala, Sweden: Nordic Africa Institute.

——. 2005. "From Thrift to Fashion: Materiality and Aesthetics in Dress Practices in Zambia." In *Clothing as Material Culture,* edited by Susanne Küchler and Daniel Miller, 107–19. Oxford: Berg.

Hansen, Karen Tranberg, Walter E. Little, and B. Lynne Milgram, eds. 2013. *Street Economies in the Urban Global South.* Santa Fe, NM: School for Advanced Research.

Hansen, Karen Tranberg, and Mariken Vaa, eds. 2004. *Reconsidering Informality: Perspectives from Urban Africa.* Uppsala, Sweden: Nordiska Afrikainstitutet.

Hansen, Thomas Blom. 2001. "Governance and State Mythologies in Mumbai." In *States of Imagination: Ethnographic Explorations of the Postcolonial State,* edited by Thomas Blom Hansen and Finn Stepputat, 221–54. Durham, NC: Duke University Press.

Hardy, Andrew. 2000. "Strategies of Migration to Upland Areas in Contemporary Vietnam." *Asia Pacific Viewpoint* 41 (1): 23–34.

——. 2001. "Rules and Resources: Negotiating the Household Registration System in Vietnam under Reform." *SOJOURN: Journal of Social Issues in Southeast Asia* 16 (2): 187–212.

——. 2003. *Red Hills: Migrants and the State in the Highlands of Vietnam.* Copenhagen: Nordic Institute of Asian Studies.

Harms, Erik. 2009. "Vietnam's Civilizing Process and the Retreat from the Street: A Turtle's Eye View from Ho Chi Minh City." *City and Society* 21 (2): 182–206.

——. 2011. *Saigon's Edge: On the Margins of Ho Chi Minh City.* Minneapolis: University of Minnesota Press.

——. 2012. "Beauty as Control in the New Saigon: Eviction, New Urban Zones, and Atomized Dissent in a Southeast Asian City." *American Ethnologist* 39 (4): 735–50.

——. 2013. "The Boss: Conspicuous Invisibility in Ho Chi Minh City." *City and Society* 25 (2): 195–215.

——. 2016. *Luxury and Rubble: Civility and Dispossession in the New Saigon.* Oakland: University of California Press.

Harper, Richard H. R. 1998. *Inside the IMF: An Ethnography of Documents, Technology, and Organisational Action.* San Diego, CA: Academic Press.

Henaff, Marcel, and Tracy B. Strong, eds. 2001. *Public Space and Democracy.* Minneapolis: University of Minnesota Press.

Hetherington, Kevin. 1997. *The Badlands of Modernity: Heterotopia and Social Ordering.* New York: Routledge.

Hetherington, Kregg. 2011. *Guerrilla Auditors: The Politics of Transparency in Neoliberal Paraguay*. Durham, NC: Duke University Press.

Hetherington, Kregg, and Jeremy M. Campbell. 2014. "Nature, Infrastructure, and the State: Rethinking Development in Latin America." *Journal of Latin American and Caribbean Anthropology* 19 (2): 191–94.

Hiebert, Daniel, Jan Rath, and Steven Vertovec. 2015. "Urban Markets and Diversity: Towards a Research Agenda." *Ethnic and Racial Studies* 38 (1): 5–21.

Higgs, Peter. 2003. "Footpath Traders in a Hanoi Neighbourhood." In *Consuming Urban Culture in Contemporary Vietnam*, edited by Lisa B.W. Drummond and Mandy Thomas, 75–88. New York: RoutledgeCurzon.

Hlinčíková, Miroslava. 2015. "The Social Integration of Vietnamese Migrants in Bratislava: (In)Visible Actors in Their Local Community." *Central and Eastern European Migration Review* 4 (1): 41–52.

Hoang, Kimberly Kay. 2014. "Flirting with Capital: Negotiating Perceptions of Pan-Asian Ascendency and Western Decline in Global Sex Work." *Social Problems* 61 (4): 507–29.

Hodgson, Dorothy L. 2001. *Once Intrepid Warriors: Gender, Ethnicity, and the Cultural Politics of Maasai*. Bloomington: Indiana University Press.

Holtzman, Jon D. 2003. "Age, Masculinity, and Migration: Gender and Wage Labor among Samburu Pastoralists in Northern Kenya." In *Gender at Work in Economic Life*, Society for Economic Anthropology Monographs, vol. 20, edited by Gracia Clark, 225–41. New York: Altamira.

Hồng Minh. 2005. "Hà Nội Giải Quyết Việc Làm Cho Lao Động Khu Vực Chuyển Đổi Mục Đích Sử Dụng Đất [Hanoi Solves Labor Issues in Areas of Land Use Transformation]." *Lao Động & Xã Hội*, no. 270:22–23, 39.

Horat, Esther. 2017. *Trading in Uncertainty: Entrepreneurship, Morality, and Trust in a Vietnamese Textile-Handling Village*. Cham, Switzerland: Springer International.

Horton, Paul, and Helle Rydstrom. 2011. "Heterosexual Masculinity in Contemporary Vietnam: Privileges, Pleasures, and Protests." *Men and Masculinities* 14 (5): 542–64.

Hou, Jeffrey. 2010. "(Not) Your Everyday Public Space." In *Insurgent Public Space: Guerrilla Urbanism and the Remaking of Contemporary Cities*, edited by Jeffrey Hou, 1–17. New York: Routledge.

Hsu, Carolyn L. 2007. *Creating Market Socialism: How Ordinary People Are Shaping Class and Status in China*. Durham, NC: Duke University Press.

Huang, Philip C. C. 2009. "China's Neglected Informal Economy: Reality and Theory." *Modern China* 35 (4): 405–38.

Hull, Matthew S. 2003. "The File: Agency, Authority, and Autography in an Islamabad Bureaucracy." *Language and Communication* 23 (3–4): 287–314.

——. 2012. "Documents and Bureaucracy." *Annual Review of Anthropology* 41:251–67.

Humphrey, Caroline. 1994. "Remembering an 'Enemy': The Bogd Khaan in Twentieth-Century Mongolia." In *Memory, History, and Opposition under State Socialism*, edited by Rubie S. Watson, 21–44. Santa Fe, NM: School of American Research Press.

Hùng Mạnh. 2008. "Trao Đổi Về Một Số Giải Pháp Tăng Cường Công Tác Quản Lý, Khai Thác Chợ Trên Địa Bàn Tỉnh Lào Cai [Measures to Strengthen the

Management and Utilization of Markets in Lào Cai Province].” Sở Công Thương, Lào Cai—Cổng Thông Tin Điện Tử [Lào Cai Department of Industry and Trade Webportal].” http://www.laocai.gov.vn/sites/socongthuong/Tintucsukien/Trang/634045949526194190.aspx.

Hüwelmeier, Gertrud. 2013a. “Bazaar Pagodas—Transnational Religion, Postsocialist Marketplaces, and Vietnamese Migrant Women in Berlin.” *Religion and Gender* 3 (1): 76–89.

——. 2013b. “Postsocialist Bazaars: Diversity, Solidarity, and Conflict in the Marketplace.” *Laboratorium: Russian Review of Social Research* 5 (1): 52–72.

——. 2015a. “From ‘Jarmark Europa’ to ‘Commodity City.’ New Marketplaces, Post-socialist Migrations, and Cultural Diversity in Central and Eastern Europe.” *Central and Eastern European Migration Review* 4 (1): 27–39.

——. 2015b. “Mobile Entrepreneurs: Transnational Vietnamese in the Czech Republic.” In *Rethinking Ethnography in Central Europe*, edited by Hana Cervinkova, Michał Buchowski and Zdeněk Uherek, 59–73. London: Palgrave Macmillan.

——. 2018. “Cho Coc—Informal Markets in Urban Hanoi.” In *The Global Encyclopaedia of Informality*, vol. 2, edited by Alena Ledeneva, 110–14. London: UCL Press.

Inhorn, Marcia C. 2012. *The New Arab Man: Emergent Masculinities, Technologies, and Islam in the Middle East*. Princeton, NJ: Princeton University Press.

Jellema, Kate. 2005. “Making Good on Debt: The Remoralisation of Wealth in Post-revolutionary Vietnam.” *The Asia Pacific Journal of Anthropology* 6 (3): 231–48.

Jenkins, Richard, Hanne Jessen, and Vibeke Steffen. 2005. “Matters of Life and Death: The Control of Uncertainty and the Uncertainty of Control.” In *Managing Uncertainty: Ethnographic Studies of Illness, Risk, and the Struggle for Control*, edited by Vibeke Steffen, Richard Jenkins, and Hanne Jessen, 9–29. Copenhagen: Museum Tusculanum Press.

Jensen, Rolf, and Donald M. Peppard Jr. 2003. “Hanoi’s Informal Sector and the Vietnamese Economy: A Case Study of Roving Street Vendors.” *Journal of Asian and African Studies* 38 (1): 71–84.

Jensen, Rolf, Donald M. Peppard Jr., and Vũ Thị Minh Thắng. 2013. *Women on the Move: Hanoi’s Migrant Roving Street Vendors*. Hanoi: Women’s Publishing House.

Karis, Timothy. 2013. “Unofficial Hanoians: Migration, Native Place, and Urban Citizenship in Vietnam.” *The Asia Pacific Journal of Anthropology* 14 (3): 256–73.

Kerkvliet, Benedict J. Tria. 1995. “Village-State Relations in Vietnam: The Effects of Everyday Politics on Decollectivization.” *Journal of Asian Studies* 54 (2): 396–418.

——. 2004. “Surveying Local Government and Authority in Contemporary Vietnam.” In *Beyond Hanoi: Local Government in Vietnam*, edited by Benedict J. Tria Kerkvliet and David Marr, 1–27. Copenhagen: NIAS Press; Singapore: ISEAS Publications.

——. 2005. *The Power of Everyday Politics: How Vietnamese Peasants Transformed National Policy*. Ithaca, NY: Cornell University Press.

——. 2009. “Everyday Politics in Peasant Society (and Ours).” *Journal of Peasant Studies* 36 (1): 227–43.

——. 2014. “Protests over Land in Vietnam: Rightful Resistance and More.” *Journal of Vietnamese Studies* 9 (3): 19–54.

Kiều Minh. 2008. "Cấm Bán Hàng Rong—Bất Cập Về Nhân Văn Trong Chính Sách [Mobile Vendors Forbidden—Problems of Humanity in Policies]." *Việt Báo*, January 22. http://vietbao.vn/Xa-hoi/Cam-ban-hang-rong-bat-cap-ve-nhan-van-trong-chinh-sach/75174511/157/.

Kim, Annette M. 2011. "Talking Back: The Role of Narrative in Vietnam's Recent Land Compensation Changes." *Urban Studies* 48 (3): 493–508.

———. 2015. *Sidewalk City: Remapping Public Space in Ho Chi Minh City*. Chicago: University of Chicago Press.

Koh, David. 2004. "Illegal Construction in Hanoi and Hanoi's Wards." *European Journal of East Asian Studies* 3 (2): 337–69.

———. 2006. *Wards of Hanoi*. Singapore: Institute of Southeast Asian Studies.

———. 2008. "The Pavement as Civic Space: History and Dynamics in the City of Hanoi." In *Globalization, the City, and Civil Society in Pacific Asia: The Social Production of Civic Spaces*, edited by Mike Douglass, K. C. Ho, and Giok Ling Ooi, 145–74. New York: Routledge.

Kovsted, Jens, John Rand, and Finn Tarp. 2005. *From Monobank to Commercial Banking: Financial Sector Reforms in Vietnam*. Copenhagen: NIAS Press.

Krupa, Christopher, and David Nugent. 2015. *State Theory and Andean Politics. New Approaches to the Study of Rule*. Philadelphia: University of Pennsylvania Press.

Kurfürst, Sandra. 2012. "Informality as a Strategy: Street Traders in Hanoi Facing Constant Insecurity." In *Urban Informalities: Reflections on the Formal and Informal*, edited by Colin McFarlane and Michael Waibel, 89–110. Burlington, VT: Ashgate.

Labbé, Danielle. 2014. *Land Politics and Livelihoods on the Margins of Hanoi, 1920–2010*. Vancouver: University of British Columbia Press.

Labbé, Danielle, and Julie-Anne Boudreau. 2011. "Understanding the Causes of Urban Fragmentation in Hanoi: The Case of New Urban Areas." *International Development Planning Review* 33 (3): 273–91.

Landa, Janet Tai. 1994. *Trust, Ethnicity, and Identity: Beyond the New Institutional Economics of Ethnic Trading Networks, Contract Law, and Gift-Exchange*. Ann Arbor: University of Michigan Press.

Larkin, Brian. 2013. "The Politics and Poetics of Infrastructure." *Annual Review of Anthropology* 42:327–43.

Latour, Bruno. 2005. *Reassembling the Social: An Introduction to Actor-Network-Theory*. Oxford: Oxford University Press.

Law, Robin. 1995. "Cowries, Gold, and Dollars: Exchange Rate Instability and Domestic Price Inflation in Dahomey in the Eighteenth and Nineteenth Centuries." In *Money Matters: Instability, Values, and Social Payments in the Modern History of West African Communities*, edited by Jane I. Guyer, 53–73. Portsmouth, NH: Heinemann.

Le, Trong Cuc, A. Terry Rambo, and Kathleen Gillogly. 1993. *Too Many People, Too Little Land: the Human Ecology of a Wet Rice-growing Village in the Red River Delta of Vietnam*. Occasional Paper No. 15. Honolulu: East-West Center, Program on Environment.

Ledeneva, Alena. 2008. "*Blat* and *Guanxi*: Informal Practices in Russia and China." *Comparative Studies in Society and History* 50 (1): 118–44.

Lefebvre, Henri. 1991. *The Production of Space*. Translated by Donald Nicholson-Smith. Oxford: Blackwell.

Leshkowich, Ann Marie. 2005. "Feminine Disorder: State Campaigns against Street Traders in Socialist and Late Socialist Việt Nam." In *Le Việt Nam au Féminin: Việt Nam; Women's Realities*, edited by Gisèle Bousquet and Nora Taylor, 187–207. Paris: Les Indes Savantes.

——. 2011. "Making Class and Gender: (Market) Socialist Enframing of Traders in Ho Chi Minh City." *American Anthropologist* 113 (2): 277–90.

——. 2012. "Finances, Family, Fashion, Fitness, and . . . Freedom? The Changing Lives of Urban Middle-Class Vietnamese Women." In *The Reinvention of Distinction: Modernity and the Middle Class in Urban Vietnam*, edited by Van Nguyen-Marshall, Lisa B. Welch Drummond, and Danièle Bélanger, 95–113. Dordrecht, the Netherlands: Springer.

——. 2014a. *Essential Trade: Vietnamese Women in a Changing Marketplace*. Honolulu: University of Hawai'i Press.

——. 2014b. "Standardized Forms of Vietnamese Selfhood: An Ethnographic Genealogy of Documentation." *American Ethnologist* 41 (1): 143–62.

Leslie, Deborah, and Suzanne Reimer. 1999. "Spatializing Commodity Chains." *Progress in Human Geography* 23 (3): 401–20.

Li, Tania Murray. 2007. *The Will to Improve: Governmentality, Development, and the Practice of Politics*. Durham, NC: Duke University Press.

Li Tana. 2012. "Between Mountains and the Sea: Trades in Early Nineteenth-Century Northern Vietnam." *Journal of Vietnamese Studies* 7 (2): 67–86.

Lincoln, Martha. 2008. "Report from the Field: Street Vendors and the Informal Sector in Hanoi." *Dialectical Anthropology* 32 (3): 261–65.

Lindell, Ilda, ed. 2010a. *Africa's Informal Workers: Collective Agency, Alliances, and Transnational Organizing in Urban Africa*. London: Zed Books.

——. 2010b. "Between Exit and Voice: Informality and the Spaces of Popular Agency." *African Studies Quarterly* 11 (2/3): 1–11.

Lindquist, Johan. 2015. "Brokers and Brokerage, Anthropology of," *International Encyclopedia of Social and Behavioral Science*, 2nd edition, edited by James D. Wright, 870–74. Amsterdam: Elsevier.

Lipsky, Michael. 1980. *Street-Level Bureaucracy: Dilemmas of the Individual in Public Services*. New York: Russell Sage Foundation.

Little, Peter D. 1992. "Traders, Brokers, and Market 'Crisis' in Southern Somalia." *Africa* 62 (1): 94–124.

Locke, Catherine, Nguyễn Thị Ngân Hoa, and Nguyễn Thị Thanh Tâm. 2012. "Struggling to Sustain Marriages and Build Families: Mobile Husbands/Wives and Mothers/Fathers in Hà Nội and Hồ Chí Minh City." *Journal of Vietnamese Studies* 7 (4): 63–91.

Lục Văn Toán. 2012. "Lào Cai Gắn Phát Triển Thương Mại Với Dịch Vụ, Du Lịch [Lào Cai Develops Trade, Services, and Tourism]." *Vietnamtourism Online*, November 21. http://vietnamtourism.gov.vn/index.php/items/10743.

Lufrano, Richard John. 1997. *Honorable Merchants: Commerce and Self-Cultivation in Late Imperial China*. Honolulu: University of Hawai'i Press.

Luong, Hy Van. 2003. "Gender Relations: Ideologies, Kinship Practices, and Political Economy." In *Postwar Vietnam: Dynamics of a Transforming Society*, edited by Hy V. Luong, 201–23. Singapore: Institute of Southeast Asian Studies / Lanham, MD: Rowman and Littlefield.

——, ed. 2009. *Urbanization, Migration, and Poverty in a Vietnamese Metropolis: Hồ Chí Minh City in Comparative Perspectives*. Singapore: National University of Singapore Press.

——. 2010. *Tradition, Revolution, and Market Economy in a North Vietnamese Village, 1925–2006*. Honolulu: University of Hawai'i Press.

——. 2016. "Rural Vietnam: Transformational Dynamics and Regional Variation." Paper presented at the international conference "Vietnam: Thirty Years of Doi Moi and Beyond," Yusof Ishak Institute, Singapore, April 7–8.

Luong, Hy Van, and Dileni Gunewardena. 2009. "Labor Market, Urban Informal Economy, and Earnings during Rapid Economic Growth: The Case of Hồ Chí Minh City." In *Urbanization, Migration, and Poverty in a Vietnamese Metropolis: Hồ Chí Minh City in Comparative Perspectives*, edited by Hy V. Luong, 211–56. Singapore: National University of Singapore Press.

Lưu Đức Khải, Hà Huy Ngọc. 2008. "Đời Sống Sinh Kế và Thu Nhập Của Người Nông Dân Bị Thu Hồi Đất Nông Nghiệp Do Quá Trình Đô Thị Hóa—Thực Trạng và Gợi Ý Chính Sách [Livelihood and Income of Farmers Who Lost Their Land due to Land Appropriation in the Process of Urbanization—Situation and Policy Recommendations]." *Tạp Chí Địa Lý Nhân Văn* 4 (21): 18–22.

Ly, Huong. 2014. "Impressive 'Made in Vietnam.'" *Vietnam Chamber of Commerce and Industry News Online*, January 29. http://vccinews.com/news_detail.asp?news_id=29974.

Lyons, Michal, and Simon Snoxell. 2005. "Sustainable Urban Livelihoods and Marketplace Social Capital: Crisis and Strategy in Petty Trade." *Urban Studies* 42 (8): 1301–20.

MacGaffey, Janet. 1987. *Entrepreneurs and Parasites: The Struggle for Indigenous Capitalism in Zaire*. Cambridge, UK: Cambridge University Press.

——. 1991. *The Real Economy of Zaire: The Contribution of Smuggling and Other Unofficial Activities to National Wealth*. Philadelphia: University of Pennsylvania Press.

MacGaffey, Janet, and Rémy Bazenguissa-Ganga. 2000. *Congo–Paris: Transnational Traders on the Margins of the Law*. Bloomington: Indiana University Press.

MacLean, Ken. 2008. "In Search of Kilometer Zero: Digital Archives, Technological Revisionism, and the Sino-Vietnamese Border." *Comparative Studies in Society and History* 50 (4): 862–94.

——. 2013. *The Government of Mistrust: Illegibility and Bureaucratic Power in Socialist Vietnam*. Madison: University of Wisconsin Press.

Malarney, Shaun Kingsley. 1997. "Culture, Virtue, and Political Transformation in Contemporary Northern Viet Nam." *The Journal of Asian Studies* 56 (4): 899–920.

Mạnh Hưng. 2015. "Dự Án Chợ Văn Hóa—Bến Xe Khách Sa Pa: Tắc Giải Phóng Mặt Bằng, Vì Đâu? [Cultural Market Project—Sapa Bus Station: Delayed

Site Clearance, Why?]" *Báo Tài Nguyên và Môi Trường Online*, May 6. http://baotainguyenmoitruong.vn/ban-doc/201505/du-an-cho-van-hoa-ben-xe-khach-sa-pa-tac-giai-phong-mat-bang-vi-dau-584260/.

Marx, Karl. (1867) 1976. *Capital: A Critique of Political Economy*. Vol. 1. London: Penguin Classics.

Massey, Doreen. 1993. "Power-Geometry and a Progressive Sense of Place." In *Mapping the Futures: Local Cultures, Global Change*, edited by Jon Bird, Barry Curtis, Tim Putnam, George Robertson, and Lisa Tickner, 59–69. New York: Routledge.

Mathur, Nayanika. 2016. *Paper Tiger. Law, Bureaucracy, and the Developmental State in Himalayan India*. New Delhi: Cambridge University Press.

Maurer, Bill, Taylor C. Nelms, and Lana Swartz. 2013. "'When Perhaps the Real Problem Is Money Itself!': The Practical Materiality of Bitcoin." *Social Semiotics* 23 (2): 261–77.

Mbembe, Achille. 2001. *On the Postcolony*. Berkeley: University of California Press.

McElwee, Pamela. 2004. "Becoming Socialist or Becoming Kinh? Government Policies for Ethnic Minorities in the Socialist Republic of Viet Nam." In *Civilizing the Margins: Southeast Asian Government Policies for the Development of Minorities*, edited by Christopher R. Duncan, 182–213. Singapore: NUS Press.

——. 2008. "'Blood Relatives' or Uneasy Neighbors? Kinh Migrant and Ethnic Minority Interactions in the Trường Sơn Mountains." *Journal of Vietnamese Studies* 3 (3): 81–116.

Michaud, Jean, and Sarah Turner. 2000. "The Sa Pa Marketplace, Lao Cai Province, Vietnam." *Asia Pacific Viewpoint* 41 (1): 85–100.

——. 2003. "Tribulations d'un Marché de Montagne du Nord-Vietnam." *Études Rurales* 165/166: 53–80.

——. 2017. "Reaching New Heights. State Legibility in Sa Pa, a Vietnam Hill Station." *Annals of Tourism Research* 66:37–48.

Milgram, B. Lynne. 2011. "Reconfiguring Space, Mobilizing Livelihood: Street Vending, Legality, and Work in the Philippines. *Journal of Developing Societies* 27 (3–4): 261–93.

——. 2014. "Remapping the Edge: Informality and Legality in the Harrison Road Night Market, Baguio City, Philippines." *City and Society* 26 (2): 153–74.

Mitchell, Carrie L. 2008. "Altered Landscapes, Altered Livelihoods: The Shifting Experience of Informal Waste Collecting during Hanoi's Urban Transition." *Geoforum* 39 (6): 2019–29.

——. 2009. "Trading Trash in the Transition: Economic Restructuring, Urban Spatial Transformation, and the Boom and Bust of Hanoi's Informal Waste Trade." *Environment and Planning A* 41 (11): 2633–50.

Mitchell, Timothy. 1991. "The Limits of the State: Beyond Statist Approaches and Their Critics." *American Political Science Review* 85 (1): 77–96.

——. 2002. *Rule of Experts: Egypt, Techno-politics, Modernity*. Berkeley: University of California Press.

Montesquieu, Charles Louis de Secondat. (1748) 1977. *The Spirit of Laws*. Berkeley: University of California Press.

Navaro-Yashin, Yael. 2007. "Make-Believe Papers, Legal Forms, and the Counterfeit: Affective Interactions between Documents and People in Britain and Cyprus." *Anthropological Theory* 7 (1): 79–98.

Newman, David. 2006. "Borders and Bordering: Towards an Interdisciplinary Dialogue." *European Journal of Social Theory* 9 (2): 171–86.

Nghĩa Hiếu. 2012. "Tuyên Án Tử Hình Phương 'Linh Hột' [The Death Sentence of Phương 'Linh Hột']." *Báo Quảng Ninh Online*, July 27. http://baoquangninh.com.vn/phap-luat/201207/tuyen-an-tu-hinh-phuong-linh-hot-2172921/.

Ngọc Ngọc. 2016. "Tiểu Thương Bất An Trước Đề Xuất Xây Mới Chợ Đồng Xuân [Petty Traders Feel Unsettled by the Proposal to Rebuild Đồng Xuân Market]." *Bất Động Sản Việt Nam*, October 6. http://reatimes.vn/tieu-thuong-bat-an-truoc-de-xuat-xay-moi-cho-dong-xuan-1408.html.

Ngọc Triển and Ngọc Bằng. 2010. "Lào Cai: Gần Chục Khu Chợ Xây Để . . . Bỏ Hoang [Nearly a Dozen Market Constructions . . . Left Abandoned]." *Báo Dân Trí Online*, August 22. http://dantri.com.vn/xa-hoi/lao-cai-gan-chuc-khu-cho-xay-de-bo-hoang-417158.htm.

Nguyễn Hữu Định. 1996. *Kinh Doanh Vàng Tại Thành Phố Hồ Chí Minh: Chính Sách và Giải Pháp* [Gold Trade in Ho Chi Minh City: Policy Solutions]. Thành Phố Hồ Chí Minh: NXB Hồ Chí Minh.

Nguyen, Minh T. N. 2014. "Translocal Householding: Care and Migrant Livelihoods in a Waste-Trading Community of Vietnam's Red River Delta." *Development and Change* 45 (6): 1385–408.

——. 2015. *Vietnam's Socialist Servants: Domesticity, Class, Gender, and Identity*. New York: Routledge.

——. 2016. "Trading in Broken Things: Gendered Performances and Spatial Practices in a Northern Vietnamese Rural-Urban Waste Economy." *American Ethnologist* 43 (1): 116–29.

——. Forthcoming. "In a 'Half-Dark, Half-Light Zone': Mobility, Precarity, and Moral Ambiguity in Post-reform Vietnam's Urban Waste Economy." *TRANS (Trans-Regional and -National Studies of Southeast Asia)*.

Nguyen, Minh T. N., and Catherine Locke. 2014. "Rural-Urban Migration in Vietnam and China: Gendered Householding, Production of Space, and the State." *Journal of Peasant Studies* 41 (5): 855–76.

Nguyễn Ngọc Kim. 2001. "Thị Xã Lào Cai Mười Năm Xây Dựng và Phát Triển [Lào Cai Town—Ten Years of Urban Construction and Development]." In *Lào Cai—10 Năm Đổi Mới và Phát Triển* [Lào Cai—Ten Years of Đổi Mới and Development], edited by Ủy Ban Nhân Dan Tỉnh Lào Cai, 265–73. Lào Cai, Vietnam: Xí Nghiệp In.

Nguyễn Sa Linh. 2014. "Vụ Niêm Phong 559 Lượng Vàng: Đẩy Nghĩa Vụ Chứng Minh Cho Dân? [The Case of Impounding 559 Gold Taels: Pushing the Responsibility of Evidence onto the People?]" *Tuổi Trẻ*, April 29. http://tuoitre.vn/Chinh-tri-xa-hoi/Phap-luat/605014/vu-niem-phong-559-luong-vang-day-nghia-vu-chung-minh-cho-dan-%C2%A0.html.

Nguyễn Thị Nguyệt Minh. 2012. "'Doing *Ô Sin*': Rural Migrants Negotiating Domestic Work in Hà Nội." *Journal of Vietnamese Studies* 7 (4): 32–62.

Nguyen Thi Thanh Binh. 2017. "Multiple Reactions to Land Confiscations in a Hanoi Peri-urban Village." *Southeast Asian Studies* 6 (1): 95–114.

Nguyễn Tuấn. 2014. "Làng Kính . . . Hại Mắt [Eyeglass Village . . . Harms the Eyes]." *Thanh Niên*, September 22. http://thanhnien.vn/suc-khoe/lang-kinh-hai-mat-455289.html.

Nguyễn Văn Sửu. 2014. *Công Nghiệp Hóa, Đô Thị Hóa và Biến Đổi Sinh Kế ở Ven Đô Hà Nội [Industrialization, Urbanization, and Livelihood Transformation in Peri-urban Hanoi]*. Hanoi: Knowledge Publishing House.

Nguyen, Van. 2016. "The King of Cyclos." *Time Out*, April 26. http://en.timeoutvietnam.vn/the-king-of-cyclos-11258.html.

Nguyen Van Chinh. 2013. "Recent Chinese Migration to Vietnam." *Asian and Pacific Migration Journal* 22 (1): 7–30.

Nguyễn-võ Thu-hương. 2008. *The Ironies of Freedom: Sex, Culture, and Neoliberal Governance in Vietnam*. Seattle: University of Washington Press.

Nordstrom, Carolyn. 2000. "Shadows and Sovereigns." *Theory, Culture and Society* 17 (4): 35–54.

Nowicka, Ewa. 2015. "Between the Devil and the Deep Blue Sea: Acculturation of Young Vietnamese Women in Poland." *Central and Eastern European Migration Review* 4 (1): 67–80.

Nugent, Paul. 2002. *Smugglers, Secessionists, and Loyal Citizens on the Ghana-Togo Frontier: The Life of the Borderlands since 1914*. Athens: Ohio University Press.

Nwapa, Flora. (1980) 1992. *Wives at War and Other Stories*. Trenton, NJ: Africa World Press.

Nyíri, Pál. 2010. *Mobility and Cultural Authority in Contemporary China*. Seattle: University of Washington Press.

O'Connor, Kaori. 2011. *Lycra: How a Fiber Shaped America*. New York: Routledge.

O'Malley, Pat. 2004. *Risk, Uncertainty, and Government*. Portland, OR: GlassHouse.

——. 2008. "Governmentality and Risk." In *Social Theories of Risk and Uncertainty: An Introduction*, edited by Jens O. Zinn, 52–75. Oxford: Blackwell.

Ødegaard, Cecilie. 2010. *Mobility, Markets, and Indigenous Socialities: Contemporary Migration in the Peruvian Andes*. Burlington, VT: Ashgate.

Ong, Aihwa. 1999. *Flexible Citizenship: The Cultural Logics of Transnationality*. Durham, NC: Duke University Press.

——. 2006. *Neoliberalism as Exception: Mutations in Citizenship and Sovereignty*. Durham, NC: Duke University Press.

Ong, Aihwa, and Michael G. Peletz, eds. 1995. *Bewitching Women, Pious Men: Gender and Body Politics in Southeast Asia*. Berkeley: University of California Press.

Ong, Aihwa, and Li Zhang. 2008. "Introduction: Privatizing China: Powers of the Self, Socialism from Afar." In *Privatizing China: Socialism from Afar*, edited by Li Zhang and Aihwa Ong, 1–19. Ithaca, NY: Cornell University Press.

Pettus, Ashley. 2003. *Between Sacrifice and Desire: National Identity and the Governing of Femininity in Vietnam*. New York: Routledge.

Pham, Nga. 2014. "Vietnam Border Shoot-out Raises Uighur Questions." *BBC News*, April 29. http://www.bbc.com/news/world-asia-27200562.

Phan Si Man. 2005. "Development of Rural Infrastructure and its Impact on the Livelihoods of People Living in Poverty." In *Impact of Socio-economic Changes on the*

Livelihoods of People Living in Poverty in Vietnam, edited by Ha Huy Thanh and Shozo Sakata, ASEDP Research Series, no. 71, 53–82. http://www.ide.go.jp/English/Publish/Download/Asedp/071.html.

Phương Sơn. 2014. "Tiểu Thương Đóng Cửa Chợ Ninh Hiệp, Vây UBND Xã [Ninh Hiệp Traders Close Market Doors, Besiege the People's Committee]." *VN Express* online, January 15. http://vnexpress.net/tin-tuc/thoi-su/tieu-thuong-dong-cua-cho-ninh-hiep-vay-ubnd-xa-2939635.html.

Piot, Charles. 1999. *Remotely Global: Village Modernity in West Africa*. Chicago: University of Chicago Press.

Poisson, Emmanuel. 2009. "Unhealthy Air of the Mountains: *Kinh* and Ethnic Minority Rule on the Sino-Vietnamese Frontier from the Fifteenth to the Twentieth Century." In *On the Borders of State Power: Frontiers in the Greater Mekong Sub-Region*, edited by Martin Gainsborough, 12–24. New York: Routledge.

Quốc Hồng. 2011. "Xây Nhiều Chợ Nhưng Hiệu Quả Thấp [Many Markets Built but Results Are Low]." *Báo Nhân Dân Online*, November 30. http://www.nhandan.com.vn/xahoi/tin-tuc/item/13527802-.html.

Rigg, Jonathan. 2006. "Land, Farming, Livelihoods, and Poverty: Rethinking the Links in the Rural South." *World Development* 34 (1): 180–202.

Riles, Annelise, ed. 2006a. *Documents: Artifacts of Modern Knowledge*. Ann Arbor: University of Michigan Press.

——. 2006b. "Introduction: In Response." In *Documents: Artifacts of Modern Knowledge*, edited by Annelise Riles, 1–38. Ann Arbor: University of Michigan Press.

Robertson, Claire. 1983. "The Death of Makola and Other Tragedies." *Canadian Journal of African Studies* 17 (3): 469–95.

Rodgers, Dennis, and Bruce O'Neill. 2012. "Infrastructural Violence: Introduction to the Special Issue." *Ethnography* 13 (4): 401–12.

Rofel, Lisa. 2007. *Desiring China: Experiments in Neoliberalism, Sexuality, and Public Culture*. Durham, NC: Duke University Press.

Rose, Nikolas. 1999. *Powers of Freedom: Reframing Political Thought*. Cambridge, UK: Cambridge University Press.

——. 2000. "Government and Control." *British Journal of Criminology* 40 (2): 321–39.

Roy, Ananya. 2004. "The Gentleman's City: Urban Informality in the Calcutta of New Communism." In *Urban Informality: Transnational Perspectives from the Middle East, Latin America, and South Asia*, edited by Ananya Roy and Nezar AlSayyad, 147–70. Lanham, MD: Lexington Books.

Roy, Ananya, and Nezar AlSayyad, eds. 2004. *Urban Informality: Transnational Perspectives from the Middle East, Latin America, and South Asia*. Lanham, MD: Lexington Books.

Rumford, Chris. 2006. "Introduction: Theorizing Borders." *European Journal of Social Theory* 9 (2): 155–69.

Rydstrøm, Helle. 2009. "Moralising Female Sexuality: The Intersections between Morality and Sexuality in Rural Vietnam." In *The Anthropology of Moralities*, edited by Monica Heintz, 118–35. New York: Berghahn Books.

Salazar, Noel B. 2011. "The Power of Imagination in Transnational Mobilities." *Identities: Global Studies in Culture and Power* 18 (6): 576–98.

———. 2014. "Anthropology." In *The Routledge Handbook of Mobilities*, edited by Peter Adey, David Bissell, Kevin Hannam, Peter Merriman, and Mimi Sheller, 55–63. New York: Routledge.

Salazar, Noel B., and Alan Smart. 2011. "Anthropological Takes on (Im)Mobility." *Identities: Global Studies in Culture and Power* 18 (6): i–ix.

Salemink, Oscar. 2011. "A View from the Mountains: A Critical History of Lowlander-Highlander Relations in Vietnam." In *Upland Transformations in Vietnam*, edited by Thomas Sikor, Nghiêm Phương Tuyến, Jennifer Sowerwine, and Jeff Romm, 27–50. Singapore: NUS Press.

Sassen, Saskia. 2000. "Spatialities and Temporalities of the Global: Elements for a Theorization." *Public Culture* 12 (1): 215–32.

Schumpeter, Joseph A. 2006. *History of Economic Analysis*. New York: Routledge.

Schwenkel, Christina. 2012. "Civilizing the City: Socialist Ruins and Urban Renewal in Central Vietnam." *positions: asia critique* 20 (2): 437–70.

———. 2014. "Rethinking Asian Mobilities: Socialist Migration and Post-socialist Repatriation of Vietnamese Contract Workers in East Germany." *Critical Asian Studies* 46 (2): 235–58.

———. 2015a. "Reclaiming Rights to the Socialist City: Bureaucratic Artefacts and the Affective Appeal of Petitions." *South East Asia Research* 23 (2): 205–25.

———. 2015b. "Socialist Mobilities: Crossing New Terrains in Vietnamese Migration Histories." *Central and Eastern European Migration Review* 4 (1): 13–25.

Schwenkel, Christina, and Ann Marie Leshkowich. 2012. "Guest Editors' Introduction: How Is Neoliberalism Good to Think Vietnam? How Is Vietnam Good to Think Neoliberalism?" *positions: asia critique* 20 (2): 379–401.

Scott, Allen J., John Agnew, Edward W. Soja, and Michael Storper. 2001. "Global City-Regions." In *Global City-Regions: Trends, Theory, Policy*, edited by Allen J. Scott, 11–30. Oxford: Oxford University Press.

Scott, James C. 1976. *The Moral Economy of the Peasant: Rebellion and Subsistence in Southeast Asia*. New Haven, CT: Yale University Press.

———. 1985. *Weapons of the Weak: Everyday Forms of Peasant Resistance*. New Haven, CT: Yale University Press.

———. 1990. *Domination and the Arts of Resistance: Hidden Transcripts*. New Haven, CT: Yale University Press.

———. 1998. *Seeing Like a State: How Certain Schemes to Improve the Human Condition Have Failed*. New Haven, CT: Yale University Press.

———. 2009. *The Art of Not Being Governed: An Anarchist History of Upland Southeast Asia*. New Haven, CT: Yale University Press.

Seligmann, Linda J. 1989. "To Be in Between: The *Cholas* as Market Women in Peru." *Comparative Studies in Society and History* 31 (4): 694–721.

———. 2004. *Peruvian Street Lives*. Urbana: University of Illinois Press.

———. 2013. "The Politics of Urban Space among Street Vendors of Cusco, Peru." In *Street Economies in the Urban Global South*, edited by Karen Tranberg Hansen, Walter Little, and B. Lynne Milgram, 115–36. Santa Fe, NM: School of Advanced Research.

Seligmann, Linda J., and Daniel Guevara. 2013. "Occupying the Centre: Handicraft Vendors, Cultural Vitality, Commodification, and Tourism in Cusco, Peru." *Built Environment* 39 (2): 203–23.

Sheller, Mimi, and John Urry. 2006. "The New Mobilities Paradigm." *Environment and Planning A* 38 (2): 207–26.

Skeggs, Beverley. 2004. *Class, Self, Culture*. New York: Routledge.

Skinner, Caroline. 2008. "The Struggle for the Streets: Processes of Exclusion and Inclusion of Street Traders in Durban, South Africa." *Development Southern Africa* 25 (2): 227–42.

Small, Ivan V. 2016. "Framing and Encompassing Movement: Transportation, Migration, and Social Mobility in Vietnam." *Mobility in History* 7 (1): 79–89.

Smart, Alan, and George C. S. Lin. 2007. "Local Capitalisms, Local Citizenship, and Translocality: Rescaling from Below in the Pearl River Delta Region, China." *International Journal of Urban and Regional Research* 31 (2): 280–302.

Smart, Alan, and Filippo M. Zerilli. 2014. "Extralegality." In *A Companion to Urban Anthropology*, edited by Donald M. Nonini, 222–38. Malden, MA: Wiley Blackwell.

Smith, Michael P. 2001. *Transnational Urbanism: Locating Globalization*. Malden, MA: Blackwell.

Sở Công Thương Hà Nội (Hanoi Department of Industry and Trade). 2012. "Định Hướng Phát Triển Chợ Truyền Thống Của Hà Nội [Orientations for Developing Hanoi's Traditional Markets]." Paper presented at conference "Mô Hình Tổ Chức, Quản Lý Chợ Truyền Thống Trong Đô Thị ở Việt Nam [Organizing and Managing Traditional Markets in Urban Vietnam]," organized by the Ministry of Industry and Trade, Hanoi, June 20.

Söderström, Ola, and Stephanie Geertman. 2013. "Loose Threads: The Translocal Making of Public Space Policy in Hanoi." *Singapore Journal of Tropical Geography* 34 (2): 244–60.

Song, Geng. 2004. *The Fragile Scholar: Power and Masculinity in Chinese Culture*. Hong Kong: Hong Kong University Press.

Star, Susan Leigh. 1999. "The Ethnography of Infrastructure." *American Behavioral Scientist* 43 (3): 377–91.

Stoller, Paul. 2002. *Money Has No Smell: The Africanization of New York City*. Chicago: University of Chicago Press.

Szanton Blanc, Maria Cristina. 1972. *A Right to Survive: Subsistence Marketing in a Lowland Philippine Town*. University Park: Pennsylvania State University Press.

Tai, Hue-Tam Ho, and Mark Sidel. 2012. *State, Society, and the Market in Contemporary Vietnam: Property, Power, and Values*. New York: Routledge.

Tang, Rose. 2014. "Murder at the China-Vietnam Border." *Asia Sentinel*, April 21. http://www.asiasentinel.com/opinion/murder-china-vietnam-border.

Tawney, Richard Henry. 1961. *Religion and the Rise of Capitalism: A Historical Study*. Harmondsworth, UK: Penguin.

TenHoor, Meredith. 2007. "Architecture and Biopolitics at Les Halles." *French Politics, Culture and Society* 25 (2): 73–92.

Thành Thế Vỹ. 1961. *Ngoại Thương Việt Nam Hồi Thế Kỷ XVII, XVIII và Đầu Thế Kỷ XIX* [*The External Trade of Vietnam in the Seventeenth, Eighteenth, and Early Nineteenth Century*]. Hanoi: Nhà Xuất Bản Sử Học.

Thayer, Carlyle A. 2014. "Vietnam in 2013: Domestic Contestation and Foreign Policy Success." *Southeast Asian Affairs* 2014 (1): 353–72.

Thomas, Mandy. 2002. "Out of Control: Emergent Cultural Landscapes and Political Change in Urban Vietnam." *Urban Studies* 39 (9): 1611–24.

Thompson, E. P. 1971. "The Moral Economy of the English Crowd in the Eighteenth Century." *Past and Present* 50:76–136.

Thorne, Barrie. 1993. *Gender Play: Girls and Boys in School*. New Brunswick, NJ: Rutgers University Press.

Thu Phương. 2014. "Văn Minh Đô Thị Nơi Thành Phố Biên Cương [Urban Civility/Civilization in the Border Town]." *Báo Lào Cai Online*, November 9. http://www.baolaocai.vn/van-hoa/van-minh-do-thi-noi-thanh-pho-bien-cuong-z8n28392.htm.

Thủ Tướng Chính Phủ (Prime Minister). 1998. "Quyết Định 10/1998/QĐ-TTg Ngày 23 Tháng 1 Năm 1998, Phê Duyệt Định Hướng Quy Hoạch Tổng Thể Phát Triển Đô Thị Việt Nam Đến Năm 2020 [Decision No. 10/1998/QĐ-TTg of January 23, 1998, Approving the Orientation of the Master Plan on Vietnam's Urban Development Through 2020]." http://vanban.chinhphu.vn/portal/page/portal/chinhphu/hethongvanban?class_id=1&mode=detail&document_id=86144.

———. 2009. "Quyết Định Số 445/QĐ-TTg Ngày 07 Tháng 4 Năm 2009, Phê Duyệt Điều Chỉnh Định Hướng Quy Hoạch Tổng Thể Phát Triển Hệ Thống Đô Thị Việt Nam Đến Năm 2025 và Tầm Nhìn Đến Năm 2050 [Decision No. 445/QĐ-TTg of April 07, 2009, Approving the Adjusted Orientation of the Master Plan on Vietnam's Urban Development through 2025, with a Vision to 2050]." http://vanban.chinhphu.vn/portal/page/portal/chinhphu/hethongvanban?class_id=1&mode=detail&document_id=86144.

Trần Cường. 2006. "Hà Nội: Tiểu Thương Chợ Thanh Xuân Bắc Lay Lắt [Hanoi: Small Traders at Thanh Xuân Bắc Market to Lead a Miserable Existence]." *Tiền Phong Online*, January 1. http://www.tienphong.vn/kinh-te/ha-noi-tieu-thuong-cho-thanh-xuan-bac-lay-lat-65314.tpo.

Trần Hoài. 2013. "Hoạt Động Buôn Bán Của Thương Nhân Người Việt Tại Vùng Miền Núi Tỉnh Quảng Ngãi Từ Sau Đổi Mới Đến Những Năm Gần Đây [Commercial Activities of Vietnamese Traders in the Mountainous Areas of Quảng Ngãi from the Time of Renovation to the Present]." Unpublished manuscript.

Trần Hữu Sơn. 2014. "Hiệu Quả Hoạt Động Của Chợ Vùng Cao Lào Cai Dưới Góc Nhìn Nhân Học [The Efficiency of Upland Markets in Lào Cai Province from an Anthropological Perspective]." *Dân Tộc Học* 3 (186): 61–71.

Trần Thị Hồng Yến. 2013. *Biến Đổi Về Xã Hội Và Văn Hóa ở Các Làng Quê Trong Quá Trình Đô Thị Hóa Tại Hà Nội* [*Social and Cultural Changes in Rural Villages During Hanoi's Urbanization Process*]. Hanoi: NXB Chính Trị Quốc Gia.

Traynor, Niall. 2015. "Contestation to Modernisation: Livelihood Strategies and Trader Resistance to the Relocation of the Sa Pa Marketplace, Lào Cai Province, Northern Vietnam." Master's thesis, University College Dublin.

Trincsi, Kate, Thi-Thanh-Hiên Pham, and Sarah Turner. 2014. "Mapping Mountain Diversity: Ethnic Minorities and Land Use Land Cover Change in Vietnam's Borderlands." *Land Use Policy* 41:484–97.

Tripp, Aili Mari. 1997. *Changing the Rules: The Politics of Liberalization and the Urban Informal Economy in Tanzania*. Berkeley: University of California Press.

Trọng Phú. 2005. "Công Nghệ Kính . . . Làng [Eyeglass Technology . . . Village]." *Tuổi Trẻ*, March 17. http://tuoitre.vn/cong-nghe-kinhlang-70569.htm.

Trouillot, Michel-Rolph. 2001. "The Anthropology of the State in the Age of Globalization: Close Encounters of the Deceptive Kind." *Current Anthropology* 42 (1): 125–38.

Truitt, Allison. 2008. "On the Back of a Motorbike: Middle-Class Mobility in Ho Chi Minh City, Vietnam." *American Ethnologist* 35 (1): 3–19.

Tsing, Anna Lowenhaupt. 2005. *Friction: An Ethnography of Global Connection*. Princeton, NJ: Princeton University Press.

Tuấn Hợp. 2014. "Hà Nội: Xây Lại Chợ Ninh Hiệp—Đừng Đùa Với Sinh Kế Của Dân! [Hanoi: Rebuilding Ninh Hiệp Market—Do Not Play with People's Livelihood!]" *Dân Trí Online*, January 18. http://dantri.com.vn/xa-hoi/ha-noi-xay-lai-cho-ninh-hiep-dung-dua-voi-sinh-ke-cua-dan-1390551477.htm.

Turner, Sarah. 2007. "Trading Old Textiles: The Selective Diversification of Highland Livelihoods in Northern Vietnam." *Human Organization* 66 (4): 389–404.

——. 2009. "Hanoi's Ancient Quarter Traders: Resilient Livelihoods in a Rapidly Transforming City." *Urban Studies* 46 (5–6): 1203–21.

——. 2010. "Borderlands and Border Narratives: A Longitudinal Study of Challenges and Opportunities for Local Traders Shaped by the Sino-Vietnamese Border." *Journal of Global History* 5 (2): 265–87.

Turner, Sarah, Christine Bonnin, and Jean Michaud. 2015. *Frontier Livelihoods: Hmong in the Sino-Vietnamese Borderlands*. Seattle: University of Washington Press.

Turner, Sarah, Thomas Kettig, Đinh Thị Diệu, and Phạm Văn Cự. 2016. "State Livelihood Planning and Legibility in Vietnam's Northern Borderlands: The 'Rightful Criticisms' of Local Officials." *Journal of Contemporary Asia* 46 (1): 42–70.

Turner, Sarah, and Natalie Oswin. 2015. "Itinerant Livelihoods: Street Vending-Scapes and the Politics of Mobility in Upland Socialist Vietnam." *Singapore Journal of Tropical Geography* 36 (3): 394–410.

Turner, Sarah, and Laura Schoenberger. 2012. "Street Vendor Livelihoods and Everyday Politics in Hanoi, Vietnam: The Seeds of a Diverse Economy?" *Urban Studies* 49 (5): 1027–44.

UBND Huyện Sa Pa (Sa Pa District People's Committee). 2014. Cộng Hòa Xã Hội Chủ Nghĩa Việt Nam. Biên Bản Họp Ngày 03/12/2014 [Socialist Republic of Vietnam. Minutes of the Meeting December 3, 2014]. Văn Phòng UBND Huyện Sa Pa.

UBND Tỉnh Lào Cai (Lào Cai Province People's Committee). 2008. "Quyết Định Số 62/2008/QĐ-UBND Ngày 02 Tháng 12 Năm 2008, Ban Hành Quy Định về Tổ Chức, Quản Lý và Phát Triển Chợ Trên Địa Bàn Tỉnh Lào Cai [Resolution Number 62/2008/QĐ-UBND of December 2, 2008, Promulgating the

Regulation on the Organization, Management and Development of Markets in the Province of Lào Cai].” http://vbpl.vn/laocai/Pages/vbpq-toanvan. aspx?ItemID=29360.

——. 2012. “Báo Cáo: Sơ Kết Tình Hình Thực Hiện Nghị Định 114/NĐ-CP Sửa Đổi, Bổ Sung Một Số Điều Của Nghị Định 02/2003/NĐ-CP Về Phát Triển và Quản Lý Chợ [Preliminary Review of the Implementation of Decree 114/NĐ-CP Amending and Supplementing Some Articles of Decree 02/2003/NĐ-CP On The Development and Management of Markets].”

——. 2013. “Quyết Định Số 06/2013/QĐ-UBND Ngày 19 Tháng 3 Năm 2013, Ban Hành Quy Định Về Tổ Chức, Quản Lý và Phát Triển Chợ Trên Địa Bàn Tỉnh Lào Cai [Resolution Number 06/2013/QĐ-UBND of March 19, 2013, Promulgating the Regulation on the Organization, Management and Development of Markets in the Province of Lào Cai].” https://thuvienphapluat.vn/van-ban/Thuong-mai/ Quyet-dinh-06-2013-QD-UBND-Quy-dinh-to-chuc-quan-ly-phat-trien-cho-Lao-Cai-181307.aspx.

UBND TP Hà Nội (Hanoi Municipal People’s Committee). 2008. “Quyết Định Số 20/2008/QĐ-UBND Ngày 16 Tháng 04 Năm 2008, Ban Hành Quy Định Về Quản Lý và Sử Dụng Hè Phố, Lòng Đường Trên Địa Bàn Thành Phố Hà Nội [Resolution Number 20/2008/QĐ-UBND of April 16, 2008, Promulgating the Regulations on the Management and Use of Sidewalks and Streets in the City of Hanoi].” https:// thuvienphapluat.vn/van-ban/Giao-thong-Van-tai/Quyet-dinh-20-2008-QD-UBND-Quy-dinh-quan-ly-va-su-dung-he-pho-long-duong-tren-dia-ban-thanh-pho-Ha-Noi-65585.aspx.

Urry, John. 2000. “Mobile Sociology.” *British Journal of Sociology* 51 (1): 185–203.

van de Walle, Dominique, and Dileni Gunewardena. 2001. “Sources of Ethnic Inequality in Viet Nam.” *Journal of Development Economics* 65 (1): 177–207.

van den Berg, L. M., M. S. van Wijk, and Pham Van Hoi. 2003. “The Transformation of Agriculture and Rural Life Downstream of Hanoi.” *Environment and Urbanization* 15 (1): 35–52.

Vann, Elizabeth F. 2012. “Afterword: Consumption and Middle-Class Subjectivity in Vietnam.” In *The Reinvention of Distinction: Modernity and the Middle Class in Urban Vietnam*, edited by Van Nguyen-Marshall, Lisa B. Welch Drummond, and Danièle Bélanger, 157–70. Dordrecht, the Netherlands: Springer.

Vu Hong Phong. 2006. “Impacts of Urbanization in a Peri-urban Area of Hanoi: The Voice of Affected People.” *Social Sciences* 5 (115): 51–60.

Vu Thanh Long, Nguyen Ngoc Huong, Khuat Thu Hong, and Chengchi Shiu. 2010. *Sexual Profile of Vietnamese Men: A Preliminary Investigation in Hanoi, Ha Tay, Can Tho, and Ho Chi Minh City*. Hanoi: Women Publishing House and Institute of Social Development Studies.

Vu Thi Thao, and Jytte Agergaard. 2012. “‘White Cranes Fly over Black Cranes’: The *Longue Durée* of Rural-Urban Migration in Vietnam.” *Geoforum* 43 (6): 1088–98.

Waibel, Michael. 2006. “The Production of Urban Space in Vietnam’s Metropolis in the Course of Transition: Internationalization, Polarization, and Newly Emerging Lifestyles in Vietnamese Society.” *Trialog* 89 (2): 43–48.

Walters, William. 2006. “Border/Control.” *European Journal of Social Theory* 9 (2): 187–203.

Weber, Max. 1978. *Economy and Society: An Outline of Interpretive Sociology*. Vols. 1 and 2, edited by Guenther Roth and Claus Wittich. Berkeley: University of California Press.

Wiegersma, Nan. 1991. "Peasant Patriarchy and the Subversion of the Collective in Vietnam." *Review of Radical Political Economics* 23 (3–4): 174–97.

Wilk, Richard R. 1996. *Economies and Cultures: Foundations of Economic Anthropology*. Boulder, CO: Westview Press.

Williams, Allan M., and Vladimir Baláž. 2002. "International Petty Trading: Changing Practices in Trans-Carpathian Ukraine." *International Journal of Urban and Regional Research* 26 (2): 323–42.

——. 2005. "Winning, Then Losing, the Battle with Globalization: Vietnamese Petty Traders in Slovakia." *International Journal of Urban and Regional Research* 29 (3): 533–49.

Winkels, Alexandra. 2012. "Migration, Social Networks, and Risk: The Case of Rural-to-Rural Migration in Vietnam." *Journal of Vietnamese Studies* 7 (4): 92–121.

Womack, Brantly. 2006. *China and Vietnam: The Politics of Asymmetry*. New York: Cambridge University Press.

World Bank. 2009. *Country Social Analysis: Ethnicity and Development in Vietnam*. Washington, DC: World Bank.

——. 2011. *Vietnam Urbanization Review: Technical Assistance Report*. Washington, DC: World Bank. http://documents.worldbank.org/curated/en/2011/11/15817674/vietnam-urbanization-review-technical-assistance-report.

Zhang, Juan. 2011. "Border Opened Up: Everyday Business in a China-Vietnam Frontier." PhD diss., Macquarie University.

Zhang, Li. 2001. *Strangers in the City: Reconfigurations of Space, Power, and Social Networks within China's Floating Population*. Stanford, CA: Stanford University Press.

Zlolniski, Christian. 2006. *Janitors, Street Vendors, and Activists: The Lives of Mexican Immigrants in Silicon Valley*. Berkeley: University of California Press.

CONTRIBUTORS

Lisa Barthelmes is a scientific curator at the House for Brandenburg-Prussian History in Potsdam. She received her PhD in anthropology from the Martin Luther University of Halle/Wittenberg in 2016 and was a member of the Max Planck research group Traders, Markets, and the State in Vietnam. Her current research project focuses on refugees and integration in the Brandenburg region.

Christine Bonnin is an assistant professor in the School of Geography at the University College Dublin. She received her PhD in geography from McGill University, Montreal, Canada, in 2012. From 2011 to 2012, Christine was a research fellow at the Max Planck Institute for Social Anthropology and member of the Max Planck research group Traders, Markets, and the State in Vietnam. She has also undertaken research on the implications of economic transformations on markets and traders in Manila, the Philippines, and Dublin, Ireland. Christine is coauthor of *Frontier Livelihoods: Hmong in the Sino-Vietnamese Borderlands*, with Sarah Turner (see below) and Jean Michaud (University of Washington Press, 2015).

Gracia Clark, professor emerita of anthropology at Indiana University in Bloomington, first studied Kumasi Central Market for her PhD in social anthropology at the University of Cambridge. She consulted for several international development agencies before starting to teach. Her books *Onions Are My Husband: Survival and Accumulation by West African Market Women* (University of Chicago Press, 1994) and *African Market Women: Seven Life Stories from Ghana* (Indiana University Press, 2010) join several edited volumes and numerous articles and chapters about gender, food security, development policy, commercial practice, marriage, motherhood, economic history, and ethnographic methodology.

Annuska Derks is assistant professor at the Department of Social Anthropology and Cultural Studies at the University of Zurich. She has conducted extensive ethnographic research in Southeast Asia, in particular Vietnam, Cambodia, and Thailand. She has researched and published on migration and transnationalism; on labor, servitude, and bondage; and on gender and sexuality. More recently, she has explored the links among commodity chains, social change, and inequality in research projects tracing the lives, movements, and entanglements of everyday objects and spices in Vietnam.

Kirsten W. Endres is head of research group at the department Resilience and Transformation in Eurasia, Max Planck Institute for Social Anthropology, Halle/Saale. She has conducted research in northern Vietnam since 1996, focusing on social-cultural transformation processes that arise from the dynamic interplay between state, society, and market. From 2011 to 2016, she headed the research group Traders, Markets, and the State in Vietnam. She is author of *Performing the Divine: Mediums, Markets, and Modernity in Urban Vietnam* (NIAS, 2011), and coeditor of *Engaging the Spirit World: Popular Beliefs and Practices in Modern Southeast Asia* (Berghahn, 2011).

Chris Gregory, an anthropologist, was a professor in political and economic anthropology at Manchester University as well as a reader at the Australian National University. His areas of regional expertise are East-Central India and the Pacific region, namely, Papua New Guinea and Fiji. His research interests range from the political economy and culture of rice growing and kinship and marriage in central India to theories of gift exchange and questions of money and morality.

Caroline Grillot is a sinologist and anthropologist currently affiliated with the Lyons Institute of East Asian Studies (IAO). From 2013 to 2016 she was a research fellow at the Max Planck Institute for Social Anthropology and member of the group Traders, Markets, and the State in Vietnam. Her research focuses on social margins in China, in particular cross-border marriages, cross-border trade, and migrant beekeepers. She is the author of *Volées, envolées, convolées . . . Vendues, en fuite ou re-socialisées: Les "fiancées" vietnamiennes en Chine* (Connaissances et Savoirs, 2010).

Erik Harms is an associate professor of anthropology at Yale University, specializing in Southeast Asia and particularly Vietnam. His areas of expertise are postwar Vietnam, urban anthropology, and theories of space, time, and social action. He is the author of *Luxury and Rubble: Civility and Dispossession in the New Saigon* (University of California Press, 2016) and *Saigon's Edge: On the Margins of Ho Chi Minh City* (University of Minnesota Press, 2011), for which he was awarded the 2014 Harry J. Benda Prize.

Esther Horat is a postdoctoral researcher and lecturer at the Department of Social Anthropology and Cultural Studies, University of Zurich. During her PhD, she was a member of the research group Traders, Markets, and the State in Vietnam at the Max Planck Institute for Social Anthropology. As part of her PhD project, she examined the dynamics within and the integration of a peri-urban trading village into wider economic structures and networks in the post–Đổi mới era. She is author of *Trading in Uncertainty: Entrepreneurship, Morality, and Trust in a Vietnamese Textile-Handling Village* (Springer, 2017).

Gertrud Hüwelmeier is an anthropologist and senior lecturer and research fellow at the Humboldt Universität zu Berlin and a senior research partner at the Max Planck Institute for the Study of Religious and Ethnic Diversity, Department of Socio-cultural Diversity in Göttingen/Germany. Her research focuses on religion, gender, urban transformation, and transnationalism in Vietnam and its diasporas in postsocialist countries. Currently, she is working on a new project, "Religion, Media, and Materiality: Spiritual Economies in Southeast Asia." She is the coeditor of *Traveling Spirits: Migrants, Markets, and Mobilities* (Routledge, 2010).

Ann Marie Leshkowich is professor of anthropology at College of the Holy Cross. Her research focuses on gender, economic transformation, neoliberalism, middle classness, fashion, social work, and adoption in Vietnam. She is author of *Essential Trade: Vietnamese Women in a Changing Marketplace* (University of Hawai'i Press, 2014), for which she was awarded the 2016 Harry J. Benda Prize, and coeditor of *Re-Orienting Fashion: The Globalization of Asian Dress* (Berg, 2003).

Hy Van Luong is professor of anthropology at the University of Toronto. He has conducted field research in Vietnam since the late 1980s and has authored and edited numerous books. His most recent publications include his monograph *Tradition, Revolution, and Market Economy in a North Vietnamese Village, 1925–2006* (University of Hawai'i Press, 2010) and a coedited book (with Amrita Daniere) titled *The Dynamics of Social Capital and Civic Engagement in Asia* (Routledge, 2012). His chapter in the present volume is based on an ongoing study on sociocultural and economic changes in rural Vietnam since 2000, conducted in seven communes in north, central, and south Vietnam.

Minh T. N. Nguyen is professor of anthropology at the University of Bielefeld. From 2011 to 2016 she was a research fellow at the Max Planck Institute for Social Anthropology and member of the group Kinship and Social Support in China and Vietnam. Her research interests include gender and class, migration and care, waste economies, and, increasingly, welfare and social security. She is the author of *Vietnam's Socialist Servants: Domesticity, Class, Gender, and Identity* (Routledge, 2015). Her second monograph, *Waste and Wealth: Labor, Value, and Morality in a Vietnamese Migrant Recycling Economy*, is forthcoming from Oxford University Press.

Nguyễn Thị Thanh Bình is a researcher at the Institute of Anthropology, Vietnamese Academy of Social Sciences, Hanoi. She obtained her BA in ethnology at the Hanoi University of Social Sciences and Humanities, her MA in anthropology at the University of Amsterdam, The Netherlands, and her PhD at the Australian National University. Her research interests are local political dynamics, social change, and culture in rural Vietnam. Recently, she has been carrying out research on urbanization in Hanoi's peri-urban areas and in the northern uplands.

Linda J. Seligmann is professor of anthropology at George Mason University. She has spent many years working on questions concerning women in informal markets, especially in the Andean region of Peru. Her books include *Peruvian Street Lives: Culture, Power, and Economy among Market Women of Cuzco* and an edited volume, *Women Traders in Cross-Cultural Perspective: Mediating Identities, Marketing Wares*. She recently contributed a chapter, "Markets," to the Blackwell *Companion to Urban Anthropology* and "The Politics of Urban Space among Street Vendors of Cusco, Peru" to the volume titled *Street Economies in the Urban Global South*.

Allison Truitt is associate professor at the Department of Anthropology at Tulane University. Her research interests cover sociocultural anthropology, economic transformations, money and other means of circulation, consumption, and globalization. She is author of the book *Dreaming of Money in Ho Chi Minh City* (University of Washington Press, 2013) and coeditor of *Money: Ethnographic Encounters* (Berg, 2007).

Sarah Turner is professor of geography at McGill University, Canada. She has conducted fieldwork in urban Malaysia, Indonesia, and Vietnam and since 1999 with upland ethnic minority groups in rural northern Vietnam and southwest China. She is editor of the book *Red Stamps and Gold Stars: Fieldwork Dilemmas in Upland Socialist Asia* (University of British Columbia Press, 2013) and coauthor of *Frontier Livelihoods: Hmong in the Sino-Vietnamese Borderlands,* with Christine Bonnin (see above) and Jean Michaud (University of Washington Press, 2015).

Index

CPSIA information can be obtained
at www.ICGtesting.com
Printed in the USA
LVHW06s2021030518
575869LV00008B/138/P